The launch of the Cunard Liner Aquitania *from the* Clydebank Shipyard of John Brown & Co Ltd on April 23 1913. She was completed in time to make three round trips to the United States before the outbreak of the First World War (National Maritime Museum).

Aquitania, *known always as 'The Ship Beautiful', displays her elegance for the first time in the Clydebank Shipyard* (National Maritime Museum).

Song of the Clyde

A history of Clyde shipbuilding

Fred M. Walker

W. W. Norton & Company

NEW YORK   LONDON

ISBN 0-393-01948-9

Photoset in 10 on 11 pt Garamond by Manuset Ltd, Baldock,
Herts. Printed in Great Britain on 115 gsm Fineblade coated
cartridge, and bound, by The Garden City Press, Letchworth,
Herts.

Contents

Preface

A story told by my late grandfather was that as a very young man, sometime in the 1880s, he paid his first unaccompanied visit to Glasgow. On alighting from the train at Glasgow Cross he climbed up from the station and found himself in busy streets thronged with tramcars, horses, carts and Saturday crowds. Noticing a policeman he made his way over to ask directions and after greeting him asked, 'Can I get from here to Kelvingrove?' The policeman looked at the young man and then with a twinkle in his eye replied, 'Laddie, from here you can get to anyplace in the world!'

The policeman's remark encapsulated two aspects of Glaswegians and, indeed, of many Scots of 100 years ago. First the humour that rarely deserts the Clydesider and which, fortunately, does not seem to have left the citizens in these changed days. Second the patriotic pride based on optimism and confidence developed from an appreciation that on the nearby riverbanks there worked men acknowledged world-wide as supreme masters in one of the current advanced technologies—the building of ships and the powering of them with steam engines of ever increasing efficiency.

Much has changed since then. The great ship-building days have passed, but despite the downturn in industrial prosperity and worldwide recession, the Clyde still produces ships of fine quality and with high technological content. Parts of the area have suffered unimaginable deprivation but the people remain generous and kindly. There are opportunities second to none in the fields of education, for the enjoyment and indulgence of cultural pursuits and appreciation of the surrounding environs of firth, sea lochs and mountains. In many respects this region has qualities of life which are the envy of Europe.

This book, which started as a challenge from a close friend nearly 15 years ago, has developed into a personal desire to write a tribute to a river which is held in deep affection, to an industrial business that has dominated Scottish life and to a group of great men, individualists all, who were leaders in the non-exclusive fields of naval architecture, shipbuilding, marine engineering and academic life. It is a matter of considerable concern that in such a tribute accuracy in text and fact must be paramount, and every effort has been made to ensure that statements are accurate.

The industrial history of Clydeside is worthy of study. While the tonnages built on the river have been eclipsed long ago by other building areas, it is doubtful if ever again, any one geographical region will be able to say that it built possibly 30,000 ships in under 200 years. I trust that this volume will be of value as a source book and that it will encourage engineers, students, ship lovers and admirers of the West of Scotland to carry out further research and hopefully publish their findings on other aspects of the life and work of this wonderful river. *Floreat Clutha!*

Fred. M. Walker
Tenterden, Kent
November 1983

TSS Queen Elizabeth 2 (John Smith Photographic Unit, UIE Clydebank).

Acknowledgements

It is a pleasure to record sincere gratitude to the many people who have directly and indirectly assisted in the preparation of this book, and to acknowledge my indebtedness to many individuals and companies who have willingly placed information and photographs at my disposal.

To my friend, Dr James Macaulay of Glasgow, for firing my enthusiasm to record the lives and times of the early Clyde shipbuilders, and to Noel Bonsor of Jersey for encouraging me to prepare the work in a format suitable for publication, thanks are due.

Of the many libraries used and consulted, pride of place must go to the Mitchell Library, Glasgow, for continuous help and co-operation in my association with them which goes back nearly 30 years. To

Mr R. Gillespie, the reference director, and particularly the staff of the Glasgow Room especial gratitude is in order.

The Library of Glasgow University and the staff also deserve especial thanks. Again my involvement with this fine library is long standing and has given me infinite pleasure over the years. While at the University thanks must be given to Emeritus Professor J.F.C. Conn, my teacher of some years ago, who introduced me to so many fresh facets of study, and to Professor Tony Slaven, a student contemporary whose judgement on shipbuilding economics and

The Clyde Anchorage, better known as the Tail of the Bank. This 19th century photograph shows the guardship HMS Aurora lying off the west end of Greenock (Wotherspoon Collection, Mitchell Library, Glasgow).

whose friendship I value. The University Archives and Mr Michael Moss have been of great assistance.

In Glasgow I have enjoyed the advantages of the Institution of Engineers and Shipbuilders in Scotland and used their former library and with gratitude remember the kindly ladies on the staff. At Kelvingrove Mr A.S.E. Browning and at Pollokshields Mr Alastair Smith of Glasgow Museums have been hospitable at all times, and I have gained immeasurably from perusing Mr Browning's 24-volume *Clyde Built Ships*. At the City Chambers Mr Richard Dell, the Strathclyde Regional Archivist, has been an unfailing source of information and inspiration.

In London I have used the libraries of the Royal Institution of Naval Architects and the Institute of Marine Engineers and, again, express my appreciation to their secretaries and library staff for these and many other services these fine institutions offer. To Derek Deere and Marine Publications International Ltd, proprietors of *Shipping World & Shipbuilder*, I acknowledge the kindness in allowing me to quote from their recent publication of National Maritime Museum Conference papers published as *European Shipbuilding, One Hundred Years of Change*.

At Greenwich I have a very special debt of gratitude owing to many friends and colleagues. The National Maritime Museum is an inspiring place for both study and for the cursory visit and it is a repository of knowledge that is of inestimable value, not only for the study of history but for use in the forward planning of our affairs. I have drawn freely on the information in the Ships Plans and Technical Records Section (probably the world's largest technical archive) and my colleagues there, and also from the staff and records of Ships Department and countless people in almost every other department of the organisation. To the Trustees and Director I record my unreserved thanks for all the help given (officially and unofficially!) and for kind permission to reproduce paintings, photographs and plans in this volume.

I have three personal acknowledgements. The first is to record that in 25 years in shipbuilding invaluable information has been given to me by countless hundreds of people. While being unable to register every incident or person, I am deeply conscious that this background is necessary to any understanding of shipbuilding and am conscious of the privilege given to me.

Mrs Brenda Ward of Tenterden has kept me on my toes with her immaculate typing and script checking. Her encouragement has been invaluable.

Lastly to my family, thanks are due for putting up with book writing. To David, Colin and Sandy for remaining interested throughout and for asking appropriate questions, and to Joan for accepting in good humour the change from having a husband whose awkward shipbuilding hours have become long hours in London and then writing at home.

I must also thank: Mr John C. Annan (T. & R. Annan & Sons Ltd Glasgow); the late Mr Bob Beattie (Glasgow); Dr Ian L. Buxton (University of Newcastle-upon-Tyne); Mr D. Caldwell (James Adam & Son (Shiprepairers) Ltd); Mr Robert G.M. Clow (John Smith & Son (Glasgow) Ltd); Mr Arthur G. Codd (Sir Robert McAlpine & Sons Ltd, London); Mr Joseph S. Craig (UIE Shipbuilding (Scotland) Ltd,

The Fairfield fitting out basin in 1898, showing the sheerlegs and the public footbridge across the bottom of the dock. The ship fitting out, nearest camera and to right, is SS Regele Carol I, *a passenger ferry for the Rumanian State Railways* (Dr I. L. Buxton).

Clydebank); Mr Victor Dare (John Brown Engineering Ltd, Clydebank); Dr Peter N. Davis (University of Liverpool); Professor Douglas Faulkner (University of Glasgow); Dr Archie Ferguson (Glasgow University Hydrodynamics Tank); Mr W. Ferguson (Scott Lithgow Limited, Kingston, Port Glasgow); Mr W. Fraser Gillespie (UIE Shipbuilding (Scotland) Ltd, Clydebank); Mr Alastair Gordon (Rutherglen Museum); Mr W.A. Greenhill (Kelvin Diesels Ltd, Glasgow); Mr Brian S. Hagan (Rugby); Mr Leslie Howarth (Campeltown Shipyard Ltd); Mr B.C.W. Lap (Prins Hendrik Museum, Rotterdam); Mr Hamish Ingram (UIE Shipbuilding (Scotland) Ltd, Clydebank); Mr John Jeremy (Vickers Cockatoo Dockyard Pty Ltd, Sydney); Mr James Kemp (Ardrossan, Ayrshire); Mrs Anne Knox (Kirkintilloch); Mr Stanley Linghorn (Shoeburyness, Essex); Mrs Maureen Lochrie (Paisley Museums); Mr Malcolm MacDonald (Seadrec Ltd, Paisley); Mr George McGruer (McGruer & Co Ltd, Rosneath);

Mr Macintosh (W. Ralston Ltd, Glasgow); Mrs Mackenzie (ClydeDock Engineering Ltd); Mr J. Allen McLachlan (Clarkston, Glasgow); Mr W.C. McMillan (Yarrow Shipbuilders Ltd); Mr W. Stanley Mackie (John Brown Engineering Ltd, Westminster); Mr D. Martin (Strathkelvin Libraries); Mr D.I. Moor (St Albans, Herts); Mr Geoffrey Penny (formerly of Furness Withy & Co Ltd); Mr J.F. Robb (Scott Lithgow Ltd, Cartsburn, Greenock); Captain F. Brian Rodgers (Andrew Weir & Co Ltd, London); Mr J.S. Shand (Govan Shipbuilders Ltd, Glasgow); Mr Brian Shaw (High Halden, Kent); Skyfotos Limited (New Romney, Kent); Mr C.A. Somerville (formerly of George Gibson & Co Ltd, Leith); Mr A.S.S. Stephen (Balfron, Stirlingshire); Mr Philip N. Thomas (Thornliebank, Glasgow); Mr John R. Tillie (Clyde Shipping Co Ltd, Glasgow); Mr Colin D. Wilson (John Brown Engineering Ltd, Westminster); and The National Trust for Scotland (Culzean Castle, Ayrshire).

Chapter 1

The River Clyde

In 1707, despite violent opposition in certain parts of Scotland, a solemn Treaty of Union was agreed and effected between the Kingdoms of England and Scotland. Many lasting benefits were to come to both countries and there was a great increase in trade, especially for the Scots who found many new markets open to them and found, too, that they could use their own ships without hindrance. Within a short period there was a considerable growth in the amount of shipping owned in Scotland, a trend which was to continue over the following 200 years.

The excitement of the launch depicted by this late 1930s photograph of the TSMV Circassia *entering the Clyde at Govan.*

Initially ships from the West of Scotland operated from Irvine and other Ayrshire ports, a situation that was moderately inconvenient for the traders of Glasgow, and in the late 17th century the magistrates of Glasgow looked around for means of rectifying this. The River Clyde at Glasgow was then little more than a broad salmon river which was fordable in various places and the idea of deepening it and canalising it, while having been discussed, seemed beyond the reasonable skills of contemporary engineers and undoubtedly at a cost well beyond the depth of the civic purse.

The alternative was to find a trading port and, in 1658, a first approach had been made to the Dumbarton Magistrates. This overture had been turned

down instantly and in 1662 the Glaswegians decided to create an artificial port 20 miles west of Glasgow on the south or Renfrewshire bank. This development was to become Port Glasgow and was where, exactly 150 years later, Europe's first steamship the *Comet* was built.

During the 18th century trade developed immensely, especially the tobacco trade. It has been estimated that in 1772 54 per cent of all British tobacco imports were through Glasgow and, indeed, were to pass through the hands of a mere four or five dozen men; the famed 'tobacco lords'. The war of 1775 and the United States Declaration of Independence of 1776 were to end this business abruptly and Glasgow, for the first time, was to come on a period of serious depression.

Just prior to this reverse the first of many Acts of Parliament for the improvement of harbour and waters was passed in May 1759 and the great work of improving the river was under way. This work has never stopped since. The river rises near Moffat in the great region now known as Strathclyde. It is quickly joined by two larger streams, the Daer and the Powtrail, and gaining strength all the time from tributaries like the Avon, makes its way through the orchards of Clydesdale and into the valley between Hamilton and Motherwell. Here the river has the first taste of its destiny as it passes industrial plant on one hand and Strathclyde Park with the famous Mausoleum of the Hamiltons on the other. The

Resplendent in new paint, the Canadian Pacific Liner Empress of Canada *leaves Princes Dock, Glasgow, before commencing her career on the Pacific Ocean. Built by Fairfield in 1922, she worked on the Yokohama to Vancouver route, but returned to Govan in 1928 for re-engining in order to partner the beautiful new* Empress of Japan *with her 21 knots service speed. The* Empress of Canada *was torpedoed and sunk in the Atlantic in March 1943.*

Mausoleum, built for the tenth Duke of Hamilton, Brandon and Chatelherault as a chapel and family tomb, tilted badly earlier this century and the surrounding ground sank and flooded from the Clyde owing to the slow collapse of mineworkings underneath. The bodies were removed and now the Mausoleum and park are open and from there one has a fine view of the river in the last stages of its pastoral run towards Glasgow.

From Hamilton to Glasgow the progress is more and more industrial and just short of Rutherglen the river becomes navigable for yachts and small craft. From Rutherglen to Glasgow Green the water is sluggish, being impounded by the weir at the bottom of the Saltmarket. Here many oarsmen from schools, university and the fine old Glasgow rowing clubs have their recreation, and in biting weather used to warm their hands in the river just off the cooling water outflows of the Dalmarnock power station.

Built at Govan in 1925, the twin-screw Anchor-Donaldson liner Letitia *was sister ship to the* Athenia, *the first merchantman to sink in the Second World War. In 1946, the* Letitia *was purchased by the Government, converted to a troopship and renamed* Empire Brent. *In 1951, she was given a full scale reconditioning on the Clyde, and with her third name* Captain Cook *became a New Zealand emigrant ship. She had her base at Plantation Quay, Glasgow, and is seen here replenishing before sailing for the Antipodes.*

Few of them recognise the old shipyard of Thomas Seath and, equally, few know that James Watt is said to have thought of the separate steam engine condenser while walking in the Green.

From the centre of Glasgow the river, now fully tidal, passes 20 miles of some of the most historic ground in Scotland. On the banks of either side, until the end of the 1960s, one saw shipyards, docks, engine works and factories. Ferries plied at many crossings and two tunnels have been driven, one during the 19th century at Finnieston now closed, and the other for modern traffic to the west of Govan.

With the growth of trade and the improvement of the Clyde the shipyards flourished, indeed in 1880 there were about 70 shipbuilding establishments on the river, a number which has steadily dwindled since, although 1880 was not the peak for Clyde shipbuilding production. That came a quarter of a

century later. Sadly this is no longer the situation with Queen's Dock now closed and partly filled in and Prince's Dock only partly open. However, one still has the pleasure of seeing major shipbuilding complexes at Govan, Scotstoun, Clydebank, Port Glasgow and Greenock and of passing under the high level bridge at Erskine.

Up to Greenock the river has been restrained, flowing between quay walls or in dredged channels sometimes marked by long banks in the centre of a broadening estuary. From Greenock the Tail of the Bank anchorage shows the river at its very best with the mountains of Argyll rising in dramatic beauty. The new Clyde Port Authority has jurisdiction over most of the Lochs and the Firth down to Arran. It includes the Hunterston ore terminal, the BP Finnart oil terminal and many other interesting developments making up a total of 450 square miles.

Since the Second World War the Gareloch has become host to a naval base and the Holy Loch to a smaller one for the United States Navy. The Clyde steamer fleet has dwindled in size and apart from the PS *Waverley* is now composed entirely of ferry type vessels. Yachting and water sports have boomed in an extraordinary way and the Clyde has reverted to being a sports centre of great repute. A period of great change is again under way and, it is to be hoped, one which can spark the inventive genius and enthusiasm of the Clydesider as did the development of the steam engine nearly two centuries ago.

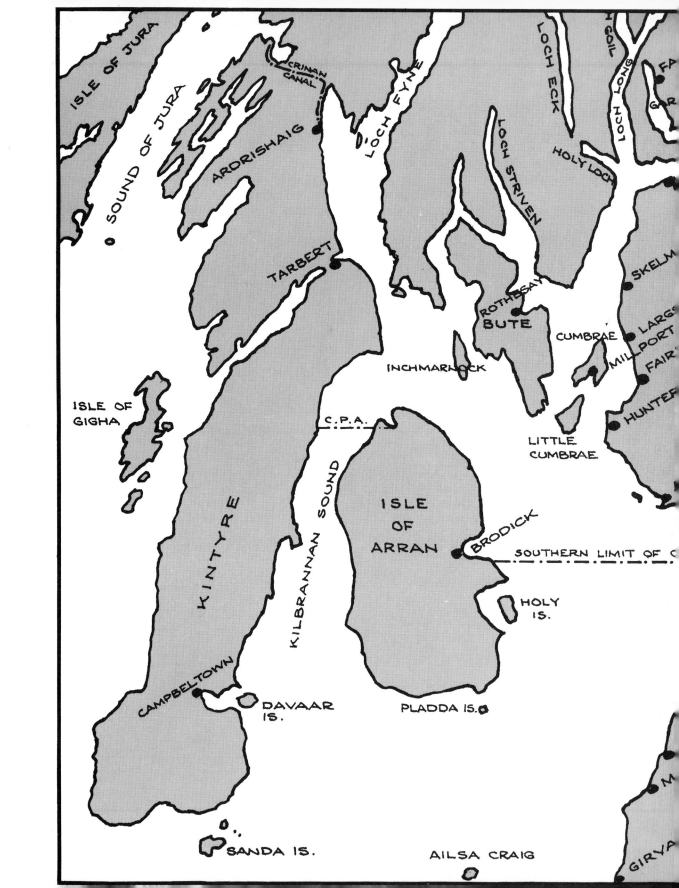

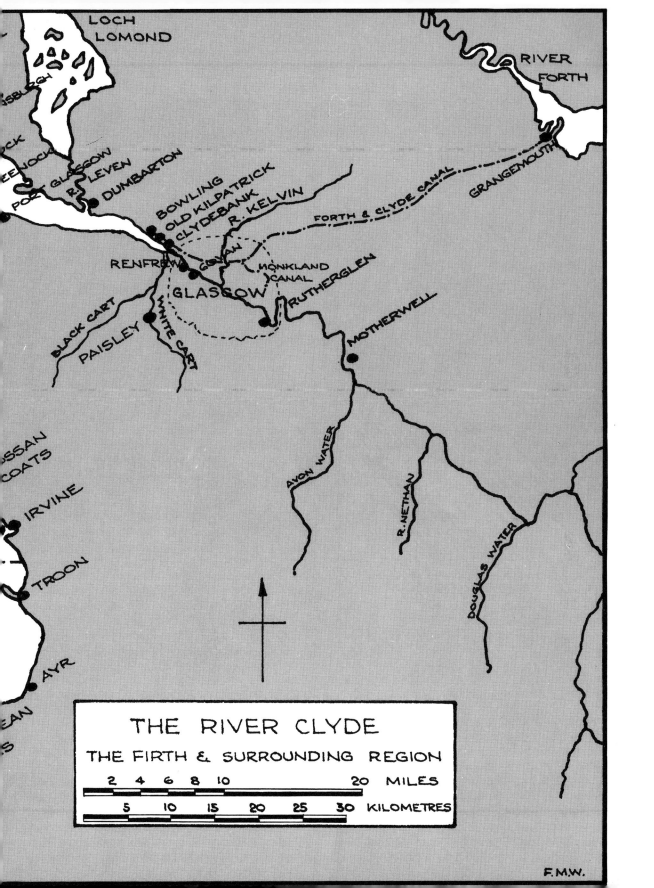

THE RIVER CLYDE

THE FIRTH & SURROUNDING REGION

Chapter 2

Early shipbuilding

Before the mid-19th century, shipyards were reasonably well distributed around the British Isles, with certain coastal areas having a distinct numerical predominance. A large number of yards were to be found on the English South Coast, and on the Thames many yards capable of building quite large vessels were in production. However, few sites capable of building anything larger than a fishing vessel were to be found north of a line from Edinburgh to Glasgow. These early yards required little more than suitable water, some experienced labour and ample storage space for vast quantities of timber. The choice of timber reflected the local grown varieties, or types easily imported into the area. It has to be appreciated that 200 years ago there were no roads suitable for the haulage of tree trunks over long distances and builders were restricted thereby in their choice. The early Scottish yards tended to use Scots oak or English oak, imported by sea from England or from the various naval bases where the material new and second hand was sold off from time to time. The opening of the Forth and Clyde Canal in 1790 paved the way for the increase in Baltic timber imports to the Clyde area, and the bringing of lumber from Canada, notably the Provinces of Nova Scotia, Quebec and Prince Edward Island commenced around the 1820s. The Wood family of Port Glasgow had two attempts at the fashionable importation of soft wood lumber in the holds of Canadian-built deep sea traders. The ships, both built in Quebec, had much timber built into their structure to avoid import duty. The first ship foundered on her return voyage and the second was wrecked on its maiden voyage.

Ships were built on age-old principles which changed little from century to century or place to place. Through the years the design of each part and the particular cut of the wood had been dictated by generations of men observing ships in action in the wild element of the sea. From this accumulated wisdom was evolved shapes of timber which were efficient and pleasing.

The wood ship building technique can be seen to this day in yards building larger traditional craft. A site is selected from which launching is easy, the keel line marked out and blocks laid on the ground on which construction will commence. The keel is selected from a series of straight, robust timbers and placed on the temporary keel blocks with accurate scarphing in way of the joints. The frames are erected at right angles to the keel and are accurately horned or held in place by wires, before being secured both at the keel and at their tops by deck beams or temporary timbers. By the time the frames are erected, stringers are in place and deck beams positioned, the shape of the ship is clear and she awaits the shell planking.

Most yards had ample storage space for timber in order that large stocks could be held or laid out for the shipbuilder to select naturally shaped pieces for particular parts like the breast hooks inside the bows or the knees connecting side frames and deck beams. The yards could operate effectively with only two items of locally manufactured plant: the sawpit and the steam box. The former could be a trench up to 2 metres deep with temporary bearers over the top. Cutting was a two-man job, one at the top, the other below, using double handed saws. In the earliest days, everything including the planks would pass through the sawyer's hands and, indeed, he might be excused for believing he had a job for life—possibly his apprentice working in the pit might have likened it to a life sentence! The steam box was the other essential. It could be constructed from timber and should be longer than the timber to be bent. Planks were inserted and the box closed apart from a steam

Above *The Clyde Gabbart* Mary *moored off Rothesay in the 1880s. These craft were seen frequently on the Firth, the River and the Forth & Clyde Canal until the end of the 19th century, when they were superseded by the Clyde puffer* (National Maritime Museum).

Below *Built by William Fife at Fairlie, in Ayrshire, in the year 1814, the PS* Industry *was first in the service of a Mr Cochrane, who shortly after sold her as a baggage boat to the Clyde Shipping Company. The rotting hulk of* Industry *was visible in Bowling Harbour, well after a century from her launch, but her second set of engines is preserved by Glasgow Museums* (Wotherspoon Collection, Mitchell Library, Glasgow).

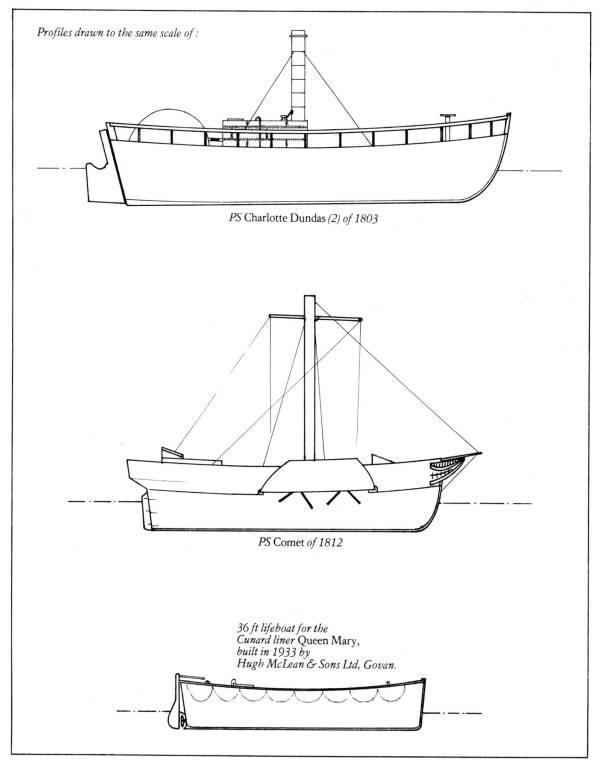

Profiles drawn to the same scale of :

PS Charlotte Dundas *(2) of 1803*

PS Comet *of 1812*

*36 ft lifeboat for the
Cunard liner* Queen Mary,
*built in 1933 by
Hugh McLean & Sons Ltd, Govan.*

The world's first excursion steamer, PS Marion, *built in 1816 by Archibald MacLachlan of Dumbarton for David Napier of Glasgow, who supplied the engines. This little vessel, named after Napier's wife, was the first to ply in Loch Lomond during the 1817 season and later was the first steamer to ply on the stretches of the Clyde above the Glasgow bridges. The* Marion *was broken up in 1828 (Wotherspoon Collection, Mitchell Library, Glasgow).*

inlet at one end and an exhaust at the other, and steam from a small boiler was passed through for up to 24 hours. Once the planks were supple, they were removed and easily pulled to shape on the hull before being permanently secured. Every other job in the yard could be achieved with the simplest of tools, although not without considerable manual effort.

In the larger shipyards the other major job was the erecting of masts. In some ports, cranes and sheerlegs were available, but in small establishments the work had to be done using lashed up spars for temporary derricks. In all, early shipbuilding was an exciting business: fortunately it can be said that despite the passage of time the need for ingenuity and alertness has not changed.

The coming of steam had one significant effect on wooden shipbuilding—in just a few years major changes came about in the structure of vessels. Steam ships with heavy boilers, unbalanced machinery and overhung revolving paddles imposed new strains on hulls and subjected them to the phenomenon of vibration which was something not associated with ships prior to the 19th century. For economy ships had to be larger, longer, deeper and broader, and this led to unusual construction details being hastily tried to overcome shortfalls in the previous technology. Cross bracing, or trussed framing along the inside of the shell, first introduced to the Royal Navy by Sir Robert Seppings in the 1800s, became a feature of some merchant construction. Inexorably wooden vessels continued to grow in length, to reach and to exceed the 80-metre mark at which point timber construction becomes distinctly inefficient owing to the problems of jointing and the mechanics of securing local pieces of material.

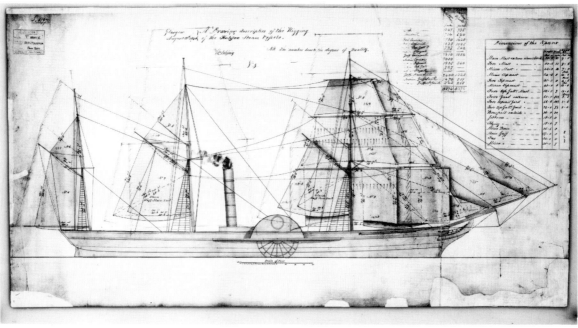

The depletion of European timber supplies, the increase in ship size and the dramatic rise in tonnage of world fleets set the stage for the change from timber to iron. This change was one of the most fortuitous events in British industrial history. Initially ships were built entirely of timber, but throughout the 19th century efforts were made to introduce metal parts to wooden boats. Keel bolts and knee bolts of iron, and even of brass or copper were fitted, and a significant step forward occurred when knees were made of forged iron, thereby saving shipwrights' time in the selecting and cutting of awkward shaped parts, and also saving valuable stowage space in holds.

Of the early shipyards, little is recorded. Many were one-off building arrangements, others were groups of people, varying from time to time in social composition as they pursued their business. There is more than just a possibility that small teams could move about different parts of an area and stay put in one locality while contracts to build ships were available. These business arrangements were not set up in any formal manner and were a far cry from today's enterprise with large capitalisation and highly structured labour arrangements. Our knowledge of these firms is scanty, they left no records and often our only brief references are from contemporary journals. From the statistician's point of view they present little problem, as their output, while significant at the time, had no long term effect on the tonnages produced by the Clyde yards in the 19th and 20th centuries.

A greater disappointment, however, is the lack of working drawings and designs of ships built in the early yards. In general terms the oldest ship plans known of in the UK are a few 17th century Admiralty plans, and for merchant vessels a few 18th century builders' plans. By far the largest and the most important holding of these is at the National Maritime Museum, and it is interesting to note that Scottish contributions to this and to other great archives effectively start in the 19th century. However, despite a late start credit must be given to the Clyde for the scientific thought that led to the preparation of plans to suit all shipbuilding needs, to their systematic recording and to analysis of ship plans with ultimate operating records.

The type of product from these early yards is known; smacks, gabbarts or trading vessels, fishing skiffs and lighters for the Clyde and later the Forth & Clyde Canal. With few exceptions the Clyde did not produce great wooden ships and it was the 19th century before the Royal Navy decided to build in these northern waters. Scotts of Greenock, the world's oldest shipbuilding organisation, founded at Greenock in 1711, started to build larger vessels in the 1760s and by 1800 had got away from the image of fishing boat builder. In 1760 a brig named *Greenock* was built in the port for trading to the West Indies, and for the first time the Clyde was moving into the league of bigger shipbuilding. This West Indiaman is now regarded as small, possibly carrying 300 tons of cargo at most, and no more than 65 metres in length, but with its successful launch the interests and aspirations of the river were in clear focus for the first time.

Above left *Despite being built in 1820, only eight years after the* Comet, *the paddle steamer* Inverary Castle *was the second ship to bear the name. The new ship, built by John Wood of Port Glasgow and engined by David Napier, has the appearance of a vessel built by men confident in their newly acquired skill. She served mostly on the Clyde and Lochfyne and was broken up in 1836 (Wotherspoon Collection, Mitchell Library, Glasgow).*

Left PS Britannia, *the first vessel in the British and North American Royal Mail Steam-Packet Company, now known as the Cunard Line. The four ships* Acadia, Britannia, Caledonia *and* Columbia *were ordered from Robert Napier of Glasgow, who in turn sub-contracted the hulls to the shipyards of John Wood, Robert Duncan, Charles Wood and Robert Steel respectively. Despite* Acadia *being the 'lead ship', the* Britannia *was first completed and inaugurated the service to Halifax and Boston in 1840. This rigging plan is inscribed 'Glasgow, August 28th, 1840' (National Maritime Museum).*

Chapter 3

A brief review of the marine steam engine

It is believed that steam power was first used on land around 1712. Owing to the efforts of Thomas Newcomen an atmospheric steam engine was constructed at a colliery in Staffordshire, and suddenly the industrial revolution had begun. The atmospheric engine was slow, cumbrous and inefficient but it fired the imagination of engineers and helped them appreciate that greater feats could become possible. The engine was studied, illustrated and working models were constructed. Not unnaturally one such model found its way to Glasgow University, and no doubt through heavy use in experiments eventually required repair and was sent off to Sisson the instrument maker for rectification.

In the early winter of 1763 the model was back at the Old College, still not working properly, and John Anderson the Professor of Natural Philosophy asked James Watt the university instrument maker to try

his hand at improving matters. As is well known Watt did not greatly improve the model, but during his deliberations realised the real deficiency lay in the great waste of steam and hence struck on the idea of the separate condenser. With this stroke of genius the steam engine became feasible for the powering of ships. Watt ultimately left the employ of the university and for some years worked as a canal engineer laying out, amongst others, the Monkland Canal before joining Boulton to commence their

Built at Renfrew in 1851, the iron PS Clyde *served the Clyde Navigation Trust well for many years. The machinery which had been constructed by A & J Inglis was purchased by William Brown of Simons and erected on the banks of the Clyde at Renfrew. William Brown's father worked in Inglis and the* Clyde *engines were their first marine engine contract (Wotherspoon Collection, Mitchell Library, Glasgow).*

celebrated business partnership in Birmingham. While not turning his back on marine engines Watt did not contribute much more to the marine field, with the possible exception of the ball governor, an older idea which he developed satisfactorily and which to this day is known as the James Watt Ball Governor.

There was an amazing interaction between engineers at that period. Despite grave difficulties in travel men covered hundreds of miles to find out more on steam engines and, with hindsight, it is interesting to reflect that most were open and frank, sharing their experiences and having none of the artificial mystique and secrecy which surrounded the older trades—not least the shipwrights in wood. Few engineers of the period patented their ideas, with the obvious exception of James Watt's notable patent of 1769, and therefore development tended to be continuous and interactive.

One of the group of young engineers at the time was William Symington (1764-1831). He was born at Leadhills in Lanarkshire not far from the source of the Clyde and, while originally destined for the

In 1857 Robert Napier and Sons, fitted a two-cylinder steam engine to the French three-decker Louis XIV. *This ship was laid down at Rochefort in France in 1811, and launched as late as 1854. The machinery of 600 nhp was installed in 1857, as depicted on an ambrotype in the possession of the National Maritime Museum* (National Maritime Museum).

ministry, he became in early life a successful engineer modifying and repairing the numerous atmospheric engines employed by the pits. Symington came into contact with a man 33 years his senior and their joint endeavours were to become world famous. The older man was Patrick Miller of Dalswinton, Dumfries. Miller had made pioneering efforts to improve the shape of ships, including his trimaran *Edinburgh* of 1786 with two sets of paddle wheels abreast the central hull. These paddles could be raised when the ship was under sail. The *Edinburgh* was driven by the effort of several men turning cranks. He tried several other revolutionary craft and at the suggestion of a friend approached Symington to see if a steam propelled craft was a possibility.

On October 14 1788 a small twin hulled vessel only 25 ft × 8 ft (7.6 m × 2.4 m) with two centre line paddle wheels steamed on Dalswinton Loch at 5 mph, and according to unsubstantiated tradition Robert Burns was one of the persons aboard. The engine was of atmospheric type with separate condenser which could well have been an infringement of the patent registered by James Watt. However, Symington had become well known and when the directors of the Forth and Clyde Canal met in London in 1800 they resolved to try an experimental steam vessel on the canal and he was invited to design the engine. According to recent researchers Messrs Harvey and Downs-Rose, a single-cylinder beam engine was fitted on a lighter supplied by Hart of Grangemouth in 1801. After unsatisfactory trials

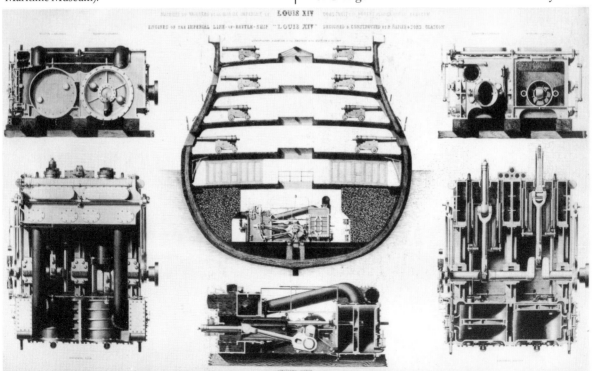

LOUIS XIV

ENGINES OF THE IMPERIAL LINE-OF-BATTLE-SHIP "LOUIS XIV" DESIGNED & CONSTRUCTED BY R. NAPIER & SONS GLASGOW

John Robertson (1782-1868), the manufacturer of the engine for the pioneer steamer PS Comet. *The cost of the order was £163, but after alterations became £365—a bill that it is believed was never paid* (Wotherspoon Collection Mitchell Library, Glasgow).

on the River Carron a second vessel was constructed again with the name *Charlotte Dundas* and on March 28 1803 this little ship towed the two sloops *Active* and *Euphemia* 18½ miles against a headwind to Glasgow in just over nine hours.

Despite conflicting stories about the number of vessels with the name *Charlotte Dundas* and about the details of build, three clear facts emerge. First, she was from the engineer's point of view an unqualified success. Second, considerable scientific thought had been brought to bear on her design, the hull forms of Captain Schank had been studied and consideration given to the optimum paddle revolutions to give best speed on the engine power. Third, the decision of the Canal Company to ignore Symington's work and to ban the ship from steaming held back the development of steam for several years in the UK and probably contributed to the poor financial returns of the Forth & Clyde Canal. The *Charlotte Dundas* had a horizontal double-acting single cylinder engine and was the precursor of later engine layouts featuring crank, connecting rods and guides. Mr G.E. Barr of Denny & Co described Symington as 'truly . . . the father of the paddle wheel engine'.

In 1780 John Wood founded a yard in Greenock

on a part of the shore known as the Rue End where many small businesses had their beginnings. His work was known to be good and he prospered to the extent that he was able to send his oldest son John south to Cumbria to serve his apprenticeship as a shipbuilder under the Brocklebanks of Whitehaven. Just before John Wood (senior) died in 1811 he had become acquainted with a gentleman, Henry Bell, a celebrated character on Clydeside who wanted to build a steam-propelled ship. Wood's son decided to carry on the project which had so attracted his father, and along with his brother Charles who joined the business, contracted to build the ship which was to become world famous—the paddle steamer *Comet*, named after Halley's Comet which had just made her predicted return to the night sky. In 1810 the business had moved to Port Glasgow East Shipyard and there the ship was built with an engine by John Robertson of Glasgow and a boiler by David Napier. The engine was of single-cylinder double acting side lever type and initially it drove a pinion which turned two shafts giving double paddles on each side but later this was changed to direct drive.

The engine of 4 nominal hp drove her at about 5 mph in good conditions but, for help in rougher weather, a large squaresail was set on the tall upright smokestack. The trials were held in August 1812 and she travelled from Glasgow to Greenock in 3½ hours. The *Comet* was just over 13 m long (43 ft 6 ins on deck) and lasted eight years during which time she travelled widely sailing through the canal to the Forth and, in 1819, establishing the first steamship route between Glasgow and the West Highlands. Her low speed and lack of reserve power led to her undoing as on December 13 1820, passing through the Dorus Mor, she was swept by the 8-knot tides on to Craignish Point on Argyll and was wrecked. Fortunately her engine survives and is now part of the fascinating marine engine collection at the Science Museum, London.

The *Comet's* success ensured John and Charles Wood steady work and over the next 41 years they produced in all 81 steam-driven ships including a replacement for the ill fated first *Comet*. Like most shipbuilders they did not build engines but purchased these from an ever-increasing number of concerns

Built by Tod & MacGregor at Partick in 1850, the SS City of Glasgow earned her place in history, by being the vessel that demonstrated the possibility of ocean-going passenger steamship operation without Goverment subsidy. The illustration is from a music plate in the possession of the National Maritime Museum, Greenwich.

which could produce them with surprising speed, efficiency and economy.

From 1812 through to the 1850s most engineering establishments built paddle engines of the tried and trusted side lever variety. They were robust, simple to operate and suitable for pressures up to about 3 bar (45 lb/sq in) and often had two independent double acting pistons exhausting directly to the condenser. A working example of this kind of engine can be seen at the National Maritime Museum, Greenwich, where the paddle tug *Reliant* has been completely reconstructed in the Neptune Hall and the machinery is now electrically driven.

David Napier was both an engineer and a ship-owner and in his latter capacity was concerned at the large amount of space in a ship's hull devoted to the engine room. In order to shorten the length of the engine room he devised a steeple engine, so called because of its high triangular configuration. The first came out on PS *Clyde* about 1836 and for nearly 30 years they were common on fast paddle steamers, and indeed were to be seen on a major proportion of the early Clyde paddle steamer fleet. In the steeple engine the cylinders were vertically under the paddle crank although the guides, crosshead and connecting rods were above, sometimes protruding above the weather deck.

The oscillating engine was the next development having been devised by Penn of Greenwich in 1825. It required more length but was low and compact and dispensed with connecting rods although requiring both sophisticated valve gear and steam connections to the cylinders. The oscillating engine was regularly fitted in paddle steamers up to the 1880s and was the type fitted to MacBrayne's classic ships *Iona* (3) and *Columba*.

From the mid-19th century through to the demise of the paddle steamer the engine which was most popular and became universal was the diagonal. It is a surprise to learn that this engine was originally patented by I.K. Brunel as early as 1822. It was a flexible design ranging from three-cylinder double acting triple expansion engines developing thousands of horse power to a single-cylinder engine driving her ship forward with quite clearly perceptible power surges.

Throughout the early 19th century much thought

and effort were expended on alternative means of propelling ships. The general principles of the screw propeller were understood but effective means of putting this theory into practice were not so clear and therefore many experiments were tried and patents taken out. In 1804 Stevens, an American, tried out an unsuccessful power plant including a Bramah type propeller, and in 1826 Samuel Brown drove a ship on the Thames with a propeller but the failure of the sponsoring company brought this promising venture to an abrupt halt. Around that time several attempts were made to drive ships with cones on the ends of the propeller shafts, each cone having a deep spiral thread cut into it.

In 1836 Francis Pettit Smith patented an elementary form of screw propeller and, with heavy financial backing from a banker, an experimental boat appropriately named *Archimedes* was built in London for a sum just over £10,000. The *Archimedes* of 106 ft × 21.8 ft (32.3 m × 6.6 m) was quite able to steam round the British coasts and indeed became a floating test-bed being, probably, the first example of a sales promotion ship. Ultimately a captain of the Royal Navy took command of the ship during the evaluation period during which she raced with Dover–Calais packets, carried out a 2,500-mile British circumnavigation and in the Firth of Forth carried out full speed turning circle trials in which she came through 360-degree turns in 2½ minutes, no mean feat for an early conventional propeller vessel!

From 1840 a steady succession of screw ships were constructed, with pride of place going to the wonderful SS *Great Britain* built at Bristol by I.K. Brunel and floated out of her dry dock in 1843. Possibly the two most significant early screw steamers to come from the Clyde were the frigate HMS *Greenock* (1849) and SS *City of Glasgow* built at Tod & MacGregor's yard in 1850. Both ships had an important role in establishing the acceptance of the screw propeller by Clyde shipbuilders and, as is mentioned later in this book, the *City of Glasgow* laid the foundation of the trans-Atlantic passenger trade by competing successfully with subsidised mail companies and still making a profit. This came through reduced coal consumption and maximised use of space for passengers and cargo. By giving improved living conditions to emigrants she sailed regularly with a high proportion of her accommodation utilised.

The change-over to the screw propeller with its fore and aft shaft posed the problem of re-orientation to the marine engine builders. This problem was compounded by the fact that early engines were much slower than the efficient speed of screw propellers and therefore required gearing up, the complete reverse from the 20th century when in general terms efficient machinery means higher revolutions and hence gearing down. As there was no laid down standard design for marine engines, the various European manufacturers (most of whom were British) tried many interesting and exciting configurations such as horizontal cylinders lying on either side of the crank, V formations and some designs which emanated from the latter variations on the established oscillating steam engine. As the years passed and as engine design reached new peaks, most manufacturers tended towards the vertical layout and ultimately placed the cylinders and columns above the crankshaft.

It is interesting to note in passing that the status of engineers in merchant ships had been low in the 1840s, but in 1863 enactments required Chief Engineers and Seconds to be certificated and this in turn led to the enhancement of their position aboard. By the time the great steamers were racing on the Atlantic and to the Cape the engineer had become equal with the appropriate deck grade and the Chief Engineer acted as an independent head of department under the Master. Recruitment of these men was from the ranks of time-served engineers from shipyards and engine works. This quietly paralleled the great British achievement of giving the world in the late 19th century an economic and totally reliable steam engine—the triple expansion.

In single-cylinder engines or engines with independently operating cylinders it was clear that steam was being exhausted which still contained untapped energy and many engineers had striven for long to work out a means of passing steam from one cylinder to another (of larger size as the partly used steam was expanded and cooler) and so on until it could be exhausted to the condenser at less than atmospheric pressure. This principle of allowing steam to expand twice in an operating cycle was known as compounding and once this had been mastered it was only some years before engines were built with triple and even quadruple expansion.

The earliest record of compounding is in 1781 with a patent taken out by an Englishman, Jonathan Hornblower, for land-based beam engines and in later years various attempts, successful and other-

Above *The Historic steamship* Agamemnon *built by Scott's of Greenock, which opened up Alfred Holt's Far Eastern trade in 1866. Powered with a vertical tandem compound steam engine, the* Agamemnon *enabled the Blue Funnel Line to compete with sailing ships on long ocean hauls. The photograph is of a model recently commissioned by the National Maritime Museum, and shows her original and later abandoned arrangement of propeller abaft the rudder* (National Maritime Museum).
Below *Waterclour of the paddle steamer* Plover, *built of iron in 1849 by Thomas Wingate & Co of Glasgow. Originally named* Maid of Lorn, *she was designed to use the Crinan Canal and is reputed to have had paddles recessed to give maximum beam on deck. Her machinery was a single-cylinder steeple engine* (Wotherspoon Collection, Mitchell Library, Glasgow).

wise, were made by Arthur Woolf and others to capitalise on the idea. However, it was to one man in particular, a former trainee of Robert Napier, that acknowledgement must be made for the design and development of a really satisfactory compound engine.

The general engineering business of Randolph Elliot & Co was joined in 1852 by John Elder, then aged only 28. The company name was changed to Randolph, Elder & Co as Elder was assumed a partner, and slowly but most surely the emphasis changed towards the expanding marine engine market. While still based at Tradeston the attention of the world was turned on them in 1854 when they completed a contract for engining a Clyde-built steamer for the British and Irish coastal service—the ship was SS *Brandon* and the engine was steam compound. In the souvenir book issued by the Fairfield Shipyard in 1909 it is recorded that instead of normal coal consumption on trials of between 4 lb and 4½ lb per hour for each indicated horse power, the *Brandon* required only 3¼ lb, a saving of around 30 per cent.

The effect of the *Brandon* was immediate and dramatic. The world beat a path to the young company as, fortunately, the young engineers had patented their developments and with brisk business they moved in 1860 to the Govan Old Yard and again in 1864 to the lands of the Fairfield Farm in Govan where a new yard was laid out. This yard continues to this day as the active centre of Govan Shipbuilders. The Pacific Steam Navigation Company in particular formed a close bond with Randolph, Elder as they recognised that without Elder's pioneering work on fuel reduction, steamship operation on long routes such as theirs from Europe to the west coast of South America would have been impossible. Over a period of 40 years they ordered 41 ships from Govan and in 1869 paid a handsome compliment to one of the Clyde's greatest engineers by naming a ship the *John Elder*.

In April 1869 John Elder, then aged 45, was elected president of the Institution of Engineers and Shipbuilders in Scotland. His opening address in the autumn of that year was awaited with especial interest, but sadly he died in London that September and the engineering community sustained an immeasurable loss.

With the acceptance of compounding two natural steps occurred. First compounding was applied to paddle ship engines and, second, strenuous efforts

were made especially on Clydeside to take compounding into the next logical stage, known by that delightful name—triple expansion.

Several developments came about quickly each in its own way establishing the marine engineering industry as one of outreach and continuous development. It was clear to the shipbuilders and engineers that technical excellence was not enough but that they must design, sell and build ships suitable for profitable trading on the known and developing world trade routes. Alfred Holt of Liverpool, the farsighted shipowner, had for some time considered steamer services to the Far East and, with clear indications that fuel savings were likely with the new style of engine, he ordered three ships from Scott's of Greenock to be named *Agamemnon*, *Ajax* and *Achilles*. The *Agamemnon* had a compound engine with the high pressure cylinder vertically under the crankshaft and the low pressure one directly above in a configuration which became known as vertical

Alexander Carnegie Kirk LLD (1830-1892), a former trainee of Robert Napier, and now honoured as the father of the steam triple expansion engine. The introduction of this engine secured for Britain pre-eminence in the maritime field for over 30 years (Wotherspoon Collection Mitchell Library, Glasgow).

Engine arrangement drawing of the triple expansion machinery for the dredger Annie W. Lewis *built by Wm Simons & Co Ltd, Renfrew, in 1927 for the Aberdeen Harbour Commissioners.*

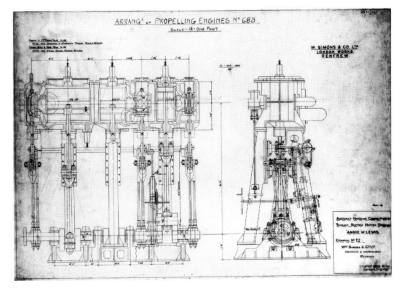

tandem and which was standard in Blue Funnel ships till triple expansion was commonplace. To even out the power surges with a single crank a large flywheel was fitted and many balancing weights fitted to moving parts of the engine.

By the 1870s several large shipping companies along with PSNC and Blue Funnel had experience with compound engines and their experience was that about 30 per cent fuel was saved by the new engine type.

Another Clyde shipyard which did early development work was Thomas Wingate of Glasgow. Wingate set up an engineering business in the city in 1823 but around 1836 obtained a major contract which was to make his name and channel his interest fully into the marine field. The order was for a 320 ihp steam engine for a ship being built by Menzies at Leith. The ship was PS *Sirius* and became celebrated as being the first ship to cross the Atlantic under continuous power, making the passage from Cork to New York in 18 days 10 hours. To the engineer she was much more significant being the first ocean going ship with fresh water in her boilers and creating a precedent by having a surface condenser to allow recycling of the feed water.

In 1837 Wingate commenced shipbuilding at Springfield Quay just west of where the Kingston Bridge is now situated and in 1848 moved to Whiteinch East and remained there for 30 years before closing. During 41 years of shipbuilding about 200 interesting ships were constructed, most bearing

the stamp of originality of this enthusiastic man. In 1844 he built the paddle steamer *Queen of Beauty* with two shafts each with drums on the ends over which an endless belt of floats passed. Regrettably this was not a success and she was converted to normal paddle configuration later. In 1849 the yard delivered PS *Maid of Lorn* an iron ship of 82 ft × 23 ft × 8 ft (25 m × 7 m × 2.5 m). The engine was a single-cylinder steeple type operating paddles recessed within the line of the hull in order to give the ship the full beam permissible on the Crinan Canal. The illustration does not make it clear whether the hull has a full recess or whether the paddle sponsons are carried through in a 'fair line' which is the more usual way to handle such a problem.

In 1872 it is said that they built a triple expansion engine designed by their manager Peter J. Ferguson, a subsequent founder of Fleming & Ferguson of Paisley. If this can be proved then Wingate's were the first engineers to build the engine which became for the best part of a century the main workhorse of the world's merchant fleets.

The first authenticated triple expansion engine was a re-engining or, in modern parlance a 'retrofit' of SS *Propontis* at Govan in 1874. The Fairfield yard had then become known as John Elder & Co and they entrusted this work to Dr Alexander Carnegie Kirk (1830-1892).

A.C. Kirk is another of the men whose destiny became linked with the Clyde and who added great

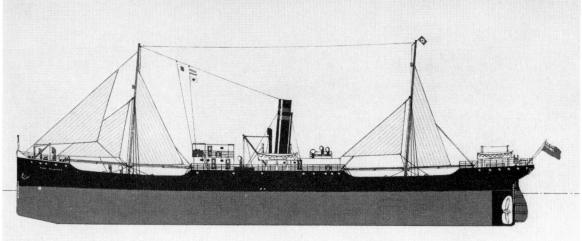

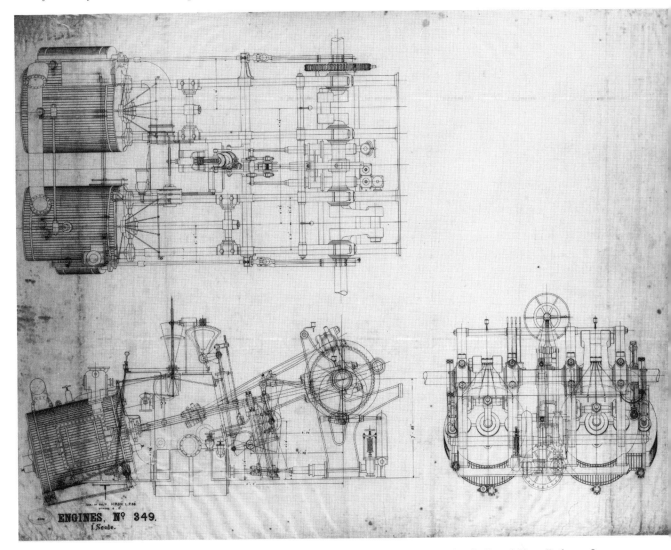

ENGINES, Nº 349.
¼ Scale.

Top left *Built by A & J Inglis Ltd, of Pointhouse, in 1951, the twin-screw steam tug* Simba *for the East African Railways & Harbours, Mombassa, was one of the last triple expansion export jobs to leave the Clyde. She is seen here in Yorkhill Basin in 1951 prior to delivery. The two sets of main machinery were supplied by Aitchison, Blair Ltd of Clydebank.*

Above left *SS* Clan Macaulay *completed in 1899 by Alexander Stephen & Sons for the Clan Line Steamers is a good representative of the British cargo ship of the turn of the century. With speeds of around 10 knots, hundreds of similar ships worked for years on the cross trades, covering immense distances and seldom touching British ports. All gear was simple and robust and machinery of triple expansion type. Sails were carried and occasionally used for fuel economy and on the infrequent times that propeller shafts fractured.*

Left *The Clyde paddle steamer* Jupiter *was typical of 20th century ships of her class in having triple expansion diagonal steam engines. Built by Fairfield in 1937, the* Jupiter *served 21 years on the Clyde and another four on war service.*

Above *The compound diagonal steam machinery manufactured by Denny & Co in 1888 for the Irrawaddy Flotilla Company paddle steamer* China. *This river steamer was built by William Denny & Brothers, the shipbuilding part of the Denny organisation in Dumbarton. (National Maritime Museum).*

lustre to the traditions of the river. A son of the manse from Angus he attended Edinburgh University, served his apprenticeship at the Vulcan Foundry, Glasgow, before becoming chief draughtsman with Maudslay, Sons & Field, London, and then returning to Scotland to work for 'Paraffin' Young, Cranstonhill Engine Works, John Elder & Co and finally as a partner with the renowned Robert Napier & Sons.

In 1881, under Kirk's superintendence and oversight, a ship was built which could be described fairly as a masterpiece. It was the SS *Aberdeen* for George Thompson's Aberdeen Line. To build for George Thompson was in itself almost an honour as, on reading over his ship lists, one sees names of some of the most famous vessels which have worn the Red Ensign. They include the iron sailing ship *Patriarch* built by Walter Hood, Aberdeen, the *Samuel Plimsoll,* the *Miltiades* and the super Aberdeen-built *Thermopylae.* Thompson must have been impressed with the *Aberdeen* as he returned many times to the Clyde and the *Australasian, Damascus, Niveveh, Moravian, Miltiades* (2) and *Marathon* bearing the traditional dark green hulls of Aberdeen ships were to leave the yards of Napier and Stephen.

SS *Aberdeen* remained on the Australian route until 1906 when sold to the Turkish Goverment and renamed *Halep.* She was damaged in war action in 1915. During her days under the British flag she could carry nearly 700 passengers and became known for being well managed with good wholesome food and general lack of ostentation.

The triple expansion engine was built in large numbers on the Clyde and quickly followed worldwide. It was a strong, robust engine capable of considerable emergency overload and is to this day regarded as an elegant and flexible product of the marine engineer. After the 1920s fewer such engines were built and ultimately went into whale catchers, tugs and other craft where their qualities were especially valuable. Few were constructed after the late 1950s.

In the early days of ocean-going screw steamships the two most common causes of breakdown were fractured propeller shafts and malfunctioning condensers. It was unusual for an engine to break down and in the few such cases the cause could be traced usually to an auxiliary. The studies carried out on steel by Kirkaldy and others ensured that greater quality control could be effected on shaft forgings and by the end of the century broken shafts were quite rare. Condenser trouble usually emanated from leakage at the screwed ends of the pipes taking cooling water. Ultimately this was overcome by better choice of materials, more original means of screwing the pipe ends and by allowance for expansion. The introduction of Admiralty brass pipes practically eliminated these problems giving steam ships an enviable record of reliability.

Built by Robert Napier & Sons, under the direction of Dr A.C. Kirk, the SS Aberdeen *for George Thompson's Aberdeen Line can be described as a masterpiece. With this ship, in 1881, the steam triple expansion engine became established and the future of the British Merchant Navy secured. The* Aberdeen *is seen here drydocked in the old graving dock of the city after which she was named* (Aberdeen Art Galleries).

Chapter 4

Shipbuilding in iron

Thomas Wilson and the *Vulcan*

While it is a matter of conjecture as to the first use of iron in shipbuilding somewhere in the English midlands in the 18th century, it is a matter of certainty as to where the first iron vessel was built in Scotland. The ship was the Forth & Clyde Canal passage boat *Vulcan* and the place was Faskine on the Monkland Canal a few miles from Glasgow. The details of the boat, her construction and history have been well recorded, and she deserves to be remembered as one of the most revolutionary vessels ever built. Her original and unique form of construction set out principles in iron and steel shipbuilding which are adhered to, even in our days.

The builder was Thomas Wilson (1781-1873) a native of Dunbar, who came to Bowling as an apprentice shipwright and later set up in business on his own account at Blackhill on the Monkland Canal. His usual product range included lighters and scows but in about 1818 he agreed to build an iron passage barge to the design of Sir John Robison of Edinburgh. To the delight of the disbelieving local lightermen he laid down the new iron ship on October 27 1818 and launched it on May 14 1819. Their even greater disbelief at its floating can be imagined!

The keel was formed of a two-ply riveted plate rising 1 ft into the ship and the plates were laid in vertical strakes each 24 in broad (608 mm) butted flush with an angle-iron frame behind each butt. The effort expended in the construction must have been stupendous as angle irons had not been rolled previous to that date and each frame was made from a flat bar bent on the blacksmith's anvil. Thomas Wilson should have greater credit than he has received to date—his *Vulcan* sailed the canal and occasionally the reaches of the Clyde until broken up in 1873, the same year as the builder's death.

The introduction of iron in the Clyde shipyards came at the best moment to ensure that the river developed and that, with the passage of some years, was poised for ultimate world leadership, which was to follow the introduction of steel in the 1880s. David Napier, a man of great intensity and imagination took a vital step when, in 1827, he decided to

The first iron ship built in Scotland, the passage boat Vulcan *launched at Faskine, near Glasgow on the Monkland Canal, on May 14 1819. The designer was Sir John Robison of Edinburgh and the builder Mr Thomas Wilson. The* Vulcan *was 61 ft × 11 ft × 4 ft 6 in (18.6 m × 3.4 m × 1.4 m) draft. She was broken up in 1873. (drawing by the author from information published by the Scottish Shipbuilders' Association 1864-65.)*

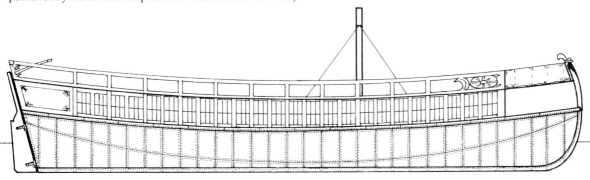

Left *Thomas Wilson, the builder of the iron barge* Vulcan *was born at Dunbar in 1781, and after serving his apprenticeship as a ship carpenter at Bowling, set up in business on the Monkland Canal. His achievement in building the* Vulcan *was remarkable, as the angle irons forming the frames had to be manufactured by blacksmiths. At that time iron works could not roll complex sections. Thomas Wilson died in 1873, the same year that the* Vulcan *was broken up* (Wotherspoon Collection, Mitchell Library, Glasgow).

Below *The lines plan of the paddle steamer* Premier *of Weymouth, built by Denny Brothers in 1846. This steamer, built of iron, was not broken up till 1938 or 1939 and at that time was almost certainly the oldest steamship still in operation. Her dimensions were 133 ft on waterline, 17 ft beam and moulded depth of 6 ft 10 in (40.5 m × 5.2 m × 2.1 m) at the time of breaking up, but it was believed that she had been lengthened in her long life. One of the great advantages of iron is that it corrodes much more slowly than steel, accounting for the great age of some ships of this type* (National Maritime Museum).

Right *Built at Govan by J & G Thomson in 1854, the* Jura *had a chequered career. The iron-screw steamship was first used on trooping duties to the Crimea, but was ultimately sold by Cunard to the Allan Line in 1861. In 1864 she struck Crosby Point on the Mersey and broke her back, becoming a constructive total loss* (Wotherspoon Collection, Mitchell Library, Glasgow).

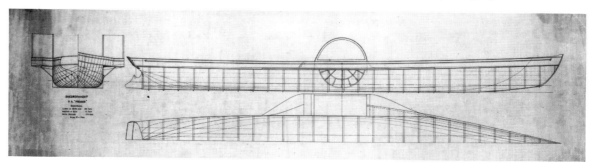

enlarge his fleet of pleasure craft by building one for that long, lovely stretch of water from the Holy Loch to Strachur in Lochfyne. Having successfully pioneered inland navigation with the *Marion* on Loch Lomond he decided to build another steamer for Loch Eck. It is difficult now to assess his reasons, but he decided to build this new ship *Aglaia* in iron and thereby must have given himself many problems with the haulage of heavy parts by horses over poorly made Argyll roads. Whatever the cost in material, labour and effort, it did allow him the opportunity to work far from the gaze of others and to participate in the creation of a new industry.

Four years later John Neilson of Garscube Road, Glasgow, built the iron paddle steamer *Fairy Queen*

at Hamiltonhill and then carried out the daunting task of transporting the hull by road to the Clyde and launching her by crane. This new steamer 97 ft × 11 ft × 8 ft (29.6 m × 3.4 m × 2.5 m) became the first iron ship to sail on the Clyde and later while serving on the Glasgow/Largs/Millport route became the first iron ship to call on the Isle of Cumbrae. Again David Napier was involved in the supply of an oscillating steam engine which was a design newly introduced by Penn of Greenwich.

The building of iron ships became more frequent and as early as 1834 the shipyard of Tod and MacGregor was set up for the exclusive production of iron ships. Their first ship was PS *Loch Goil* delivered in 1835 and it was to be followed by a

Below *The Cunard iron mail paddle ship* Persia *under construction in the Govan shipyard of Robert Napier & Sons in 1855. At the time the* Persia, *which had dimensions 376 ft × 45 ft (114.6 m × 13.7 m), was the largest ship in the world. This is one of the earliest known photographs of a Clyde shipyard, and depicts Napier's at the time when they were rising into prominence. The photograph clearly illustrates the problems of the old shipbuilders in erecting shell plates, paddle boxes and masts without effective craneage* (Annan, Glasgow).

Above *Built by J & G Thomson at Govan in 1866, the iron paddle steamer* Gondolier *had a remarkable life of well over 70 years, serving first David Hutcheson & Co and then David MacBrayne on their Caledonian Canal service. In 1939 she was stripped of all fittings and her immaculate oscillating engines removed, before she was towed to Scapa Flow and sunk there as a blockship. The photograph shows her at Fort Augustus with Loch Ness in the background* (National Maritime Museum).

Below *An early photograph of the steam ferry* Leviathan *which inaugurated the world's first train ferry service between Burntisland and Granton on the Firth of Forth in Febuary 1850. This service continued until the opening of the Forth Railway Bridge in 1890. The photograph shows that the principles of the link span were mastered at the outset. This ship was so successful that the second vessel was named* Robert Napier *in honour of the designer and builder* (National Maritime Museum).

A view of Water Row, Govan, in the 19th century. Across the River Clyde can be seen the stocks of the Meadowside shipyard of Tod and MacGregor on the west bank of the Kelvin. To the right of the picture are the masts and funnel of a steamer, probably in the drydock (Wotherspoon Collection, Mitchell Library, Glasgow).

succession of about 160 ships before their sale to Hendersons in 1873. Among the ships was PS *Queen* built to their own account in 1838 for service in Cork.

Tod and MacGregor had an advantage over their competitors in that they set up the new shipyard untrammelled by an inconvenient layout dictated by the needs of wooden production. It is indeed an interesting reflection that the same year, 1834, saw the formation of the embryo of the Boilermakers' Society indicating that there has been parallel growth between industry and the unions for 150 years.

The new technology spread like wildfire and there must have been great excitement as people experimented with hull shape, iron structures and with steam engines which became further developed and more sophisticated as every month passed. Yards which embraced the new techniques were faced with many problems ranging from recruiting suitable labour to obtaining necessary machine tools, and from organising stock piles of iron to erecting furnaces.

Shipyards which did not have railway links quickly decided to arrange this as deliveries from the ironworks of Lanarkshire were most convenient in this way. Craneage became a matter of urgency and stockyards were found essential for several reasons. The first and most obvious one is that most yards decided to carry a certain percentage of their iron plates and bars as ready-use stock allowing for ship repairs and also for replacement of plates found faulty. The high standards expected from today's steelworks were not available in the first half of the 19th century and, indeed, the strength of iron plate varied quite dramatically and in a random manner.

The other main reason for stockholding in the open air is that plates and sections which have been rolled hot in the ironworks have millscale on the top surface. This must be removed as it breaks down later removing paint and leaving the surface open to rusting and corrosion. The easiest known technique up to, say, 30 years ago was to stand the plate in the open air, and by weathering, the millscale would fall off leaving a rusted plate. The variable weather of Clydeside could be said to be an added bonus in this case. The rust could be removed more easily by wire brushing and the plate then protected by old fashioned red-lead, that is an oxide of lead in a linseed oil mix.

Each yard required some quite expensive tools including plate rolls, a machine with variable heavy turning rollers through which a plate could be 'mangled' to ensure its flatness or by adjusting the rolls can be bent to a pre-arranged shape. Shears were an early invention and effectively are guillotines which can be used to crop the ends of plates to accurate size. Punches were also introduced early in the yards and, despite increased sophistication over the years, their main purpose remained the same— to punch small holes for bolts and rivets. Many of these machines were operated by belt and pulley drive from steam-driven overhead shafting.

In the early days the cutting of manholes was a manual job carried out by caulkers using hammers and chisels. The hardness of the iron resulted in much arduous work which was eliminated much later in the century by the use of oxy-acetylene and, later again, oxy-propane cutting gases.

Riveting was a known technique and initially was carried out by squads of men skilled in fitting the rivet in the appropriate holes, then capping it and finishing it by hand. Later the use of hydraulic riveting machines increased productivity in flat areas with many rivets and, later again, this was superseded by hand-held pneumatic riveting hammers. Owing to their key role the riveters became the best paid tradesmen on the River Clyde, a position they held until the 1920s. Their high earnings reflected their grip on production and their ability to negotiate good piece rates, that is a payment based entirely on work completed with allowances for special factors like difficulty in access.

The other major feature of the iron shipbuilding yard was the need for furnaces. Until recently the only means of bending the frames of a ship was to heat them and then, after withdrawing them from the furnace, bend them on the slabbed floor of the workshop. Similarly, awkward plates had to be heated and then hammered into shape by the platers.

The more these yards are studied the clearer it becomes that early shipbuilders showed considerable initiative and by their efforts of both mind and hand created an industry.

Paddle steamer Sheila *built and engined in 1877 by Caird & Co of Greenock. She was renamed* Isle of Bute *and later joined the North British fleet as* Guy Mannering *Her machinery was a single-cylinder diagonal engine, and this gave her a regular thrusting motion, especially at speed* (Wotherspoon Collection, Mitchell Library, Glasgow).

Chapter 5

Sailing ships

The earliest ships of the Clyde, apart from dug outs and small boats, were the smacks, skiffs, gabbarts and busses required for local trade. This tradition of building goes back centuries and is recorded at Ayr, Ardrossan, Dumbarton, Greenock and elsewhere. The smacks, gabbarts and their near relatives, the busses, were bluff-bowed craft designed to carry the maximum of cargo within a hull of small dimensions and to offer qualities of easy sailing, sea kindliness and the ability to beach on reasonable sand or shingle. Strangely, the opening of the Forth & Clyde Canal at the end of the 18th century imposed a restriction on their overall dimensions.

The gabbarts, as is obvious from their shape, were not exciting sailers but were very useful craft and good sea boats. Generally they were confined to the Clyde estuary and were sloop or cutter rigged with a single pole mast and gaff mainsail. The stern was rounded with the rudder set outboard. They lost ground to the onslaught of the steam coaster, the puffer and the relatively efficient coasting topsail schooner but especially to rail and road competition.

It has been said that improvements in the boat builders' skills on the Clyde came about through the examples seen of East Coast building. Some authorities date this from 1822 when the Caledonian Canal was opened, making it the only true sea-to-sea link established for larger vessels across the British Isles. The influence of the beautiful ships of the Moray Coast began to be felt and it is not improbable that the lovely lines of the Lochfyne skiff were influenced in this way. The skiff, with its raked keel and stern-post, loose footed standing lug sail and easy sheer, was a powerful yet gentle sailing vessel. Now all have gone as, indeed, has much of the long line herring fishery which took its name from the longest sea loch on the Clyde estuary.

With the growth in trade and the repeal of the Navigation Acts the launching of larger ships became more frequent on the river with two trades in particular being catered for, the West Indian and the Canadian. Despite the great distances covered, remarkably small vessels founded important trade routes and, indeed, the great Allan Line (later incorporated in CPR) started its Canadian sailing with the wood brigantine *Jean* built at Irvine in 1819 by Gilkison, Thomson & Co. The dimensions of the *Jean* are amazing by any standards, 78 ft 6 ins × 22 ft 6 ins × 13 ft 4 ins (23.9 m × 6.9 m × 4.1 m) —not much bigger than a gabbart or a Clyde puffer. Captain Alexander Allan made two remarkable round trips with her in 1819, the first leaving Greenock on June 5 he discharged at Quebec, loaded lumber and was home on August 4. On August 21 he sailed for Canada, calling at Dublin en route and was back in home waters on October 11.

However, the demand for cargo space coupled with an understanding that safety was enhanced by size in the North Atlantic brought about the building of consistently larger vessels and, as we have seen, the introduction of composite, iron and finally steel construction. The ultimate in sailing ships was the building by companies like Henderson, Russell, Reid and Rodger of the steel four-masted barques of the 1890s, ships which were able to sail at up to 15 knots in fair conditions, carry cargoes in excess of 6,000 tons deadweight and operate with small, low paid crews. By this time the Clyde yards had been producing ships for many years for every world route and the design of sailing ships was beginning to be approached scientifically and, above all, passenger accommodation was regarded as an important feature. By the 1870s when Robert Duncan & Co could boast that they 'built more ships for the New Zealand trade than any other Scottish shipbuilder', the standard had become high in ship construction

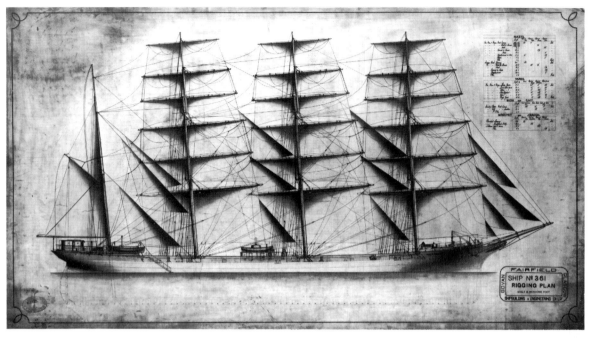

The rigging plan of the four-masted barque Pass of Melfort *built by the Fairfield S & E Co Ltd in 1881 for Gibson Clark & Co* (National Maritime Museum).

and maintenance in the effort to attract passengers. James Nourse of London built many fine sailers on the Clyde each with a specific trade in mind and yet each able to change at short notice from bulk grain to, say, the Coolie trade or from the unpleasant carriage of nitrate to the Australian wool business. Nourse built over 20 ships with Charles Connell of Scotstoun, five of which were big sailing ships the last being the *Mersey* in 1894.

To many people the most glamorous part of mechant sail was that short interlude involving a surprisingly small percentage of world cargo carrying capacity, known as the Clipper Era. Its origins can be traced first to the East Coast of the United States where, in the 1840s, shipbuilders from Virginia, Maryland, Massachusetts and Maine developed fine lined fast sailing ships crowding on square rigged canvas and competing in the high value cargo markets of the world. Prominent among these shipbuilders was Donald McKay (1810-1880) a 'bluenoser' of loyalist stock who ultimately returned to Massachusetts setting up a yard, Currier & McKay at Newburyport in 1841, later worked on his own account at Boston and finally died at Newburyport. Despite his poor record in business he

left as a legacy the inspiring story and the superb designs of some of the greatest US ships of all time including the *Lightning*, the *Champion of the Seas* and the *James Baines*. Many of his ships were 'extreme clippers' designed solely for speed, a requirement encouraged by the California gold rush of 1849 and with no serious consideration given to cargo carriage. However, exigencies of trade later forced him to design medium clippers and others that were just fast sailing ships. The *Lightning*, a full rigged ship built for James Baines of Liverpool in 1854 was, and still is, regarded as one of the fastest sailing ships in the world had a direct influence on the thinking of British shipowners and shipbuilders who have always acknowledged the supremacy of the Yankee Clippers and the originality of their design.

The other origin of the Clipper Era was Aberdeen. Here in 1839 Alexander Hall produced for about £1,900 the fast topsail schooner *Scottish Maid* for packet service on the East Coast from London to Lerwick. Her hollow lines and unique bow were noticed and emulated by other Aberdeen builders such as Duthie and Hood and in the following 25 years the Granite City was to build a fleet held in awe to this day and headed by ships like *The Caliph*,

The new rigged ship; the five-masted barque France *is towed down the Clyde in 1890 after completion by D & W Henderson of Partick. One of the largest sailing ships in the world, the* France *could load a cargo of 6,200 tons* (National Maritime Museum).

Coulnakyle, Black Prince and *Thermopylae*. The Clyde were not slow to follow and two or three shipyards were to try this kind of work with Robert Steele taking the undoubted lead.

Robert Steele Senior was born in the year of turmoil, 1745, when Bonnie Prince Charlie was raising his army in the West Highlands. However, being of Ayrshire stock it is doubtful if the Jacobite cause troubled his family and he became a builder of fishing smacks at Saltcoats before going in 1796 to join John Carswell in forming a yard at the Bay of Quick, Greenock. Robert Steele Junior joined the business which was restyled Robert Steele & Co in 1816. By then they had built the *Princess of Wales* for the excise fleet—possibly a sister craft for Scott's *Prince of Wales* of 1794 and some other fast vessels. No doubt the young proprietor's interest already was fixed on speed at sea!

The yard was changed in 1816 to the Rue End area where for 39 years fine vessels were built and in 1851 they expanded into Cartsdyke West closing the other yard four years later. With the order in 1821 for PS *Eclipse* of 87 tons for Robert Napier, the company was set for obtaining orders of a better

quality than the other yards round about. This was aided by the friendship developed between the Steele Company and the slowly growing band of enthusiastic yachtsmen on the Firth, the forebears of what was to become the Clyde Corinthian Yacht Club. Orders for yachts were forthcoming including that for the *Wave* in 1834 which, according to G.L. Watson, was the first with a metal keel.

Napiers remained friendly and passed many ship hulls to Steele's as subcontracts including the PS *Columbia*, one of the original four Cunard ships, and many more in the later 1840s. In 1855 Robert Steele built his first clipper ship, the *Kate Carnie*, and followed it in 1858 with the *Ellen Rodger*. The young Robert Steele (1821-90) developed a taste for the clippers and the yard was to produce many in the coming years including *Falcon, Taeping, Serica, Ariel, Sir Lancelot, Titania* and *Lahloo*. In 1866 the celebrated tea race was headed by three Greenock Clippers *Taeping, Serica* and *Ariel* all racing up the English Channel together. Steele's sons Robert (3) and William joined the business and after 1870 they worked more on steamships building for PSNC, Donald Currie's Castle Line, and Ben Line, Anchor and Allan. At the same time they started to construct machinery. In 1880 the use of shipbuilding steel was introduced, but in 1883 with severe cash problems and heavy debts the yard was closed and Scott's took over the ground, equipment and records. The name of Steele will never be forgotten for they built 300 ships some of which were the loveliest vessels which ever left the Clyde.

Two other shipyards must be mentioned in respect of fast sailing ships. The first is the Dumbarton yard of Scott & Linton formed on May 31 1868 by the partnership of Hercules Linton, naval architect, born in Inverbervie, Kincardineshire, 1836, and William Dundas Scott, nine years his junior. They obtained the woodyard from Denny's in Dumbarton and there built nine ships, six being steamers, and the last three being the iron sailing ship *Invereshie*, composite ship *Cutty Sark* and the composite schooner *Linn Fern*. Difficulties were apparent from the start and of the nature all too common in shipbuilding—cash flow. Within a year the company was in difficulties and in January 1870 ceased operation. The *Cutty Sark* was launched on November 22 1869 and moved later to Denny's Leven Shipyard. She sailed from the Clyde for London on January 13 1870. Linton had a family background of shipbuilding and had worked in the Aberdeen shipyards. The foreclosure was a tremendous personal tragedy for him, but he is remembered as the designer of one of the half dozen truly historic ships preserved in the world.

The other great sailing shipyard may come as a surprise to many; the Scotstoun shipyard of Charles Connell & Co Ltd which was founded in 1861 and continued under family management until 1968 when absorbed into Upper Clyde Shipbuilders Ltd. In that period of time the yard built just over 500 ships although between 1931 and 1937 there was no production and the shipyard was idle. Throughout the company history hulls were built and outfitted but no machinery was ever manufactured.

The founder was Charles Connell who came from Ayrshire and served his apprenticeship with Robert Steele & Co as a shipwright before becoming foreman and later manager with Alexander Stephen at Kelvinhaugh. It is understood that on terminating his employment with the Stephens they felt he would not be successful as a yard proprietor—on his death 23 years later the estate was recorded as being over £1¼ million!

Very quickly the Connell yard started to build fine sailing ships mostly for the China trade including *Taitsing* and *Spindrift*, *Fiery Cross* and the composite *Wild Deer* for Paddy Henderson's Albion Line. Many owners came back over and over again and these included Harrison, Brocklebank, Wilhelm Wilhelmson, Nourse and the Ben Line. The MV *Inventor*, delivered in 1964, was the 48th ship for that company from Connell and, indeed, far from the first *Inventor* to have been built on the Clyde.

The Connell family developed extensive shareholdings in shipping ventures and through these had connections with William Thomson & Co, the Ben Line of Edinburgh and Denholm's the ship management company of Glasgow. Over 30 ships were built at Scotstoun for the Ben Line and associated companies and in the real tradition of clipper ship builders had among them the steam turbine ship *Ben Loyal* of 1959 and the motorship *Ben Ledi* of 1964 which were amongst the fastest British merchant vessels on the Far East route and part of the 'speed war' which developed between the Ben Line and their great rival the Glen Line of London.

Composite ships

It was an accepted fact of life in the early years of Queen Victoria's reign that there was a limiting length for ships built of timber and various ideas on construction were tried to overcome the problem. George Blake describes the period from 1850 to 1870 as 'an overlap between wood and iron . . . with investigations going on in two fronts'. By the 1870s practically all large ships were built of iron but prior to that many of the largest sailing craft, particularly from Aberdeen, the Clyde and to a lesser extent from Sunderland and the North East were of composite construction.

Composite construction consists of the keel, frames and certain other main structural parts being manufactured of iron and the sheathing or outer skin of the ship being of timber. This arrangement was found to have many advantages, not least that the transverse strength and the longitudinal strength of the ship were greatly increased. As the iron frames were smaller and fewer in number than the wooden ones there was more space for cargo or, in the words of the ship's officer, there would be an increased bale capacity. Some owners switched to this form of construction as it gave qualities of strength and also the insulative value of timber cladding, thereby reducing sweating when valuable or perishable cargoes were being carried.

Several clipper ships were so constructed including

Andrew Weir's four-masted barque Olivebank *built by Mackie & Thomson, Govan, 1892. Ultimately she passed into the fleet of Captain Gustaf Erikson, and while sailing under Finnish colours struck a mine off Jutland on September 8 1939 and went down with considerable loss of life* (Andrew Weir & Co).

the *Cutty Sark* built by Scott & Linton and later completed at the beginning of 1870 by Denny of Dumbarton. This fine ship, the only surviving true clipper, is permanently drydocked at Greenwich and a visit aboard quickly conveys the need for professional skill and daring to drive these surprisingly small vessels on their round-the-world dashes for luxury cargoes like tea.

On examining the undersides of the *Cutty Sark* one notices copper plates secured over all the hull. The original reason for this was as a protection against growth of weed and the ravages of the teredo or timber boring ship worm. Experiments to protect ship bottoms had gone on for many years with the use of zinc, lead, copper and later Muntz metal being tried for sheathing, (Muntz metal is a brass alloy formed of 60 per cent copper and 40 per cent zinc and is named after the metallurgist G.F. Muntz). Around 1800 the Royal Navy were finishing the massive task of coppering all their ships, a programme of great administrative genius and one which created

considerable wealth around Swansea, where the main copper smelters were situated.

With the need for great speed by the clipper ships the coppering ensured the continuance of perfectly smooth underwater hulls and in this and other respects their overall concept and design could not be bettered. *Lloyd's Register of Shipping* recognised the commercial importance of this small fleet and introduced 'Rules for Ships of Composite Construction' in the mid-1860s. These were largely the product of Bernard Waymouth, a surveyor of the Society and also the designer of the great Aberdeen clipper *Thermopylae* (1868) which was *Cutty Sark*'s close rival.

Iron sailing ships presented one great problem: the fouling of their bottoms by weed and barnacles. For many years there was no totally dependable material which could be painted on the bottom and iron, it was discovered, was prone to gathering large quantities of growth especially in sailing ships which spent considerable time in docks, moored in tropical ports and frequently becalmed in the doldrums. During a year at sea in which moderate fouling takes place the energy required to drive a ship increases by over 10 per cent so the need for adequate protection against this unwelcome problem was of primary importance. It is not possible to put copper plates outside iron or steel plates owing to the immediate

galvanic action between the two in sea water but experiments were tried on the Clyde and elsewhere in the 1860s by sheathing iron ships in wood and then coppering the wood sheathing ensuring that at all times there was an adequate timber separation between the two metals. This was moderately satisfactory and does work. Such systems can be seen to this day on certain lightships which are permanently moored round our coasts.

The problem of fouling has been dealt with over the years with increasing effectiveness by the development of paint systems which inhibit marine growth. In fact modern systems which require considerable technology for their application are designed to 'self polish' when at sea, leaving the ship's underside continuously offering a smooth surface to the sea through which it passes.

Two other problems concerned early 19th century shipbuilders and shipowners. Until Airy and Kelvin had mastered the theory and practice of compasses it was inadvisable to depend on a compass in an iron

A typical product of Charles Connell & Co, the Ben Line motor vessel Bendearg *heads up the English Channel* (Skyfotos Ltd, New Romney, Kent).

ship. Owing to the hammering, vibration and other effects of shipbuilding while lying for a period of time in a fixed position the ship picks up a complex and permanent magnetic field acquired from the Earth's lines of force and this adversely affects the compass until neutralised by soft iron spheres on either side of the compass and Flinder's Bars fitted in the base. The second problem was of galvanic action: early steamships had iron hulls and iron propellers, but once other metals were introduced into the structure adjacent to the sea, the reaction set about pitting and corrosion on the surface of one of the metals. This was overcome by the fitting of zinc 'sacrificial' anodes which are eaten away while protecting other metals around. In recent years this has been taken over in some advanced ships by systems where electrical charges are impressed on parts of the hull.

Chapter 6

Building on a sure foundation

One of the manifestations of the patriotic mood of the country in the mid-19th century, was the setting up in every large town of volunteer units—auxiliary soldiers willing to be called to the colours. No doubt the motives of the volunteers were varied and mixed, but their early enthusiasm laid the foundations for the citizen army of the First World War and what was later to become the Territorial Army. In 1859, a unit was founded and shortly thereafter integrated into the 1st Lanarkshire Volunteers, and now well over a century later still exists as the Glasgow Universities Officers Training Corps. This latter unit has served the country well in a training role, but never on the battlefield and is thereby bereft of battle honours. However, they can claim a distinction which no other military unit can equal, that their two earliest company commanders left their names on the recognised scales of absolute temperature, namely degrees Rankine and degrees Kelvin. With Watt's name being used for the unit of power in the SI system, the University of Glasgow is well represented in the list of names internationally used for scientific measurement.

The founding spirit for the Rifle Volunteers was the professor of civil engineering and mechanics at the university, William John Macquorn Rankine—described aptly and succinctly by a recent biographer as 'no ordinary man'. He succeeded the first holder of the oldest chair of engineering in the world, Lewis Gordon in 1855, and like his predecessor had to overcome antipathy and resistance to the teaching of applied science in a university which had survived 400 years without such confections. However, by virtue of his commanding position in the international field and by the support of a group of brilliant men including Sir William Thomson (later Lord Kelvin), Rankine not only taught engineering, but defined the teaching syllabus for the classical course, wrote basic text books which stand good to this day and simultaneously carried out fundamental research in thermodynamics and naval architecture. It was through Rankine's continued efforts that the university ultimately offered a degree in engineering and the Faculty of Engineering was founded.

It is said that Glasgow made the Clyde, and that the Clyde made Glasgow. It is just as true to say that the university provided a backbone for the development of industry in the West of Scotland, and that industry in turn provided incentives in many forms for the university to strive in the fields of science. Founded in 1451 the university had survived some of Scotland's turbulent history and indeed had created no small part of it. But is was not until the 18th and 19th centuries that it came into a position of world eminence. Men like Adam Smith, James Watt, Joseph Black, Macquorn Rankine, Lord Kelvin and Joseph Lister put it into that select few centres of study (including the sister University of Edinburgh) which were at that time assisting in the shaping of thought in Western Europe.

The influence of a university is pervasive, and there is a strong case for the point of view that Glasgow's role was vital to the life and development of the Clyde shipyards. This is borne out by comparative studies of the shipyards of the Thames and Clyde: the former were establishments of considerable antiquity, they had changed from building in wood to the use of iron, and again later to steel, and yet for mysterious reasons which attract historians and economists to this day, they virtually ceased production at the close of the 19th century— the last major yard to close being the Thames Ironworks in 1912. The conditions under which they operated were not so dramatically different from the Clyde—wages were higher in the London area, steel had to be transported further and ship repairing had a sapping effect—but none of these alone or collectively explains the demise of Thames shipbuilding during the period of expansion of the industry on Clydeside.

It is likely that the real reason lies in the deep rooted traditions of good education enjoyed by almost every Scottish child which in turn gave social acceptance to research, and made every shipyard worker conscious of and indeed proud of the fact that he was working at the limits of known technology. The influence of good shipyards like Napier's, Denny's, Wingate's, Stephen's and latterly John Brown's ensured that research and scientific analysis were regarded as an every day matter.

Most senior personnel and many juniors aspiring to greater things were members of one of Britain's earliest engineering societies, the Institution of Engineers and Shipbuilders in Scotland. Their 'Transactions' commencing in 1857 and continuing to this day, give a superb commentary on the changing scene in shipbuilding and general engineering. The close identification of many university men ensured that the 'Transactions' were not just the records of a professional club, but in reality the proceedings of a learned society. There are over 1,450 papers on almost every aspect of engineering and ship science. The full run of volumes is treasure trove for the man of scientific bent as well as the local or industrial historian, as no other run of volumes is so liberal in outlook or catholic in taste. Several papers are milestones and reflect the open-handed manner in which shipbuilders and others have disseminated research material to those interested. The Institution meetings were largely in the evenings to ensure no impediment was placed on the young person wishing to gain from the papers and discussion.

From the Institution there came from time to time the articulation of ground swells of opinion from among the shipbuilding community, one of which in the 1870s was for the establishment of a lectureship in naval architecture at the university. In 1881, the president J.L.K. Jamieson, made the following welcome announcement:

'It will be remembered that at our last General Meeting the Institution gave its hearty and cordial support to the scheme for establishing a lectureship in Naval Architecture & Marine Engineering in the University of Glasgow. Mr. J.G. Lawrie had then generously offered to give the first course of lectures, and arrangements have since been made for these to commence early in November.'

Jamieson, a former superintendent engineer of the Pacific Steam Navigation Company, and a partner of John Elder & Company made another forward looking statement later:

'The point I wish to draw attention to is that whilst the Clyde is justly called the birthplace of Steam Navigation and on its banks Naval Architecture & Marine Engineering have received their greatest development we do not possess any establishment where it can be determined experimentally, by model, the amount of power necessary to propel a given form of vessel at a certain speed per hour. It has already been suggested that a basin for this purpose should be established in the Clyde district, and I hope our shipbuilders and engineers will take united action and soon have this suggestion carried out. It is specially with this view that I have alluded to this subject in the manner I have done.'

In the period of a couple of years, the Clyde was to boast the world's first commercial experimental tank, followed quickly by another, but 80 years were to elapse before one was built for the university itself.

The proposal for a lectureship in naval architecture received financial support from Mrs Isabella Elder, the widow of John Elder of Fairfield. This lady gave many gifts to Glasgow and to the Burgh of Govan

Right *Mrs Isabella Elder, wife of John Elder, shipbuilder, Govan. After her husband's death in 1869, Mrs Elder gave many gifts to Glasgow and Clydeside, and in 1883 endowed a chair at the University of Glasgow which to this day is held by the John Elder Professor of Naval Architecture. On the 450th anniversary of the founding of the University in 1901, Mrs Elder was made an Honorary Doctor of Laws* (Wotherspoon Collection, Mitchell Library, Glasgow).

Below left *William John Macquorn Rankine LLD, FRS, born in Edinburgh 1820 and died 1872. In 1855 he was appointed Regius Professor of Civil Engineering and Mechanics at Glasgow University and in 1857 was appointed first President of the Institution of Engineers in Scotland for two years, a post he was to hold again from 1869-70. One of the greatest engineers of the 19th century, he was described by Professor James Small in the words: 'Great as Rankine's achievements were as physicist and practising engineer, it is yet possible that at the bar of history he will be judged to have been greatest in his development of the education of the engineer, and his elevation of the dignity of the engineer's studies'* (Wotherspoon Collection, Mitchell Library, Glasgow).

Below *The ship model tank that never was. This ground plan of Glasgow University dated 1904 indicates the position for a proposed building for the ship model tank and naval architecture department on the green slopes of Kelvingrove. Had this development come about, the role of the department would have been dramatically altered* (Glasgow University Hydrodynamics Laboratory).

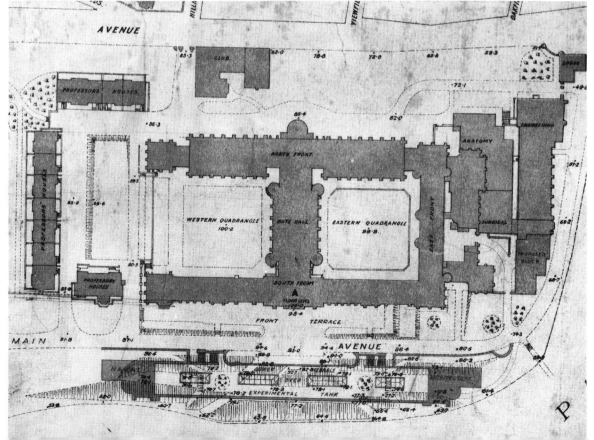

including the Elder Park and the Elder Cottage Hospital, but none were to have such far reaching effects as the gifts to the university. In 1883 the funds were such that the lectureship established in 1881 was uprated to a professorship, and the second chair of engineering at Glasgow and the first chair of naval architecture in the world were created, appropriately named after Mrs Elder's late husband. This munificence did not go unmarked or unrecorded as Mrs Elder became one of the first ladies to receive an honorary LL D from a grateful university.

In the first hundred years there have been only seven incumbents of the John Elder Chair. Francis Elgar, Philip Jenkins and Sir John Biles each with a Royal Naval background and with training either at South Kensington or the RN College, Greenwich, were followed by three 'home grown' professors, Percy Hillhouse, Andrew Robb and John Conn, and they in turn by a Greenwich man and member of the Royal Corps of Naval Constructors, Douglas Faulkner. Each man made a separate contribution to the development of the school—Biles with the wide views of a consultant (his company still operates from Paisley and London), Hillhouse with the practical viewpoint of the man deeply immersed in the affairs of the Clyde shipyards and with the memory of being

trapped and ultimately becoming a survivor of the submarine *K13* after its accident on trials in the Gareloch in January 1917. Andrew Robb, like Sir John Biles, wrote a mammoth textbook and is remembered for his interesting expositions and dry wit. He was succeeded by Professor Conn, a former apprentice of Alexander Hall of Aberdeen and late naval architect to the then named British Shipbuilding Research Association. During his period in office, the department expanded dramatically and the long awaited test tank facility became a reality. Under Douglas Faulkner, the department has become increasingly involved in the new technology required for offshore work and to the name of the department has been added 'Ocean Engineering'.

The close connection between the university and the Institution was further cemented when in 1923,

While not the largest in Britain, the ship model experimental tank at Glasgow University is certainly one of the most modern. Opened at Garscube Estate in November 1963 by Dr John Brown, it has made notable investigations into ship resistance, the behaviour of offshore structures in bad weather conditions and especially into the 'squat' effect of ships in shallow water (Glasgow University Hydrodynamics Laboratory).

as the Faculty of Engineering became self governing, the Institution founded two additional engineering professorships known to this day as James Watt chairs.

Another strand in the connections between formal education and shipbuilding is discernible in that, in 1796, an effort was made to found another university in Glasgow. Professor John Anderson of the Natural Philosophy Department (known as Physics in many colleges) had had a long and, at times, stormy relationship with his colleagues on the Senate of Glasgow University, largely brought about by his revolutionary ideas on technical and adult education. On his death, £1,500 was left to found the rival four-faculty John Anderson's university, but even this sum, large at the time, was inadequate for the purpose envisaged. However, true to the founder's requirements the new Institution started to cater for the working man and, indeed, could be seen as a precursor of today's Open University.

The history of the new organisation was more than eventful, but ultimately having been closely allied with the Working Man's Institute movement, which was powerful in Scotland at the time, a role was developed, and as the years passed the new body became more and more of a rival to the older 'varsity, particularly with their greater willingness to grant places to older students irrespective of their educational background. In 1882 lectures in naval architecture were commenced and in 1909 this course became available on a full time basis. Throughout this history various names were used, but undoubtedly the best known and most popular was Royal Technical College, otherwise the 'Tech' to generations of appreciative students.

The relationship between the Technical College and Glasgow University was not always harmonious, and was considerably strained in the 1950s and '60s as the two bodies sought to find a mutually agreeable arrangement for entrance and graduating qualifications. On the granting of a university charter to the younger body, there was disappointment at their choice of name—University of Strathclyde—and for a while transactions between the two universities were rather formal. Happily those days are passing and now the two departments of naval architecture, which have gone different ways, are complementary in the overall scheme of teaching and research. Two men have held chairs in naval architecture at Strathclyde—Ian Bridge who was succeeded by Chengi Kuo both Glasgow graduates and former apprentices of Denny of Dumbarton.

The City of Glasgow is fortunate in having two universities and many colleges of further education. It is doubtful if any other city in the world can claim two universities with a combined life approaching seven and a half centuries!

The shipyards themselves had an enviable reputation for research and development work. Several early Clyde shipbuilders had attempted to assess the effect of change of shape on hull form by testing small scale models in streams and ponds. David Napier, a cousin of the more celebrated Robert, experimented with models in the Camlachie Burn, and designed the Dumbarton built paddle steamer *Rob Roy* in 1818 after trying various hull forms in small scale. The Scotts of Greenock tested 5 ft long models in Loch Thom above Greenock around the same time and no doubt those involved derived some benefit and considerable pleasure from these efforts. Few other tests seem to have been carried out in Scotland, apart from those done by the Halls of Aberdeen in small glass-sided tanks, with two fluids, water and red turpentine, which assisted in their design of what was to become their virtual trade mark, the Aberdeen Bow, in the 1840s.

It became apparent to all scientific men that model tests were not to be the full answer until the science of hydrodynamics was further advanced. This step forward came from one of the world's greatest naval architects William Froude (1810-1879) who persuaded the Admiralty to finance the building of a proper ship model test tank at Torquay in 1872. Froude's work placed test tank work on the highest levels of scientific thought and laid down the principles for the correlation of results between small models and full size vessels which stand good to this day. Most of Froude's effort was for the Admiralty, but his work did not go unnoticed on Clydeside, or elsewhere for that matter, and within 30 years nearly 20 further test tanks were constructed. A century later the number of tanks was to number hundreds in the service of shipyards, navies and universities on every continent.

The Dutch followed by constructing their tank at Amsterdam, and under the direction of Dr Bruno Joannes Tideman (1834-1883) quickly established themselves as an alternative to Torquay.

It is interesting to note that probably the first Clyde hull to have its design investigated by a towing tank was the Russian Imperial Yacht *Livadia* which was launched by the Duchess of Hamilton from John

Elder's Fairfield shipyard on July 7 1880. The amazing turbot-shaped ship was designed under the supervision of Captain E.E. Goulaeff of the Russian Navy on the principles first laid down by Vice-Admiral Popoff, and advocated by John Elder the Clyde shipbuilder. Once the Russians decided on the building of this strange vessel (to replace the previous Royal Yacht lost in the Black Sea) they naturally came to Govan to discuss the matter, and placed the order for a ship of 'Popoffska' design. Sir William Pearce, principal of the Fairfield yard, was concerned lest his company fail to meet their obligation of building a ship capable of 14 knots—to have the contract rejected would leave an expensive and virtually unmarketable object on their hands, and he contracted with the Amsterdam test tank to have the *Livadia* form tested. Their report was encouraging, and further confirmation came from a tenth full size model, complete with three screws, tried on Loch Lomond. Work went ahead and the new yacht was launched, outfitted and taken to the Tail of the Bank for trials. Lord Kelvin personally supervised the adjusting of compasses all made to his new design, and then on trials the Royal Yacht achieved 15.73

Glasgow Museums' magnificent model of the Imperial Russian Yacht Livadia *built by John Elder & Co at the Fairfield Shipyard, 1880* (Glasgow Museums).

knots on indicated horse power of 12,354 and displacing just over 4,000 tons.

The *Livadia*, named after a town in Yalta, sailed for the Black Sea and, despite encountering fierce conditions in the Bay of Biscay, arrived after a very steady journey and only minor hull damage. However the death of the Czar in 1881 after an assassination attempt ended the need for the ship— her rose garden, illuminated fountains and wine racks for 10,000 bottles were never used, and ultimately it is said she became a coal hulk.

The third tank to be set up was at the Leven shipyard of William Denny & Brothers of Dumbarton. William Denny (3)* persuaded the partners of the need of the facility, and it turned out to be a far-

*William Denny was the third generation of the family to have the founder's name. Born in 1847, this brilliant shipbuilder died aged 39 while representing the company in Buenos Aires.

sighted move. Denny's in the 1880s were discovering that, owing to the restrictions of the River Leven into which they launched, the larger orders were moving away to Govan and Clydebank, and they were becoming more and more dependent on medium sized ships of high value and high technical content. To compete in such a market required first class design work and very accurate cost estimation.

The new tank opened in February 1883 and quickly established its reputation for accurate work with the Denny partners. Work became short for all Clyde yards in the early to mid 1880s and at this stage the Denny's made an all-out attempt to obtain the contract for the Belgian Government's Dover–Ostend cross channel passenger steamer *Princesse Henriette*. The ship 91 m (300 ft) long and on a draft of 2.6 m (8 ft 8 ins) was to attain 20½ knots on trials, a requirement which was, to say the least, daring a hundred years ago. Denny's signed a contract which gave the owners £500 reduction in price for each 0.1 knot less than 20.5 and agreed that the ship could be rejected if the speed was less than 19.75 knots. However, for each 0.1 knot in excess of 20.5 knots a premium of £500 was paid.

Denny's had an anxious time until the trials but the care lavished on the ship and engines paid off, and the clear advantages of the tank results vindicated the investment. The *Princesse Henriette* 'ran the lights' at just over 21 knots and with paddles turning at 50 rpm. Overnight the yard discovered they had success on their hands and for the next 60 years were the undisputed world leader in cross channel ship and specialist vessel design. They capitalised on this by every means—advanced technical training for staff, scholarships for study, suggestion schemes and, above all, granting more university/college apprenticeships throughout the years than probably all the rest of the Clyde yards put together.

In 1904 John Brown & Co Ltd opened a 136 m (445 ft) tank at Clydebank. It was to be in existence for about 70 years and was Brown's answer to the challenge of the German liners on the North Atlantic. The Norddeutscher Lloyd Company (NDL) of Bremen had been instrumental in building and running a tank at Bremerhaven, and Brown's realised that while they wished to co-operate with Denny's it was in their interests to have tank facilities to hand. Among their early experiments were those on the *Lusitania* which were also part contracted out to other tanks, Dumbarton included. For the *Lusitania* the parent hull form was eventually

taken from the Clydebank *City of Paris*, and this tank also developed its own highly successful operation.

The Glasgow University tank was opened in the 1960s and has concentrated on rather different work including investigations of the effect of shallow water on ships, on the tethering of oil rigs, and on the stresses in their structures in North Sea conditions. It is similar to some Continental and American tanks in that research work and teaching are carried out side by side.

Throughout the 19th century, other experiments were carried out by the shipyards. Following an order for high pressure boilers, Robert Napier instructed his Chief Draughtsman and Calculator, David Kirkaldy (1820-97) to conduct experiments into the strength of various ferrous materials. Kirkaldy was the right man for the job—meticulous, painstaking and mathematically inclined. Educated at Merchiston Castle School before going on to Edinburgh University, he related in later life his pleasure at discovering as a schoolboy that he occupied the bedroom once used by Napier the mathematician and author of the system of logarithms.

In 1860 he published his findings to the Scottish Shipbuilders' Association and in 1862 they appeared in book form. During 1858 to 1861 he designed and operated a testing machine for the plates of Robert Napier's HMS *Black Prince*. In 1861 he left and went to London, setting up an engineering consultancy which continued with an international reputation until 1965. In the National Maritime Museum is the 'as fitted' profile of Napier's iron PS *Persia* built for Cunard. It is one of the most beautiful ship plans ever drawn, has been exhibited at the Royal Academy and is signed in the corner 'David Kirkaldy'.

The work of Lord Kelvin is well documented. This intellectual giant of a man not only guided the destiny of a university, but was deeply involved in the industrial work of the Clyde as well. One of his most famous inventions was the Kelvin compass which came about in an unusual manner. In 1871 while still Sir William Thomson, he was asked by a friend, the Rev Norman Macleod, to write a short article on the mariner's compass. With his usual thoroughness Kelvin first assembled the facts, then criticised the shortcomings and finally suggested remedies to make a new and effective compass. Kelvin had some made and tried on ships, and even shown to the Astronomer Royal. His biographer, Silvanus Thompson, recounts the story that on the

Left *A view of the ship model testing tank of William Denny & Brothers Ltd, Dumbarton. The first experiment was made in February 1883, and the last one for British Shipbuilders Hydrodynamics Ltd in 1983. This tank has been purchased by a consortium of museums and is to be preserved* (D.I. Moor, St Albans).

new Kelvin compass being shown to Sir George Airy at the Royal Observatory, Greenwich Park, the Astronomer Royal thought for a moment and said, 'It won't do'. Kelvin, on being told of this, said with a trace of contempt in his voice, 'So much for the Astronomer Royal's opinion!'. In 1889 the 10-inch Kelvin compass was adopted as the standard compass for the Royal Navy! Kelvin had his compasses manufactured by James White, a Glasgow optician, and in 1900 they formed a limited liability company known as Kelvin and James White Ltd. To this day the name is perpetuated in Kelvin-Hughes Limited.

The *Lucy Ashton* trials

A wonderful opportunity presented itself in 1949 to the British Shipbuilding Research Association (BSRA). They had been anxious to carry out full-scale systematic resistance tests on a ship hull, and preferably without the water being disturbed by propellers, paddles or even a tug nearby. Such experiments had not been carried out in Britain since the tests on HMS *Greyhound* in 1874 and scientific reasoning had come a long way since then.

In 1949, British Railways decided to dispose of their oldest Clyde steamer, the PS *Lucy Ashton*. She was purchased by BSRA and stripped down, engines and paddles removed, and just abaft of midships a bridge fitted by Denny of Dumbarton on which were placed four Rolls Royce Derwent jet engines for propulsion. During 1950, with ear piercing screeches, the *Lucy Ashton* ran on the Gareloch mile during which time information was amassed on

Below *Profile of the former Clyde paddle steamer* Lucy Ashton *after conversion to jet propulsion for scientific enquiry purposes. The results of these, now world famous tests, were published in the 1951 Transactions of the Royal Institution of Naval architects.*

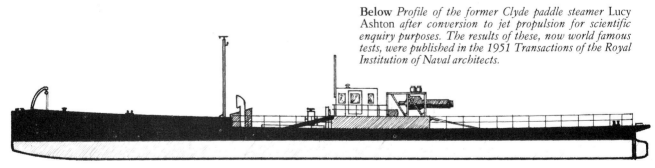

The paddle steamer Lucy Ashton *lying in Bowling Harbour in 1949, and awaiting the shipbreakers after 61 years of service on Clyde passenger routes. Shortly after this photograph was taken she was reprieved, and fitted with Rolls Royce jet engines carried out a programme of scientific research for BSRA. The* Lucy Ashton *was built by Seath of Rutherglen in 1888, and finally broken up in 1951.*

speed, power output and, by deduction, considerable information on the resistance of ship's underwater skin to motion through the water.

Six exact scale models or 'geosims' were manufactured correct down to the 5¾ in sag on the *Lucy Ashton*'s keel, and these were tested in various ship model tanks. When T.B. Seath built this fine little steamer at Rutherglen in 1888 and when the North British Railway bestowed the name *Lucy Ashton* taken from Scott's novels, little did they anticipate the fame she would eventually acquire in the worldwide technical press!

Classification societies and other authorities

Merchant ships are built to meet strict international safety standards and the responsibility for ensuring these are met falls mainly on the Department of Transport (formerly known as the Board of Trade) and other bodies overseas including the United States Coast Guard. However, the standard of design and workmanship on a vessel is a matter which has to be continuously monitored during building by an independent examination body known as the Classification Society. It is on the report and final certificate of the society that the insurance of a ship and many other matters depend. This certificate is obtained by submitting the plans of a ship to the society and having them corrected and approved according to the rules in force, and then requesting that a surveyor of the society attend the construction of the vessel and check that the work is carried out correctly and satisfactorily. For this service the Classification Society charges a fee to cover its running expenses, overheads and especially its heavy marketing and research and development commitments. By tradition the surveyors are recruited from shipyard staffs and nowadays almost every recruit is an engineering graduate.

The main Classification Societies are Lloyd's Register of Shipping—not to be confused with the independent Lloyds of London insurance market—

Det Norske Veritas of Oslo, Bureau Veritas of Paris, the American Bureau of Shipping, Germanischer Lloyd of Hamburg and Nippon Kaiji Kyokai of Tokyo. Most societies are independent and officially non-profit making, but while co-operating on a grand scale they are in direct competition with one another.

Regrettably Britain, which had two Classification Societies up till 1949, now has only one with a probable loss of competitive edge but it is still the largest, oldest and undoubtedly most prestigious organisation of its kind in the world. The history commences in 1760 when the celebrated Edward Lloyd had a group of underwriters as patrons of his London Coffee Shop, and they produced ship lists or registers which were the precursors of today's Lloyd's Register. The listing of ships became more systematic and scientific as the years passed and ultimately a stage was reached when an independent group of men found themselves able to create a rule book for the design, construction and upkeep of ships.

Throughout the early years Lloyd's Register had trouble with shipowners and shipbuilders in provincial outports—often trouble caused in the long term by both parties. The Port of Liverpool formed its own register but in 1845 settled any differences with London and joined the main society and, by the end of the 19th century, things seemed to be placid until proposed Government legislation in 1890 created a storm which had far-reaching and yet overall good effects for shipbuilding.

The legislation was regarding the Load Line, that is the amount of freeboard a ship may have and thereby the positioning of the 'Plimsoll Mark'. It was proposed at Westminster that only two authorities be empowered to oversee this work—the Board of Trade and Lloyd's Register of Shipping. This news was received in Glasgow and indeed throughout Scotland, the North of England and Ireland with incredulity. The centre of the shipbuilding world at that time was Clydeside with the North East of England running as a close competitor and this decision was seen as retrograde, unimaginative and likely to allow the continuance of obsolete practices. In his bicentenary work on Lloyd's Register George Blake points out that the protest movement in Glasgow 'was formidably backed'.

Directors of shipping companies included Allan, Anchor & Burrell with prominent Belfast and Clydeside shipbuilders and Professor Jenkins set up a rival Classification Society called the British Corpora-

tion. The weight behind the committee must have been formidable indeed as the Government gave way and included the new and untried society and, also, Bureau Veritas in the list of assigning authorities. The British Corporation went further, while only weeks old it persuaded the Government to accept the principle that further changes in Load Line regulations were to be made only after the Government had consulted the classification authorities. Lloyd's Register, while smarting at the implied criticism of their housekeeping, equally must have admired the style and open-handedness of their new competitor.

The BC, as they were known, went from strength to strength. They adopted standards which were designed to encourage progress and technical development, and their first rules of 1890 allowed a saving of 10 per cent on the weight of steelwork on a ship in comparison with Lloyd's Rules. To a tramp ship owner this was vital as it meant reduced initial cost and the ability to carry, say, 300 tons more cargo on a 10,000-ton displacement vessel for the rest of her lifetime.

The first ship built under a special survey was SS *Turret*, a Turret Deck Vessel built in 1892 by William Doxford & Sons Ltd of Pallion Shipyard, Sunderland. However, the vessel, which was revolutionary, was also surveyed under construction by Lloyd's Register and according to another authority was ultimately classed with Bureau Veritas!

The British Corporation never looked back, many fine ships were inspected and classed by them including *Jutlandia*, *Virginian* and *Victorian* and the greatest compliment they received was when the Italians and the Japanese modelled their societies on the BC way of working. In 1912 they instituted a Liverpool Committee but, by this time, Lloyd's had taken stock of the situation and created a Glasgow (now known as Scottish) Committee.

In 1932 the first move to heal the division came when Lloyd's and BC fused their aircraft inspection departments and after the Second World War, during which the two societies worked harmoniously in every theatre of the globe, the decision was taken to amalgamate. Sadly the British Corporation name has been lost and reading recent short histories of Lloyd's Register, it appears they have forgotten a vital part of their own history as the great contribution made by BC to the classification of ships is never mentioned.

Chapter 7

The cradle of steam navigation

The shipbuilding traditions of Greenock and Port Glasgow stretch back at least two and three quarter centuries and within their bounds there have been at least 90 shipyards in that period accounting for over 20 per cent of all shipyards in the Clyde area. On close analysis over half these shipyards operated for less than ten years, some were in fact 'one ship' yards, others scratched a poor living from the Greenock waterfront which had seen many business ventures come and go. Despite the transient nature of many of these businesses nothing can dim the achievement of the Inverclyde area in producing Europe's first steamship, in having the oldest shipyard in the world and in producing an abundance of ships as diverse as West Indiamen and submarines, pilgrim ships and four-masted barques or light cruisers and VLCCs.

As the known Clyde shipyards are listed in the Appendix there will be no need to list every shipyard in this chapter but the names of the earliest are worthy of recording. These early yards bore no resemblance to current shipbuilding establishments but were small riverside sites where a family and their associates and a few employees constructed small, wooden ships for fishing or for the coastal trade:

John Scott, later Scott's S & E Co, founded 1711 (now Scott-Lithgow)
S. Halliday, Westburn W, Greenock, 1740-60
MacPerson & MacLachlan, Bay of Quick, Greenock, 1740-60
Porter & Morgan, Westburn W, Greenock, 1740-60
James Munn, Westburn W, Greenock, 1760-1820
John Wood & Co, Greenock & Port Glasgow, 1780-1853
Steele & Carswell, Bay of Quick, Greenock, 1796-1816
Love, Greenock, late 18th century

The busiest period in the towns was from 1860 to 1880 when at least 34 yards operated sometime during that 20-year spell. To obtain a clear perspective on the development of the various businesses it will be sufficient to consider only seven or eight companies as their histories reflect the growth of the towns and the industry in the area. John Wood, the builder of the *Comet*, has been discussed elsewhere in this volume.

The Greenock yards
Pride of place in all shipbuilding narrative must go to the Scott's of Greenock, a company which commenced trading in 1711 and with an unbroken succession of family directors was managed despite a series of different names through until 1969 when the merger was effected with Lithgows Ltd of Port Glasgow. During this period the population of Greenock had risen from around 1,500 to close on 80,000 at the time of the merger, and it can be inferred that Scott's workforce grew at an even greater rate than that. The company commenced at Westburn East to the West of Greenock and with additions and changes over the years found in 1934 that they were operating the Cartsburn Dockyard and adjoining Cartsdyke West Yard as well as Cartsdyke East which was separated from the main business by the Greenock Dockyard Co Ltd then occupying the intervening Cartsdyke Mid Yard. In an unusual and original exchange agreement the Greenock Dockyard moved east and Scott's took the Cartsdyke Mid Yard giving them for the first time in over 200 years a continuous river frontage.

From the beginning Scott's have built ships and tried new ideas well in advance of other establishments. They opened the first graving dock in 1767 and again had a first in 1806 by launching the *John Campbell* fully masted and rigged. In 1815 they produced two paddle steamers *Active* and *Despatch* of 59 and 58 tons respectively and in 1819 made history by building the PS *Talbot*, the first ship with feathering floats. During this period all machinery had been purchased from the Napiers or from James Cook of Tradeston, Glasgow, but in 1825 the iron and brass foundry of William Brownlie was purchased by Scott and trading under the name of Scott, Sinclair & Co began the long history of marine engineering within the group. In 1859 the name was changed to the Greenock Foundry and in 1904 it was absorbed into Scott's S. & E. Co Ltd. Two particular milestones are important; the building of the iron screw frigate HMS *Greenock* for the Royal Navy and the Blue Funnel Liner SS *Agamemnon* for Alfred Holt & Co of Liverpool.

The frigate to be named *Pegasus* was ordered at Greenock in 1845 and broke new ground by being of iron and screw propelled as, until then, this mode of construction and means of propulsion were novel in the Navy. Iron in particular created problems in larger ships owing to compass deviation created by the inherent magnetic field within the ship's hull. The work of Sir George Airy, later Astronomer Royal, had solved the major problems and iron became an acceptable material for the Queen's ships. The name of the frigate became *Greenock* before her launch in 1849 and ultimately she sailed with twin-cylinder horizontal geared steam machinery, as in the *Great Britain* built a year or two earlier in Bristol, the propeller speed was stepped up from that of the machinery.

The SS *Agamemnon* and her sisters *Ajax* and *Achilles* were built of iron in 1865 and 1866 and for the time were of considerable size being 309 ft (94.2 m) in length bp, 38 ft 6 ins (11.7 m) breadth and 29 ft 8 ins (9.0 m) in depth. Alfred Holt felt that with increased thermal and mechanical efficiency of engines, ships on long hauls with sufficient capacity for bunkers and an economic cargo could break even and end the monopoly of sailing ships on the Far East trades. The three ships proved immensely successful and the timely opening of the Suez Canal enhanced their value. The machinery which proved so invaluable was of tandem compound design with the high pressure cylinder under the shaft and the low pressure above. To even out the working of the engine a massive flywheel was built on to the crankshaft. Within 16 years the SS *Aberdeen* was to follow from Napier's at Govan with triple expansion machinery and the marine steam reciprocating engine had come of age.

From then on there was a wide range of work which included building for the Royal Navy, John Swire's China Navigation Co and Alfred Holt & Co, all of whom had long lasting relationships with the company. Many vessels were built for service on the Yangtse River. The four-masted barque *Archibald Russell* was completed as late as 1905 and the following year the first submarine depot ship, HMS *Maidstone*, was delivered, incorporating revolutionary ideas for the time including repairs facilities, stores, services and accommodation for submarine relief crews. In 1928 another 'first' was scored in the building of the tanker *Brunswick*, the largest diesel electric vessel to date, the first on the Clyde and unusual in having all superstructure aft, an arrangement which is routine nowadays.

The wars saw Scott's with a 100 per cent workload for the Royal Navy including a very full run of submarines, cruisers and destroyers and their Second World War production included HM cruiser *Scylla* of 1942 adopted by the City of Aberdeen. Post-war activities have been wide ranging with work of all

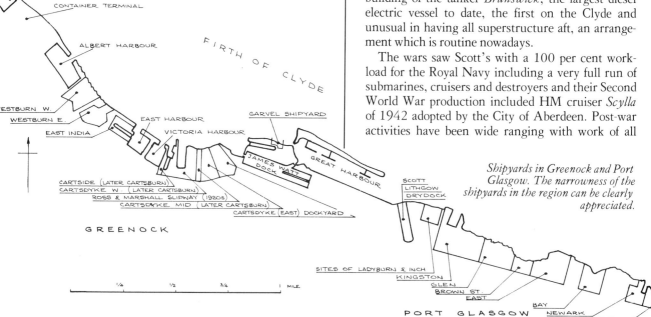

Shipyards in Greenock and Port Glasgow. The narrowness of the shipyards in the region can be clearly appreciated.

kinds, passenger/cargo liners for the Far East, tankers, bulk carriers, general cargo ships as well as submarines and frigates.

In 1883 Scott's purchased Steel's Cartsdyke yard and in 1934 switched yards with the Greenock Dockyard Around 1925 they purchased Ross & Marshall's slip making their complex compact and unified.

In 1966 the Greenock Dockyard Company merged with Scott's S. & E. Co Ltd and the ultimate aim of having one complete yard from Cartsburn to Cartsdyke East was achieved. The dockyard had become established in Greenock in 1900 when the Grangemouth Dockyard bought over Russell's Cartsdyke Mid Yard, and on the Clyde they operated for the first eight years as the Grangemouth & Greenock Dockyard Co producing during that period over 40 ships including the sailing ship *Mozart* of 1904. During this period they became known on Clydeside as 'The Klondike' probably as a result of the good piece work rates available during the years of the Klondike rush. From 1908 till 1920 the company, recognising that the Clyde yard was the more important of the two, changed its name to the Greenock & Grangemouth Dockyard and in this phase they built nearly 50 ships. In 1920 the name Greenock Dockyard Co was finally adopted and from then until 1966 nearly 110 ships were built including many for the Clan and latterly the Union Castle Lines. In 1924 Cayzer Irvine & Co secured a large part of the shareholding and by the 1940s the whole of the equity had been transferred to Clan Line Steamers Ltd. The takeover in 1966 brought about rationalisation of facilities with the Cartsdyke East end becoming a steel fabrication area with the last launch from the yard in 1979 the MV *Maron* for the Ocean Group.

During the transition from Greenock Dockyard to Scott's in 1966 there were, among the ships completing, two for the Geest Line, and as their ultimate owners were not involved in the shipyard transactions, it was decided to float a company to complete this deal. Therefore they were handed over by the Cartsdyke Dockyard Co Ltd which therefore merits inclusion in the List of Clyde Shipbuilding organisations as a two-ship 'yard'. The ships *Geestcape* and *Geesthaven* are recorded in Lloyd's Register as products of Scott's S. & E. Co Ltd, however!

Before leaving Scott's it is interesting to note that in the 1950s the motor bulk carrier *Crystal Cube* was designed for the carriage of sugar, the first such ship in the world. This was not inappropriate as Greenock is a major centre of sugar refining and the town is succinctly described by the epigram: 'Ships, Sugar—and Showers!'

*   *   *

Thomson and Spiers are believed to have employed John Scott Russell as their manager around 1840. This was a formative period for young Russell as he devoted time to the study of hull form, tidal phenomena, wave motion and civil engineering design. His active intellectual exercises coupled with his practical experience helped him to change the traditional views around him and his influence on the Clyde in general was probably greater than is now realised. His legacy of works and writings and his candidature for the Chair of Mathematics at Edinburgh University bear witness to his great ability. At this time Caird & Co then operating only as engineers found themselves in receipt of many ship orders and, as was the custom at the time, subcontracted the hulls to Duncan, Thomson & Spiers and others. The loss of revenue involved irritated James Caird, the local director, and he decided to take over a shipyard. Ultimately Thomson & Spiers was purchased and John Scott Russell retained as manager.

James Caird was a kinsman of John Caird the founder of Caird & Co engineers and ironfounders in Greenock. James served his apprenticeship with the company and then left to do other work but returned on the death of John Caird to be first chief draughtsman and later a partner. He was worthy of the opportunities offered him and under his guidance Caird & Co became a power in the shipbuilding world and, indeed, the virtual 'retained yard' for the great P & O steamship fleet. Caird and Russell were reputedly good friends but Russell knew that he could never become more than an employee and probably felt that with both shipbuilding and academic life appearing to have closed doors to him he should try his fortune in London. It is a matter of interesting conjecture just how Cairds might have developed if these two capable men had remained together.

For 82 years Caird & Co built under their own name and for 40 of them built about two P&O vessels a year. They were superb ships, part of the great black-funnelled fleet serving all places east. Among the smallest were the 22-knot *Isis* and *Osiris* built in the 1890s for the passenger and mail shuttle service between Italy and Port Said, part of the overland route to the east. They were 300 ft long (91m) and were limited to 78 passengers and 123 tons of baggage and mail and, owing to the exigencies and strict timetable of the service, developed a name for being uncomfortable, wet ships. Larger ships included the 6,900 gross ton *Himalaya*, Caird's largest ship up to 1892, the *Moldavia* of 1903 and the three troopships built around 1900—*Sobraon*, *Plassy* and a ship with a well chosen name, *Assaye*, the supreme battle honour of the Highland Light Infantry or RHF as it is now known.

James Caird died in 1888 and his three sons converted the business to a limited liability concern but continued as managers. The third son, Robert, had been the most dynamic and on his death in 1916 the remaining brothers sold the business to Harland & Wolff Limited. The name Caird did not disappear overnight and existing contracts were finished under Caird's name. However, by 1922 they were but a memory and the legacy remaining was of superb ships and half block models indicating their style and beauty.

Harland & Wolff developed the yard but, with the recession biting and possibly a management more concerned at keeping Belfast busy, work fell away and after 12 H&W ships the yard became idle in 1928. In 1936 it was sold to National Shipbuilders Security Ltd.

*   *   *

In the 1897-98 Transactions of the Institution of Engineers and Shipbuilders in Scotland' the address of a member, Peter Taylor, is given as Garvel Shipyard, Greenock. It is one of the few published references to the yard of Taylor & Mitchell which existed from 1898 to 1900 before being taken over by the Brown family and becoming known as George Brown & Co and around 1936 as George Brown & Co (Marine) Ltd. The founder, George Brown (1859-1933), was trained at Stephen's, was an assistant manager at Denny's and found time to be the first evening class teacher of naval architecture in Scotland. He started building with contract No 5 keeping the same system running as had been used by the predecessors. When the yard went into voluntary liquidation in 1983 the contract numbers stood around 285.

The yard was known as 'The Siberia' and built ships up to 4,000 tons deadweight concentrating on small cargo vessels, coasters (including many for Everard & Sons), tugs and a few fishing vessels. The sons and ultimately a grandson continued the business but in 1963 discontinued shipbuilding owing to falling demand and utilised their plant and equipment on the manufacture of cargo handling gear marketed by their subsidiary, Cargospeed Equipment Limited. This market, too, became dull in the 1970s and the shipyard surprised everyone on

SS Clan Sutherland *leaves the Greenock Dockyard in 1951 for sea trials. A close relationship existed between the Dockyard and Clan Line Steamers Ltd, and ultimately the Clan Line held considerable equity in the yard.*

the Clyde in 1981 by accepting orders for two tugs and buoy tenders for Mexico. Further orders followed but, sadly, for financial reasons in 1983 this last family business on Clydeside finally closed and the last ship was produced by The Siberia.

The Gourock yard

The one yard which is to the extreme west of the three towns is that of James Adam & Son (Ship-repairers) Ltd. Founded in 1871 as yacht builders and repairers, they experienced varying fortunes until 1951 when taken over by the Caldwell family and their role changed. Currently the yard carries out steel fabrication work and also does a limited amount of voyage repair work.

The Port Glasgow yards

In 1853 the Inch Shipyard was taken over by one of the colourful men that are attracted to thriving industry. His name was Laurence Hill, born 1816 at Dalkeith and educated at schools in England and Scotland before going to Glasgow University. He twice visited America, an unusual trip to make in those days, before joining Professor Lewis Gordon—the world's first engineering professor—to design the Loch Katrine water supply system in 1845. He also worked with Professor Rankine and lectured for three years at the Andersonian College. The setting up of the shipyard was the fulfilment of an ambition which allowed him the satisfaction of production work coupled with the challenge of research. At the Inch yard he worked on propeller design and other theoretical matters as well as building 76 ships in just 17 years. Around the yard were shallow water and narrow channels and according to his obituary in the 1892-3 'Transactions' of the IESS 'he used curved ways in launching'. What is meant is not clear but could indicate the use of cambering on the ways, a feature that is now common. In 1869 or 1870 the yard was taken over by D.J. Dunlop and J.L. Cunliffe and in the subsequent 12 years they built over 80 ships including SS *Esbjerg* for DFDS and the first tug *Scot* for the Caledonian Canal. In 1881 Cunliffe retired and Dunlop continued with the business name amended to David J. Dunlop & Co. Altogether over 100 ships were built prior to 1911 when Dunlop died. The name was felt to be valuable and a new company was formed with Donald Bremner as managing director. During the war the yard was sold to Lithgows but, after the last ship SS *Baron Hogarth* was built in 1926, the yard

closed ultimately to be taken over by National Ship-builders Security Ltd in 1933. Donald Bremner went on to join Hugh MacMillan and found the Blyths-wood Shipyard.

Another of the great river characters and the proprietor of a shipyard was Henry Murray. He was a completely different type from Laurence Hill, having been born in poor circumstances in Paisley in the year 1838. After serving his apprenticeship as a joiner and working for a time with Blackwood and Gordon he went into partnership with Hugh Paton and James Crawford and in 1867 they formed the shipyard of Henry Murray & Co at Kingston, Port Glasgow. They built in all about 100 ships all under 2,000 tons and had a thriving business which was sold out to Russell & Co in 1882. However, in 1875, Henry Murray separated and along with James Murdoch (1821-98) founded Murdoch & Murray at Brown Street, Port Glasgow. The yard had steady production for the next 37 years apart from a short period of closure during the slump of 1895. Over 250 ships were built, all small, and with a particular emphasis on shallow draft vessels. Two well known products were the Clyde paddle steamer *Queen Empress* of 1912 and the Anchor Line tender *Paladin* built in 1913. After James Murdoch's death Murray ran the business till his retirement in 1909 and then Murdoch and Murray became a limited company continuing as such till 1912 when it was reconstituted as the Port Glasgow Shipbuilding Co Ltd. In 1918 John Slater Ltd, a London group, took over the yard along with neighbouring Ferguson Brothers but did not sustain activity beyond 1923 when work ran out. In 1927 an unusual happening took place, the derelict industrial land was cleared and transformed back to a green field site for recreation!

Henry Murray was very much a small ship man and was associated with Henry Murray & Co of the Sandpoint Yard which operated in Dumbarton from 1881-4 and Murray Brothers who operated the nearby Phoenix Park Yard from 1883-91. The former company built a complete yard and among the ten ships built was the early twin-screw steamer *Richmond Hill* for the Twin Screw Line.

Another interesting group of companies has operated for over 100 years on the Castle Street site at Port Glasgow. The yard was developed by Blackwood & Gordon in 1860 after their move from Paisley—a decision taken in order to build larger ships. After 27 years of moderately successful

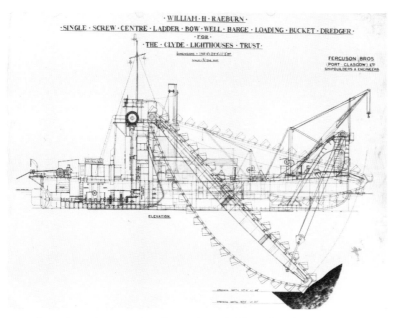

WILLIAM·H·RAEBURN·
·SINGLE·SCREW·CENTRE·LADDER·BOW·WELL·BARGE·LOADING·BUCKET·DREDGER·
FOR
THE·CLYDE·LIGHTHOUSES·TRUST·

FERGUSON BROS
PORT GLASGOW LTD
SHIPBUILDERS & ENGINEERS

ELEVATION.

Left *the self-propelled bucket dredger* William H. Raeburn *built in 1913 for the Clyde Lighthouses Trust by Ferguson Brothers (Port Glasgow) Ltd* (National Maritime Museum).

Below right *Capacity plan of the twin-screw motor tanker* Athelviscount *built in 1929 by Robert Duncan & Co Ltd of Port Glasgow, for United Molasses Ltd. The capacity plan is of great assistance to the officers of a ship, giving practical information on drafts, storage and deadweight* (National Maritime Museum).

operation they became insolvent in 1887 and temporarily closed after arranging with Murdoch and Murray to complete their outstanding contracts. The problems were resolved in 1889 and the company restarted with four partners, Messrs Blackwood, McGeoch, Wallace and Purvis. The latter gentleman had served in William Froude's testing tank and had been involved in the setting up of Denny's tank at Dumbarton. The position of the company had been precarious throughout but this new arrangement carried on for 11 years until further difficulties brought about ultimate closure in 1900.

Blackwood and Gordon left a record of over 200 ships built including SS *Strathclyde* for Burrell in 1871 and the engines for SS *Strathleven* the first vessel built for the carriage of frozen meat from Australia using Bell-Coleman refrigeration. In 1870 the Duke of Hamilton took delivery of the steam yacht *Thistle*. His Grace, a man of immense power and a British Viceroy, must have been satisfied as he returned to the reconstituted yard for the paddle steamer *Lady Mary* in 1868 and another *Thistle* in 1882.

In 1900 the Clyde S. & E. Co Ltd, with a registered capital of £30,000, took over the yard which was modernised and they then built over 100 ships in the following quarter century. The Clyde Company built several US and Canadian Great Lakers, a market that has largely been the province of the Great Lakes and the Clyde shipyards alone. In

1919 they were taken over by Amalgamated Industrials Ltd it being fashionable then to set up diversified groups but this company crashed in 1927 and the Castle Yard ultimately was sold to James Lamont.

James Lamont & Co became established at East India Harbour, Greenock, in 1870 a site they have continuously used for ship-repairing operations. They purchased the Castle Yard in 1929 but did not commence shipbuilding there until 1938, and again the yard reverted to repairs during the war becoming a full shipyard again once hostilities were well over. In 1979 the company announced that it was to give up shipbuilding and concentrate on repair work which had been expanded by their 113 m drydock opened in 1966. Altogether over 70 ships have been built including for the Associated Humber Lines *Darlington*, *Harrogate* and *Selby*, for Glasgow City Council the sludge hoppers *Dalmarnock* and *Garroch Head* and ten Caledonian-MacBrayne landing-craft type ferries.

In 1903 four brothers named Ferguson decided to leave Fleming & Ferguson of Paisley and to set up on their own at Newark Shipyard, Port Glasgow. The current contract number at Paisley when they left was 152 and for reasons not at all clear the Fergusons starting building in Port Glasgow with the next yard number. Hence both Ferguson Brothers and Fleming & Ferguson had ships No 153 building simultaneously. Ferguson Bros also became associated with Amalgamated Industrials but despite that set-back continued building throughout. In 1955 Lithgows obtained shares and full control was effected by them in 1961. In 1969 Ferguson Brothers became part of the Scott-Lithgow Group and in 1977 a member company of British Ship-builders. The Corporation separated them from the Port Glasgow group in 1981 and with Ailsa of Troon they set up a joint management company named Ferguson-Ailsa—to the great annoyance of many Troon citizens who argued that on grounds of alphabetic priority or yard seniority the names should have been the other way round!

Over 300 ships have come from Newark including about 20 tugs for the Clyde Shipping Company and associated companies, ferries for the Clyde Navigation Trust and in 1929 the SS *Discovery II* for the Falkland Isles. This latter ship, run as a scientific and exploration vessel, was singularly successful and happy and succeeded the RRS *Discovery* built by the Dundee Shipbuilders Company in 1901 and currently being fully restored by the Maritime Trust in London. The present *Discovery* in the fleet of the Natural Environmental Research Council was built by Hall, Russell of Aberdeen keeping alive the tradition of building north of the Border.

The Lithgow heritage

The story of the several companies which have come together to form the Lithgow shipyards is as complex as it is inspiring. While few of these constit-uent groups ever aspired to build the costliest ships on the market, they did in all cases construct craft which were suitable for their purpose and economic-ally priced. With the ever-growing sophistication of merchant ships the group, like all other major ship-builders worldwide, was forced into re-assessing its market strategy, and owing to this has in the past 15 years successfully completed ships as diverse as giant tankers and heavy lift cargo carriers. To gain an appreciation of the background to the setting up of Lithgows Ltd each history must be looked at in turn.

The oldest link in the chain is formed by Robert Duncan & Co, an organisation that was to have two lives in the Inverclyde area. The first was from 1830 when Robert Duncan left the shipyard of James MacMillan of Greenock, where he was a partner, to found his own yard in Greenock which continued till his death from typhus in 1841. In 11 years he was to build some interesting ships and his products increased in size as his name became known and he could tackle bigger jobs. Probably the most

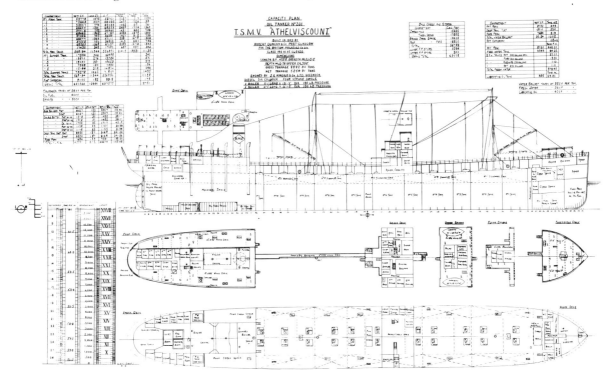

important job to come from the yard, and certainly the best known, was the PS *Britannia* built on hull subcontract to Robert Napier. This ship opened the North Atlantic mail service by Cunard and along with other Clyde-built sisters *Acadia, Columbia* and *Caledonia* started the long history of what was then called the British and North American Royal Mail Steam Packet Company. Duncan built the hulls for the paddle steamers *Clyde* and *Teviot* for the Royal Mail Line but, again, as subcontractors to Caird & Co who manufactured the engines. The relationship between John Scott Russell and the Cairds has already been noted but it is interesting to discover that Duncan built a ship, the *Flambeau*, to J.S. Russell's design as a means of checking the efficacy of his wave line theory.

Robert Duncan's son, also named Robert, trained as a shipbuilder, spent some time at sea and then worked as manager for his father's old partner MacMillan. However, in 1862, he decided to strike out on his own and using his father's company name took over the East Yard in Port Glasgow. The company was successful far beyond Robert Duncan Jr's wildest hopes or dreams. Nearly 400 ships were built in the East Yard from its start through until the last ship was delivered in 1931. Robert Duncan had the pleasure of seeing his three eldest sons join the business, and in public life was greatly honoured by becoming President of the Institution of Engineers and Shipbuilders in Scotland for the 1872-4 sessions. He was another of the many shipbuilders with an inventive turn of mind and produced many ideas which either were patented or which earned considerable sums of money for himself or associated shipowners. From 1882 mild steel replaced iron for all work in the shipyard making Duncan's one of the first companies to commit themselves to this extent. Robert Duncan Jr died in 1889 and left behind excellent relationships with the Anchor Line, with P. Henderson of Glasgow and their subsidiary the Albion Line which later amalgamated with Shaw, Savill & Co. For some years his associations with the Anchor Line were closer than appeared on the surface as he was manager of the Barrow Shipbuilding Company and was responsible for the layout of their yard.

In 1900 the last sailing ship left their yard and in either 1914 or 1915 the yard was taken over by Russell & Co. Duncan's continued in their own name and produced some fine vessels including the SS *Dalriada* of 1926 for the Glasgow-Campbeltown

service. Around 1934 the yard was finally closed.

The next thread in the complicated Port Glasgow set-up is of John Reid & Co who operated in three yards, the East, the Glen and Newark at various times between 1847 and 1891. John Reid was related to John Wood the builder of the *Comet* and was in partnership with him between 1838 and 1857. One of his first major contracts was around 1847 when he accepted an order from trustees and managers of a parish of the Free Church of Scotland for a floating church for use in Loch Sunart in the district of Morvern. The great disruption of 1843 had split the Church of Scotland and those dissenting on conscientious grounds were faced with leaving their manses and churches and starting anew. To overcome hostility from landlords still giving allegiance to the Auld Kirk, the members of the Free Kirk held services in strange places such as on one Hebridean Island between the high and low water marks. The floating church disappeared long ago and, most fortunately, with the reunification of the Scottish Kirk the need for it has passed.

Reid's son, James, joined the business and being an enthusiastic yachtsman tried to popularise yacht construction in iron and later steel. He was successful in that in 1885 the America's Cup challenger *Galatea* was built of steel and sailed the Atlantic in her vain bid to wrest the elusive cup from *Mayflower* in 1886. The work output of the yard ranged from the pioneer SS *Collier* in 1849 to the largest steel full rigged ship of the 1880s—the *British Isles*.

In 1891, after building the paddlers *Marchioness of Bute* and *Marchioness of Breadalbane* for the Caledonian Steam Packet and the auxiliary yacht *White Heather*, the company suspended both work and payments with liabilities of £103,000 with, however, an estimated surplus on uncompleted contracts. In 1891 the yard was sold to William Hamilton & Co.

James Reid continued in business running a limited liability business on the old name. From 1891 to 1909 he was in Whiteinch, Glasgow, concentrating on pleasure steamers, sailing vessels and yachts, some of which were designed by Alfred Mylne. The four-masted barque *Colonial Empire* of 4,000 tons dw was launched in 1902 and was one of the first such sailers to be fitted with bilge keels. In 1903 the four-masted *Mneme* was launched—she is still afloat as the *Pommern* at Mariehamn in the Åland Islands. In 1909 the yard was taken over and absorbed by Barclay, Curle & Co Ltd.

Two new ships are seen together on the Clyde during the early summer of 1904. The 5,300-ton dwt four-masted barque Kurt *leaves the Port Glasgow shipyard of William Hamilton & Co, attended by the new steam tug* Cruiser *built by Alexander Stephen & Sons for the tug owners Steel & Bennie. The* Kurt *entered the nitrate trade under the flag of G.J.H. Siemers of Hamburg. Later renamed* Moshulu, *she is afloat 80 years after her delivery in Philadelphia* (William Lind/Glasgow University Archives).

In 1871 William Hamilton founded a shipyard which in 1891 absorbed John Reid's Glen Yard. Hamilton's was a yard concentrating on trading ships. Their products include several small vessels for Turkey, several standard trawlers and, in 1904, two famous four-masted barques—the *Hans* and the *Kurt*, later renamed *Moshulu*. William Hamilton retired in 1919 and Lithgows took over with the shareholding ultimately being almost 50/50 with the Liverpool shipowners Thos & Jno Brocklebank Ltd. From about 1920 almost all Brocklebank liners with their distinctive black hull and white band came from the Glen yard and, indeed, many of the smaller members of their associated fleet, the Cunard Line. In 1963 the yard was closed and ultimately merged into the reconstituted Lithgow East Yard.

The real Lithgow legend began in 1874 when

Joseph Russell (c 1833-1917) and Anderson Rodger (c 1843-1909) formed a partnership called Russell & Co and took over the Bay Shipyard from McFadyen. They concentrated on building hulls only and on achieving high steelwork tonnages as a means of efficient overhead recovery. In 1882 they expanded and took over Murray's Kingston Yard with the existing staff including W.T. Lithgow (1854-1908) the chief draughtsman. Lithgow was invited to become a partner and with his enthusiasm and the very able service of the Shipyard Manager, Alexander Lambie, the yards went from strength to strength. In 1890 with three yards and about 14 building berths they obtained the world 'blue ribband' of 70,370 tons gross from 26 sailing ships and eight steamer hulls. Lambie was an enthusiast for standardisation, a feature which was aided by the company policy of building different ship types at each yard. It is said that he built close on 50 sailing ships from the same mould loft scrieve, achieving considerable savings in man-hours and increased efficiency through the familiarisation which such production gave to the workforce. His fertile mind thought up many productivity ideas and he designed a hydraulic frame joggling machine.

The regular clients of Russell & Co included Andrew Weir's Bank Line, Nourse, Burrell and

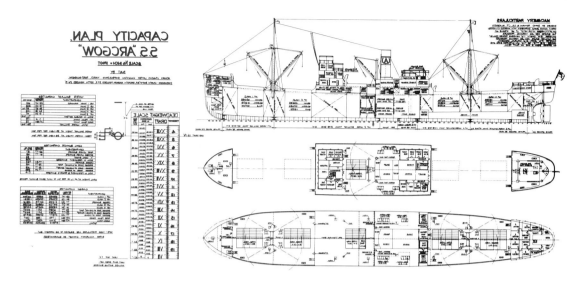

For many years it was appreciated that a ship with a nearly rectangular midship section was inefficient. In an effort to overcome this, the late Sir Joseph Isherwood devised the ARCFORM with the idea of reducing resistance to motion through the water. Several ships were built in Britain and overseas, one of which, SS Arcgow, was built by Lithgows Limited in 1934 for a company set up by Isherwood. While savings in fuel were recorded, the additional building costs, and increased difficulties in cargo stowage, deterred further purchasers of this ship form. The body plan shows the shape of this 9,248-ton displacement tramp steamer. (National Maritime Museum).

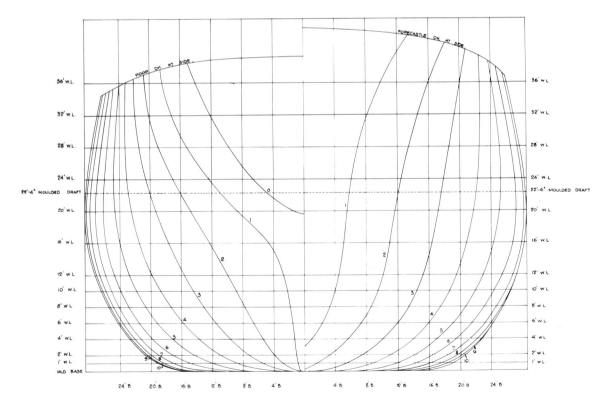

Above *A typical Lithgow tramp ship of the inter-war years.* MV Tolten *was built in 1930 and engined with an 8-cylinder Kincaid diesel for the Compania Sud Americana de Vapores* (Scott Lithgow Ltd).

Right *During the 1970s, Scott Lithgow built some very large crude carriers (VLCCs) and made history by launching them in two halves. After careful alignment, they were joined afloat and the final closure of the shell butt made by welders working in a watertight cofferdam under the ship.*

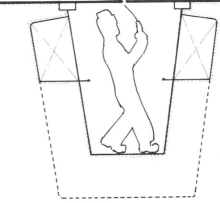

Bruugaard Kiøsterud of Drammen. In their long history only one order came from the Admiralty for the fast patrol craft *P 21* of 1916. One of the outstanding ships was the case oil carrier *Brilliant* built in 1901 for the Anglo-American Oil Company. She was the largest of four sailing ships, all four-masted barques being built for the owners by Russell & Co and William Hamilton & Co and, indeed, was the largest four-masted vessel afloat being 352 ft 5 in × 49 ft 1 in (107.4 m × 15.0 m) and capable of carrying 6,000 tons dw. The other ships were called *Daylight* (Russell) and *Comet* and *Nonpareil.*

In 1891 Russell retired. Lithgow took over the Kingston and Greenock yards which continued as Russell & Co until 1918 when Lithgow's sons renamed them Lithgows Limited. Anderson Rodger took the Bay Shipyard which operated until 1912 as A. Rodger & Co. At the dissolution of the partnership Rodger and Russell both kept in step number wise, both continuing with ship No 298. Rodger built about 120 ships including the famous Anglo-American Oil Company's four-masted barque *Arrow* in 1902, later renamed *Parma.* Most ships were tramp steamers for Hogarth, Kyle, Burrell and others. Mr Rodger died in 1909 and by 1912 the yard had reverted to Russell & Co.

Two small yards are worthy of mention; the Greenock Cartsdyke mid yard was operated from 1874 to 1879 by J.E. Scott. Despite misconceptions this is not part of Scott's of Greenock, and in 1879 their yard became part of Russell & Co. The other is Carmichael MacLean which occupied Russell's Kingston Yard from 1895 to 1898, but they failed and Russell had to finish their contracts before handing the yard over to the Grangemouth & Greenock Dockyard in 1900.

William Todd Lithgow died in 1908 and the Lithgow concern came on the shoulders of two remarkable sons, James (later Sir James) and Henry Lithgow. They were forthright and, to the outsider, brusque but this concealed a desire to have a thriving business and to give good employment in the West of Scotland. Proof of this can be seen in their wartime gross tonnages of 315,141 in the First World War and 1,200,000 in the Second, a greater tonnage than any UK shipbuilder in that period, and to quote J.M. Reid's biography of James Lithgow:

'The Lithgow yards indeed had never been idle. In the ten years after 1919 they had built, on an average 1.8 per cent of the tonnage launched in the world. In the depression years 1932-4 this percentage was between 5.7 and 5—almost one new vessel in every 16 launched anywhere was produced by them. In 1932 their output was 61.8 per cent of all built on the Clyde.'

The company and its associates were products of their time—good shipbuilders backed by aggressive sales drives who had only one match in the United Kingdom, that being the redoubtable brothers Sir Amos and Sir Wilfrid Ayre in Burntisland, Fife.

In both wars Henry Lithgow ran the yards while James served as Director of Merchant Shipbuilding, on his return from France in 1916, and then in the Second World War as Controller of Merchant Shipbuilding and Repairs. During the inter-war period the Lithgows increased the companies under their control like the steel stockists James Dunlop (to ensure their supplies), the North British Welding Company in 1936 and also a period of speculative building in Irvine at the Ayrshire Dockyard in the 1930s. The brothers' most astute and, for the country, the most beneficial move was the purchase of the Fairfield Shipyard when it was threatened with collapse in 1935.

Their customers remained loyal, none more than the fledgling Scindia Steam Navigation Company of Bombay which had its first new building launched at Port Glasgow on July 14 1927 only eight years after its founding. In 1969 when Scott's and Lithgows combined it was to form a large group with a veritable background of shipbuilding expertise unsurpassed throughout the world. They were equipped with very modern shipyards and with the 150,000-ton capacity Scott-Lithgow drydock, an acquisition from the ill-fated Firth of Clyde Drydock Co Ltd of the early 1960s.

Chapter 8

Ship design

It is doubtful if any branch of engineering can offer a stimulus as satisfying and yet as demanding as designing a ship. It is work which can be carried out by one man at a drawing board or by a large unified team with the back-up of computer-aided design systems but, in either event, it requires knowledge, skill, experience and dedication. In ship design no single aspect can be considered on its own as it reacts with other contributory factors and influences the final result. '

Ship design has motivated great men and over the centuries we have been left with their thoughts and, more important, their plans and drawings as in the case of *Architectura Navalis Mercatoria* depicting the studies of F.H. of Chapman whose work was published in Stockholm in 1768. By that date the commonly accepted conventions in ship drawing were in force ensuring that future generations of draughtsmen were comparing like with like. One of the most important customs is that all ships are 'steaming' to the right-hand side of the drawing

board and displaying their starboard side, and this arrangement must be applied rigorously for all details. The concept of scale was understood and by that date British plans were usually drawn 1:48, ie, ¼ in represents 1 ft.

At the beginning of the 19th century the principles of orthographic projection were accepted and the engineer's standard three views of profile, plan and section became universal. Since then drawing office practice has changed to the SI system allowing for more convenient scales like 1:100 or 1:50, there have been better qualities of draughting material introduced and drawings themselves are more explicit while being easier and simpler to construct.

Through the 19th century the business of naval architecture was developed steadily. Aspects were researched and many systems developed to solve problems. Early textbooks like Rankine's *Shipbuilding, Theoretical & Practical* of 1866 produced elegant solutions which were then accepted

Cut-away profile of the double ended Clyde passenger ferry boat built by Harland & Wolff Ltd, Govan in 1923. With a length of 57 ft (17.4 m), this vessel could transport 140 passengers at 7 mph. The machinery was a 2-cylinder simple vertical steam engine manufactured by the Clyde Navigation Trust workshops. Two clutches ensured that the engine could drive either propeller as required. The unusual skeg at each end was to allow landing at riverside steps.

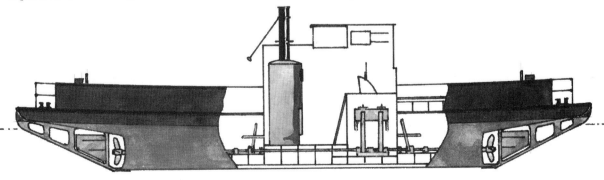

Above *The Clyde Navigation* Ferry No 1 *was the third passenger ferry of that name, and set a new pattern by having a Gleniffer 4-cylinder diesel engine. Most of her working life was at Kelvinhaugh, or as seen here at Govan. She was sold in 1968 and broken up at Bowling. Ferry No 1 was built by Barclay, Curle & Co Ltd, and was licensed to carry 140 passengers.*

Below *Built in 1938 by Ferguson Brothers (Port Glasgow) Ltd, the* Vehicular Ferryboat No 4 *was the first diesel-electric ferry on the River Clyde and operated at Govan till the service ceased in November 1965. She had four screws, and an elevating vehicle deck. In September 1940, this ferry went alongside the blazing cruiser HMS Sussex to assist in the firefighting at nearby Yorkhill Quay. In the left background is the plate shop of Harland & Wolff Ltd and to the right the riverside building berths of Fairfield.*

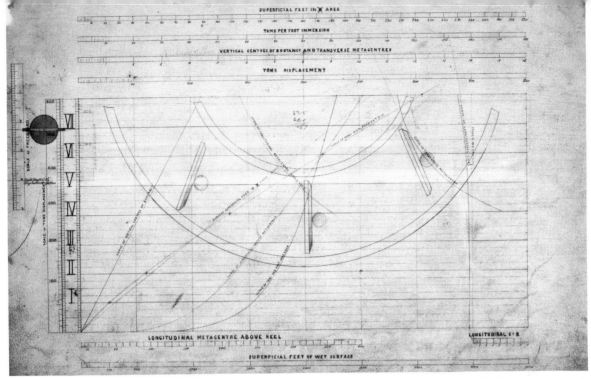

Above *A hydrostatics plan of the river paddle steamer* Diana, *built at Denny of Dumbarton in 1880 for the Buenos Ayres & Campana Railway Company. On the left is the main draft of the ship with the bottom of each figure representing the draft at that dimension and the top of the figure the draft six inches higher. By reading across on the ship's draft one can have information on displacement, hull wetted surface, paddle wheel immersion, the position of the centre of buoyancy and some details on stability* (National Maritime Museum).

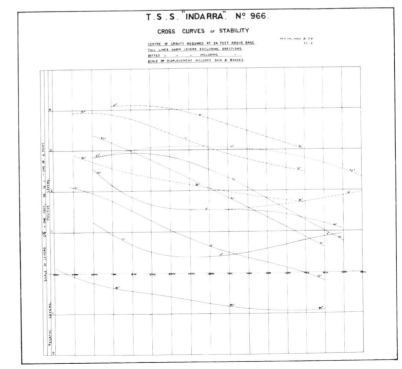

Right *Cross curves of stability of the Australian United Steam Navigation Company's TSS* Indarra *of 1912. Before handing the ship over, Denny arranged that this plan be drawn showing the righting levers keeping the ship upright at different conditions of displacement and angles of heel* (National Maritime Museum).

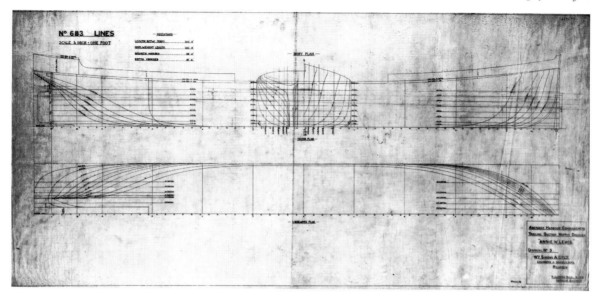

The Lines Plan is the representation on a plane surface of the complex and subtle shapes of a ships hull. For 200 years it has been the convention to draw ships 'Steaming' to the right, and to show them with a profile depicting bow and buttock lines, a body plan showing sections and a plan view showing waterlines. This lines plan is of the Simons-built centre well dredger Annie W. Lewis *of 1927.*

as standard by the profession. Every student is aware that there are many empirical methods for obtaining information but usually only one which is neat, tidy and economical of effort which is, as often as not, named after its inventor such as Atwood's, Riddlesworth's, Kirk's or the Denny-Mumford formulae. The solution to these problems owes much to the staff of the Director of Naval Construction and to staff in a handful of shipbuilding establishments of which Denny's of Dumbarton, followed by Clydebank, must take a clear lead. From the earliest times Denny's had chief executives with scientific background who insisted that design work must be done in an ordered way and that there was good feedback from ships on trials to their design office—which significantly in that yard was known as the Scientific Department. Denny's developed very specialised forms of hydrostatic plans and were one of the first yards in the 19th century to draw out cross curves of stability for every ship.

In 1883 the Dumbarton commercial ship model testing tank was opened and it could be said then that they had the most advanced design team in the world, with the possible exception of the Admiralty team working under the Froudes in the South of England.

A brief description of ship design may be of interest. To make a really constructive design a naval architect must consider the total environment in which his projected ship will operate and first assess the commercial, financial and practical requirements of the owners. From this he can then move to check the constraints that are placed on the design, like dimensions which are limited by locks, drafts by shoal or tidal conditions and air draft by bridges and anticipated conditions of loading.

From the overall dimensions an estimate of capacity for cargo and fuel can be made and then allowances made for machinery spaces, fresh water, crew accommodation and so on. The basic hull shape has to be selected, the size, shape and speed of propeller chosen and, with these known, the type of main machinery nominated and this in turn will confirm the space required for the engine room.

With experience built up over the years most design offices can produce a design proposal at short notice and this is used as a basis for more advanced studies. Often shipyards will produce scores of these proposals before one is accepted and ultimately becomes the reality of an order. In the early 1960s the Cunard Company considered replacing the QSS *Queen Mary* and asked several shipbuilders to

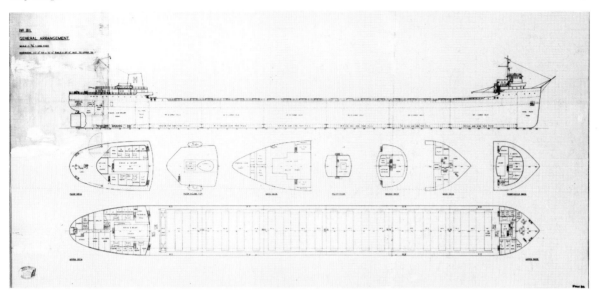

The General Arrangement is an outline drawing showing the external appearance of the ship, as well as the layout of accommodation and cargo spaces. This single-screw steam turbine bulk carrier, Leecliffe Hall, *was built by Fairfield at Govan in 1961 for the Hall Corporation of Canada. With an overall length of 711 ft (217 m) this ship was the largest possible that could be built in the UK for operation on the North American Great Lakes. The launching of this ship was monitored carefully by Fairfield to obtain data of use in the event of a replacement Cunarder being ordered at Govan.*

submit design proposal for a North Altantic mail and passenger liner. These were known as the *Q3* proposals and from the Clyde submissions were made by both John Brown & Co and by Fairfield. They were in considerable detail as it had to be established early on that the schemes were feasible and that not only could the liner be built, but she could be safely launched, moved in the river and would meet all stipulations laid down by the owners. In the Fairfield submission the directors decided to show a plan of river movements to reassure the Cunard Company that it was possible to manoeuvre a large ship in the Port of Glasgow and it indicated that the western corner would have to be removed from the Fairfield outfitting basin to allow the ship to depart at the end of outfitting. As it turned out this expensive exercise was to no avail as the *Q3* project was dropped in favour of the design that became *Queen Elizabeth 2.*

Once the proposals are taken further the full economics of the design are studied including cargo potential, operating costs, likelihood of increased earnings and so on, and then the operational route has to be checked for unforeseen snags like ice conditions or shallow water which slow a ship or, alternatively, demand additional power. There are

many facets of design work which develop into what is called a 'design spiral' which should end with a hard and fast design satisfying the owners and being potentially cheap to build.

One major part of the procedure is the testing of a self-propelled model in a test tank to determine hull resistance and, therefore, power requirements. The tank test may be used also to check steering, manoeuvreability, stopping and sea-keeping qualities of the new hull. If the ship travels considerable distances in ballast the tests may be repeated for a model in light condition in order that the best overall results can be obtained.

The resistance of the water to a ship is basically made up of energy losses through skin friction and energy losses by the generation of waves. The most economical ship will have a smooth, even polished bottom and a shape that slips through the water leaving as little disturbance as possible. In some conditions of draft, speed and loading, a bulbous bow has a beneficial effect as the bulb can create a train of waves which cancel the bow waves of the ship.

As the shape is becoming finalised structural designs are prepared for the Classification Society— usually Lloyd's Register of Shipping—showing the

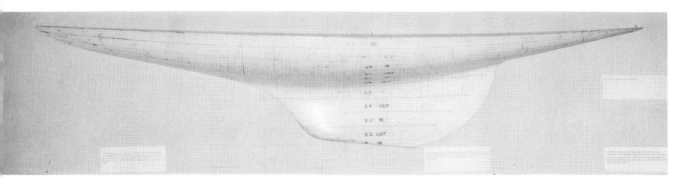

Above *The shipbuilders' half block model of Sir Thomas Lipton's yacht* Shamrock III *of 1903. This America's Cup challenger was designed by Fife of Fairlie, tank tested at Dumbarton and then built as Contract No 685 by William Denny and Brothers at Dumbarton. The half block is of especial interest in this case, as the yacht was constructed of alloy steel with aluminium decks, and this model would have been used frequently by the draughtsmen preparing the constructional plans. The model can be seen at the National Maritime Museum, Greenwich* (National Maritime Museum).

Below *It was usual on Clydeside for funnels to be the responsibility of the engine works in shipbuilding companies, and in this case the basic plans for whistle and siren are detailed by Denny's engine works for the LMS Railway cargo steamer* Slieve Bloom *of 1930. Immense care was taken in their initial design to ensure efficient smoke dispersal and a standard of appearance that would be a credit to the ship, her owners and the shipbuilders* (National Maritime Museum).

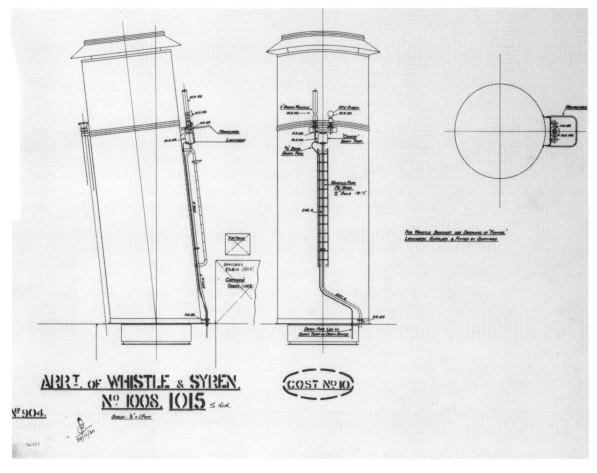

main steelwork and defining the 'scantlings' or overall standard of steel sizes. With approval for the scantlings the detailed work commences with draughtsmen making plans of each main steel unit of the ship and plans also showing layouts, pipework, ventilation, electrics and so on. In particularly congested areas or in small complex ships the drawing office often prepare a composite plan in large scale showing every service in a compartment. If this is not satisfactory then a tenth scale model is made, a usual feature in congested areas like factory decks in fishing vessels.

Each draughtsman lists the material in his drawings and this is ordered by the shipyard purchasing department. Simultaneously the design department are making detailed calculations on hydrostatics, stability, strength, launching, vibration and a host of other matters.

In the past 20 years there have been great changes in drawing offices with modern, tilting drawing boards, the introduction of computers, visual display systems and even computer-generated instructions to the shipyard machine tools. Plans which used to be on long rolls of tracing linen are now on modern plastic film and in international sizes based on the metric AO sheet. Despite all these changes and the infinitely improved working conditions the challenge of ship design remains as exciting as ever.

In October 1937 the Union Steam Ship Company of New Zealand took delivery of the Kakapo *from Stephen's shipyard.*

Chapter 9

Paisley and Renfrew—birthplace of dredgers

Few persons motoring from Glasgow to the airport, give any thought to a 60-metre high flyover crossing the River Cart near Paisley, and sadly few people can tell much of the friendly town below, barring its long association with the thread mills and the manufacture in days gone by of the world-famous Paisley shawls. The purpose of the bridge is to allow access by ships to the centre of Paisley, but more important the delivery of new vessels from the once busy shipyards which, in a span of 130 years, constructed close on 2,000 vessels which were to serve in every corner of the globe. Sadly the last ship has sailed down the river and the shipyards are closed, but the high bridge is a permanent memorial to the brave days now past.

The river flowing through Paisley is the White Cart which after a mile or two is joined by the Black Cart coming from the south-west. Together they are known as the Cart and enter the Clyde directly opposite the Clydebank shipyard, in the wide mouth which was kept dredged for the launch of the largest liners and warships. It is ironic that the Cart, the birthplace of so many small vessels, was instrumental in the delivery of the *Queen Elizabeth 2.*

The many efforts of the Burgh of Paisley to create a harbour and encourage seawise trade to the town centre seemed to have been doomed from the start. Attempts to raise capital for the project go back at least as far as 1753 without real effect, and it was not until the civil engineers Messrs Bell & Miller wrote a glowing report of Paisley's potential as a seaport, in 1884, that public imagination was fired and strenuous efforts made to obtain the necessary parliamentary sanction in 1885. The Cart Navigation was planned, dredging of the river commenced and proper quays constructed at Paisley, but lack of finance precluded the full potential being realised, and although riverborne passenger traffic started in a

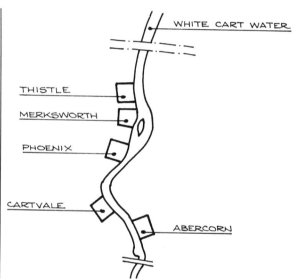

Map showing the relative positions of five shipbuilding sites in the Burgh of Paisley.

serious way in 1899, Paisley never became a bustling seaport.

For the five shipbuilding sites around the Burgh, the work of deepening the river was most fortuitous as they had always worked under the restrictions of building and moving ships in water with limited depth and breadth and with a tidal 'window' of just a short time on either side of high water. The dredging eased the depth problem, and draft ceased to be a serious consideration bearing in mind the small size of the shipyard products, but another restriction was the limited width of 45 ft or just under 14 m available at Inchinan Bridge. This impediment had been overcome from time to time by the shipyards delivering newly built paddle steamers to the Clyde with their paddles, paddle boxes and sponsons being left off for

An illustration of Old Renfrew Harbour in the 19th century. The ship furthest away appears to be resting on a gridiron (Wotherspoon Collection, Mitchell Library, Glasgow).

later fitting. In 1921 the Paisley Corporation (Inchinan Opening Bridge) Order received Royal Assent, and shortly thereafter a new bridge was constructed widening the passage to 90 ft or 27.4 m.

For the towing companies, too, the Cart produced problems, as tugs are on the whole heavy and deep vessels. Certain tugs with reduced draft were kept for this purpose and, of course, up until their disappearance just after the Second World War, paddle tugs with their minimal requirement for water were ideal, and regularly seen plying to Paisley.

In the 1960s the number of shipyards on the river had fallen to one, and Paisley Town Council became active in trying to rid itself of the encumbrance of a river fast dying in the commercial sense. In 1969 the last ship to be built in the town was delivered, the suction dredger *Bled* sailed to the Firth of Clyde for trials and delivery to Yugoslavia, and the real need for the Cart Navigation and the high flyover came to an end.

The earliest shipbuilder of any importance on the Cart was J. McKenzie who started in 1837 and Barr and MacNab who set up the following year, but later transferred to Renfrew. Shipbuilding in the accepted Clydeside sense started in the 1850s with

Hanna & Donald (1851) and Blackwood & Gordon (1852), and from then shipbuilding was continuous until 1969. The major shipbuilders, in date order, were: J. McKenzie, 1837; Barr & McNab, 1838; Hanna & Donald (and successors), 1851-95; Blackwood & Gordon, 1852-60; John Fullerton, 1866-1928; Donald & McFarlane, 1867-8; H. McIntyre, 1877-85; Campbell & Co, 1880-1; J. McArthur, 1882-1900; Fleming & Ferguson, 1885-1969; Bow McLachlan, 1900-33.

In addition to these, vessels were constructed by Millen Brothers, Reid & Hanna (the predecessors of Hanna & Donald), P. & W. McLellan and a company with the improbable name of Milne, Milne, Milne & McGilvary!

The yard furthest from the Clyde and the only one on the east bank of the White Cart is the Abercorn Shipyard. There, in 1838, Barr & MacNab set up as iron shipbuilders for a short time, building Clyde steamers, but shortly after transferring to Barr's West Yard at Renfrew which was renamed Barr & MacNab. It is said that their last ship the PS *Blue Bonnet* capsized on launching, but details of this are hazy.

The next recorded occupiers of the site are Messrs Hanna & Donald who moved there around 1868. The company's principal was James Donald (1826-1901) who became a partner of the long established firm of Reid & Hanna in 1851. They had been founded in 1816 and ultimately became iron boat

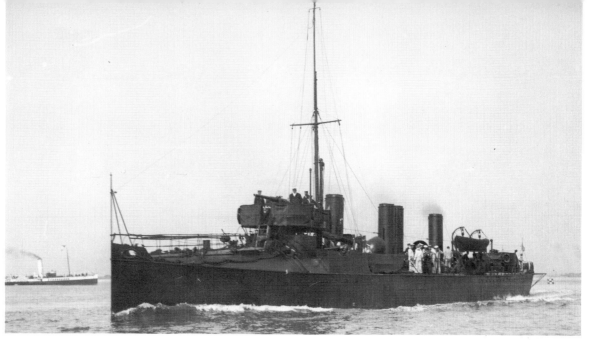

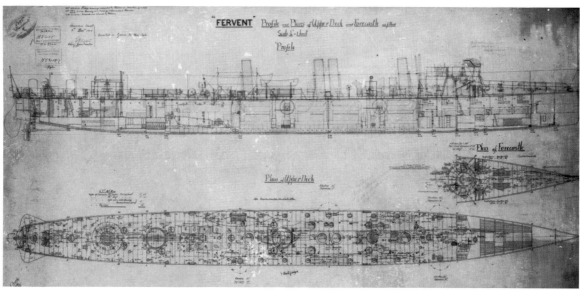

Left and Below left *A photograph and a general arrangement plan of HMS* Fervent *showing the modifications carried out jointly by the Navy and the liquidators of Hanna, Donald & Wilson prior to the destroyer being accepted into the fleet in 1900* (National Maritime Museum).
Bottom left *HMS* Fervent *as originally constructed by Hanna, Donald & Wilson of Paisley. She is seen here on trials off Skelmorlie Her poor speed forced the Navy to reject acceptance, and ultimately the shipbuilders became insolvent* (National Maritime Museum).

builders. The title was changed for a third time to Hanna, Donald & Wilson in 1870, but whoever Wilson was, he was shortlived in the business as, by 1880, it was solely in the hands of James Donald and his three sons. They built up a specialised, but strangely diversified business in hydraulic engineerings for slipways, gas plant as well as the building of high speed naval craft and light scantling passenger ships. Typical of their products was the *Countess of Breadalbane*, a very early steel vessel, transhipped to Loch Awe in 1882 for the Loch Awe Hotel Company. They also built two floating docks, *Sourabaya* and *Chiselhurst*, the first being lost on a coral reef while on delivery voyage, and the subject of costly litigation in the Scottish Courts. The form of construction must have been novel to overcome the shallow water of the river and the narrowness of the bridge, but presumably they were small, or were constructed in parts for reassembly once floated out to the Clyde.

Their engineering background encouraged attempts to build in unusual ways, and they are reported as having built a lightweight longitudinally framed hull as early as 1876. Tragedy befell the company in the placing of an order by the Royal Navy for two torpedo boat destroyers in the current vogue of 27 knots. They were follow-ups to two earlier Royal Navy torpedo boats and the *Delos* and *Sappho* for the Greek Navy. The two new ships, later to become HMS *Fervent* and HMS *Zephyr*, were ordered following the 1893-4 estimates and launched in March and May 1895 at a contract price of just over £33,000 each. With their previous experience of small, light and fast vessels, no problems were anticipated, and as was the custom at the time the Admiralty left Hanna, Donald and Wilson very much to their own devices, provided they remained within the general framework of their remit. Such hopes were dashed when neither *Fervent* nor her sister could reach anything close to 27 knots despite repeated attempts on the Skelmorlie Mile. The problem lay with the use of locomotive type boilers which could not generate the steam required and were overweight by several tons—a serious

problem in a ship with a light displacement of only 275 tons. The final arrangements are not clear— either the shipyard went into voluntary liquidation or the Navy rejected the ships—or indeed a combination of these, and after negotiations it is understood that the liquidators, with Admiralty assistance, completed the contract by lengthening the hulls, reboilering and fitting additional auxiliaries. The two ships were not a success and barely reached their speed and were accepted with reluctance into the Royal Navy as late as 1900 and 1901. The unique one-funnel configuration had gone, to be replaced by four and the costs had risen to just short of £42,000 each.

In the latter years of Hanna, Donald & Wilson the returns were given as for the Abercorn Shipbuilding Co Ltd. It is possible that this appelation was used after the liquidation and while the two destroyers were finishing. Many other shipyards throughout Britain were to suffer a similar fate while striving to break into the lucrative but fickle defence contract market.

The second oldest site and the one second furthest from the Clyde is the Cartvale Shipyard. It was here in 1852 that Thomas Blackwood and Andrew Gordon set up their business. They had served their apprenticeships together in Barr & MacNab's yard, had become friends and then set up an engineering business, and in the progress so frequent in 19th century Scotland, from there moved to founding a shipbuilding establishment. Their first product was a two-funnelled, 11-knot iron paddle steamer called *Reindeer*. It was followed by 33 more ships before Blackwood and Gordon decided to move to Port Glasgow in 1860 to obtain more space and be free of the irksome restrictions of the river. The yard remained empty for a few years and then was busy for a few months in 1867 when Messrs Donald & McFarlane built a few (believed four) small ships. The Donald involved a relative of the principal of the Abercorn Shipyard.

The Phoenix Shipyard was the longest surviving shipbuilding site on the Cart. It was opened in 1877 by Hugh McIntyre, then aged 37, who had served his apprenticeship with Barclay Curle before gaining further experience with Charles Connell, William Hamilton and then Thomas Wingate at their respective yards. Some authorities mention that he started in partnership with a D.R. MacBrayne. For eight years he ran the yard, and certainly it must have been a success as in that time he produced no less than 123 ships before vacating the site in June 1885. Most of the ships were under 1,000 tons and included lighters and coasters as well as the Clyde steamer PS *Brodick Castle* of 1878 and P. & A. Campbell's PS *Waverley* of 1885. On selling the yard, he set up a consultancy business, then a shipyard at Alloa. He died in Jamaica in 1901.

For the following 84 years the new proprietors were to make themselves an imperishable name and nearly 700 ships were to slide down their ways. The new company, Fleming & Ferguson Ltd, was founded by various members of the two families, and as such remained until 1903 when the Fergusons (all brothers) left to form Ferguson Brothers of Port Glasgow and the Paisley company was left in the hands of W.Y. Fleming. Rather interestingly, Ferguson Brothers commenced building using the next contract number from the last ship at Paisley, so both shipyards appear to claim the true numerical succession from 1885!

One of the original founders of Fleming and Ferguson was Peter J. Ferguson (1840-1911) who had been manager of Thomas Wingate & Co at Whiteinch, where it was claimed they had built the world's first triple expansion engine in 1872, two years before SS *Propontis* was re-engined and nearly nine years before the great SS *Aberdeen* sailed from Govan. Be that as it may, the climate of experimentation was such at Wingate's that P.J. Ferguson was motivated in the field of research and development of steam reciprocating engines, and from this Fleming and Ferguson were to become masters in this product, and to remain builders of them right up until the 1950s. At the turn of the century they developed their own triangular connecting rod engine which claimed to require a reduced floor area. As shipbuilders, they produced specialist ships— dredgers, survey ships, chain ferries, elevating deck vehicular ferries, buoy vessels and pilot cutters, with a high percentage of the work going overseas.

A photograph believed taken early this century at Paisley shipyard of Fleming & Ferguson Ltd shows an early bow thruster. The idea of such manoeuvring aids is quite old, and indeed was proposed in the 19th century by Lord Kelvin (National Maritime Museum).

In 1964 the yard was taken over by the American Marine & Machinery Co Inc and while still operating under the old name produced a few more ships. In 1969 the last ship left the Phoenix Shipyard, and the great tradition was over.

In the cruise northwards along the White Cart, the next yard was the Merksworth which was operated by John Fullerton & Co from 1866 to 1928. The founder died in 1905 and his younger son, James, continued the business until his death in 1925. The last ship, contract No 279 *Greta Force* was launched in 1928. The ships were coasters, small cargo vessels and the odd passenger steamer, never very distinguished technically, but all carrying the hall-mark of sturdy construction, like the iron steamer *Earl of Zetland* built in 1877 for the Shetland north isles service. It was to have a particularly long and adventurous life, being spared the breakers until 1950. It is recorded that Fullerton's, like most Paisley shipbuilders, launched sideways from time to

time and in this manner the SS *Hilda* was set afloat in August 1884.

The final yard was Thistle, which was opened by Campbell & Co in 1880, built four or five ships before becoming bankrupt in 1881. The yard was reopened by James McArthur of Abbotsinch in 1882 and from then until 1900 turned out over 100 coasters and small passenger steamers. Despite the death of the proprietor in 1891 and a serious fire in 1895, the business prospered and was sold as a going concern to Bow McLachlan & Co.

At this stage it is worthy of mention, that shipyard fires were much more frequent in the latter half of the 19th century than at any other time. The large quantities of wood stored in the proximity of blacksmith shops and plate shops where furnaces for the heating of plates and frames had some effect, especially as few small yards at that time had layouts which were anything but haphazard. A serious fire could destroy good timber, but a major catastrophe would involve the loss of mould loft scrieve boards and many hundreds, or even thousands, of manhours.

The third and last occupier was Bow McLachlan & Co Ltd who took over in 1900 and ran the yard until its demise and purchase by National Shipbuilders Security Ltd in 1933. The company was formed in

The lighthouse tender Relume *enters the River Cart around the end of 1951 after launching from the Paisley shipyard of Fleming & Ferguson Ltd. This ship, operating under the British flag, helped to maintain the Persian Gulf Lighting Service* (National Maritime Museum).

Above *A group of officials, draughtsmen and foremen photographed at the Fairfield shipyard in August 1880. The occasion is the leaving of Mr James McArthur, the shipyard manager, to set up his own shipyard at Inchinan (McArthur is seated centre front row). J. McArthur & Co took over the Thistle shipyard of the bankrupt Campbell & Co in 1882, so McArthur must have operated elsewhere in the district for some months. He died in 1891 and the company ceased building in 1900. The half block model to the right is of HMS Nelson (Strathclyde Regional Archives).*

Below *A dumb barge under construction at the shipyard of Bow, McLachlan and Co, Paisley in 1923. It is likely that this was a 'knock down' job for re-erection overseas (J.A. McLachlan).*

1872 by William Bow and John McLachlan and were manufacturers of steering gear and other auxiliaries. It has been suggested that they manufactured small ships at their 20-acre site at Abbotsinch prior to 1900, but there is at present no hard evidence for this, and this is also borne out by the fact that they continued with McArthur's numbering system—their first ship being No 137 on taking over the yard.

William Bow was a benefactor of Paisley and district with gifts to Paisley College, assistance with

Andrew Brown (1825-1907) was an engineer of originality and distinction. At the age of 25 he was appointed engineering manager to A & J Inglis of Whitehall Foundry, where he designed efficient dredging machinery. In 1860 he became a partner of William Simons & Co and shortly thereafter became head of the company. Under his guidance revolutionary designs of ships were tried and through his efforts Renfrew became the established and accepted building place for the highest class of dredging plant. Over the years many millions of pounds were spent in Renfrew on this specialist equipment (Wotherspoon Collection, Mitchell Library, Glasgow).

public parks and he is remembered especially for his offer of £500 to the first airman to shoot down a German zeppelin over Britain in the First World War. The offer was honoured in 1916, and through this and other activities he became well known, a fact which presumably smoothed the way for the arrangements leading to King George V's visit to three Paisley shipyards in 1917 when he launched three ships within one hour!

Bow McLachlan & Co had a name as tug builders and continued to supply these interesting craft into the 1920s with, in fact, two each for the competing Clyde Towage companies of Clyde Shipping and Steel & Bennie. Many barges were built for overseas often as knock down jobs. As the 1920s drew to a close many of the experienced senior staff were dead and, as the managing director had other business commitments, the purchase and closure of the yard was accepted all round.

The end of Cart shipbuilding is a matter for sadness and some regret. With the passing of these slightly rough and ready companies, the nation lost specialist skills and a body of men of independent mind. Such yards were excellent training grounds, as most apprentices, and certainly any young man lucky enough to be an assistant manager, saw every aspect of the shipbuilding business.

Other companies worked at Paisley: during the Second World War, P. & W. McLellan built landing craft on the Thistle yard site and Millen Brothers built knock down craft right up to the 1950s, in an off-river works.

*   *   *

It is unusual to write of a shipyard which commenced life in Scotland before moving overseas and then returned to become an important and innovative business. Such a firm was founded in Greenock by one of their townsmen, William Simons in 1810, on a site now integrated into Victoria Harbour. Their first ship, a brig of 180 tons named *Janet Dunlop*, was launched in 1811.

The lure of Canada with its great forests and growing shipbuilding industry attracted Mr Simons and, in 1812, he suspended operations on the Clyde and moved to Isle Aux Noix at Montreal. There 12 ships were constructed of which four were for the King's service. However, as with the Wood family later, the time in Canada was limited and Simons returned to the Clyde, recommencing shipbuilding in 1818 on ground next to Robert Steele's yard, and until 1826 there built various sailing craft.

In 1826 William Simons made another move to a yard at Whiteinch in Glasgow setting up on land between Thomas Wingate and Aitken & Mansell. A steamship *Fingal* was constructed for Belfast and then a series of interesting vessels including the PS *Erin* for Dublin, the G.L. Watson designed yacht *Tiara* which was a successful all weather craft and, in 1851, the paddle tug *Clyde* with independent engines on each paddle. In the same year Simons built the sailing ship *William Connal,* claimed to be the first vessel fitted with wire rope rigging supplied by Newall & Co from Gateshead-upon-Tyne.

After 34 years in Glasgow the company made two more changes, both of which were to prove of the greatest importance as the years progressed. Firstly their building site was changed yet again to the East Yard, Renfrew, which they took over from J.W. Hoby & Co who had been there for ten years. Simons also purchased the iron foundry of Fox Henderson & Co known as the London Works, a title which was to remain thereafter on their postal address. The second and far-reaching change was the invitation to Provost Andrew Brown of Renfrew to become a partner. Andrew Brown (1825-1907) had served his apprenticeship at John Nielson's Oakbank Foundry and then had gained further experience as a draughtsman and foreman patternmaker with William Craig & Co who had taken over Claude Girdwood & Co before working with Tod & McGregor, the Caledonian Railway and finally A. & J. Inglis where he had designed dredging equipment to work to depths of 37 ft or just over 11 m. He had been instrumental in pioneering work on link motions for the valves of steam engines.

Within a short time William Simons retired and effective control was in the hands of Brown and was to remain with him and his family for many years. By 1861 it was clear to see on the Clyde that a new era had arrived in the old company: the paddle steamer *Rothesay Castle* achieved 20.25 knots on trials (it later became a blockade runner, and later still served as the *Southern Belle* on Lake Ontario), the shipyard had constructed a diving bell and Andrew Brown made the first descent in it and construction started on four self-propelled hopper barges for the Clyde Navigation Trust, the first of their type ever built.

Between 1866 and 1872, Simons built 11 bucket ladder dredges as well as nine other types. During this short period the Anchor Liner *India* was

constructed and was the first vessel on the North Atlantic with four-cylinder compound engines of the surface condensing type—a great step forwards in the search for efficient marine propulsion then underway. The problem with a narrative of this kind is that it becomes a long list of firsts—but this indeed was the situation and therefore it will be sufficient to mention three significant Simons designs, each of which had worldwide application.

The Mersey ferry *Oxton* was launched in 1879 and established the efficiency of hulls with twin screws at each end for manoeuvring in tidal and restricted waters. This was taken a stage further in 1890 with *Finnieston*, another four-screw double ended steamer but with an elevating deck which could be raised or lowered to suit the tide on the Clyde Trust's ferry crossing between Finnieston and Mavisbank. In 1895 the yard built the TSS *Salford* an enclosed hopper-type ship for dumping of sewage waste at sea. Again a prototype had been established and this design, with modifications, is used to this day universally.

'The Ring', as Simons was known locally, had become a recognised world leader in dredger and specialist work by the turn of the century. This is work that demands accurate but rugged engineering and a high input of technical expertise in the design side, as seldom are dredgers either simple structures or uncomplicated engineering jobs.

During the two wars the output was steady and dramatic. In the period 1914-18 a total of 46 ships were produced, that is one every month, and while allowing that some were less complicated affairs, it was still a great achievement which speaks greatly of the efforts of all staff and in particular the managers in the yard. In 1957, after completing 800 ships, William Simons amalgamated with the next door neighbour Lobnitz & Co Ltd.

The West Yard at Renfrew possibly was first used for shipbuilding around 1838 when J. Barr was the proprietor. An iron paddle steamer, the *Monarch*, is given in their returns for 1846, but details become difficult to pin down when one realises that at some stage between 1838 and 1847 Barr and MacNab of Renfrew took over the yard. There is every likelihood that the Barr constituent in both companies was either the same man or the same family.

In 1847 the yard changed hands and became the property of James Henderson who, with his son, built about 40 ships. They were related to the Henderson family which ultimately opened the

The first Clyde steam hopper barge delivered in 1862 by William Simons & Co. This commenced their long association with the Clyde Trust, and was also the start of their specialisation in dredging plants. (Wotherspoon Collection, Mitchell Library, Glasgow).

Anchor Line and several of their ships had family money invested in them. In 1857 a Dane named Mr Henry C. Lobnitz joined the staff and gradually was promoted up to the most senior level. From 1861 to 1874 the company was known as Henderson, Coulborn & Co and then, as Henry Lobnitz was a partner, Lobnitz, Coulborn & Co.

Lobnitz was born at Fredericia, a small town on the east coast of Jutland, in 1831. His family were professional engineers with the ordnance department of the Danish Army but Henry Lobnitz, while wishing to be an engineer, decided on the then called 'civil' branch as distinct from military. He came to Britain, was ultimately naturalised, and worked with Penn & Sons of Greenwich and for a while with J. Scott Russell. He died at Renfrew in 1896 and by then the west yard had a new name, simply Lobnitz & Co Ltd. He left as a legacy another specialist yard on the Clyde, deeply involved in dredger building and with more emphasis on rock breaking and cutting than Simons, their neighbour and rival.

Lobnitz & Co were slower at moving into specialisation than Simons, but by the 20th century were just as committed. In the 1880s many small ships were built for Denmark but, as the years progressed and family ties became less binding, the yard set out to surpass their neighbours. In 1887 they built a 20-ton floating crane *Alexandre Lavalley* for the original French Panama Company. It was taken over by the Americans, used in their Panama operation, and in 1914 became the first ship to sail across the isthmus of Panama coast to coast.

Throughout the 20th century their production was unceasing and when amalgamation with Simons came about nearly 1,200 ships had been built by Lobnitz and their predecessors in the West Yard.

In 1957 the two companies recognising their common interests and the value of integration of many aspects of their work decided to amalgamate forming Simons-Lobnitz Ltd. Such unions can be successful given time, patience and goodwill. The greatest benefits can accrue from the strengthening of the sales and technical side and, in this area, the new company with two distinct but complementary backgrounds had much to offer. In 1959 the shipyard was acquired by the Weir Group and, sadly, in 1963 for what were described as financial reasons the decision was taken to close the operation. In

Clyde tugs & hopper barges in Queen's Dock, Glasgow 1964. The basic design of hopper barges has not altered in over 100 years.

terms of job losses it meant the unemployment or redeployment of several hundred people, possibly an acceptable price from some viewpoints, but with the advantage of hindsight it was in national terms a tragedy almost unequalled on the Clyde. A unique service which was international in scope and possessed hard-earned expertise in the design, building and selling of dredgers was lost to Britain.

The goodwill of the name and of the massive spares business was sold to Alexander Stephen & Sons Ltd and a few further and very large dredgers were built under Simons-Lobnitz name in the upper reaches of the Clyde. But with the setting up of UCS and its eventual demise, the Simons-Lobnitz business slowly tailed off.

One brighter aspect of the closure was the forming in 1969 of Seadrec Limited, a consultancy formed by several former executives of the old shipyard. This young thrusting company, set up in Paisley, is prepared to act for clients in the full execution of dredger orders carrying out feasibility studies, doing the design and drawing office work, ordering material and supervising construction in the builder's yard. This is an area in which our country excels and where the organisational and technical talents of engineers should be encouraged.

Before leaving Renfrew, two other small shipyards have to be mentioned. One is the repair slip of the Clyde Port Authority near the Renfrew Ferry. This small works was opened in 1908 at a cost of £122,000 to service the large fleet of dredgers and hoppers of the Clyde Navigation Trust and it replaced the works sold in 1905 at Dalmuir to William Beardmore. Through the long history of

this and the previous repair works very little in the way of new construction has been attempted, they have constructed steam engines from time to time for some of the double-ended passenger ferries. The ownership of this yard was passed on January 1 1966 from the 107-year-old Clyde Navigation Trust to the newly created Clyde Port Authority, which also took over the responsibilities of the Greenock Harbour Trust and the Clyde Lighthouses Trust. Nowadays they are competing in the commercial market.

Almost next to the Navigation Works is the small shipyard which for many years produced small craft and, in particular, ship's lifeboats. The company, later known as Hugh McLean & Sons Ltd, commenced in Govan in the 1880s and until its closure nearly 90 years later was managed by members of the McLean family. In the 1930s they took over a small yard in Renfrew and some years later also extended their operations to Gourock but closed Govan in 1943. At the time of final closure their contract numbers had reached a phenomenal 5,009. In 1972 the yard recommenced under a new company, the Argyll Ship & Boatbuilding Co Ltd, but this ended after the completion of about four ships, two of which were 74 ft (22.6 m) stern trawlers, very similar to the popular Aberdeen *Sputnik* Class. Later the yard was taken over by the Ritchie's of the Clyde ferry and boat services.

Chapter 10

The shipbuilding process

No information brings as much pleasure to the work-force of a shipyard as confirmation that an order has been placed. Equally, nothing can be more irritating to senior staff than to hear this vital news from sources on the 'shop floor' and to have it authenticated shortly after by an official statement. It is difficult for people close to the chief executive not to be aware of the likelihood of an order and there is a great temptation for people with close friends and relatives in the yard to make optimistic remarks in their company. The short-lived Fairfields (Glasgow) Ltd did try to combat this and to prevent rumours spreading in the shipyard by a clearly laid down briefing system with the chief executive meeting senior managers and giving them material for dissemination and they, in turn, meeting a group of deputies, and so on, until within a couple of hours several thousand people were aware of company news or important changes in policy.

The original profile proposed in 1928 for the new Cunard North Atlantic liner. The classic outline was retained through all design processes, with the exception of the counter stern which was discarded in favour of the cruiser stern, giving more accommodation and a longer effective waterline (National Maritime Museum).

The placing of the order is usually the climax of a carefully orchestrated sales and marketing drive. The serious way in which this is treated is a reflection of the importance which a large contract can have on the well-being of possibly thousands of people, their families and also the locality. Throughout the years the aggressive approach to selling ships has not changed, only the handling of some aspects of the technique. Gone are the days of the travelling chief executive with his personal ready reckoners designed to enable him to give budgetary costs to likely clients. The introduction of marketing, of large sales teams and of excellent communications have made selling more positive but much tougher. Instead of ship owners being visited and asked if there is a likelihood of work arising, now they are given helpful suggestions as to a good pattern of purchasing with the potential shipbuilder stressing his speciality and proposing vessels which can be fitted into his forward building programme.

The proverbial story of the designing of a ship on the back of a dinner menu card is seldom true but on rare occasions flashes of old worldly business techniques are seen, as exampled overleaf by a letter received by a Glasgow shipbuilder just after the Second World War from Liverpool shipowners:

Dear Sirs,
We shall be obliged if you can build us one cargo vessel, similar to those previously supplied to us by yourselves, and to your usual high standard. Terms and delivery to be agreed mutually.

Yours faithfully,

———————————————

Changes in technology make such things unlikely in present day conditions but when one examines the diaries of 19th century shipbuilding masters like Robert Napier one sees that, even then, orders went to those who made the opportunities.

The first stage in the shipbuilding cycle is the issue of the lines plan to the mould loft. Here, traditionally, on a floor on the top of a building the lines of the ship already designed in the drawing office are laid out full size on the loft floor. The floor is often painted black and the lines drawn in with chalk. Once the loftsmen are satisfied that the lines are 'fair' or true and sweet in every direction, a body plan of sections of the ship is drawn full size on a special board, and these lines then gouged or scrieved to preserve them for all time. This board becomes the master dimension control and from it all yard templates are prepared.

In modern times this has been superseded by the mould loft working to one tenth full scale and, even more recently, by computer with great savings in time, labour and space.

The Planning Office has become the key to modern shipbuilding production as the industry is, by and large, one of assembly. With the exception of steelwork and joinerwork almost every other trade is involved in assembling bought-in components to such an extent that few items on the new ship are manufactured in the yard. The Planning Manager and his staff ensure that each item is purchased at the right time, that delivery is on schedule and that to meet the programme of building the yard has sufficient labour at each stage in the construction. This may sound straightforward but it rarely is owing to unforeseen exigencies like late deliveries of parts and to the overriding requirement of keeping several other ships up to-date on the programme as well.

One of the world's most complex planning exercises was that required for the United States Polaris programme of the 1950s. To ensure very widely separated groups were on target, or at least meaningfully monitored, a new system of manage-

Left *The mould loft at Clydebank around 1910. This photograph shows clearly the lines and sections of a ship drawn out full size on the floor. With the advent of first, one tenth size lafting, and second computer techniques, the need for full size sketching and simulation is practically gone. (National Maritime Museum).*

Above right *Construction of the fast cargo liner* Benledi *at the Scotstoun shipyard of Charles Connell & Co (Shipbuilders) Ltd in October 1964. The P & O Tanker* Opawa *built by Barclay, Curle & Co Ltd can be seen outfitting at the North British Quay.*

Right *The steel stockyard of John Brown and Co Ltd, Clydebank, around the beginning of the 20th century. The neatly laid out area is typical of most shipyards of the period, with the plates weathering to loose all traces of millscale. With modern techniques of shotblasting, the need for prolonged weathering is not so important, and with modern craneage using either suction pad lifts or magnetic pads, most plates are stowed horizontally (National Maritime Museum).*

31.

Left *Construction of Benledi at Scotstoun in November 1964 showing the revolutionary triple hatch layout for fast cargo handing.*

Below *A 'Hugh Smith' plate bending machine at John Brown's Clydebank shipyard around 1910. Machinery of this kind could endure as long as 100 years in a shipyard and still remain efficient. However, over the years layouts have to be altered and the moving of a machine like this, with deep foundations, can be a costly business* (National Maritime Museum).

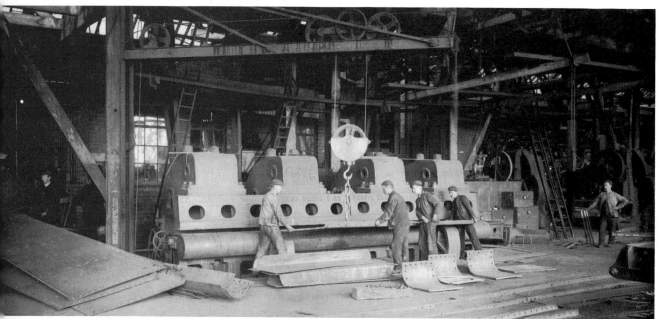

Left *Construction by the old piece-meal methods, highly inefficient and labour intensive, partly brought about by lack of suitable craneage. This photograph is of the Aquitania at Clydebank around 1913.* Right *As launching approaches, the shape of the new ship becomes apparent, and on completion of painting the forest of staging uprights and planks is steadily removed* (National Maritime Museum).

ment control was devised by a management consultancy company in the United States of America. This was known at the time as Program Evaluation & Review Technique (PERT), but is now universally known as Network Analysis. In 1963 this technique was applied to the outfitting of the Bibby Liner *Lancashire* at the Fairfield yard and the exercise was supervised by a team jointly recruited from Fairfield and the British Ship Research Association. The results were interesting in that the ship was completed well on schedule and without difficulty but, as was quickly realised, the foremen and junior managers paid special attention to this 'one-off' in the middle of a normal building programme. Network analysis did not become a permanency in shipbuilding being tried in Aberdeen, Elsinore and other places and ultimately discarded— but it did awaken management to a new way of thinking and added phrases like 'critical path' to the modern manager's vocabulary.

The first stage of construction is known as preparation. Here all plates and sections are shot-blasted clean of rust and millscale and then, after being painted with a metallic primer, are marked, cut and bent into their final shape for assembly in the ship. In modern shipyards this is almost automatic with all processes being carried out on cold steel by hydraulic machinery. The use of semi-automatic shot-blasting equipment capable of removing mill-scale ensures that steel need not be left in stockyards longer than is convenient for the yard.

The second stage of construction is known as fabrication. This concept has been attempted in various ways for the best part of 100 years, but was accepted on the Clyde in 1933 during the construction in Dumbarton of the Diesel Electric Paddle Ferry *Robert the Bruce*. This ship was probably the first all-welded ship built in Scotland and it was quickly realised that welding was cheaper and more effective if done by the operative in a 'down hand' position. Each deck was built separately, turned as necessary to accommodate the welders and then erected. The ship was a great success and from this early experiment a new technique developed which is still improving to this day.

The final steelwork stage is erection on the berth. Here dramatic changes have taken place. Instead of the laying of keel plates and keelsons, the erecting of frames and a generally piecemeal building of a ship, large parts—often up to 100 tons—can be placed on the berth and the edges carefully merged or 'faired' into the next to give the shell its required smooth appearance. Lithgows Limited at Kingston have built very large ships by commencing laying stern units at the water's edge and slowly moving their crane up

Launch of the P & O Liner Malwa *from Caird's of Greenock, 1908. The Greenock Yard built two such liners every year, as well as other work, and were the main builders for P & O for many years* (National Maritime Museum).

the yard as the steelwork nears completion. However, no Clyde yard has copied Burmeister & Wain of Copenhagen who developed 600-ton units in 1960 and built ships with them in a dry dock designed for Panamax bulk carriers. During the building of the Baltic passenger ferry *Bornholm* they must have reached the ultimate in this form of construction in 1961 when the ship was constructed using only six main hull units.

On the berth the ship must be inspected and the watertight tanks pressure tested and, prior to launch, all main structural parts carefully checked to ensure the ship is strong enough for the severe stresses induced during launching.

The steel trades

Briefly the steel trades are those directly connected with the building of the structure of the ship. The past years have seen a vast reduction in the numbers of these trades with certain skills becoming obsolete and other trade groupings merging. The oldest trade is that of shipwright. Current members of this group can claim descent from the wooden shipbuilders of previous years. Their responsibilities are in general the erecting of large parts of the ship, in aligning the units, launching and certain aspects of outfitting including the laying of wooden decks. Closely associated are loftsmen, the men who draw out the ship either full size or in reduced scale in the mould loft and who also are responsible for sighting and alignment.

Platers are the men who mark, bend and generally shape plates, who construct small fabrications and are responsible for the 'fairing' of plates which is, as a well known Clyde shipyard director described it, a euphemism for brutally forcing the edges together. Despite the joke at the platers' expense it is a technique requiring skill and knowledge.

The welders are a newer trade, only fully recognised less than 50 years ago—they have the task of bonding steel together using electric welding, by hand tongs, by superintending automatic processes such as panel flow lines, or by using semi-automatic hand feed machines.

The riveters, once princes of the river have gone, and any small jobs using this technique are carried out by squads who also burn (cut with oxygen and gas), drill and caulk (chamfer and cut with pneumatic hand tools).

Riggers and blacksmiths, both greatly reduced in

Below *Harland & Wolff Ltd, Govan, launch the Motor Vessel* Thessaly *on May 29 1957 for the Royal Mail Lines. The angle to the centre line of the river is clearly visible: this alignment allows ships a longer unobstructed run* (Furness Withy Group).

Below right *The whale catcher* Anders Arvesen *being slowly winched down the slipway of Inglis' Pointhouse Shipyard in August 1951. Some ships were launched in a conventional manner into the mouth of the River Kelvin, others by the use of their 'marine railway', a system coming back into favour in many parts of the world.*

numbers, make up this group and are all members of the Boilermakers' Society.

Among the important semi-skilled men attached to them are the stagers who erect the staging or scaffolding around a ship and whose function is to ensure that every workman has good, safe and well guarded access to any job he is called on to perform.

Launching

George Blake's epic novel *The Shipbuilders* opens with a description of a Clyde launch day. The colour and excitement is vividly portrayed of the preparations and ceremony for the naming and launching of the fictitious *Estramandura* but, sadly, the book goes on to describe the consequences and effects in the yard and its workforce as it becomes clear that there will be no possibility of further work.

The launch day is one of the most important stages in the construction calendar of a ship. It is often the one time that the Boards of Directors of the two contracting companies meet in what is to be hoped is a relaxed atmosphere, entertain their guests and quietly assess their mutual involvement. In earlier years it was the day on which a substantial stage payment was made to the builders (sometimes up to 33 per cent), and even in modern times with changed patterns of cash flow is a recognised moment in the financial contract. After many a successful launching a cheque is handed by one director to another in a discreet but nevertheless formal manner on the launch platform.

The traditions and conviviality of launch days go back centuries—in fact from earliest times men have regarded launching as important, requiring that the new ship on which they have invested time and money, and on whose performance the lives of their associates, their families and themselves may depend, will enter its element under the most propitious circumstances. Such age old customs and superstitions which are now being researched are not fully understood, nor well documented, but come from times long before the Clyde was a navigable river. In Scotland traditional arrangements are relatively simple: the ship has a brief naming ceremony, usually performed by a lady sponsor invited by the ultimate owners, a bottle of wine or other beverage is broken on the bows and the signal given to release the ship from her ways. The sponsor often receives a gift of jewellery and, as in many commercial transactions, the value of the gift may be commensurate with either the first cost of the ship

involved, or reflects the importance the shipbuilders attach to the friends of the lady concerned. At the launch of the *Queen Elizabeth 2*, Her Majesty the Queen was presented with a speedboat for the Royal Yacht *Britannia*.

It is unusual on Clydeside for the launching to be preceded by a religious service, although recently more and more well known owners request that this be done. Some overseas owners bring priests of religions other than the Christian faith to bless the new ship. The Royal Navy have a short but moving service laid down for use before the launching of one of the Queen's ships, ending with the Sailor's Hymn and all presented in a standard order of service— spoiled only by the unimaginative printing of the MOD form number 'D10' on the front page! For naval ships the wine used is invariably from the Commonwealth, and on this one occasion the shipyard has the privilege and duty of dressing the ship with naval flags—the Union Flag on the jackstaff, the Lord High Admiral's Flag on the main- mast and the White Ensign at the stern. It is customary for no other flags to be used on such days.

In merchant launches the flag etiquette is different. The ship at that stage belongs to the shipbuilder and is therefore to be launched with the Red Ensign at the stern, the white bordered Union Flag (or Pilot Jack) at the bow and the shipyard houseflag on the mainmast. It is usual to wear the future owners national ensign and his houseflag at the courtesy position on the foremast. Prior to the launch the name and port of registry of the ship have to be decided, and British ships require to have this checked out and approved by the Registrar General of Shipping and Seamen at Cardiff. The British Registry does not encourage closely similar names and, indeed, severely discourages identical names except in special circumstances.

The whole procedure marks a happy event and the small courtesies on the occasion come about as much by thoughtfulness as by a rule book. On April 16 1953 one simple courtesy was extended by Stephen's and their clients, the Greek Line, when it was discovered that their new liner required the same tide for launching as the Royal Yacht. In order to give precedence to the Queen and her yacht, it was agreed that the 17,000-ton liner be known and launched as Ship 636 and that only later be known by her name, which was to be *Olympia*. At the time of the launch it was said on the Clyde of 636 that 'the Greeks have a name for it!'

Above *An unusual launch at Fairfield in 1962. The dock gate for the Firth of Clyde Drydock, then under construction. The gate was floated to Greenock and then ballasted into her position at the dock entrance and secured.*

Right *A diagrammatic section showing the standing and sliding ways under a ship on the building berth. Usually the ways are spaced about one third of the ship's breadth apart, and some hours before the launch take the weight of the ship once the long wedges in the sliding ways are 'rammed up'. Side shores, bilge blocks and keel blocks all shown with dotted lines are removed prior to the launch. The sliding ways often stay under the ship after launching and have to be carefully pulled clear and then every one accounted for.*

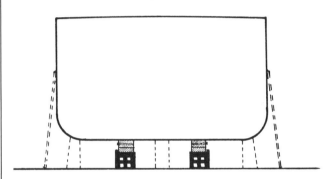

In recent times, owing to the expense of bringing foreign guests to launch days, many companies hold launching ceremonies on the same day as naming ceremonies for sister ships launched without formality on other occasions.

The practice of launching is a well tried and proven technique with clearly understood principles. Before construction the position and height on the berth have to be ascertained and the safety of the launch assured by preliminary calculation. When building has commenced the standing ways or fixed part of the slides are laid under the ship and the top surface coated with a proprietary material which is heated, poured over and allowed to cool and form a solidified smooth surface. On top of this a soft lubricant is applied and then the sliding ways run in to form the base of the cradle on which the ship rests.

On top of the sliding ways timber 'make up' is fitted coming to the underside of the ship and on this the weight of the ship will rest once it has been rammed up before the launch. Just before the launch all other shores, blocks and so on are removed and ultimately the ship will stand free, held from sliding only by two daggers or triggers on each side. The design of daggers varies from yard to yard, but two main forms are used—the first a system of complex bell crank levers, eccentrics and weights which when freed lowers a lip on the standing ways and frees the sliding ways above. The second is a very simple set of two timber baulks so positioned that while one is held immovable by a wire anchored to the ground, the second is in compression between the standing and sliding way. The second system, while simple to a point of absurdity, has the added advantage of being foolproof.

On release the ship slides backwards into the water travelling in some cases faster than she ever will again. Stopping is effected in different ways; by drags, that is bundles of chain which progressively exert a greater frictional force as the ship moves away, by

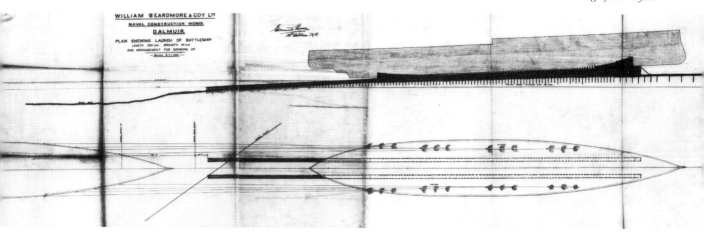

Above *The launch diagram for the battleship HMS* Benbow *built by William Beardmore & Co Ltd, Dalmuir. The ship was launched successfully on November 12 1913* (National Maritime Museum).

Below *TSS* Caledonia *is taken in charge by Clyde Shipping Company tugs after a smooth launching from Stephen's Linthouse yard in 1925. Behind the tug* Flying Condor *one has a glimpse of Barclay Curle's shipyard. Prior to the Second World War, few yards had much of the ground made up or cemented, and this added to the credit of the shipbuilders in producing such lovely craft sometimes in quite primitive conditions.* (National Maritime Museum).

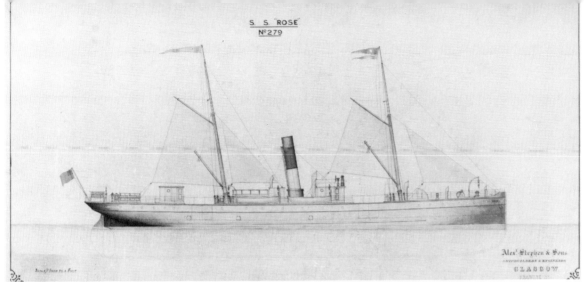

S. S. "ROSE"
Nº 279

Alex Stephen & Sons
GLASGOW

After being raised and repaired, the Daphne *was renamed* Rose, *and shortly thereafter was sold* (National Maritime Museum).

water brakes, and in Dumbarton by the simple expedient of dropping suitable anchors. Once stopped the drag cables can be dropped from the side as tugs take charge of the new ship and guide it to the outfit berth.

Over the years the Clyde has built up an enviable record for safe, incident-free launches, but one accident was tragic and is never to be forgotten. On Tuesday July 3 1883 the small steam coaster *Daphne* was launched from the Linthouse Shipyard of Alexander Stephen & Sons of Glasgow. She was a single screw ship of iron construction, with a length of 177 ft (53.9 m) and a beam of 25.3 ft (7.7 m) giving her, even for those days, an unusually high L/B ratio of 7.0. The *Daphne* had been ordered by the Glasgow, Dublin and Londonderry Steam Packet Company for their Irish and Scottish coastal services. This company was later incorporated in the Burns and Laird Lines, now part of the P&O Group. The specification for the new ship had been drawn up by the Superintendent Marine Engineer, and he had also given rigid instructions regarding the type of equipment to be used, and the overall dimensions to be adhered to. As he was not a naval architect, all this was decided after an examination of previous ships in the fleet, but it was expected that the builders could carry out detailed design and fully investigate stability problems despite being restricted in their ability to alter form or the height of the centre of gravity. Up until the 1880s many shipyards accepted such contracts after only cursory investi-

gations into the capability of a hull to meet its requirements and by and large accepted the specialist knowledge of their clients.

The launch preparation and planning was carried out with all the care and attention which was the hallmark of Stephen's and as the shipyard did not own a convenient fitting out quay, the two-cylinder compound engine of unusually high configuration was installed. The boilers were not put aboard, but an opening was left in the deck for shipping once the vessel had been moved to a quay near the Broomielaw. Fitting out was so well advanced that it was anticipated the ship would be at work for her owners at the beginning of August, and to ensure speedy completion nearly 200 workmen remained on board during the launch in order that they could continue work as the ship was towed upstream. Just before noon, two tugs were on stand-by off the shipyard, several work boats were on the Clyde, the regulation launch flag displayed and a small crowd assembled on the bank. After a brief ceremony the ship was released, slipped quietly into the Clyde and was brought to a standstill by the action of the drag chains.

Within seconds of coming to rest, the ship suddenly heeled several degrees to port, and after a momentary pause and slight recovery, heeled more and more and to the horror of everyone watching, rolled over completely. Despite frantic efforts by all concerned only about 70 people were saved and ultimately it became clear that a total of 124 men and boys had lost their lives in the accident. The speed of the capsize was aided by 30 tons of loose gear on the decks, by 200 men sliding to the port side, and by water entering the boiler access hole as the main deck edge came under the water level.

Shortly after launching on July 3 1883, the steam coaster Daphne *rolled over and sank with the loss of 124 lives, making it one of the worst tragedies in the shipbuilding industry. The effects of this accident were profound and far reaching, and did much to ensure that on the Clyde ship design and shipbuilding practice were of the highest professional standard* (Wotherspoon Collection, Mitchell Library, Glasgow).

The ship was righted in a few days and taken to Salterscroft Graving Dock—now known as Govan No 1 Dock, and after cleaning and examination was refloated for a carefully monitored inclining experiment to ascertain the full stability particulars of the ship. A commission from the Home Secretary and issued by the Lord Advocate for Scotland, appointed Sir Edward Reed, one of the foremost naval architects of his time, to make an enquiry and report back on the cause of the disaster. He inspected the ship, examined the launchways and drag chains, supervised the inclining experiment, took evidence from the builders and also from other leading Clyde shipbuilders and made his report a bare six weeks later.

The report was incisive: Alexander Stephen and Sons were commended, as were other shipyards, for the assistance they gave the enquiry, and for producing information and details of previous stability problems for open discussion. No fault was found with the launch arrangements at Linthouse and despite many novel and ingenious reasons for the capsize being put forward at the hearings, the cause was found to be small initial stability, coupled with an excess of persons and loose equipment aboard.

In the 1880s British shipyards were technically advanced but despite this, a commonly held view was that high sided vessels could be launched with safety and that from the stability point of view, there was no need for exhaustive weight assessment prior to launch. Nowadays this may seem deficient thinking, or at best naive, but the sad fact is that it took this accident to the *Daphne* to bring the matter to the forefront of naval architects' considerations and for the enquiry to highlight a near accident on the Clyde of similar nature some months before.

John H. Biles (later Professor Sir John) the naval architect of Messrs J. & G. Thomson of Clydebank reported that the steamer *Hammonia* had on launching settled in the water with a 40-degree list. The ship was examined, her stability particulars calculated in full and then an inclining experiment carried out, from all of which it was discovered that the *Hammonia* in launch condition had no positive righting lever when heeled beyond 53 degrees. This matter had caused no small amount of consternation at the Clydebank shipyard and the problem was being considered actively by other Clyde shipbuilders.

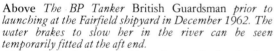

Above *The BP Tanker* British Guardsman *prior to launching at the Fairfield shipyard in December 1962. The water brakes to slow her in the river can be seen temporarily fitted at the aft end.*
Above right *A close-up of launch water brakes fitted on the tanker* British Guardsman.

Stephen's employed Francis Elgar to represent their interests and he rightly said that previous to the accident no curve of stability had been constructed for a merchant ship at launch.

The results of this disaster were many: ships had their positions of centre of gravity estimated before launch, and provisional stability particulars worked out, all weights aboard were assessed, evenly distributed and secured, and the numbers of men aboard limited to those necessary for the mooring and post launch examination of the ship. The stringent Clyde regulations were tightened and other ports introduced similar arrangements.

The *Daphne* was renamed *Rose* and within a few months of delivery was sold. Her high, powerful engine was removed and a smaller and lower one of half the power purchased from marine engineers in Dundee.

Since the *Daphne* well over 20,000 ships have slipped into the Clyde and, while minor incidents occur from time to time, injuries to persons and damage to ships have been negligible. Indeed the planning of launches has become such a fine art that the final position of large ships on the river can be foretold with great accuracy, as in the celebrated case of the Cunarder *Queen Mary*.

The greatest effect of the disaster was on the attitude of shipbuilders. The concept of ultimate responsibility for their product was brought home and from 1883 even quite routine and mundane shipbuilding practices were questioned and subjected to the scrutiny of scientific analysis. The *Daphne* incident can be taken as the coming of age of ship-building in the United Kingdom and the time when builders realised that their judgement was ultimate in the question of design.

The outfitting process

This name is given to the process which changes a bare steel hull to a ship fully equipped and outfitted for sea. It can be complex work made difficult on smaller ships by large groups of men having to work simultaneously in every compartment. The task of the outfit manager or the ship manager in charge of the vessel is an onerous one as he has to ensure that each compartment and system is finished in the correct sequence and that the long programme of tests leading up to trials is kept on schedule.

The main trades involved in outfitting include the

Above left *John Brown's blacksmith shop in the early part of the 20th century. The basic tools have not changed much since then, although with the introduction of high tensile steel into lifting gear and the simplification in shipbuilding practice, the need for smithwork has greatly reduced* (National Maritime Museum).

Left *For some Clyde shipyards, outfitting after launching was a particularly heavy burden as they did not have outfit quays of their own. The SS Benlomond, shown here in 1957, is a case in point, lying in Queen's Dock, Glasgow mid-way between the shipyard of Charles Connell and the engine works of David Rowan.*

Above *The good name of a shipyard is associated with the standard of finish in the accommodation. No effort is spared, especially in passenger liners, to ensure the highest standards are maintained, as in this Grill Room in John Brown's Aquitania* (National Maritime Museum).

painters whose main role is the finishing of accommodation and other parts to a high standard. They are associated with the redleaders, the semi-skilled section of their department—men who have not served apprenticeship and whose responsibility is the painting of steelwork, the coating of double bottom tanks and so on. Their name comes from the days when red lead was a commonly used preservative.

Pipeworkers form a large group, nowadays composed of plumbers and coppersmiths. Working from the plans they measure on the ship, prepare pipes in the pipeshop and finally fit up the massive and complicated systems now required on the modern ship. The pipeshop, particularly of modern layout, is eminently suitable for dealing with non-marine contracts and, indeed, large shops like that at Govan have often worked in petro-chemicals and occasionally at supplying pipework for other shipyards.

Left *This view from the top bridge of MV* Elysia *gives a clear indication of the large amount of rigging and deck outfitting work required on a conventional cargo vessel. The* Elysia *was built in 1945 by Lithgows Limited, Port Glasgow, and was powered by a Barclay, Curle-Doxford diesel engine. She served the Anchor Line for many years on both their New York and Bombay routes, with Yorkhill Quay, Glasgow (pictured here) as her base.*

Below *A 72-tonne unit about to be erected on a new ship at Govan. The detailed outfit can be seen clearly, and will assist in ensuring that the ship is built as quickly as possible on berth. This technique has been developed specially in Govan (Govan Shipbuilders).*

The joiner's work is by far the most impressive part of the whole process. Their skill changes steel lined spaces into elegant lounges and dining rooms, and using carefully selected timbers can make even small cabins warm and restful. Their work is very different from the shore joiner or shopfitter in two respects: first the standards in general are much higher, comparable with those required of cabinet makers ashore and, second, the ship outfitter has to be able to work allowing for deck sheer and camber. In recent years it has been customary for loose items of furniture like tables and chairs to be brought in from companies like Rowan & Boden and in very large ships like Cunarders and union Castle Liners to sub-contract parts of the public rooms to specialist firms like Archibald Stewart of Glasgow.

Attached to the joiner's shop are french polishers with spray booths and advanced equipment to aid their professional skill. To a lesser extent every year one finds modelmakers capable of making the half block models once necessary in the drawing offices and the beautiful finished models seen in board rooms, head office windows and ultimately in museums. Lastly the upholsterers, once an integral part of the shop, have all but vanished from British shipbuilding.

The last main group are electricians, or 'sparkies', whose responsibility has grown vastly in recent years. They were introduced to most yards in the 1900s while some companies, including Charles

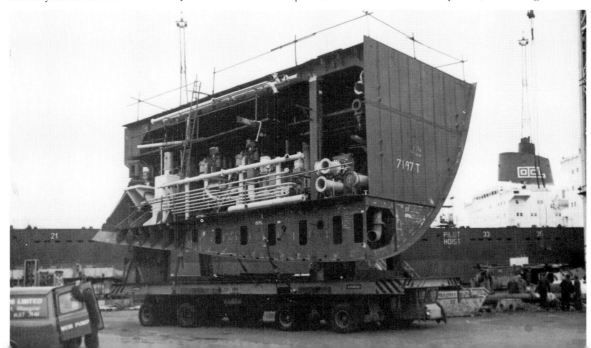

Above *The massive rudder, propellers and sternframe of the QSS Aquitania pictured at her first drydocking, in 1914. The work at first drydocking includes cleaning and repairing the paint on the undersides prior to applying a fresh coat of anti-fouling paint. The propellers are burnished to enable the ship to produce the best results possible on the measured mile* (National Maritime Museum).

Below *Attended by the tug* Paladin, *the Anchor Liner* Cilicia, *resplendent in new paint, leaves Govan for her trials in the Firth of Clyde.*

Connell, did not have ship electricians and subcontracted their work out to other firms.

All modern ships have ventilation systems with hot and cold air trunking. This is drawn up in the office, checked at ship and then manufactured either in the sheet metal shop (if the shipyard possesses one) or at a contractor's works.

It is a known fact that the cost of a job in the shipyards varies with where it is carried out. For example, a simple job carried out in the shops has a basic charge but the same job on the building berth,

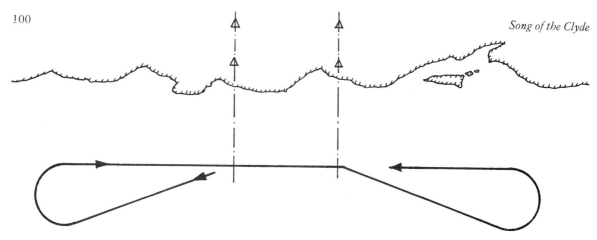

The route taken by a ship on the measured mile, showing the long straight run required to bring the vessel to a steady state of motion prior to entering the accurately measured nautical mile.

owing to weather influences, walking time, more restricted craneage and other factors can cost three times as much. The same job carried out on an afloat ship can cost up to three times as much again for similar reasons. This drop off in productivity has long caused concern to management and is severe enough for sundry attempts to have been made to alter the styles and techniques in building. In recent years Govan Shipbuilders have developed a simple technique which has reduced this costing; the outfitting of prefabricated units while still in the building bays and enabling an almost complete unit to be lifted on to the berth.

Sea trials

Over the years, the testing of a ship in working conditions has become a sophisticated process aimed at extracting the maximum technical information from the new vessel in the shortest time. As few people have had the opportunity of attending sea trials, a brief description of the work and objectives may prove helpful to an understanding of the need to test ships.

As ship outfitting proceeds in the builders' yard, the planning of sea trials commences, and with the ship carrying a larger than normal complement, agreements are made with the Department of Transport for alternative lifesaving arrangements to be effective during the trial trip. As completion nears, more and more equipment is placed aboard and much of it has to be tested on site. The first major test is usually the alternators, and from then the ship may be lit and serviced by its own electricity. Near the end of the testing schedule, the main engines are first turned over, and if all appears well, they are then fired and run in an exercise called the dock trial, during which the moorings are well secured and special care taken

to ensure that the propeller wash will not affect quays, boats or even ships in the vicinity. For the engineer manager this is the closest he will witness his machinery in operation until the passage down river and the trials themselves. The ship or hull manager is equally busy with a punishing load of smaller tests and is also burdened by the setting up of the paperwork and administration for the trials.

Attended by tugs, the new ship leaves the quay, and makes her way to the place appointed for the first test, which is usually the dropping of anchors and then their recovery, an operation involving the lifting of two anchors often weighing several tons and up to 200 m of heavy studded steel link chain cable on each side. From then on tests follow to a preset pattern, with compass adjusting, the testing of steering gear by a set of tough manoeuvres and only then to the miles, to the crash stops, the astern running and the checking for vibration.

It is usual for ships on trial to remain the property of the shipbuilder, and to sail with the builder's house flag on the main mast and the Red Ensign at the stern. Most Clyde shipyards appoint a River Pilot to take command on behalf of the builders, and he, working closely with the manager, goes through the agreed programme which can be as short as one day, but often as long as one week. The managers have also to keep a strict record of all personnel aboard, and to ensure that safety requirements are met.

When a ship runs over the measured mile, it is arranged that it runs straight and steady for three or four miles before going through the transits. This ensures that there are no avoidable changes in steering or acceleration forces on the propeller detracting from an accurate speed on the mile. On completion of the first mile the course is changed and the ship prepared for a run back at the same power and engine revolutions, allowing tidal and wind effects to be neutralised.

The speed of the ship can be computed in various ways and the three calculations below show how different results varying by about ½ of 1 per cent can come about on two double runs at constant power, through different types of calculation.

1 Using averages

Run No	Direction	Time min	secs	Speed over ground knots	1st average	2nd average
1	South	4	57	12.12	11.565	
2	North	5	27	11.01		11.63
3	South	5	00	12.00	11.695	
4	North	5	16	11.39		

2 Using mean of means

Run No	Direction	Time min	secs	Speed over ground knots	1st mean	2nd mean	mean of means
1	South	4	57	12.12	11.565	11.535	
2	North	5	27	11.01	11.505	11.600	11.568
3	South	5	00	12.00	11.695		
4	North	5	16	11.39			

3 Using 1331 multiplier method

Run No	Direction	Time min	secs	Speed over ground knots	Multiplier	
1	South	4	57	12.12	1	12.12
2	North	5	27	11.01	3	33.03
3	South	5	00	12.00	3	36.00
4	North	5	16	11.39	1	11.39
						92.54

$$\text{Speed} = \frac{92.54}{8} = 11.568$$

The second and third methods are more correct mathematically and either of these or similar type calculations are used by naval architects.

A sea mile or nautical mile is the length of a minute of arc measured along a meridian. It was defined originally as 6,080 imperial feet, but has been redefined and accepted internationally as 1,852 m. The speed of a ship is given in nautical miles per hour, terminology shortened to the familiar word 'knots'.

Sea trials have been on the go for a long time. The journals of learned societies in Britain alone, have over one hundred papers on the subject written in the past 100 years. Among the first properly documented records were the Reports on Sailing Qualities on HM Ships, followed in 1790 by the fascinating comparative tests of a conventional hull form and that of a shallow drafted centre board hull by Captain John Schank at Deptford on the Thames. The Royal Navy understood at an early stage the importance of full scale testing.

The coming of steam highlighted a need for systematic trials, first to compare one engine against another, and to evaluate the benefits of change to hull form. Again the Admiralty started to document steam trials around 1840, but it is certain that before then Clyde shipbuilders were developing crude means of assessing the speed and power of the new steamships. The Woods of Port Glasgow built something like 80 steam vessels between 1812 and 1859 and they were conscious of change and improvement, and even more aware of the need to supply product information as an early form of salesmanship.

The most widely used test on the Clyde was known as 'running the lights' between Cloch and Cumbrae, a process, if done in two directions, involved steaming 30 sea miles. The great distance created the problem that by the time the ship had travelled one leg and turned for the return trip, the tidal conditions would have changed and the weather and wind altered. It was important to obtain a shorter testing distance, and this was done in 1866 by Robert Napier & Sons of Govan. The announcement of their achievement was made in a letter to other Clyde shipbuilders and is reproduced here in full:

Lancefield House, Glasgow,
30th August 1866.

Dear Sirs,

We beg respectfully to state that having long felt the want on the Clyde of a correct measured nautical mile for testing the speed of large steamers (similar to what the Admiralty have near Portsmouth and elsewhere), we had the shores of the Clyde examined for a suitable place for laying off a knot; and finding that from Skelmorlie Pier southwards would answer the purpose, we applied to the Right Hon the Earl of Eglinton for liberty to erect beacons on his property. This the Earl at once most kindly gave full permission to do. We then employed Messrs Kyle & Frew along with Messrs Smith & Wharrie, Land Surveyors,

Glasgow, to measure and lay off a knot, which they did; and thereafter we made application to the Lords Commissioners of the Admiralty, begging as a favour that they would send one of their officers to remeasure and test the correctness of this knot, and we would willingly bear the expense. Their Lordships were pleased to accede to our request, and afterwards intimated to us that the knot had been duly tested by their officers and found correct. At the same time they declined to make any charge.

Their Lordships have caused a printed notice to mariners to be issued from the Hydrographic Department of the Admiralty, of which the annexed is a copy. We are, dear Sirs, your obedient servants,

R. Napier & Sons

This mile is in steady use to this day, and until well into the 20th century was regarded as the most important measured mile in the UK.

As scientific knowledge increased it became understood that shallow water can have a serious slowing effect on a ship steaming through it. For this reason several measured miles around the coasts of Europe fell into disfavour as the size of ships increased. Even Skelmorlie at 33 fathoms, that is around 60 m in depth and then the deepest in use in the world, had limitations and ultimately the two great consecutive Arran miles were marked off on the East Coast of the island in moderately sheltered water and with depths of around 110 m available. The greatest ships in the world, built on the Clyde and elsewhere come to these miles which have seen the *Queen Mary*, the *Queen Elizabeth*, HMS *Vanguard* and many others steaming past the majestic peaks of Arran.

One of nine identical ferries for the Bosphorus, the Kuzguncuk *built by Fairfield in 1961 proceeds on trials. These Turkish ships were driven by twin 4-cylinder Christiansen & Meyer compound steam engines built at Fairfield. This system was chosen as it was felt to be more flexible and responsive for ships that had considerable amounts of close manoeuvring to contend with. Duplicate controls were fitted on each bridge wing, and the draft marks are given in metric units.*

Chapter 11

The steam turbine

The coming of turbines

Mass transportation had become a sophisticated and competitive concern in the late 19th century, and throughout the British Isles almost uncontrolled railway development had spread its sinews of steel, culminating in intense inter-company rivalry. Nowhere was the proliferation of routes and lines greater than on the Clyde Coast, where frenzied competition ensued and railways sought by every means to attract business and thereby aid in their serious problem of financial overhead recovery. The Caledonian Railway had been strained by the building of the Gourock tunnels, and part of their plan for attracting custom and widening their sphere of influence was to operate a steamer fleet from their rail terminals. To overcome irksome legal obligations imposed on railway companies they instituted an independent but totally subservient shipping company known as the Caledonian Steam Packet Co.

On the Isle of Arran service the Caledonian steamers were in earnest competition with the steamers operated directly by the Glasgow and South Western Railway. Indeed arrangements were ultimately agreed to end much of the unnecessary and expensive racing across the Firth on this route. However, with severely curtailed plying limits imposed on them by their charter, the G & SW fleet felt it necessary to come to a working arrangement with independent steamer operators especially to help them share in the lucrative long distance sailings such as the Campbeltown route. To cream off this traffic, one would require efficient rail services from Glasgow to the coast, and thereafter a really fast and comfortable steamer for the outer Firth. As paddle steamer design had reached a plateau in development and design, and such vessels were expensive to operate over, say, 17 knots it was time

to look to a novel design. The *King Edward* was to be the answer, and a new company came into being to co-operate with the G & SW Railway and bring this to fruition.

Apart from the railway company's desire to widen its sphere of influence, several other parties were interested in the new development. Denny of Dumbarton had been enthusiastic about turbine development in ships. The Parsons Marine Turbine Co Ltd was anxious to enter the field of merchant shipping, and the go-ahead Clyde steamer owner, Captain John Williamson, wished to further improve his fleet, obviously with as little commercial risk as possible.

As the shipbuilding industry was a positive and volatile affair, especially on Clydeside at the turn of the century, it was not long before representatives of Denny and Parsons met Captain Williamson and ultimately concluded an agreement setting up the Turbine Steamer Syndicate of 1901. The arrangements were interesting: William Denny & Brothers, the Parsons Marine Steam Turbine Co Ltd and Captain John Williamson jointly undertook to meet the cost of building a revolutionary new steamer and of finding initial legal and other expenses. The National Bank of Scotland (now incorporated in the Royal Bank) provided Captain Williamson with a loan, that in turn was guaranteed by the G & SW Railway subject to certain conditions on the use of the new ship. The overall sum involved was £33,000.

In February 1901, Charles Parsons gave a paper on Marine Steam Turbines to the Institution of Engineers & Shipbuilders in Scotland. In the recorded discussions, Mr Archibald Denny acknowledged that both Parsons and Denny had desired to work together for some time, and until the Turbine Steamer Syndicate had been created, they had almost

despaired of obtaining a contract for a merchant ship. Denny mentioned that 'they approached the railway companies in the first instance, but they affected a terrible amount of modesty, and each company was anxious that somebody else should make the first experiment'. It is now clear that to Captain John Williamson belongs the honour of being the first man to venture into commercial turbine exploitation.

Technically speaking the *King Edward* was the second merchant vessel to have a turbine fitted as the Denny-built paddle steamer *Duchess of Hamilton* built in 1890 had a turbine to drive a dynamo for her highly unusual electric supply.

The *King Edward* was similar to the *Duchess of Hamilton* in dimensions, both vessels being 250 ft long and 30 ft broad, but there the resemblance ceased. The new turbine ship had clinically trim lines, flush main deck, with the exception of a mooring deck aft, a bridge and separate boat deck and white elliptical funnels, black topped. This steamer set standards of appearance which were to influence Clyde and West Highland steamer design for three decades; the vast bulk of Clyde turbine steamers were to come from the Leven shipyard and they had the marque first stamped on the fleet by *King Edward*.

Denny and Company, the engineering associate William Denny and Brothers supplied the boiler working at 150 lb square inch (approximately 10 bar) and the Parsons Marine Steam Turbine Co Ltd three turbines in a simple arrangement with the high pressure turbine driving the centre line shaft, and exhausting to two low pressure cylinders driving the wing shafts. Astern turbines were incorporated in the wing turbine casings. The main shaft revolved at around 500 rpm and the wing shafts at about 900. As no gearing was involved, the propellers turned at these extraordinarily high speeds. From the start it

TrSS King Edward, *built by William Denny & Brothers Limited in 1901, was the world's first turbine-powered merchant ship. Her layout became a model for further excursion steamers, and the machinery arrangement, despite lack of reduction gearing, became standard in merchant ships for many years. The* King Edward *was withdrawn after 51 years of service, and a turbine was preserved by Glasgow Museums. The photograph shows her turning at the entrance to Princes Dock in August 1950, prior to steaming astern to her berth at Bridge Wharf.*

was appreciated the propeller surface area and their high peripheral tip speed would cause cavitation problems and in the original design the wing propellers were augmented by additional propellers situated on extended wing shafts, making her in effect a five-screw ship.

Between June 1901 and April 1905 when the side propellers were reduced to two, altogether 34 double runs on the Skelmorlie Mile were carried out along with numerous endurance and other trials, during which several propeller configurations were tried. This great effort in design work, cost in docking and modification and loss of revenue during the days of trials gives some idea of the dedication and determination of Denny and Parsons to get it right.

Williamson bought the ship outright for his new company, Turbine Steamers Ltd and ordered an enlarged sister, to be named *Queen Alexandra*, from Dumbarton within the year. The *King Edward* sailed on the Clyde all her life except for troopship duties in the First World War and as a hospital ship running to Archangel in Russia. In 1952 she was towed off for breaking, and now all that remains is one turbine held by Glasgow Museums.

The effect on Denny's was dramatic, within the

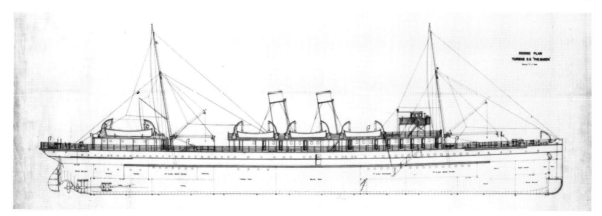

Above *The South East & Chatham Railway inspected the* King Edward *and in 1902 confirmed an order with Denny of Dumbarton for the first cross-Channel passenger ship powered by steam turbines. The new ship, named* The Queen, *was delivered in the summer of 1903, and was an enlarged version of* King Edward *including twin propellers on the outboard shafts as is shown on this rigging plan. After a period of trials, she was reduced to normal triple-screw configuration. Capable of 21 knots,* The Queen *served on the Dover Calais service, cutting the times to under one hour. She was sunk by German gunfire in October 1916 (National Maritime Museum).*

Below *In September 1926, Turbine Steamers Ltd, of Glasgow took delivery of the twin-screw turbine steamer* King George V *for their Clyde passenger services. Following their renowned* King Edward *—the world's first commercial turbine ship—the new addition to the fleet also made history by being driven by turbine using superheated steam at 550 psi and 750°F (60 bar and 400°C). For the first nine seasons she was on the Campbeltown or Inverary service, but in 1935 she was changed to normal turbines and transferred to the West Highland Fleet of David MacBrayne Ltd. During the war she operated as a Clyde tender after serving with distinction at Dunkirk. For the vast bulk of her life with MacBrayne's, she served on the Oban-Tobermory-Staffa-Iona route, and when withdrawn in 1975 was one of Scotland's best loved ships. The illustration shows her as rigged in her last few years.*

period 1901-6 they built no less than 17 turbine ships, and pulled off a series of remarkable turbine firsts including the first cross channel vessel, first for the Irish Sea, first ocean going merchantman, first on the Pacific and first on the UK India route.

Their third vessel was *The Queen* for the South Eastern & Chatham Railway's English Channel service. There were two particular problems involved in this design, first the need for a restricted draft and secondly ample stopping power. The shallow harbours of the English and French coasts were suitable for paddle ships, but the deeper immersion of screw ships, particularly powerful ones partly led to the triple screw solution with the Parsons classical turbine layout. The small terminal areas required that ships travelling fast on tight and competitive schedules could be stopped quickly in harbour. Considerable thought was given to this and around 1902 astern and stopping trials became a critical feature of ship testing, and commenced the rigorous study of this field, which 80 years later is of even greater importance and still not fully mastered.

The theory of the turbine is very old, but the

practical harnessing of the idea was carried out in the 1890s by two remarkable men, Charles A. Parsons (1854-1931) and Gustaf de Laval (1845-1913). It is true to say that neither man had ship propulsion in mind when they first approached the rigorous study of turbines.

Gustaf de Laval, a Swede, studied at Stockholm and Uppsala and by his invention of the single wheel impulse turbine, brought very high rpm to the notice of the engineering profession. His first turbine patent was in 1883 and for double helical reduction gears in 1889. In 1892 he constructed a reversing turbine of 16,000 rpm (to this day a quite remarkable speed) developing 15 hp, and with his own reduction gearing drove a small launch on lovely Lake Mäleren, the propeller turning at 330 rpm. It could be claimed that this was the world's first turbine-driven craft, and also the first with gearing. Dr de Laval did not capitalise on the marine side and his life ended, sadly, with serious business problems.

Charles Parsons came from the family of the Earl of Rosse, and was brought up in a profoundly academic atmosphere at the home Birr Castle, Ireland. Parsons was educated privately, but in a liberal manner which enabled him to develop his quite phenomenal powers as a mathematician, scientist and practical engineer. Two years at Trinity College, Dublin, was followed by a spell at St John's College, Cambridge, before serving a premium apprenticeship at Armstrong's of Elswick on the Tyne. In 1884 he joined Clarke, Chapman and Company at Gateshead as a junior partner in charge of the electrical department. His first problem was to design a steam-driven ship's lighting set where the optimum dynamo speed was much in excess of the top speed attainable by a steam reciprocating engine. From this came Parsons' 1884 patent and ultimately the birth of the steam turbine.

In 1888 Parsons severed his connections with Clarke Chapman and in 1889 set up a new company, the Parsons Marine Steam Turbine Co Ltd. His work on patented turbine designs was in the name of Clarke Chapman, and therefore he was forced to design a new turbine system to avoid infringing existing patents. Initially this was overcome by designing radial flow turbines, although of less developed form. Despite his desire to produce electrical generators, Parsons decided to work in parallel with another development, the marine turbine, and in 1894 produced the epoch-making *Turbinia*. Ultimately changed to axial flow units, this

fine yacht in 1897 attained over 34 knots and a new chapter in marine engineering commenced. Also in that year he followed de Laval's example and engined a small steam pinnace with a turbine and reduction gearing. Through this Charles Parsons again realised that one could have turbines working at that optimum speed and gearing to produce the much slower revolutions required by a ship's propeller.

Two further developments far from Clydeside must be recorded. The torpedo boat destroyer *Viper* was ordered for the Royal Navy from Hawthorn Leslie, Newcastle in 1896, 210 ft long, 21 ft beam and displacing 370 tons. She was powered by four turbines on four shafts. On trials at a displacement of 380 tons she made over 36 knots on trial at propeller revolutions of 1,180. On acceptance HMS *Viper* was the fastest destroyer in the Royal Navy— 15 months later while on exercise off Alderney on August 3 1901 she struck a reef and broke between boiler rooms three and four.

Another vessel *Cobra* was being built to ship-builder's account at Armstrong Whitworth's works at Elswick, Newcastle. This company were trying to create a market demand and hoped for a ship of 31 knots, then one knot faster than Admiralty require-ments for a destroyer of her size. On trial her 'mean of means' was 34.89 knots and subsequently, subject to minor modifications, she was accepted into the Royal Navy. In September 1901 on delivery voyage from the Tyne to Portsmouth, the weather deteriorated, but despite speed reduction she broke in two and sank immediately with heavy loss of life. The court martial findings recorded structural weak-ness and, indeed, a recent re-assessment of the incident using modern scientific analysis would bear this out. The theory that she had a hull fracture after striking her forefoot on the sea bed whilst pitching heavily, is unsubstantiated.

The Admiralty made the destroyer *Wolf* available for experiments on hull strength. The work was supervised by Professor J. Harvard Biles of Glasgow University and the work done by a team of Glasgow undergraduates. Biles remarked later, 'It will be seen that the vessel successfully stood stresses in dock much higher than those found at sea. It may be inferred that the bending moments which come upon a ship at sea are less than those assumed in the standard condition.'

Despite the loss of two new ships, the Admiralty quickly regained confidence in turbine ships and by August 1914, 53 per cent of all horsepower

The TSS Canterbury *was a single order received by Denny's for a one class ship for the 'Golden Arrow' service on the English Channel. Capable of 22 knots, and powered by Parsons turbines with single reduction gearing, the* Canterbury *quickly established herself on the route, and served 37 years before going to the breakers. In later years she reverted to two classes. Completed in 1928, she set new standards for the English Channel.*

developed in Admiralty ships came from turbines. By September 1939 this had risen to 98 per cent.

Even the most ardent Clydesider would acknowledge the role of the Tyne at this stage in turbine development but both rivers co-operated remarkably and welcomed ideas from all over. The turbine's pre-eminence was quickly established and the accolade of distinction conferred when the Royal Yacht *Alexandra* was ordered from A. & J. Inglis of Glasgow. This was the first Royal Yacht ever built by a commercial company, and with the turbines was a major breakthrough in 1905 for Inglis. Their success can be gauged by the fact Parsons allowed Inglis the first license to manufacture their turbines in Scotland.

First on the Atlantic

Until recently the beautiful 'White Empresses' of the Canadian Pacific Steamship Company were a well known sight in the waters of the Mersey, the Clyde and the St Lawrence and, indeed, until the outbreak of the Second World War their gleaming white hulls, buff funnels and red and white chequered flag were known worldwide. Few persons admiring their elegance could realise that in their very survival lay a battle between two companies which to a great extent had opened the worldwide shipping trades to the steam turbine. The chill wind of necessity had forced their larger rival, the Allan Line of Glasgow and Montreal to invest in new fast, expensive turbine ships. This decision ultimately led to the Canadian Pacific gaining control of the North Atlantic passenger trade to Canada.

Liverpool has been and remains the principal port in the long standing Canadian trade. Early shipowners purchased vessels in the Dominion, built of native timber, fitted the holds with the same produce and sailed their new ships to North West English and other ports. This trade in the early and middle parts of the 19th century led in no small way to Liverpool's prestigious growth and laid the foundations of Canada's export business—a business vital to the development of the country where cash flow was of prime importance in the conquering of a vast land where distances and at times hostile climatic conditions stretched the exchequer to the limit. To this day shipbuilding is found in developing countries and is often associated with early industrial might. Canada may be regarded as the first of many such countries.

Many shipping companies seized opportunities to trade with Canada. Cunard's long lasting connection began with the arrival of PS *Britannia* on July 17 1840 at Halifax, and many others were to follow and to trade for varying lengths of time. The Anchor Line were to commence Canadian operations in 1859, Donaldson in 1870 and others including the Furness Lines and the State Line of Glasgow. However the doyen of the trade was the Allan Line which started in the Scotland/Quebec trade with the Clyde built brigantine *Jean* in 1818, and who were to purchase the Montreal built brig *Favourite* straight from the builders in 1824.

The founder of the company was Captain Alexander Allan, a cousin of Robert Burns the poet and father of nine children, five of whom in 1854 were to found the Montreal Ocean Steamship

Company, known in the UK as the Allan Line. The five sons were to make their homes at the terminal points, two in Montreal at Ravenscrag (now part of McGill University), two in Glasgow and in Mull, and one at Liverpool, and yet by virtue of their fleet were able to maintain close family ties and affection.

Allan Liners, with black hulls, red funnels topped with a white band and black above became a familiar sight in Liverpool and Glasgow. From 1890 their houseflag was flown back to front, at the request of the French Government as it had been identical with the French tricolour, and with blue to the fly and red to the mast it was less easily confused!

The obtaining of the UK mail contracts and the development of trade brought fortune to the Allan's and by the end of the 19th century they were the principal passenger carriers to Canada with one and a half times the capacity of their nearest rivals. This clear lead was cemented in 1891 with the purchase for £72,000 of the six ships and the goodwill of the State Line. In 1897 to mark the departure from their fleet of the last sailing vessel, a further trading name was registered, the 'Allan Line Steamship Co Ltd' with one of the Montreal family as chairman.

Another company to appear on this exciting scene was the Canadian Pacific Railway, which entered shipping in a serious way in 1887, and two years later was to bid for and be successful in obtaining the first empire mail route across the Pacific. This trade west from Vancouver gave intense satisfaction to the Canadian and British governments as it completed the round world 'all red' mail route. It also introduced the 'White Empresses' and was to mark a turning point in the affairs of both CPR and the Allan Line. In 1903, CPR took over the Atlantic service of Elder, Dempster & Co Ltd, their 14 ships with the prefix *Beaver* to the name and also firmly entrenched themselves in Liverpool.

The purchase of the Beaver Line from Elder, Dempster's and the setting up of the Pacific mail service on the prestige Hong Kong and Yokohama route satisfied CPR and indeed stretched them financially, as they were still expanding their railroad routes on the continent.

It was at this stage that the Allan directors decided the time had come to take over the North Atlantic trade in a decisive manner. Taking cognisance of the Canadian government's desire to have mail ships with speeds approaching 20 knots, the Allan Line considered new designs of ships for their mail contract. They faced two severe problems; first the

state of transition in marine engineering at the beginning of the 20th century with the expansion steam engine almost at the zenith of its design, and secondly the navigational hazards presented by the North Atlantic with ice, fogs and storms to be contended with in ships with no aids to navigation as now accepted as commonplace. High speed and the North Atlantic were not regarded as synonymous by prudent owners. In later years the tragedies of the *Titanic* and of the *Empress of Ireland* were to underline this problem, as was indeed the Allan Line's potentially serious incident in 1912 when the TSS *Corsican* struck an iceberg, fortunately with no loss of life and minimal damage.

In 1903 the Allan Line decided to order two twin screw steamships of conventional type, but with exceptionally high standards in passenger accommodation. Negotiations were carried out with several companies, but principally with a Belfast shipyard, Workman Clark & Co in the initial stages, as the technical director Mr Charles Allan was one of the three non-shipping sons of the late Captain Allan. By 1903 Charles Allan had persuaded his relations to consider triple-screw turbine ships, and later that year the two ships were ordered, one in Belfast and the other from Alexander Stephen's shipyard. The overall design of single funnel two masts, vertical stem and counter stern was similar to that set by Denny's *Bavarian* of 1899 and Stephen's *Tunisian* of 1900. The new ships were pacesetters in every way.

The new ships, carrying 1,500 passengers each, transformed the trade. Stephen's ship *Virginian* was launched at the end of 1904 and was ready for the summer season of 1905. She averaged 17.05 knots on an Atlantic crossing in June and by August had reduced the time from Moville to Rimouski to five days 20 hours 22 minutes. The *Virginian* was to become one of the most remarkable ships of the Atlantic. Requisitioned in November 1914, she served as a troopship, appropriately with the Canadian Expeditionary Force, later as an armed merchant cruiser in the tenth squadron. Arriving in Glasgow, 14 years and one day after her launch she was thoroughly refitted for the Canada trade, but while still on the Clyde was sold to the Swedish Amerika Line and sailed from her home renamed *Drottningholm*. The Swedes re-engined her with de Laval single reduction geared turbines and put her into their Atlantic service. During the Second World War she often acted as a hospital ship for her neutral owners and repatriated many injured servicemen on behalf of the Red Cross. In 1945 she was sold to the Home Lines, renamed *Brasil* and again later *Homeland*. After 50 years of superb service the grand old Stephen's ship went to the Trieste breakers.

The Canadian Pacific Company had good reason for alarm at the Allan Line's dynamic attack on the Canadian passenger market, and immediately ordered two twin-screw conventionally powered passenger ships, the first to be ready for May 1906. They were named *Empress of Britain* and *Empress of Ireland*. Despite conservative design they were popular and sea kindly ships, almost as fast as their rivals—the *Empress of Britain* was able to sail from Moville to Rimouski on one occasion in five days 21 hours 17 minutes.

In 1906 the Allan Line mail contract was renewed on a six-year term with the princely sum of £3,000 per round trip at stake. Onerous conditions were imposed, however, including the supply of four ships of equal standing and all capable of 18 knots. Neither the Allan Line nor CPR could stand further building costs, which were rising rapidly at the time, and an agreement was reached whereby CPR's Empresses joined the *Virginian* and her Belfast sister *Victorian* on a sub-contract basis.

The end of the road for the Allan Line came quicker than expected. In 1909, while outwardly the two lines were competing, arrangements had been made for the Allan Line and agencies to be sold for $8.5 million. In 1913 the Allan South American service was sold to the Donaldson Line and on January 1 1916 a new Canadian Pacific company, CP Ocean Services wholly absorbed the Allan Line which was formally dissolved in 1931. Sadly the Allan flag never reappeared after the war and the ships were renamed in the system of CPR.

The search for efficiency

As has been mentioned already, very considerable experimentation was required to supply the right kind of propellers for the *King Edward* owing to their abnormally high speed. Sir Charles Parsons was well aware of the short-comings of a system where for efficiency a turbine requires high revolutions, but a relatively slow turning propeller. In 1909 he purchased a cargo vessel *Vespasian* a coal-fired ship with triple expansion machinery, and carefully measured power, coal and steam consumption and so on, over a voyage from the Tyne to Malta. After removing the machinery and replacing it with

turbines geared to the main shaft, Parsons once more took the ship to sea for the manual data logging exercise: his verdict, published by the Institution of Naval Architects in 1910, showed a distinct fuel saving coupled with other lesser advantages. The turbine/propeller speed problem had been solved.

To the layman the solution of this problem may appear deceptively simple, but in reality it was complex and involving advanced technology of the time. The problem in manufacturing large gears was to cut them with accuracy so that they would be able to transmit the power required without undue wear on the teeth, and without unacceptable levels of noise and vibration. Gear cutting had not reached the position of today when loss of efficiency can be measured by a fraction of one per cent, and to capitalise on his developments Sir Charles Parsons again demonstrated his wide-ranging abilities by designing and manufacturing suitable machinery.

It must have been pleasing for the Parsons Company to receive an order immediately for geared turbines from the London and South Western Railway Company for two twin-screw cross channel ships building at Fairfield. To the design of J.H. Biles & Company of London and Glasgow, the new twin-funnelled ships were elegant and fast, both doing over 20 knots. The *Normannia* was launched at Govan in November 1911 and the *Louvinia* renamed *Hantonia* shortly after in December. The former ship was lost at Dunkirk while the latter served ultimately on the Channel Islands service until 1952.

Cunard's resurgence

The now practically defunct passenger trade of the North Atlantic has always been an unique business, with expensive ships, high overheads and the problem of marketing, requiring shipping companies to forecast business in order that their ships can remain in demand and be viable for the whole length of their economic lives. Officially regarded as a special trade, the North Atlantic witnessed the maritime aspirations of most European nations until the Second World War, and then the final struggle between the French, the Americans, the Italians and the British into the late '60s. The British, the earliest in the field, are now the sole survivor with one great liner tenuously maintaining the effort pioneered by Samuel Cunard in 1840.

The vast movements of people, mostly westwards, was the reason for the growth of shipping companies in the 19th century, and a growth which was to differentiate in a marked form the companies which carried the wealthy, the less affluent and ultimately the poverty-stricken migrants to their destinations. The top end of this market had the important feature of traffic both ways, which gave a stimulus to the fashionable companies—failure to them was relegation in the league table and the ultimate struggle of surviving with only emigrants on a one way basis. White Star, Collins, Cunard and the ill-fated Guion Line competed and indeed the latter company failed it is believed by entering the field where high investment risk was an actuarial decision.

For the top competing companies the balance sheet was an involved and complex equation involving many technical and marketing functions. For these operators decisions revolved around mail contracts, government subsidies for ships earmarked as wartime auxiliary cruisers, low operating costs, high speed, fast turnround and above all the ability to remain fashionable in the fickle market of public demand. The decisions involved in the building of ships included consideration of the service, the frequency and thereby the number of sisterships running on the route. For the Cunard Line, the desire to run a two ship week about service had always been their aim—something they achieved before the First World War, but strangely not again until the advent of the two 'Queens' in the late '40s.

At the end of the 19th century the Germans, French, Americans and British were the main competitors in the North Atlantic passenger market. The French activity was confined to the Compagnie Générale Transatlantique which was not putting intense pressure on the others, the British effort was mainly in the form of the popular but ageing Cunarders *Campania* and *Lucania* while the American effort was more in the form of business

with the growth of the International Mercantile Marine Company. This latter company, the brainchild of J. Pierpoint Morgan, was acting in one of history's first takeovers purchasing under the holding company various transatlantic operators, retaining their name and flag with a view to ultimately monopolising this trade and then naturally maximising profits. It was the intent of Pierpoint Morgan to control the whole operation to the New World, and possibly it was owing to his publicly stated desire to own the Cunard Steam Ship Company that he ultimately failed.

The German competition came from the Hamburg-Amerika Line and the Bremen based rival Norddeutscher Lloyd and with their *Deutschland* and *Kaiser Wilhelm der Grosse* were to gain the Blue Ribband for the first time for Germany in 1897 and to hold it until 1907.

The German successes caused concern in the boardrooms of shipping companies and also public indignation at the loss of national prestige. Above all the threat of the International Mercantile Marine Company spurred Cunard to precipitate action which led to Lord Inverclyde, their Chairman, approaching the UK government for support in replacing his older ships and in wresting back the Blue Ribband and its accompanying prestige. Negotiations were successful and in 1903 the government entered into

Just too early for turbines! The first Cunard liner to be unencumbered with spars was the twin screw mail ship Campania *built at Fairfield, Govan, in 1893. The two tall funnels assisted the natural draught from 13 boilers and 100 furnace grates, and the steam generated drove twin 5-cylinder triple expansion engines. On trials the* Campania *achieved 22.09 knots. This ship and her Fairfield-built sister* Lucania *were to hold between them the Blue Riband of the Atlantic from 1893 to 1898 until beaten by the German liner* Kaiser Wilhelm der Grosse.

an agreement with Cunard whereby the shipowners were to build two 24- or 25-knot steamships and in turn the government would grant a loan of £2.6 million at the rate of 2¾ per cent pa, and an annual subsidy of £150,000. Subsidiary clauses required these ships to remain British in flag and control, to be available to the Navy in certain eventualities, and that all Cunard ships of over 17 knots to be built to Admiralty approved plans.

In 1903 John Brown's shipyard at Clydebank were proceeding with the preliminary work for two intermediate liners for the Cunard Co. They were 19-knot vessels of 20,000 gross tons and 12,000 tons deadweight—that is cargo carrying capacity with some deductions, they were destined for the Liverpool to New York trade and were envisaged as twin-screw ships with steam reciprocating machinery. The names *Caronia* and *Carmania* had been reserved for them in keeping with Cunard's tradition of naming ships after Roman states with the letters 'ia' as an affix.

In August 1903, the directors of the Cunard Steamship Company decided to refer the problems of propulsion of their new 25-knot ships to a committee, and the committee's attention was to be drawn to the success of Parson's turbines in smaller ships, notably the Clyde steamer *King Edward*. The names of the committee are revealing: Mr James Bain, Cunard Co Superintendent; Rear Admiral H.J. Oram, Admiralty; Sir William H. White, Swan, Hunter & Wigham Richardson; Mr Andrew Laing, Wallsend Slipway; Hon C.A. Parsons, Parsons Marine Steam Turbine Co; Mr J.T. Milton, Lloyd's Register of Shipping; Mr Thomas Bell, John Brown & Co; Mr William Brock, Denny Brothers, Dumbarton; Lieutenant (E) W.H. Wood RN, Secretary.

Possibly not unnaturally the committee, with Charles Parsons and a representative from Denny of Dumbarton sitting on it, recommended that the propulsion of the new Cunarders be direct drive steam turbine and that pending Admiralty permission one of the two new Cunarders under construction at Clydebank be changed to the new form of propulsion.

The building of the twin-screw steamer *Caronia* continued without change. When ordered she was the largest ship in the world, and her designed profile indicated a fine looking two-funnelled ship in the classic Cunard mould. The launch was on July 13 1904, and on February 25 1905 she set off on her maiden voyage and in fact 27 years of trouble free running. Her quadruple expansion engines drove her

at 19.62 knots on trials at Skelmorlie in the upper Firth of Clyde while displacing 30,000 tons at a draft of 33 ft 3 ins. Her passenger accommodation was for approximately 2,400 persons.

The sister ship *Carmania* missed the title of first turbine Atlantic ship to the Allan Lines *Victorian* and *Virginian*, which was possibly unfortunate as the *Carmania* and *Caronia* were to remain in harness together for many years and were to be known most deservedly as the 'Pretty Sisters'. During construction the decision was taken to change the stern configuration of the *Carmania* and to adopt triple screws as this enabled the propellers to develop less power each and operate in a more satisfactory way. However, with the rpm increasing to 175 as compared with *Caronia*'s 80 it can be readily understood that neither propellers nor turbines which prefer high revolutions, were working at optimum speed.

The advantages of *Carmania* included a 5 per cent reduction in machinery weight, a clearer machinery space with lower centre of gravity allowing in compensation more weight on the passenger accommodation above. The machinery consisted of a high pressure turbine on the centre shaft and low pressure turbines with astern turbines on the wing shafts. The turbines were of the largest diameter possible to help reduce the shaft revolutions giving far better propeller efficiency—they were prodigious fitting and balancing jobs with over one million blades required. The low pressure turbines weighed 340 tons each!

Launched on February 21 1905, the *Carmania* went on trials at Skelmorlie late that year and achieved 20½ knots. Her performance was excellent in all respects and gave confidence to Cunard in their decision on the new ships. In a paper to the Institution of Naval Architects in 1914, Mr Leonard Peskett, the naval architect of Cunard said:

'While on the subject of turbines, attention may be drawn to the bold experiment made by the Cunard Company in building two ships of equal dimensions and displacements—the *Caronia* and *Carmania*—one fitted with reciprocating engines and the other with turbines. The boiler power in both ships is identical; the forms are as near alike as it is possible to make them. The *Caronia*, fitted with quadruple-expansion reciprocating engines is propelled by twin screws, running at an average of 80 revolutions per minute. The *Carmania*, fitted with compound turbine engines, is driven by triple screws, running at an average of 175 revolutions per minute. These ships

The Cunard Liner Lusitania *shortly after leaving John Brown's shipyard in 1907. Eight years later she sank after being torpedoed while steaming home from the United States* (John Smith Photographic Unit, UIE Clydebank).

have now been in service for over eight years, and the results do not warrant the adoption of direct-acting turbines to drive a ship of this type at a speed of 18 knots, the coal consumption for the *Carmania* being considerably greater than that of the *Caronia*.'

Mr Peskett's words are harsh, and now with the benefit of hindsight we know that turbine and propeller development were to improve, and above all the ultimate introduction of reduction gears were to open the field, allowing turbines and propellers each to run at its own most efficient speed.

However, the 'Pretty Sisters' were to sail together for 26 years, and the *Carmania* was to operate throughout very largely in the original form as built at Clydebank.

Fully to understand the background to the building of the magnificent *Lusitania* and *Mauretania* we must retrace our steps to three years before the successful launching of *Carmania* and *Caronia*. The Cunard Board had been giving serious thought to the building of two powerful liners, capable of maintaining an exacting schedule between them on the Liverpool to New York service. In November 1902, after much discussion, they approached four British shipbuilders for their views. The companies were: John Brown & Co Ltd, Clydebank; The Fairfield Shipbuilding & Engineering Co Ltd, Govan; Swan Hunter & Wigham Richardson, Wallsend; Vickers, Sons & Maxim, Barrow.

The negotiations which followed were model in their approach and, in later years, many shipbuilders commented on the straightforward approach of Cunard and on the fact that they did not at too early a stage involve the shipbuilders in heavy outlay which obviously not all of them could hope to defray later.

Each company was given an outline general arrangement and specification for a triple-screw steamer 750 ft × 76 ft × 49 ft displacing 33,000 tons of sea water with ihp of 55,000 and a speed of 25 knots. (For academic interest the outcome was the *Mauretania* and *Lusitania* 760 ft × 88 ft × 60 ft (231.6 m × 26.8 m × 18.3 m) displacing 44,000 tons, ihp of 70,000 and speed of 25 knots.)

This approach was novel at the turn of the century as it was quite often left to shipbuilders to submit their proposals, involving them in delay, expense and the loss of key personnel in what might well be a fruitless venture. The Cunard design department then started consultations with the builders concerned and separately with Sir Philip Watts, then Director of Naval Construction for the Admiralty. Watts, aged 56, had been newly appointed, was a practical shipbuilder and naval architect of repute, and above all was clear headed and able to discern trends in design having lived through the greatest period of upheaval yet known in naval history. He readily assented to being involved and directed that the facilities of the

Admiralty Experimental Tank at Haslar be made available and the work superintended by Mr R.E. Froude the son of William Froude, the father of modern naval architecture.

Experimental work began in earnest and was instigated largely by the Admiralty at Haslar, by John Brown's using the testing tank of Denny's of Dumbarton, and also by Swan Hunter's using a $\frac{1}{16}$ full size model in the Northumberland Dock. In model hull testing it is usual to use a known form with tabulated actual speeds and powers and test it and then make adjustments and retest, checking with the original at each stage. The original form was that of the successful Cunard Liner *Campania* of 1893, a ship 600 ft long displacing 18,000 tons and with a service speed of 21 knots, but it was soon found that this form extrapolated up to 750 ft long was totally uneconomic at 25 knots and a new 'parent' had to be found. The answer was the hull form of the *City of Paris* a 528 ft long ship built at Clydebank in 1888. In later years John Brown & Company were to use the *City of Paris* hull form at their own Clydebank tank for a methodical set of hull comparisons, known not too surprisingly as *City of Paris* Methodical Series, denoting the effect of alterations to the breadth, draft, trim and block coefficient (or fullness) of the parent form. At Haslar and in Dumbarton the tests proceeded and soon it became apparent that a broader hull form was required. To obtain the speeds required, a vast increase in power in the region of 15,000 ihp was agreed and at this stage the proposal to change from triple to quadruple screws was taken. As the Cunard turbine committee already had found in favour of turbine machinery the initial design work was complete.

Owing to the increased beam, the Barrow shipyard of Vickers, Sons & Maxim were forced to withdraw owing to dock restrictions in Cumberland and, as the Fairfield Company did likewise, the main and only contenders for the order were the Newcastle and Clydebank Shipbuilders. The Clyde Navigation Trustees were prepared to widen the Clyde and ease one of the bends on the river so that no physical impediment to the building was presented to Brown's, as was also the case for Swan Hunter. Fortuitously the New York Harbour Authority advised on a minor deepening of their port which allowed Cunard the fullest opportunity to exploit this new design.

In 1904 the Cunard Company placed the order for one ship each with the remaining contenders and, with the now mandatory approval of Sir Philip Watts for the Admiralty, the building of two of the world's most historic ships began.

At the Cunard Office and in Clydebank and Newcastle further studies were made to check, amongst other things, the watertight subdivision and the strength of the new liners, and then design and drawing office work proceeded on the biggest ship-building contracts yet attempted anywhere.

The design of the turbines followed closely to the pattern of *Virginian* and *Carmania*, but with turbines developing 70,000 shp on four shafts at 180 rpm. There were six turbines in all, two high pressure ones on the wing shafts exhausting to low pressure ones on the centre shafts. Reverse turbines (high pressure) on the main shafts only were fitted forward of the driving turbines. This arrangement was for many years the most powerful turbine direct drive arrangement known.

The *Lusitania* was launched on June 7 1906 by Lady Inverclyde, the widow of the man who first enabled this great project to start. Like many other illustrious ships she was launched across the Clyde into the River Cart, stopped and was then towed to Brown's basin, to lie for nearly a year as outfitting progressed. The official trials were conducted from July 29 to August 1 1907 when a mean speed of 26.45 knots was obtained and then under her new owner's colours she sailed to her berth at Liverpool before setting out on her maiden voyage on September 7 1907.

The first double crossing did not gain the Blue Ribband, but to the relief of many this was obtained on the second double crossing in 1907 with average speeds of 23.99 knots westwards and 23.61 knots eastwards. The prized trophy was to stay in the hands of the two Cunarders for more than 20 years, but for the vast amount of that time with the sister *Mauretania* with whom *Lusitania* ran in partnership and friendly rivalry.

While the running of *Lusitania* was incident free and calculated to win her support, her end was tragic and sudden. In 1915 while on passage from New York, she was within sight of the Old Head of Kinsale in Ireland, when without warning on May 7 she was torpedoed and sank in 18 minutes going down by the head. 1,201 persons lost their lives in calm seas that day and Britain suffered the loss for the third time in three years of a very large vessel with heavy death toll. The two previous ones,

unconnected with war, were the *Titanic* and the *Empress of Ireland*.

The life aboard majestic liners in this era was of unparalleled luxury for first class passengers, and of close confinement and, indeed, on some ships misery, for the hordes travelling third class or emigrant. The crew accommodation was cramped and the stokehold staff in particular had tough conditions with eight hours of gruelling toil per day. The *Lusitania* required nearly 1,000 tons of coal on a normal day on the Atlantic and 400 odd stokers and their immediate superiors were required to trim and deliver the fuel in unrelenting fashion. After the war the grim stokehold was removed from most large liners and oil fuel substituted with benefits of cleanliness, better control of furnaces, reduced costs and often a reduction as large as 50 per cent in the complement of engine rooms.

With the loss of the *Lusitania*, Cunard reverted to a three ship arrangement after the war on their

Built by Fairfield in 1930, the Empress of Japan *has been described as the finest Pacific Liner ever built. With twin screws and geared turbines, she made the transpacific crossing from Yokohama to Victoria in 7 days 20 hours and 16 minutes (22.27 knots). In 1942, following the declaration of war with Japan, her name was altered to* Empress of Scotland *and when released for peacetime duties she was brought out in this distinctive livery. Until sold to the Hamburg-Atlantic Line in 1958, her route was Liverpool-Greenock-Montreal (Canadian Pacific).*

premier service, using *Mauretania*, the German-built *Berengaria* and the ship that many people believe to be one of the most beautiful ships ever to leave the Clyde—the *Aquitania*. This trio concentrated on reliability rather than on pure speed, and for close on 15 years in unison they were highly successful. The building of the *Aquitania* by Brown's in 1914 was the ultimate vindication of the turbine. At that time it eclipsed all other machinery in the marine field.

Chapter 12

Dumbarton

For centuries the Rock of Dumbarton has been regarded as the dividing point at which the River Clyde changes in character and becomes an estuary. It also marks the entrance of the River Leven into the Clyde, the last main tributary before the ever-widening stream can be regarded as totally saline. The town of Dumbarton claims the distinction of having been a capital of one of the ancient kingdoms of Scotland and is in its own right historic. Reference to Dumbarton as a shipbuilding town goes back as early as the 14th century with the semi-retired King Robert the Bruce being credited with constructing ships in the vicinity during his declining years. The great forests of Luss at Loch Lomond supplied ready timber and as early as the 12th and 13th centuries it was floated down the Leven to the Clyde, finding its way to Glasgow and some to the new roof on the cathedral.

Formal records are few and far between but it can be assumed that small shipyards existed in Dumbarton from the time of King Robert until the 19th century when the town developed as a modern shipbuilding centre. To the east of Dumbarton, at Dumbuck, the Clyde shoaled and owing to this the Burgh of Dumbarton was the natural termination point for coastal ships coming to the Clyde. Dumbarton could well have become the main port for the river had the magistrates of Dumbarton and Glasgow reached agreement in the mid-17th century, but this was not to be, and instead Dumbarton and the Leven became a shipbuilding river developing rapidly after 1820. The numbers of shipbuilding establishments at different periods is estimated as: 1820-40, 8 different shipbuilders operated; 1840-60, 10 different shipbuilders operated; 1860-80, 16 different shipbuilders operated; 1880-90, 12 different shipbuilders operated; and in all something like 40 shipbuilders have worked in Dumbarton during the 19th and 20th centuries. Many of them were important and well known but all were overshadowed by two great yards, McMillan's and Denny's. Both were important as employers and, as shipbuilders, and it can be said without fear of contradiction that the latter Denny of Dumbarton can be placed in a unique group of three or four iron and steel shipbuilding

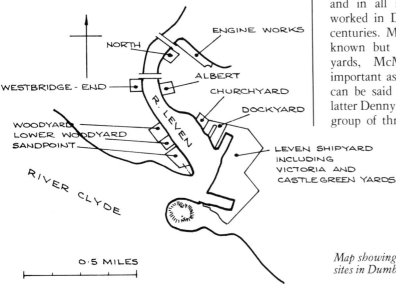

Map showing relative positions of the various shipbuilding sites in Dumbarton.

companies whose influence has been vital to the development of world shipbuilding as we now know it.

Sir James Marwick, the Town Clerk of Glasgow until 1903 said:

'The development of Dumbarton, especially in connection with shipbuilding since 1840 has been remarkable, and has necessitated a large increase of house accommodation for the rapidly growing population. As the number and size of the ships which left the yards increased, the need for having the channel of the River Leven into the Clyde enlarged and deepened became apparent and in 1851 a movement to effect this was commenced. A sum of £2,177 was raised and speedily expended in carrying out remedial plans . . . in 1854 the Burghs Harbour (Scotland) Act was adopted as a means for river improvement.'

In the same reference Marwick mentions that Irving's *History of Dumbartonshire* contains a list of 364 ships built in Dumbarton during the 20 year spell from 1839 to 1859.

To those not accustomed to the area it is worthy of mention that the name of the town in modern days is Dumbarton, but of the former county centred on the town is Dunbartonshire, with its distinctive spelling.

There have been about a dozen recognised shipbuilding sites in Dumbarton on both banks of the Leven. In the early days they were ill defined and, according to David Moor the noted shipbuilding historian of Dumbarton, were often the result of surreptitious occupation, extension, shipbuilding and ultimately given some credence by boundary fence construction! Yards had common boundaries and over the years merged, as in the particular cases of McMillan's Dock Yard and Church Yard and Denny's very large area ultimately known as the Leven Shipyard but encompassing Dockyard, Leven, Victoria and Castlegreen yards—the latter being the area used by Denny's for their main outfit basin.

One of the earliest steamship builders at Dumbarton was Archibald MacLachlan who occupied the Woodyard from some time after 1810 until 1818 when it is said he moved to Port Glasgow. From 1814 the shipyard produced a steady stream of steamships starting with PS *Trusty*, only the fifth steamer from the Clyde. In 1816 they built the hull for David Napier's PS *Marion* the first ship to steam up the River Leven to Loch Lomond. In later years the yard was managed by William Denny who took over the business in 1818, moved to the Albert Yard in 1819 and returned to the Woodyard from 1826-

1833. In 1818 William Denny built a very early paddle tug for the Clyde Shipping Company and it was given the name *Samson*, an appelation which was to become popular for towing vessels in the following years. While this was not the forerunner of the later company it was the start of the Denny shipbuilding tradition.

In Port Glasgow the remarkable brothers John and Charles Wood had developed great influence on Clydeside through their vital part in the introduction of steam ships from which the river was to benefit so greatly. The two men were always willing to dispute a technical point but despite this worked harmoniously. However, they also carried out business ventures on their own and Charles Wood ran the Dock Yard at Dumbarton from 1835 to 1840 and then the Castlegreen yard for three years. There he built the PS *Caledonia*, the third of the original four mail ships for the Cunard Line.

Another early shipbuilder was Archibald McMillan who commenced in the 1830s and ultimately established a yard in 1834 at Westbridge-End, a district later known as Dennystown owing to the large amount of Denny shipyard housing erected there. McMillan was joined by his son John and, in 1845, they made the first of their moves to the Dock Yard recently vacated by Charles Wood and were to remain there for 85 years until their closure in 1930. In 1867 they extended into the Church Yard and laid out a fine unencumbered shipyard with ways conveniently situated for launching up the River Leven. Considerable sums of money were spent improving the site and building a dry dock which became busy and gave years of profitable service until closed in 1895 owing to the ever increasing beam of ships.

Iron was introduced in 1866 with the building of three puffers *Cameo*, *Amethyst* and *Topaz* for Robertson of Glasgow and in 1881 they changed to steel construction with SS *Lydian Monarch*, a ship for the London-New York service which had high volume cargo space and extensive emigrant accommodation.

They never built engines and developed a great name for large sailing vessels building them with cellular double bottoms and even riveted by machine. Among their better known vessels was the iron full rigged ship *Coriolanus* of 1876 whose figurehead and wheel are preserved in the National Maritime Museum and displayed along with a splendid recently commissioned model. Apart from three sailing

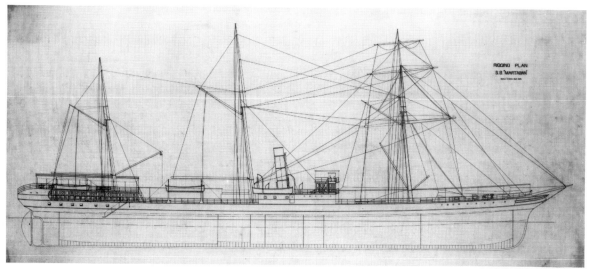

Rigging plan of SS Martaban, *built in 1873 by William Denny & Brothers, Dumbarton, for the closely associated British and Burmese Steam Navigation Co Ltd. This ship was managed by P. Henderson & Co of Glasgow* (National Maritime Museum).

barges their last sailing ship was the barque *Gostwyck* of 1904. By that time the company had experimented with the construction of ships using Isherwood's longitudinal framing system.

Archibald McMillan died in 1854, his son John continued the business and took his own sons into the shipyard. Various family matters and a death brought about changes between 1885 and 1890 with a member of the Steele family joining as a partner and, in 1890, the business was registered as a limited liability company. During the First World War one McMillan died on active service and the company became associated with the Royal Mail Steam Packet Co with, at different times, Lord Pirrie and Lord Kylsant sitting on the board. Despite considerable investment in the yard and great loyalty shown by old customers, the work load ran down drastically. Among the last orders two were for Elder, Dempster of Liverpool, the West African trade motor vessels *David Livingstone* and *Mary Slessor.* In 1930 the yard closed, a disposition in favour of National Shipbuilders Security Ltd was made out on April 29 1932 and the following year the plant sold. It was a sad end for a shipyard with a sterling tradition.

The Denny family were involved in several small undertakings, some of which are briefly described:

1 James Lang operated the Dock Yard from around 1815 to 1822 when he joined with Peter Denny of Castlegreen and until 1839 they operated as Lang and Denny. They built the PS *Comet* (2) to replace the ship of the name lost in 1820. The new ship was the first steamship to pass through the Caledonian Canal. (The *Dido* built by Blackwood & Gordon, Paisley, in 1858 was the first UK ship through Suez in 1869 and the *Alexandre Lavalley*, built by Lobnitz in 1887, was the first ship through Panama in 1914.)

2 Denny & Rankin was formed by Peter Denny after dissolving his partnership with Lang and while Provost of Dumbarton joined with David Rankin. Denny died in 1856, James Rankin son of David became a partner, he died in 1861 and David Rankin continued alone till 1865. The company operating at Woodyard and Victoria built over 200 ships.

3 Alexander Denny & Brother was set up by Alexander (1818-65) and Archibald (1825-66). The company built 48 iron ships and 11 sets of machinery at the Albert Yard from 1849-59.

4 Archibald Denny worked with his brother, Alexander, in Alexander Denny & Brother until 1853 when he severed his connection and set up on his own account at Church Yard joining with a John Mclean. About 40 ships were built. On Alexander Denny's death in 1866 the yard was taken over by John Spence, a relative, and John Henderson and under the name Henderson, Spence & Co operated from 1866-70.

Other well known Dumbarton shipyards include Birrell, Stenhouse & Co builders of nearly 50 sailing vessels, mostly barques for well known owners including Andrew Weir and the Scottish Shire Line. Burrell & Son, the shipowners and better known in present days as former art collectors, operated the Lower Woodyard in the early 1880s and built about 20 steamers, some for their own fleet. Owing to the bad recession at the time they closed the Dumbarton operation and concentrated on the yard at the Forth & Clyde Canal. J. & R. Swan was another business which had a yard in Dumbarton and another at Maryhill on the canal banks.

Near the bridge there was a renowned engine building business in the late 19th century known as Matthew Paul & Co. They had an enviable reputation as marine engineers but particularly in the 1880s built some small screw yachts. In 1900 they supplied the triple expansion machinery for the *Sir Walter Scott* which is used to this day for excursions on Loch Katrine.

In 1881 Henry Murray, formerly of Murdoch & Murray and of Henry Murray & Co, Port Glasgow, set up yet another shipyard in Dumbarton at Sandpoint. He built a few ships including the *Richmond Hill* of the Twin Screw Line before going out of business in 1884. However, in 1883, another company, Murray Brothers, was set up and with the same Henry Murray as common factor built ships till 1891 at Westbridge-End, later called the Phoenix Park Yard. Altogether 16 vessels were built including four *Cluthas.*

Scott & Linton operated in the late 1860s and are more fully discussed elsewhere in this book.

*   *   *

The name of Denny of Dumbarton must rank among the all time greats of British shipbuilding and along with Napier, Rankine and possibly two or three other family names of great distinction will be remembered as one of the most remarkable maritime concerns ever organised from the shores of Scotland.

The influence of Denny stretched far beyond the boundaries of Dumbarton or, indeed, of the Clyde ports and left a clear and discernible effect on the development of steel shipbuilding and on the maturing of the profession of naval architecture. The Leven Shipyard was a pioneer in the use of systematic evaluation of trials results and in the careful recording of scientific data.

From the beginning William Denny & Brothers encouraged training and technical development, an emphasis which ensured every draughtsman understood that he was expected not only to master his trade or craft, but to have a fair understanding of the principles of engineering involved in the construction and operation of ships. Of those younger men privileged to be students with the company even more was expected and, indeed, on return from university or college to the shipyard they could anticipate a penetrating interview with a partner or director on the sometimes embarrassing subject of the stewardship of their time while on release from the company.

To ensure that there was a clear code of conduct, Denny's instituted around 1884 a book entitled *Code of Procedure* which laid down in considerable detail the requirements for the smooth running of the technical, constructive and commercial departments of the firm. It was a model of clarity which suggested matters as different as the required scales for drawings to the abbreviations to be used on steel plates to identify their purpose in the shipyard. It gave details of occasions that tap riveting was acceptable in the shipyard and laid down the duties of officials prior to the launching of a new ship. No company matter escaped the 'Code of Procedure' which encouraged staff to make proposals for the improvement of methods, a feature that was enlarged later and incorporated in a Suggestion Scheme which awarded cash premiums and, on more than one occasion, patented the ideas of a member of staff in

The diesel-electric paddle ferry Mary Queen of Scots *built by Denny of Dumbarton for their ferry service on the Queensferry Passage on the Firth of Forth, north of Edinburgh. This centuries-old service ended in 1965 with the opening of the Forth Road Bridge. Three other ferries were operated here by the builders:* Robert the Bruce, Queen Margaret *and* Sir William Wallace *all being almost identical in design.*

the joint names of himself and the company. Denny's clearly appreciated that their open handedness was not without risk and resultingly included an 'honour clause' in the Code book:

' APPROPRIATION OF DATA OR DRAWINGS
As there is growing in our offices a large amount of special and organised information, procured and organised at considerable expense by us, it must be clearly understood by every member of our staff that we consider this information private and to be used only in our service.

Any member of our staff found copying or removing any of this special and organised information, or any information obtained in the experimental tank, will be considered to have acted against honour, and will, on our coming to know of his action, be immediately and without further warning, expelled our offices. To such a person we will decline to give either reference or character.

We consider that the opportunities afforded to the members of our staff in their ordinary work, and for private study by our library, and the use of our office in the evenings, are sufficient to enable them to acquire a knowledge of all methods of working, by means of which, should they leave our service for that of some other firm, they can collect and organise information for themselves or their new employers. There is no excuse for their acting against honour in the way we have now forbidden.

In the case of our head draughtsmen, the firm grants them permission to copy portions of our data. But it must be clearly understood as a matter of honour that such information is only to be for their own use and not for transmission to others.'

The shipyard encouraged systematic recording of information, not of mere facts, but of details that with the help of careful analysis could assist the researches of future naval architects. They looked at measured mile trials and started progressive trials, they made comparative analyses of fuel consumption and hull resistance and gave particular attention to scantling strength and hull weight. Much of this can be seen to this day in the intact Denny collection at the National Maritime Museum, Greenwich.

A close relationship was established with educational establishments like Glasgow University, the Royal Technical College (now Strathclyde University) and the Massachusetts Institute of Technology. It was to Cambridge, Massachusetts, that Sir Maurice Denny went for his undergraduate training, and this link was further strengthened when James Robertson Jack, a former manager of Denny's, was appointed professor in 1920 and then stayed as head of department for 16 years. As his immediate colleague was the redoubtable Professor William Hovgaard, it was said that to get on at MIT one had to learn two languages—Danish and Scottish!

The management of the company was kept in family hands, but at every stage one or two outsiders sat on the board—usually men who had been with the company all their days and were respected in the town of Dumbarton. Such men included the Wards, the Brocks, the Russells and latterly William P. Walker. The relationship with Dumbarton was unique, not just as the largest employers, but as kindly benefactors of the burgh avoiding too much patronage. The company and the family supported worthy local causes, offered university scholarships of various kinds and, also, held apprentice places in the shipyard for sons of employees and certain local people. While this is unfashionable nowadays, it was a matter of concern during the various depressions that struck the Clyde in the 120 years that the yard was in operation.

The welfare work, suggestion schemes and training typified Denny's approach and this was further outlined by the words of William Denny (3) in the 1880s when he wrote: 'The worst element in

SS Buenos Ayrean *built by William Denny & Brothers in 1879 for the Allan Line's services from Scotland to the St Lawrence and to South America. When built, this was the largest vessel of mild steel construction, and was only a few months younger than Denny's* Rotomahana, *the first ocean-going ship constructed of mild steel. The* Buenos Ayrean *was broken up in 1911 (National Maritime Museum).*

the employers and the employed question just now is a very detestable caste feeling, making the former look down with an assumed superiority and a good deal of fear and dislike on the latter, the compliment being returned with interest . . . You will only eliminate this ugly element by a constant habit of meeting as equals . . . I believe a permanent conference is the only solution. Anyway it is worth a trial on the Clyde.'

The succession of Denny shipbuilders commenced with William Denny (1) (1779-1833) whose first company, William Denny & Son, started the family shipbuilding enterprise. However, it was the subsequent company, Denny Brothers of 1844 and reconstituted in 1849 as William Denny & Brothers, which is the true start to the enterprise.

In 1851 Peter Denny, a second generation member of the family, set up an engine works in Dumbarton along with John Tulloch of Greenock. The company continued as Tulloch & Denny and built engines for the shipyard and other clients. In 1862 on the retiral of Tulloch, the engine works became known as Denny & Co and remained so until 1918 when both the shipyard and engine works combined in the title William Denny & Brothers Ltd.

From the beginning with PS *Lochlomond* built in 1845 to the order of the Dumbarton Steamboat Company, the shipyard used iron in almost all work. Indeed in 1879 the yard delivered the SS *Rotomahana* to the Union Steam Ship Co of New Zealand and the SS *Buenos Ayrean* to the Allan Line and could claim that they were the first reasonable sized ships ever built of mild steel. These two contracts were so successful that the yard moved over to steel construction, the first ever to do so in entirety. By then they had established long lasting relationships with the British India Company, the Irrawaddy Flotilla, P&O, the Union Steam Ship Company, various Indian River Navigation Companies and La Platense Flotilla Company operating from Buenos Ayres. The relationship with the Irrawaddy Flotilla became close and, ultimately, Denny directors sat on their board and on that of the closely associated British and Burmese Steam Navigation Company and their managers 'Paddy' Henderson & Co of Glasgow.

In 1881 William Denny (3) presented a case to his fellow partners for the building of a ship model test tank, and with their approval the work went ahead. Some of the structural calculations were carried out

by Professor W.J.M. Rankine and early in 1883 the tank commenced work. This was one of their most far reaching decisions involving the diversion of capital and skilled personnel into a project that could not have an immediate return. However, the first real reward came in 1888 with the award of a cross channel steamer contract with extremely tight specifications. As described earlier in this book the PS *Princesse Henriette* surpassed all expectations, vindicated the construction of the tank and established Dumbarton as cross channel experts. Like Denny's shipyard the tank produced many notable characters one of whom, Frank Purvis, tank superintendent, went to Tokyo University as professor of naval architecture when Professor Hillhouse returned to Glasgow at the turn of the century. On the closure of the shipyard, the tank was taken over by Vickers and worked in conjunction with their other hydrodynamics laboratory at St Albans. After nationalisation in 1977, it became part of British Shipbuilders Hydrodynamics Ltd, and continued to operate until 1983, having given 100 years of service.

In 1905 the company was placed on the Admiralty list, a situation previously impossible owing to a partner being a Member of Parliament. The Royal Navy quickly ordered at the yard and from 1907 till 1959 when HMS *Jaguar* left Dumbarton the Navy were seldom absent for long. During the Second World War two unusual craft were built for the Merchant Navy, but with the war effort in mind. They were Merchant Aircraft Carriers, diesel engined cargo vessels of about 8,500 tons dwt, 13 knots and capable of transporting fighter bombers. The original designs and two ships were produced at Burntisland Shipyard in Fife and two ships each then produced at Lithgows Ltd and Denny of Dumbarton. The Dumbarton ships were MV *Empire MacAndrew* and MV *Empire MacDermott* both managed by the Hain Steamship Company and which regularly crossed the Atlantic with 7,200 tons of grain and five swordfish aeroplanes for convoy protection. The disparity between their 8,500 tons potential deadweight capacity and the 7,200 tons of grain is caused by the poor stowage rate per ton of wheat.

The loss of the Denny-built TSMV *Princess Victoria* in the North Channel while crossing from Stranraer to Larne on January 31 1953, had a dramatic effect on the company. This loss, with 133 lives in some of the worst weather of the century was felt deeply, as the specialised ferry was of their

A 10-cylinder Denny/Sulzer diesel engine is taken down the River Leven in 1957 for installing on TSMV Bardic Ferry. *Denny's tug* The Second Snark *tows the well known Clyde Barge* Bojum *from the Engine Works to the Leven Shipyard. The funnel of the Norwegian ship SS* Valetta *can be seen to the left of Dumbarton Rock*

developed design. Despite the shipyard being cleared of all responsibility, the memory of the *Princess Victoria*, or Ship No 1399 as she was known, hung like a shadow over the cross channel builder for some years.

The Atlantic Steam Navigation Company under Lieutenant Colonel Frank Bustard was responsible for introducing the 'Roll-on, Roll-off' principle of ferry operation to Britain. It was natural that the first ship specifically designed and built for this service should come from Denny of Dumbarton. The photograph shows TSMV Bardic Ferry *on trials off Skelmorlie, and is unusual in showing Denny's 'Elephant' house flag. This ship was delivered to her owners in August 1957.*

Throughout their career Denny's produced unusual craft and experimented frequently. Battery-driven small ships were tried before 1900, vane wheel propulsion was introduced, welding commenced, stabilisers designed in conjunction with Brown Brothers of Edinburgh and new ship types developed ahead of market demand—like Ro-Ro vessels, hovercraft and newsprint carriers. Sadly, in the early 1960s it was decided to go into voluntary liquidation. W.P. Walker in somewhat controversial words described it as: 'a courageous and prudent decision . . . and thereby mark the end of British shipbuilding practice as we first new it and indeed the end of the domination of world shipbuilding by the UK.'

This was the saddest closure in the history of the Clyde and ended the yard that had built nearly 1,500 ships and had seen giants like William Denny (3), Dr Peter Denny, Sir Archibald Denny and Sir Maurice Denny (who died only in 1955) leading an industrial company which created standards that were accepted without question throughout the shipbuilding world.

Chapter 13

Small craft

Clyde and West Highland steamers

Depending on one's choice of definition the numbers of Clyde and West Highland ferries and pleasure steamers varies between 400 and 500. For 170 years these ships have served on the West Coast with conspicuous credit carrying mail, passengers and the highly seasonal holiday traffic to the Clyde ports, the Hebrides and the less accessible parts of the Western mainland. Traditionally few companies competed on the Western Isles services but many were involved in the cut-throat competition on the Clyde.

The early Clyde steamer fleets were privately owned, often in single ship companies which, if they survived the intense rivalry of the 1850s, merged into larger operating groups to combat the threat of railway steamers or of steam packet companies set up by the railways to overcome the more irksome aspects of railway company charters.

The Western Isles were served by David Hutcheson & Co, and McCallum Orme & Co, both of which came under the control of David MacBrayne. No wonder the West Highlander never forgets the jingle:

The earth unto the Lord belongs
and all that it contains
Except, of course, the Western Isles
and these are all MacBrayne's.

Not every shipyard on the Clyde was involved in building small passenger steamers and, indeed, a survey carried out on the particulars of 390 steamers indicated that the most important builders were on a percentage basis: Denny and other yards operated by the family, 13 per cent; Wood, Port Glasgow, 10 per cent; Tod & MacGregor, 6 per cent; Duncan, 5 per cent; Barclay Curle, 5 per cent; Inglis, 4 per cent; J. & G. Thomson, 4 per cent; Caird, 3 per cent; Seath, 3 per cent; Wingate, 3 per cent.

On closer examination one can discern that these ships were built at certain yards over comparatively short periods of time and, of course, almost all early ships from the Woods served as Clyde steamers at the beginning. The role of Denny is interesting in that these ships came from Dumbarton from early in the 19th century and continued until the 1950s.

The American Civil War commencing in 1861

Below left *A scene at Crinan on the western end of the canal in the early part of this century. The TSS* Linnet *has brought passengers over the canal from Ardrishaig and they are about to be transferred to David MacBrayne's beautiful two-funnelled paddle steamer* Chevalier *for onward passage to Oban, Fort William and elsewhere. Many of the passengers would have left Glasgow that morning on the PS* Columba, *and on the following day will continue up the Caledonian Canal on PS* Gondolier. *The small cargo coaster or puffer is SS* Countess of Kellie (Wotherspoon Collection, Mitchell Library, Glasgow).*

Right *An unusual view of the Clyde paddle steamers* Jupiter *and* Juno *under construction on one berth at the east end of the Fairfield yard. The* Jupiter, *nearest the camera, was launched on April 9 1937, and the* Juno *entered the water on May 25.*

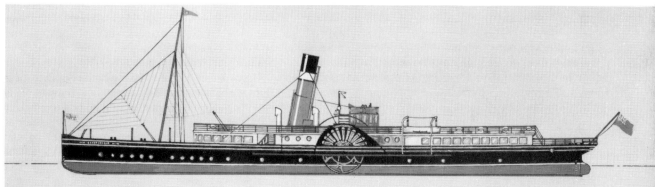

Above *The North British Steam Packet paddler* Redgauntlet. *Built in 1895 by Barclay, Curle & Co, this paddle steamer was the largest in the NB Fleet, but was sent to the River Forth in 1909 and did not return to the River Clyde.*

Right *The high plateau of 19th century river steamer design. PS* Mercury *built in 1892 by Napier, Shanks & Bell of Yoker for the Glasgow and South Western Railway (National Maritime Museum).*

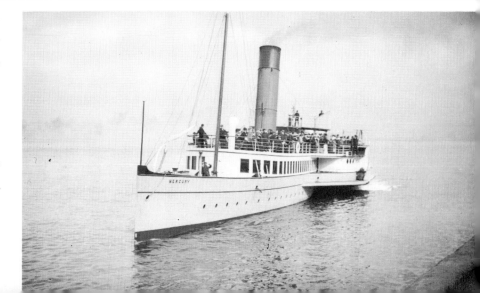

had the same effect as all wars of pushing up rates by creating a demand for shipping. In particular the Confederates required fast, long, light, high speed craft to run the blockade of the Southern ports. Their agents purchased ships from all over the UK and, indeed, hundreds of ships left the Thames, Mersey and Clyde manned by British seamen to carry out this task. Many sailed for Halifax, Nova Scotia, others for the Caribbean and from there under cover of dark they would dash for the south with their cargoes of luxury goods and military stores. It is on record that a Liverpool built blockade runner, PS *Banshee* of 1862, made eight successful round trips of the Atlantic and netted 700 per cent profit for her owners.

As available spare Clyde steamers dwindled the shipyards turned their hand to this profitable business. Few yards did not become involved. Aitken and Mansell designed and built fast steamers and Kirkpatrick McIntyre of Greenock built a ship 231 ft long with the name *Let-it-Rip*. Several yards experi-

mented with steel hull construction to reduce weight, an acceptable idea in such vessels where the owners were willing and able to pay enormous costs to obtain steel which was then a rare material and usually stronger than the mild steel of today. Shipowners staked large sums on this high risk venture and the crews were well rewarded financially. The training that the engine room of a blockade runner gave was excellent and this in turn raised the professional standards of engineers.

The end of the war saw another minor boom as the yards built to replace the tonnage sold from the country and now advanced designs for coastal ships were the norm. The beautiful paddlers built by J. & G. Thomson of Clydebank showed the influence of the Civil War years—ships like *Glen Sannox, Iona* and *Columba*. These high standards in paddle ship design were never lost.

The next major change came in 1901 with Denny's *King Edward* and with it the pattern was set for using Clyde steamers as test beds for changes in

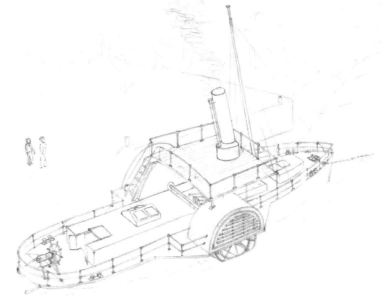

design and engine room layout. Examples include the high pressure turbine ship *King George V*, the diesel electric paddle ship *Talisman* and the turbine steamer *Atalanta* built as a precursor to the Cunarder *Lusitania*.

A little known experiment was carried out in 1908 when a gyroscopic stabiliser was fitted in MacBrayne's steamer *Dirk* and then transferred to the *Lochiel*, both built then by Scott's of Bowling. As the scheme was not repeated one can assume that it was not regarded as a success.

With the purchase of the *Queen Alexandra*, which became *St Columba*, and the *King George V* in 1935 MacBrayne's could claim to have the widest range of marine engines in the world with steeple, oscillating, diagonal, vertical reciprocating, turbine and diesel all being represented.

The Clyde steamers were the products of the shipyards but as offspring they repaid the industry handsomely by sailing as test beds and by advertising the excellent products of the river.

Shallow draft vessels

Exploration and military operations in the 19th century gave British shipyards a captive market for shallow draft ships for use in the colonies and protectorates and in other areas where there was strong British influence. Literally thousands of ships were sent overseas, dismantled or as deck cargo, and

quite a few travelled remarkable distances under their own steam. The destinations were the rivers of South America, Africa, India, Burma and China and there they were to serve in inland fleets belonging to trading companies and government departments.

Initially these ships were side paddlers as paddle floats require smaller immersion than propellers for efficient operation. The design requirements were small draft, good steering, longitudinal strength, light construction and simple machinery using easily obtained local fuel. Over the years both British and American naval architects were to master this problem independently and it is amazing to discover the close similarity to the solutions as depicted in the American river steamer, the Canadian Yukon sternwheeler and British-built vessel similar to those of the Irrawaddy Flotilla Company of Rangoon. The illustration of Denny's *Namtu* overleaf shows the use of the upper deck as a girder to give the shallow hull strength and give ample deck space for cargo and passengers. The Clydeside builders specialising in

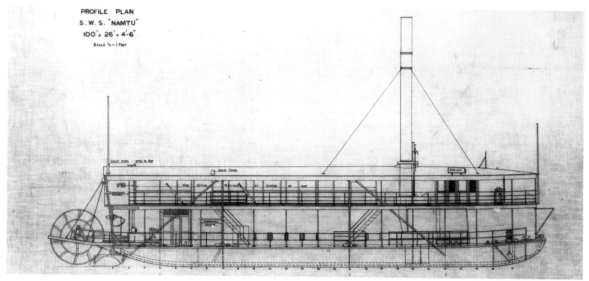

PROFILE PLAN
S. W. S. "NAMTU"
100'x 26'x 4'-6"
SCALE ¼ = 1 FOOT

this work were: Denny of Dumbarton; Ritchie, Graham and Milne of Whiteinch; Seath of Rutherglen; Yarrow; and some of the Paisley shipyards.

As the years passed it was found that side paddlers were not the most efficient types of ships with sponsons sticking out the sides and the sternwheeler developed with the paddles in line with the ship and with an excellent flow of water up to the stern.

A variation was the quarter wheeler with two side paddles within the line of the ship, one on each quarter, taking advantage of the first class research that was done by Denny's experimental tank on the design of feathering paddle wheels.

It is ironic that one of the world's best known sternwheelers, now serving on the Mississippi and Ohio Rivers as an old fashioned 'period piece' tourist ship was, in fact, a product of the Clyde. The *Delta Queen* was built by Denny in 1925 for reassembly at Stockton, California, and since the Second World War was brought round the coast through the Panama Canal and into the Gulf of Mexico to start her new life. Few Clyde vessels served on these waters and none were to become so world famous as the *Queen*.

In the 1920s Denny's attempted to bring a quite revolutionary form of propulsion into the world of shallow water navigation. It was called vane wheel drive and consisted of two propellers set on the stern of the ship with only part of their lower blades in the water. This concept had the advantage that the hull could be given an efficient afterbody shape and the two propellers or vane wheels which operated at

The passenger and cargo stern wheel steamer Namtu *built by William Denny & Brothers of Dumbarton for the Irrawady Flotilla Company in 1917. The ten float stern wheel was turned at 30 rpm and her maximum speed was 8½ knots. The* Namtu *was lost when the Flotilla was scuttled in advance of the Japanese capture of Burma in 1942 (National Maritime Museum).*

around 65 rpm could be driven by simple steam engines. As ships tend to 'squat', or increase their after draft when being driven, it gave the wheels increased immersion and improved their propulsive performance. Only a few vane wheel ships were built and by the 1930s almost all vessels were designed as tunnel types.

The idea of the tunnel is quite old. As early as 1856 patents were taken out for hulls with arched tunnels under them amidships in order that propellers of greater diameter than the draft of the ship could be fitted. Yarrows started to apply the principle in the 1890s in London and since then have constructed well over 100 such vessels. The design of the tunnel is such that the propeller, even if partly in air, starts to draw water when the ship moves and soon is operating in what is called 'solid water'. Yarrows patented a tunnel flap to increase the efficiency of the propellers.

The fascination of shallow draft ships is a reflection of their unusual field of operation but, sadly, less time is spent on this kind of design and research work as the hovercraft has been proved to be the most efficient type of transport in these regions.

A barque in the upper reaches of the Clyde with the Steel & Bennie tugs SS Thunderer *and PS* Brigadier.

Unless a very cost effective shallow draft design can be produced the air supported craft will continue to dominate the market.

Tugs

John Scott Russell, one of Glasgow University's illustrious sons, left a legacy of papers and memoirs mostly printed in the Transactions of the Institution of Naval Architects which are informative and thought provoking. In a delightful paper entitled 'On the Late Mr John Wood and Mr Charles Wood, Naval Architects, of Port Glasgow' read in London on March 1 1861, he recounted the lives and achievements of the two men to whom the later Clyde shipbuilders were all indebted. In the text is the interesting comment:

'In 1817 they built the first towing steamboat, which from her intended employment was named the *Tug*; hence the name of a well known useful class of steam vessels.'

The appendix to the paper states that *Tug* was 70 ft in length, 17 in breadth, had engines of 32 horse power and 'went to Leith'. A small ship indeed but one which was to create an international business based on thousands of vessels of which, even after over 160 years, the largest are only two or three times longer and broader although equipped with engines several hundred times more powerful.

The prestigious journal *Engineering* in March 1876 had less friendly remarks to make about the Clyde:

'Notwithstanding the eminent position which the Clyde has long enjoyed in connexion with shipbuilding and marine engineering, it has hitherto done comparatively little in supplying its own ports, and those of other parts of the country with steamers for towing purposes.'

This quotation drew attention to the remarkable fact that in the mid to late 19th century the design and building of tugs, especially paddle tugs, had become centred on Tyneside. Every Clyde tug fleet had vessels built by Eltringham, Marshall, Chisholm and others from around the Shields. However, as the screw tug took over from paddle steamers the Clyde yards came back into the picture and several establishments developed a reputation for building these fine craft endowed, not with elegance, but the simple beauty of being designed for a specific and utilitarian purpose. James Howden & Co, the marine engineers, designed a double ended tug with a large diameter propeller at both ends each of which could be worked independently, and this vessel was supplied to the Screw Tug Company of Glasgow in 1874.

In recent years Clydesiders are accustomed to seeing tugs in two liveries on the river, the black funnelled ships of the Clyde Shipping Company and the black and white funnels with a black diamond of Cory Ship Towage (Clyde) Ltd. It is surprising to note that the following companies have served on the river and, indeed, possibly others not recorded here.

Left *The iron paddle tug* Vanguard *built by the short-lived shipyard of Robertson & Co at Greenock in 1868 for Steel & Bennie of Glasgow. This ship served her owners well until disposed of in 1917, a period of 49 years. The machinery was a side lever engine, often known as a 'Grasshopper Engine'* (Wotherspoon Collection, Mitchell Library, Glasgow).

Below left *Steel & Bennie's steam tug* Warrior *seen at Yorkhill Quay in 1952. Built by Scott's of Bowling in 1935, the plans of this tug were adopted during the Second World War for the manufacture of large numbers of* Warrior *and* Modified Warrior *coastal tugs. In the background are two tugs of the Clyde Shipping Company's fleet, the Anchor Liner* Eucadia *and the Queen's Dock entrance.*

Most of these companies were short lived 19th century businesses, but the Clyde Shipping Company claims to go back as far as 1815 and Cory through its purchased interests to 1851: Clyde Shipping Company (operating at present); Glasgow & Greenock Shipping Company which became Steel & Bennie Ltd and later Cory Ship Towage (Clyde) Ltd (operating at present); Clyde Towing Company; River Towing Company; New Clyde Towing Company; Bowling & Greenock Towing Company; City of Glasgow Towing Company; Greenock Towing Company; Screw Tug Co Ltd; Port Glasgow Towing Company; Caledonian Towing Company; Messrs A.L. Simpson; Messrs Davie; Clyde Navigation Trust; Ardrossan Harbour Co Ltd; Irvine Harbour Company.

In addition to these companies can be added the Anchor Line with their tug and passenger tender *Paladin* built by Murdoch and Murray of Port Glasgow in 1913 which served the Line till 1939 when sold to the Clyde Shipping Company.

The Clyde Shipping Group has interests in Shetland Towage, Forth Towage and took control in 1983 of Lawson-Batey Tugs Ltd of Newcastle.

Cory Ship Towage is part of the Ocean Group—better known in earlier years as Blue Funnel and Elder Dempster—but now widely diversified. Prior to their control the company was known as Steel and Bennie and from 1917 this had been part of Houlder Brothers, a company now in the Furness Withy Group.

By the turn of the century most of the Clyde tugs were being built on home waters and presumably with an eye on trials and launch contracts Steel & Bennie and the Clyde Company ordered in Ayr, Paisley, Bowling and Glasgow. The total number of tugs on the river has always been around 20,

The Clyde Shipping Company's tug Flying Buzzard *leaves Ferguson Brothers' Port Glasgow shipyard in 1912 for trials and handover. In those days there was more atmosphere of a social event on trials, something often impossible to achieve in modern days with highly complex vessels and tightly scheduled performance assessment. The load line mark amidships shows the initials* BC *awarded by the assigning authority—the British Corporation* (Wotherspoon Collection, Mitchell Library, Glasgow).

indicating an order of replacement possibly slightly faster than one per year. During the Second World War the total number of tugs rose to over 40.

Within the United Kingdom tugs fall into reasonably clearly defined classes. The first is the deep sea tug, a ship designed for long periods at sea and to be able to tow awkward objects like a lightly ballasted tanker many thousands of miles over wild oceans. This type of tug is called on for salvage duties and should possess the engine power and the hull shape to rush to the assistance of a stricken vessel.

The second group are the coastal, river estuary and large harbour tugs. Generally the tugs of the Clyde and indeed the Thames, Mersey and Tyne also are of this type. In order to be efficient pullers in bad weather such tugs require displacement—to be heavy and to have powerful engines with efficient paddles, propellers or water tractor units. For coastal voyages a reasonable turn of speed is essential and also accommodation is necessary for the crew. The tow hook is usually fitted about amidships and is

invariably a patent device designed to shed the tow line if the tug is in danger of being overturned. In modern tugs a power winch has replaced the tow hook.

The third group are small harbour and dock tugs of which, with odd exceptions, there have been few on the Clyde, but do include the Clyde Port Authority's tug *Clyde* which replaced a larger vessel with twin inward turning screws some years ago.

There is no doubt that the style of towing adopted in European ports has developed from the vessels designed for the British rivers. The most famous design was that of Steel & Bennie's SS *Warrior* built by Scott & Sons of Bowling in 1935—she was an elegant and powerful tug with triple expansion engines which were at that time a novelty for the owners as they had until then relied on compound units for their fleet. At the beginning of the war the Admiralty Merchant Shipbuilding Department decided to standardise on three or four tugs for batch or mass production, and with modifications the *Warrior* was one of those chosen as a prototype. An interesting feature of her design was the central position of bunkers which allowed the ship to stay on a steady trim no matter how much fuel had been expended.

Since the Second World War the Clyde shipyards have delivered tugs all over the world and built many for UK and, indeed, Clyde owners. Towing companies displayed some reluctance to give up the

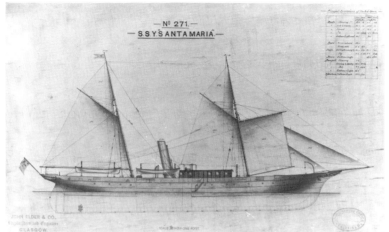

— № 271 —
— S S Y S A N T A M A R I A —

Left *The steam yacht* Santa Maria *built by John Elder & Co, Govan, 1883 for Lord Alfred Paget. Up to the First World War, the Fairfield yard built 16 fair sized yachts and many other yards on the River were deeply committed to this line of business* (National Maritime Museum).

Below *The elegant relief and inspection steamer* Pole Star *built by Fairfield in 1892 for the Commissioners of Northern Lighthouses.*

well tried and relatively trouble free steam reciprocating engine, but ultimately fuel costs drove them to the direct diesel and to diesel-electric units. Tugs for overseas, especially Africa, were built with old fashioned engines until the 1950s, largely owing to the fuel situation in their home ports and availability of labour trained in the use of steam plant.

The past 20 years have seen a revolution in tug design, particularly with the introduction of the Voith Schneider propeller unit and the widespread use of hydraulic and electric gear aboard. Gone are the days when tugs were built to ensure that maintenance was negligible, for to be competitive in an increasingly international market tugs have to be capable of outstanding service often in hazardous conditions.

There have been several accidents on the Clyde; tugs have been 'girthed' and overturned by their own tow lines, rammed by the vessels they are assisting and so on, but the few fatalities indicates the professionalism of the crews and, especially in recent years, the excellence of design. The introduction of towing winches has been important not only for the long life of the tow rope but, also, as a speedy method of recovering the rope from the bottom of the river where it used to be dropped by outgoing steamers. The effect of this was to brake the tug while in front of its tow which may well have been increasing speed.

Since the early 1970s a new class of tug has been evolved with the offshore oil fields in mind. The design of supply ship/anchor handling tugs owes much to the American and Dutch experience but is now a full branch of British expertise and several such vessels for Seaforth Maritime Ltd of Aberdeen have been built in Port Glasgow.

Chapter 14

The Clyde, wars and the Royal Navy

Ships for the defence of the realm have been built on almost every part of the British coastline and have come in large numbers from the Royal Dockyards of Chatham, Woolwich, Deptford and Sheerness on the Thames and Medway, and from Devonport, Portsmouth, Pembroke and in earlier days from Hawlbowline in Ireland. Some ships were built in North America, many in India and a few in other places where British interests were at stake. Over the years there has been a closing and rationalising of dockyards and an increasing dependence on commercial shipyards for the production of HM ships. The Royal Dockyards in the UK were four in number—Chatham (now closed), Devonport, Portsmouth and Rosyth in Scotland. Rosyth never built ships and the other three have not laid down a keel since the 1960s. In the past few years the Royal Navy has come to an arrangement with British Shipbuilders whereby certain shipyards are designated for naval building like Yarrow Shipbuilders Ltd of Glasgow, Vickers S & E Ltd of Barrow and Vosper-Thornycroft Ltd of Southampton as well as merchant yards with recognised standards like Hall, Russell Ltd of Aberdeen and Brooke Marine Ltd of Lowestoft.

In 1794 the shipbuilding industry was in its infancy on the Clyde when Scotts' of Greenock received two orders, one for a timber carrier *Caledonia* to service the naval dockyards and, also, deliver wood to the many private builders working for the King, especially around Hampshire. This ship may have been the first naval order in Scotland, but the credit is more often given to the *Prince of Wales.* The latter ship is variously attributed as the first Clyde-built man of war for the Royal Navy, but the story is more likely that in 1794 she was built as the revenue brig *Prince of Wales* and around 1803 was sold to the Navy, rerigged as a full rigged ship and renamed HMS *Thrush.* The *Thrush* is recorded as being 24 m

(78 ft 10 in) on the keel and 8.2 m (27 ft) broad with 18 guns and having a crew of 121 men on Naval Service. From this small beginning rose an enormous volume of work and the development of the armament business on Clydeside. According to J. Harvard Biles, 22.8 per cent of all naval ships built 1868-78 were from Clydeside and for the period 1898-1908 the comparable figure was 23.6 per cent. This reflects great credit on the young iron shipbuilding industry of West Scotland, and also on the Admiralty who were prepared to put out work from their own dockyards and from the tried and proved commercial rivals on the Thames. In the 20th century the River Clyde was to justify the faith shown in it by building 19 of our greatest battleships or battlecruisers including *Ramillies, Renown, Hood, Duke of York* and the last British battleship *Vanguard* which left Clydebank in 1946.

Robert Napier can take much credit for making the Clyde a shipbuilding area acceptable to the Admiralty. He was punctilious in his dealings with the Naval authorities, was energetic in his design work and made a point of following up ships and assessing their service performance. As has been said elsewhere, Govan was an area where experimentation was accepted as the norm, and there Napier and his staff experimented on ship structures and made considerable efforts to produce original designs. While mainly oriented towards merchant construction the burgeoning naval market in Britain, and in Europe, was not neglected and Napier produced ships and sometimes only engines for the Danes, Dutch, French and others, as well as for the Royal Navy. One of the most interesting designs was that of the floating battery HMS *Erebus* built in 1856, an iron vessel of 1,825 tons displacement with a two-bladed propeller driving her at 5½ knots. The *Erebus* was armed with 16 68-pounder guns and was

protected by a belt of 6 in (150 mm) teak under a layer of 4 ins (100 mm) armour plating extending from the gunwale to a point more than 0.5 m below the waterline. The *Erebus* was ahead of the French armour frigate *Gloire* by three years. Four years later the Royal Navy were to build HMS *Warrior* at the Thames Ironworks & Shipbuilding Company at Blackwall, London, and then HMS *Black Prince* at Napier's in Govan.

HMS *Black Prince* was launched in February 1861, completed in 1862, and was then the largest ship built on the Clyde. Her armour was considerably advanced on that of HMS *Erebus* but was of the same basic type with an intermediate layer of hardwood. She made history not only as the second true ironclad in the Royal Navy, but as the first with a steam capstan. Her sea service was uninspiring and included six years from 1868 to 1874 as guardship on the Clyde. Around 1874 her wooden lower masts were replaced by iron masts from the *Ocean* and as Admiral Ballard dryly remarks: 'It was rather paradoxical that the timber sticks of an iron hull should be removed to make way for iron sticks from a hull of wood.' The *Black Prince* was renamed *Emerald* in 1903 and later *Impregnable III* before being broken up at Dover in 1923. Her sister HMS *Warrior* is still afloat, the only survivor of her age in the Royal Navy and currently is being rebuilt at West Hartlepool.

In 1868 Napiers built the twin-screw armoured ram *De Buffel* for the Dutch Navy. This ship, too, remains afloat, at Rotterdam a testimony to fine engineering and the longevitous qualities of iron as a shipbuilding material.

The heir and successor to Robert Napier & Sons

HMS Black Prince *was launched at Robert Napier's Govan Shipyard on February 27 1861, and with a displacement of 9,800 tons was then the largest ship to have been set afloat on the River Clyde. After 62 years of unadventurous existence, she was broken up at Dover in 1923. The* Black Prince *is remembered for being the second armour-plated ship built for the Royal Navy, and for having a massive and beautiful figurehead of the Prince after whom she was named* (Wotherspoon Collection, Mitchell Library, Glasgow).

was the company known as William Beardmore & Co Ltd. In 1900 the name of the Govan shipyard was changed and imperceptibly the role changed from that of the most versatile of shipbuilders to that of the shipbuilding adjunct of an armament and armour plating company. The new directors were conscious of the arms race developing and with large sums at stake in preparation for war were anxious to build all factories and yards on a grand scale and with ample capacity to hand.

In 1905 the Govan yard was moved to a green field site on the north bank just west of their rivals John Brown of Clydebank. Ground was purchased from the Clyde Navigation Trust and the new yard laid out and plans developed for a mammoth dry dock capable of handling all known and projected ships. The dock was to be run by the Dalmuir Dry Dock Co Ltd and the land for this purpose alone was acquired for a sum in excess of £50,000. The scheme did not proceed—a decision which was regrettable as dry docking facilities on the river lagged behind demand and requirements from the beginning of this century. The Dalmuir Company was later wound up.

The shipyard of Beardmore's, however, was carefully planned with a superb tidal dock and building berths with side gantries and overhead lifting capability. In a 30-year period they obtained well over 60 contracts for the Royal Navy varying from the battleship *Conqueror* to volume orders for seaplanes. There is no question that Beardmore's role was a vital one in the First World War and their contribution of national importance. At the peak of production the Beardmore company produced ships of all kinds, airships, aeroplanes, steel products, special forgings, marine and general machinery, armour plating, heavy ordnance as well as vehicles including the taxicabs to be seen on the streets of London and Glasgow. It is possible that the company overstretched in diversification, but no one would claim that they lacked initiative or zest. On the engineering side the British patent rights were held for Caprotti Valve Gear for steam engines as well as the Bauer Wach low pressure exhaust steam turbine. The Caprotti gear was an elegant and simple form of valve gear for reciprocating steam engines which avoided the necessity for fitting cumbrous valve gear connecting rods. An example can be viewed in the Falmouth steam tug *St Denys* now open to the public in her home port. Not many examples of this are to be found as Beardmore's exclusive rights may have inhibited wider usage.

The tragedy of Beardmore's resulted from their expansive attitude in the First World War when they purchased their way out of production bottlenecks, as typified by the case of the Speedwell Works in Coatbridge acquired solely to improve their turnover in marine steam engines. In the early 1920s they held many businesses, some of which had not had time to repay their initial investment. The final blow was the Washington Treaty of 1922 and the cancellation of the British four battlecruiser orders three of which were placed on the Clyde at Beardmore's, Brown's and Fairfield. The other two companies weathered this blow better than Beardmore's who were reduced to building tugs, motor yachts and sludge hoppers on berths designed for battleships like HMS *Agamemnon*. The last ship built at Dalmuir was the lighthouse tender *Pole Star* for the Commissioners of Northern Lighthouses. In 1930 the yard was closed and in 1933 the machinery and plant sold. In 1938 Arnott Young & Co purchased the land and set up shipbreaking in the basin and on part of the old yard.

While not ships of war it is reasonable to discuss two very fine vessels built by Beardmore at Dalmuir. In 1913 the Allan Line took delivery of the beautiful *Alsation*, a two-funnelled, quadruple-screw turbine steamer for their UK Canada service. With a service speed of 18½ knots and particularly smooth running engines the *Alsation* was a success from the start. At the end of war service as an armed merchant cruiser she returned to the Clyde for refit, and subsequent upon the Canadian Pacific Railway having gained control of the Allan Line she was renamed *Empress of France*. One of the notable features of this liner was that her hull had no expansion joints and her superstructure was made 'effective', that is contributing to the strength of the hull girder. This was a novel technique at the time and indicated the forward looking and co-operative approach of the British Corporation—the Classification Society involved in this ship.

The other unusual Beardmore ship was the icebreaker *Krisjanis Valdemars* built for the Government of Latvia in 1925. This vessel was one of the very few ice-breakers built on the Clyde and was distinguished by an ice breaking bow, propellers fore and aft and the broad hull configuration of the ice-breaking ship. Machinery was in the form of two triple expansion engines, one for each shaft. Her generous beam of 54 ft (16.5 m) was to keep open sea passages in the Baltic to the Port of Riga and this breadth was regarded at that time as satisfactory for ships calling at that Lettish port.

Towards the end of the 19th century several other Clyde yards were beginning to obtain Admiralty orders and, in 1905, William Denny & Brothers became eligible to quote for naval work, once one of the partners resigned his seat in Parliament. As a result of their specialist background over 100 destroyers, frigates and other craft were built for the white ensign in just over 50 years.

At the same period A. & J. Inglis obtained the order for HM Destroyer *Fury*, their first naval contract and the only such vessel till then built within the boundaries of Glasgow. (This situation was the result of Partick, Govan, Hillhead and other Burghs being then independent of the City!)

The Fairfield shipyard produced nearly 180 ships for the Royal Navy including the battlecruisers *Indomitable*, *New Zealand* and *Renown*, the battleships *Commonwealth*, *Valiant* and *Howe* and the aircraft carriers *Implacable* and *Theseus*. Their greatest contribution was in the cruiser and destroyer field with 26 cruisers, two fleet scouts, two guided

Left *HM Destroyer* Fury, *built by A & J Inglis in 1911. This was Inglis' first warship contract for the Royal Navy and the only RN vessel to that date launched within the official boundaries of the City of Glasgow (Wotherspoon Collection, Mitchell Library, Glasgow).*

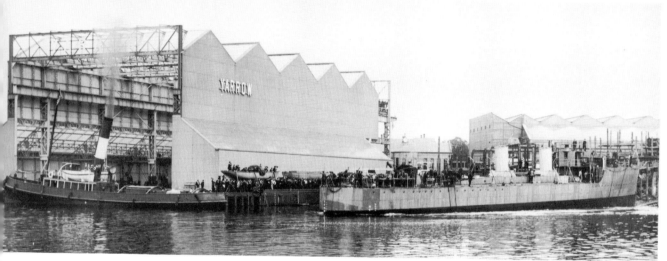

Above *Launch of Brazilian torpedo boat destroyer* Para *from Yarrow's Scotstoun Shipyard on July 14 1908 (Yarrow Shipbuilders Ltd).*

Left *The launch of HMAS* Warrego *at the Government Dockyard, Cockatoo Island, Sydney, New South Wales, on April 4 1911. The Warrego was built at the Fairfield Shipyard, Govan knocked down and delivered to Cockatoo Island for re-erection and launching. As the Royal Australian Navy was created in 1911, the Warrego is of special importance in their story (Vickers Cockatoo Dockyard Pty Ltd, Sydney, NSW).*

missile destroyers, 75 destroyers, two frigates and a host of lesser but equally interesting craft all built between 1878 and the 1960s.

One most interesting warship contract was placed in 1909 by the Australian Commonwealth Government for three destroyers. The first, *Yarra*, was built at Dumbarton, the second, *Parramatta*, at Fairfield, Govan, and the third, *Warrego*, was erected and bolted up at Govan, then dismantled and shipped to Australia for re-erection at Cockatoo Island Dockyard, Sydney in New South Wales. The Royal Australian Navy had been created on July 10 1911 and as the *Warrego* was launched on April 4 1911 and commissioned on June 1 1912, she can claim a special place in the annals of the new Navy.

The Great War was to alter for all time the pattern of life on our islands. When judged long term, the effect on the River Clyde was equally dramatic and, unquestionably, had a direct bearing on the contraction of British shipbuilding when compared with world output over the next 60 years. The short term effect of the wave of patriotism was two-fold; a gearing of the yards to meet the demands of war with conversion work, ship repair and naval work looming large in the plans of shipbuilders, and then the loss from the shipyards of experienced managers and skilled men who were called to serve in their territorial and reserve battalions.

In 1914 the Royal Navy ordered their ships from both the Royal Dockyards and from approved privately owned shipyards. This system was satisfactory in that the dockyards were assured of a steady flow of similar work and maintained their tradition of service by remaining efficient shipbuilders and at all times keeping a skilled workforce employed and available for use in emergencies. The private yards in the higher quality bracket enjoyed the benefit of Admiralty vessels being ordered when work loads were uneven or slack, giving them a work cushion and the ability to maintain a relatively unchanging number of men in their labour force. Defence contracts are often tighter and more closely monitored than appear to the outsider and, at times, create problems by drawing off labour from lucrative short-term merchant work and by introducing a double standard of workmanship in the shipyard. Overall, it is apparent that shipyards with mixed naval and merchant output on the Clyde have done well financially during most of the 20th century.

The gearing of the yards to meet war requirements meant, in many cases, the appreciation that the style of work would alter, that the proportions of different trades in the workforce would change and that unprecedented demands for specialised services would suddenly appear. Early on, many passenger liners were brought in for conversion to armed merchant cruiser, a process demanding detailed planning if speed were to be obtained. Such conversions often involved removing accommodation, the fitting of guns and appropriate stiffening, the introduction of additional bunkers and the shipping and securing of hundreds of tons of ballast. As the war proceeded, the pattern on the river settled with some shipyards like Beardmore's totally committed to defence contracts, while others like Charles Connell concentrating almost exclusively on the equally vital role of building vast numbers of easily produced and inexpensive cargo vessels. In this area D & W Henderson were lead yard for the War Standard A and B cargo ship designs which were notable for their efficiency and cheapness, but notorious for their plainness which verged on the inelegant.

The requirements for certain outfit trades became less in shipbuilding during the hostilities, but other opportunities for these trades usually presented themselves. William Bow, the individualistic Paisley shipbuilder, was instrumental in the setting up of a production facility, using joiners and others, for artificial arms and legs for injured servicemen. Many yards had arrangements whereby they made aircraft parts and in some cases were involved in munitions work. As the war progressed new types of ships were produced like X-lighters for troop landing, shallow draft hospital ships and specialised tugs, many of these designs exhibiting originality stemming from the working together of the Director of Naval Construction's staff and the ship designers of the country's merchant shipyards.

The tragedy for the shipyards, as for many other national enterprises, was the short and long term loss of manpower. Skilled men and able administrators left to fight in France and Mesopotamia, many never to return, and few to return in time to assist the industry in its vital role. William McMillan, the chairman and managing director of Archibald McMillan & Son Ltd of Dumbarton, fell while serving with the Argyll and Sutherland Highlanders in France, James Lithgow served with the Gunners before being recalled for more appropriate duties at national level with regard to ship production, and they were accompanied by members of almost every

Clyde shipbuilding family irrespective of role including directors, draughtsmen, tradesmen and helpers. For the experienced owner and director, many of whom were officers in the reserve, the decision to serve the colours must have been taken with great difficulty knowing that their friends already had responded to the call of Lord Kitchener, but also knowing that their shipyard, employees' families and localities required steady and unflinching management in times of stress. In the Second World War this decision was not left open to many as shipbuilding was designated a reserved occupation. However, the memorials and rolls of honour of many a Clyde shipyard carry the names of men lost overseas, mostly serving with the regiments which recruit traditionally in the West of Scotland—the Royal Scots Fusiliers, the Cameronians, the Highland Light Infantry and the Argyll and Sutherland Highlanders.

In the long term the loss was even greater. As the industry struggled in the inter-war depression it did so with an older and an ageing administration. It suffered also from lack of recruitment as many families were reluctant to encourage their more able youngsters to make a career in an industry with so many 'hungers and bursts'.

Submarines

Over a period of 70 years six Clyde shipyards have built about 78 submarines for service in the Royal and Commonwealth Navies. This is not a large number and pales into insignificance when compared with the hundreds which have been produced since the beginning of the century by Vickers of Barrow-in-Furness. However, submarine construction, particularly by Scotts of Greenock was almost continuous from 1912 to 1978, and ensured that a specialist submarine building capability with its strict regulations and conventions, remained alive on the Clyde through two wars. The numbers of submarine launched on the river are believed to be: Scotts' of Greenock, 44; Wm Beardmore, 15; Fairfield S & E Co, 10; Wm Denny & Bros, 5; John Brown & Co, 3; Yarrow & Co, 1. Several further vessels were cancelled around 1918 and 1919 and, of those built, a few were towed away for completion in the Royal Dockyards, principally Devonport.

The first submarine ordered in Scotland was *S1*, laid down at Greenock in 1912 and launched in February 1914. Scotts' had worked hard to obtain this business, having arranged a sole licence from the Fiat Company of Spezia to construct submarines of Italian design for both the UK and all British possessions. The Admiralty had ordered all previous submarines (around 80) from either Vickers or the Royal Dockyard at Chatham and had adopted a naming system of *A, B, C, D* and *E* classes prior to *S1*—the S presumably stood for 'Scotts''. Scotts' were granted considerable freedom in the design and building, as the Admiralty believed that there would be some advantage in comparing the work of a renowned shipbuilder, yet untried in submersible work, with the traditional approach of the more experienced submarine shipyards. The *S1* was small, being 148 ft 1½ ins (45.14 m) in length and displacing 324 tons submerged. Her speed on the surface was 13.25 knots driven by twin Scott-Fiat 2 stroke diesel engines and 8.5 knots submerged using battery powered electric motors. *S1* was followed by orders for two further vessels of the class and all three were sold to the Italian Navy in 1915 and saw little service with the British Forces. The overall cost of all three was around £200,000.

In August 1913 the Navy placed a fourth order with Scotts' for a new submarine named *Swordfish*. This new ship was only the second submarine in the Royal Navy with a traditional ship's name and was the first British steam-driven submarine. She had two propellers each powered by a single set of Parsons turbines running at 3,500 rpm and geared to reduce to a shaft speed of 530. Again her operational experience was short, but she increased submarine surface speed of 17 knots and paved the way for the steam 'K' Class which were to have a surface speed of 24 knots, well in excess of the then required 20 knots for vessels accompanying the British Fleet.

Of the 17 'K' Class submarines, four were built on the Clyde, *K13* and *K14* at Fairfield, *K15* at Scotts' and *K16* at Beardmore's in Dalmuir. These new ships were large being 339 ft (103.3 m) long and displacing 2,566 tons submerged. By the beginning of the First World War both Fairfield and Beardmore's had successfully built four 'E' Class submarines each and were adjudged suitable for being designated 'K' Class builders. However, the construction of these vessels was to tax the ingenuity and resources of the three companies.

The new submarines were impressive, indeed aggressive in appearance, and were comparable in size and almost in speed with current European destroyers. The main machinery, driving two screws, was two sets of Brown-Curtis steam turbines using steam generated by two oil-fired Yarrow type boilers. Submerged the shafts were driven by four 360 bhp electrical motors, and as an innovation an 800 hp diesel engine was fitted, that in turn drove a dynamo to supply motive power for the short period after surfacing when the engineers were raising steam.

The first of the Clyde-built *K* ships, *K13*, left the Govan shipyard at Fairfield on January 29 1916 manned by a naval crew and several shipyard representatives, with a view to formal handover on completion of trials. During her third dive in the Gareloch the boiler room flooded and *K13* sank out of control in nearly 20 m of water. Four boiler room ventilators had been left open and, as a result, the ship was incapable of raising herself by the normal means. Thirty-one naval personnel and civilians died, 29 trapped at the aft end and two in an attempted escape from the engine room hatch. Forty-eight others were imprisoned in the fore end for two and a half dreadful days in cold dark and filthy conditions as attempts were made to pump air to the stricken ship and by this means elevate her bows to the surface. During this period the Captain of *K14*, who was aboard as an observer, attempted to go to the surface and was lost, and *K13*'s Commanding Officer was accidentally swept up during the attempt but saved.

Ultimately with hawsers from surrounding ships supporting the submarine her bows were raised and a hole was cut in her pressure shell and the 46 remaining survivors pulled clear. Among them was the Fairfield naval architect Professor Percy Hillhouse who, according to his fellows aboard, worked quietly with his slide rule and along with William Wallace, a director of Brown Brothers of Edinburgh, assisted the second in command in shutting all watertight doors before making their escape. *K13* went back to Govan for refit and ultimately joined the fleet as *K22*. Fairfield, in all, built only ten submarines and after the war their submarine berth and west yard were closed.

Denny of Dumbarton built five during the First World War, the last of the group *L54* being towed away to Devonport for ultimate completion in 1924. John Brown built three and Yarrows only one, the *E27*, completed in August 1917. It is surprising that these three companies with their tradition of innovative building and high class naval construction did not produce more than nine vessels of this type.

William Beardmore & Co Ltd built 15, the last

two being HMS *Olympus* and HMS *Orpheus* both commissioned in 1930 and among the last ships to be launched at Dalmuir. *Olympus* and her sister were both to be lost in the Mediterranean in the Second World War.

With the closure of Beardmore's, submarine building effectively was carried out at four establishments: Scotts' on the Clyde, Vickers at Barrow, Cammell Laird of Birkenhead and Chatham Dockyard. About 25 years after the Second World War, Cammell Laird discontinued submarine construction, and in 1970 the policy decision was effected to cease the centuries long tradition of building in the Royal Dockyards—the last dockyard ship was the Portsmouth-built 'Leander' Class frigate HMS *Scylla*. This left Vickers and Scotts' sharing conventional submarine work and with Vickers responsible for all nuclear submarines.

The policy of increasing the British nuclear fleet submarine strength and the fact that the conventional 'Oberon' and 'Porpoise' Classes are efficient and adequate for our long-term needs has left Scotts' without submarine construction work for some years, and indeed, only refit work in very recent times. This is an unfortunate turn of events as it could lead to the unhealthy situation of only one submarine shipyard in the UK, and to the loss of submarine expertise on the Clyde, the very river which has the main Royal Naval nuclear base of Faslane and the United States nuclear base at Holy Loch.

*   *   *

The inter-war years were devastating for many parts of the United Kingdom but nowhere more than in the traditional steel and shipbuilding districts. The Washington Treaty and the run down in defence spending brought naval shipbuilding to a virtual standstill. The few fine ships built for the Royal Navy assumed a significance which reflected more their rarity value than their technical development. Designed and ordered during the Great War, the last great vessel to be completed for the Royal Navy before the moratorium on building commenced was the battlecruiser *Hood*. Launched in August 1918 at Clydebank HMS *Hood* was undoubtedly the greatest naval ship to be delivered from the Clyde between the two wars and, in the eyes of many, was amongst the four or five finest vessels ever to be commissioned into the Senior Service. Despite her sad end she was almost the ultimate in the big gun capital ship, being

well protected, heavily armed with a wide diversity of guns including eight of 15 ins and was capable of over 30 knots. This awesome vessel was a milestone also in naval engineering and was driven at top speed by four propellers with a massive total shaft horse-power of 144,000 (or 107,490 kw). Each shaft had two turbines, first a high pressure unit exhausting to a low pressure unit both coupled to a gearbox, but as a special embellishment had cruising turbines so designed that on full power they could drive the *Hood* at nearly half speed using only 15 per cent of normal steam consumption—a salutory lesson regarding the costliness of speed at sea.

From the delivery of HMS *Hood* through till the delivery of the 'King George V' Class at the beginning of the Second World War, only two battle-ships joined the British fleet—the *Nelson* and the *Rodney*, both products of English yards and both

Above *HMS* Hood (John Smith Photographic Unit, UIE Clydebank).

severely cut down as fighting ships followed the International Naval Treaties. However, the greatest body blow to Scotland came in 1922 when the 1921 battlecruiser programme of four 'super *Hoods*' was cancelled of which three had been placed on the Clyde one each at Beardmore's, Fairfield and John Brown's. This devastating cancellation was one of the many misfortunes which led to the ultimate closure of Dalmuir. In 1939 four further battleships

Below *HM Battleship* Vanguard *leaves her Clydebank birthplace on a spring high tide for her journey to the open Firth of Clyde in 1946* (John Smith Photographic Unit, UIE Clydebank).

Above *One of the handsome prewar Tribal Class destroyers, HMS* Gurkha, *slips down the Clyde for Contractor's Sea Trials in 1938. Within 18 months this fine Fairfield ship was lost in the North Sea as a result of enemy action. The Tribal Class were built in various shipyards and were notable for their high speed—the Denny-built* Ashanti *and* Bedouin *both achieved well over 37 knots on light displacement trials.*

Right and Below right *Spectacular war damage to the Anglo-Saxon motor tanker* Alexia *drydocked for repair by Barclay, Curle & Co Ltd* (W. Ralston Ltd Collection in Strathclyde Regional Archives).

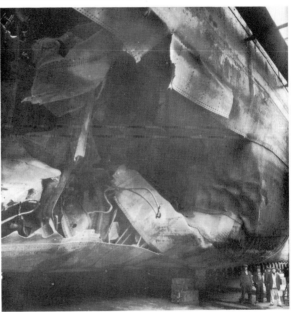

were ordered of about 40,000 tons displacement and in general similar to the 'King George V' Class. Two of these ships (to be designated 'Lion' Class) were ordered again at Fairfield and Clydebank and again shortly after the outbreak of war were cancelled, but this time the work was replaced by orders with a shorter building time span that could more usefully be employed in the war.

The Clyde were to build three more battleships, the *Duke of York* a product of Brown's and the Fairfield-built *Howe*, both of which served actively during the war and then the last British battleship, HMS *Vanguard*, which slid down the ways at John Brown's on St Andrew's Day 1944. This 51,000 tons displacement ship never fired a shot in anger and was broken up less than 15 years after her commissioning.

Reverting to the inter-war years there was a gradual improvement of shipbuilding orders from 1930 with a growing number of contracts from the Admiralty. Destroyers and small vessels were ordered and later the river was asked to build three of the outstanding 'Southampton' Class cruisers and HMS *Southampton*, HMS *Glasgow* and HMS *Liverpool* were all delivered in time for the war.

The experiences of the Great War may have helped Clyde shipbuilders in their planning for conflict once war seemed to be inevitable from 1936 onwards. However, no person could have foreseen the vital role that the river was to play from 1939 to 1945 as the key sea port of the United Kingdom. In six years Clyde Pilots moved 500 million tons of shipping on the river, the tug fleet was greatly augmented, a barrage boom fitted across the river and a small armada of auxiliary ships assembled including water barges, fuel tankers, lighters for coaling and former pleasure steamers for passenger tenders at the Tail of the Bank. The constant arrival and departure of troopships, warships and freighters placed considerable strain on all services including water, gas, electricity and railway transport and the River Authority already coping with air raid damage had to contend with a dramatic turnover in shipping whilst arranging berths for coaling, loading explosives, quarantine and for lay-by after serious war damage. Incidents occurred like the bomb landing on HM Cruiser *Sussex* while in Yorkhill Basin in September 1940. As fire spread through the ship the decision was taken to scuttle her, thereby preventing her magazines from exploding in a densely populated part of the city.

The shipyards moved into top gear and in six years produced nearly 2,000 new ships, carried out about 600 major conversions and countless thousands of drydockings, voyage repairs and minor war damage repairs. Despite heavy bombing in Glasgow and massive damage to the burgh of Clydebank where only seven houses were undamaged, work continued in the shipyards. Charles Oakley recounts that in Clydebank 55,000 people had to leave the Burgh after the blitz and only 2,000 could remain, and yet despite men and women having to travel up to 50 miles to work, 75 per cent of Clydebank's industrial output was back close to normal within 48 hours of the raids.

During the war several long-closed shipyard sites were re-opened for final fabrication of mass produced hulls like landing craft at Meadowside, Paisley, Old Kilpatrick and other positions. Slowly shipyards had learned that shipbuilding was an industry based on assembly and that steelwork fabrication, whether for a marine or land environment was a specialist job. The urgent needs of war greatly assisted this new thinking and, when 700 escort vessels had to be built on top of an existing and agreed construction programme, serious consideration was given to building in an unconventional manner. For the 'Loch' Class frigates (120 in number) and the 'Castle' Class corvettes (80) a revolutionary style was developed.

Firstly about 30 motivated draughtsmen were seconded from shipbuilders all over the UK to a central drawing office in Glasgow and here the plans of the two ship designs were drawn up quickly and in detail. The simplifications anticipated by both the Royal Navy and the shipbuilders were difficult to achieve as operational requirements often conflicted with constructional interests and it was found that each ship required up to 1,300 composite parts of structure. A progress office was set up in Edinburgh and from there orders for large fabricated parts were sent out to engineering companies in all parts of the country. Each unit was carefully jigged and checked for tolerance before going initially to three lead yards: John Brown & Co Ltd, Swan Hunter and Wigham Richardson Ltd of Wallsend-on-Tyne and the Burnt-island Company. As the flow of fabricated units increased more shipyards were involved and each was expected, on top of their current programme, to join up the units, make and launch a watertight structure. As outfitting would have been too great a burden for these yards the steel hulls were towed off to two outfitting bases which had been specially set up—the Dalmuir Basin on the Clyde on the site of Beardmore's long-closed battleship complex, and the Hendon Dock, a non tidal basin in Sunderland at the entrance to the River Wear.

A race developed between the three lead yards and John Brown & Company successfully maintained the Clyde's lead with the production of HMS *Loch Fada*.

The Royal Fleet Review, held at the historic Tail of the Bank Anchorage in 1946, not only recognised the valiant wartime roles of both Royal and Merchant Navies but gave recognition and cheer to tens of thousands who had served the Allied cause by their efforts on Clydeside.

A period of prosperity ensued after the war and the river received its share of destroyers, frigates, submarines and other ships. In the 1950s, with the Russian *Sverdlov* cruiser programme becoming common knowledge, public opinion forced the Government to increase its conventional cruiser strength, and the never completed war-built *Blake* and *Tiger* were sent to Fairfield and Clydebank respectively to be finished and updated. Both these companies had interesting naval work with Brown's obtaining the two most glamorous jobs, the Royal

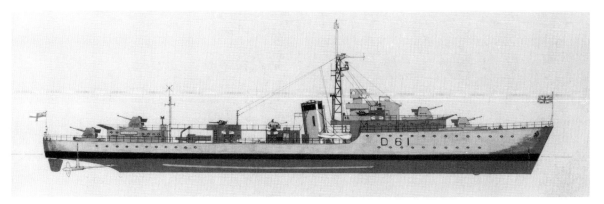

The destroyer HMS Chequers *built by Scotts of Greenock, 1944. HRH Prince Philip, Duke of Edinburgh, served on this ship as navigating officer for a period after the Second World War.*

Yacht *Britannia* and HMS *Intrepid*, an assault ship with stern docking facilities for landing and assault craft.

The last Royal Navy contracts to come from Govan were the 'County' Class destroyers *Fife* and *Antrim*. The latter ship was completed by successors to the old Fairfield Company. The present proprietors of the yard, Govan Shipbuilders, are not serious contenders for this kind of work as they do not mix naval work with specialist freighter production. After 1970 fewer orders were placed in general shipyards and the Admiralty displayed a distinct preference for specialist builders, particularly

in view of the cessation of naval building at the Royal Dockyards. On the Clyde the specialist yard was Yarrow with a long experience of destroyers, frigates, survey vessels, shallow draft and unusual ships of all kinds, including four diesel electric paddle tugs for the Royal Navy in the late 1950s. In this last mentioned contract Yarrow was lead company and builder of four ships in a class of seven designed to have small draft and also low 'air draft' to enable them to work under the overhangs of aircraft carriers.

HMS Implacable, *the third ship to bear the name in the Royal Navy. Completed August 28 1944 by the Fairfield S & E Co Ltd, Govan, this ship of 23,000 tons displacement located the German battleship* Tirpitz *off Tromsö and later served as a prisoner of war evacuation ship in the Far East. Her complement was 2,000 men and over 60 aeroplanes.*

At this juncture it is important to look briefly at the background of Yarrow & Company and to consider the fascinating history that has taken them to their position of supremacy in warship building and design. The story commences in 1865 on the Isle of Dogs almost opposite what is now the Royal Naval College at Greenwich, when Alfred Fernandez Yarrow set up business as an engineer. Working with a Mr Hedley for ten years they built what were for the time quite advanced machines including steam ploughs, steam horseless carriages and ultimately steam launches. The business really prospered once Yarrow freed himself from the partnership and established himself on his own. He built repetitive easily costed jobs including steam launches and finally moved to the Poplar Shipyard in London. Here the company graduated to the two specialist ships that were to make them world famous—the knock down shallow draft ship for tropical use and the torpedo boat destroyer. Their experience, particularly in Africa, quickly made them specialists in lake craft, their pedigree dating from October 1875 when the SS *Ilala* was launched in Lake Nyasa (now Malawi) as a slavery suppression vessel and memorial to David Livingstone, and continued by *Le Stanley* ordered by the indefatigable Welsh-born H.M. Stanley for his explorations of the Congo. Alfred Yarrow was equally assiduous in pleasing the Admiralty and the War Office with, for example, preparing designs for river craft to relieve General Gordon and Khartoum—craft which, had they been requested by the authorities in time, might have changed the course of one chapter of our history.

While being a product of the Thames it is nevertheless essential to record the background to the development of the torpedo boat and the torpedo boat destroyer. The origins of the torpedo and of torpedo warfare are in the American Civil War, and within a short space of time all the European powers were considering the best means of using small fast ships with spar torpedoes, that is, explosive charges on the end of poles sticking well beyond the attacker's bows. Much effort was expended in perfecting torpedoes and in considering means of defence against torpedo attack. By the late 1870s the self-propelled Whitehead Torpedo had been developed to the extent that it could be fired with fair accuracy over a distance of several hundred metres. This development changed the scene again and Yarrow & Co, which had been making a good living from high speed steam launches adapted for spar torpedoes, suddenly realised that there was a market for a larger and equally fast torpedo launching craft and in 1878 launched what was to become *Torpedo Boat No 14* for the Royal Navy. From this beginning Yarrow & Co were to develop a great tradition of building for the Navy.

To counteract the torpedo boat menace, larger and more heavily armed vessels named torpedo boat gunboats were produced and very quickly they were superseded by torpedo boat destroyers, the first in the world being HMS *Havock* and HMS *Hornet* from Yarrow and HMS *Daring* and HMS *Decoy* from Thornycroft. The Yarrow ships on a displacement of about 240 tons steamed at 26.1 and 27.3 knots and overnight the shipyard moved from being a successful supplier of small, fast naval ships to a world recognised designer, builder and indeed innovator of modern warships. By 1911 Yarrow had built several important torpedo boat destroyers for Japan, Russia and other countries and among them the *Sokol*, a flush-decked four-funnelled destroyer for the Russians, which was memorable for being the first ship to achieve 30 knots, and for having weight saving high tensile steel used in her hull construction. In 1911 HMS *Lurcher* was built, the precursor of modern destroyer design with what was to become traditional—the raised fo'c's'le—a speed of 35 knots and capability of working in the worst conditions anticipated around the British coasts. By 1911 Yarrow was in Glasgow and *Lurcher* was Clyde-built.

Shortly after the turn of the century Alfred Yarrow began to consider the situation in which his yard found itself. Business was good, excellent in fact, but the Thames was in obvious decline and more serious the skilled labour force in the London area was contracting. He let it be known that he wished to move his business to another site in the British Isles, and within a short space of time received in all four hundred invitations or enquiries from authorities all over including Dundee, Hull, Manchester and Newcastle. He selected Scotstoun on the north bank of the Clyde which, in 1906, was outwith the Glasgow boundary and had a completely rural setting. The decision to come to Glasgow was undoubtedly influenced by the excellent reputation the Clyde enjoyed internationally, the good labour force, the professional back up of an organised employers association and the professional standards largely attributable to the University and several

The Yarrow fitting out basin under construction in 1907 with the Clyde Navigation Trust bucket dredger *Craigiehall at work* (Yarrow Shipbuilders Ltd).

outstanding shipbuilders. However, equal to all of these must have been the knowledge that on the Firth of Clyde there was an excellent measured mile in deep water at Skelmorlie which had sheltered conditions. This was of especial importance at the time as the efficacy of testing ships in shallow water was coming under close scrutiny. A celebrated case brought the matter to the attention of naval architects in the 1909 Transactions of the Institution of Naval Architects. The destroyer HMS *Cossack* was tested on the measured mile off the Maplin Sands on the Thames and, again, in similar conditions but much deeper water off Skelmorlie on

the Clyde. It was found that at 32 knots the total shaft horse power while running in water 7½ fathoms deep was 86,000 while that for running off Skelmorlie in 40 fathoms it was 105,000. This shallow water effect was partly unpredictable but did vary with depth of water, trim of the ship and so on. To be sure of accurate and consistent figures all shipbuilders were forced to prove their fast ships in the deepest channels possible and only the Clyde offered this facility.

The move north was relatively uneventful, the office staff transferred in their entirety to Glasgow and a new yard was laid on the Scotstoun fields. The

Brazilian torpedo boat destroyers under construction at Yarrow's Scotstoun Shipyard in July 1908. The light construction is clearly visible in this photograph (Yarrow Shipbuilders Ltd).

yard has seldom been idle and the order book quite diversified. Since coming north the total number of ships built is approaching 400 of which 40 per cent have been for the Royal Navy, 40 per cent for export and 20 per cent for British commercial companies. In addition the company built up a marine and land boiler business, and at different times over the years had associated companies and shipyards in Yugoslavia, Canada and South Africa.

Since the Second World War Scotstoun has been a hive of activity with two yard extensions taking in the Blythswood shipyard and the Barclay Curle Elderslie drydocks. A covered facility at Elderslie has been set up for the manufacture of glass reinforced plastic mine counter measure vessels or MCMV's.

The post-war frigate programme in which Yarrow and other Clyde shipbuilders have been deeply involved was the result of design studies in 1944 for what was described as a '25-knot escort sloop' largely with the North Atlantic in mind. From these initial studies there has been a build up of successive designs for anti-aircraft and anti-submarine work, and ultimately general purpose ships designed for all round offensive and defensive work geared to the requirements of the large British contribution to NATO.

The Yarrow contribution has included ships of the 'Rothesay' and 'Leander' Classes and more recently Type 21 and Type 22 frigates included among the former being HMS *Ardent* lost in the Falklands campaign.

The frigate HMS *Ashanti* was delivered in 1962 as lead ship in the 'Tribal' Class and broke new ground by being a single-screw vessel with alternative means of power, a gas turbine and a steam turbine each coupled to a gearbox. This was the first large gas turbine ship in the fleet and, while it was not appreciated at the time, was the first move in weaning the Navy away from the steam turbine whose monopolistic grip had built up over nearly 50 years. The engine room of *Ashanti* was described officially as Combined Steam and Gas, COSAG for short, and variations on this take us through to the present day COGAG (Combined Gas and Gas) where two sets of gas turbines are fitted in warships, one set for economical cruising and the other for high speed requirements.

The Type 22 frigates were led by HMS *Broadsword* and are twin-screw gas turbine ships, again with cruising gas turbines for economical 'steaming'. The Type 22s are only 131 m in length, displace 3,500 tons but can operate at over 30 knots carrying Exocet and Sea Wolf Missiles. The Falklands conflict reinforced the argued case that warships must have a full range of armament, and this is to be rectified in *Broadsword* and her sisters by the retro-fitting of conventional guns.

The current programme of advanced warship-building marks total commitment by Yarrow Shipbuilders Ltd—as the yard has become known since nationalisation. The varied building of post-war years including RNLI lifeboats, knock down ferries for African Lakes and stern trawlers has ended and the company continues as a world name in one specialised field.

On nationalisation Yarrow Shipbuilders Ltd and Yarrow (Training) Ltd passed into public ownership but the original holding company, Yarrow & Co Ltd, remained outwith British Shipbuilders. Their main asset is Y-ARD Ltd a consultancy company with an international name in defence, engineering and advanced naval architecture studies. Starting as a research group on high pressure steam in the late 1940s the project work has so developed that it is a company in its own right employing several hundred people in their central Glasgow office block. The scope of work carried out is wide and like similar groups has offshore engineering as an ever increasing component.

Above *The Type 21 Class frigate HMS* Ardent *photographed off Arran and the Holy Island shortly after being handed over to the Royal Navy by Yarrow Shipbuilders in 1977. Powered by Rolls Royce gas turbines, this class of frigate has all round armament including, Exocet missiles, Seacat missiles, automatic rapid fire 4.5-in gun, anti-submarine torpedo tubes and a helicopter. HMS* Ardent *was lost in the South Atlantic during the Falklands campaign.* (Yarrow Shipbuilders Ltd).

Below *The Yarrow Shipyard Complex looking upstream towards Glasgow centre. First the covered GRP building berths, the 70,000-tonne drydock, the covered drydock for outfitting work, the frigate drydock complete with sonar pits and two Type 22 frigates on the River Wall. Beyond is the main yard, part of which was taken over from the Blythswood Company. The drydocks were formerly those of Barclay, Curle & Co and came to Yarrow's in 1974* (Yarrow Shipbuilders Ltd).

Chapter 15

The Clydebank story

Despite the fact that John Brown's, Clydebank, is a household name, few people realise that Brown's history as a shipyard is relatively short, a mere 69 years compared with longevitous companies like Scott's of Greenock, Hall's of Aberdeen or Stephen's of Linthouse. Similarly it is little known that the name of the Burgh of Clydebank came to that region of Clydeside only a hundred years ago as the result of a move by the original Clyde Bank Shipyard of the Thomson brothers.

The story began in 1847 at Finnieston Street, Glasgow, when two brothers, James and George Thomson, secured ground and set up an engine and boiler works. They were well trained and started their business at a time when engineering had become well established on Clydeside and there was a steady expansion in demand for engineering goods and services. Their enterprise was rewarded and in three years, they were hunting for a new site on which to expand their business and to commence shipbuilding. In 1850 they opened a new establishment at Govan (where the dry docks are now situated) and this move presumably influenced their choice of name for the new works—the Clyde Bank Shipyard.

The life story of the two brothers is well documented and is typical of men of that period. James, the oldest of three brothers, served an apprenticeship as a joiner in Glasgow and, in 1826, joined Robert Napier as a patternmaker. This is a skilled and demanding occupation involving, among other things, the manufacture of timber moulds for iron and metal casting. For good consistent results with the minimum of finishing work to the casting, thoughtfulness and resource is required, coupled with a knowledge of wood, and an understanding of the behaviour of metal. James must have displayed these and other qualities as he rose to be foreman,

and finally assistant manager working under another Napier man, David Elder. George Thomson served an apprenticeship, followed by time at sea and he, too, ultimately joined Napier as a foreman fitter.

While not within the compass of this story it is of significance that a third brother, Robert Thomson, also had a similar training, spent time at sea as an engineer before coming ashore to become the first superintendent engineer of the Cunard Line. Little can the three brothers have realised that the paths of their successors were to cross many times and that jointly the two companies were to build and run revolutionary and famous ships like *Servia* of 1881, *Carmania* of 1905, *Lusitania* launched in 1906, the *Aquitania* of 1913 and the world famous ships *Queen Mary*, *Queen Elizabeth* and *Queen Elizabeth 2*.

In a span of 21 years, Thomson's built over 120 ships at the Govan yard. As success breeds success, so the affairs of the firm prospered, a regular clientele was established and above all a name for high engineering standards earned. Undoubtedly the presence next door of their former employer, Robert Napier, must have been both an inspiration and a challenge to the two men. Govan was the undisputed centre for experimentation, and the work of Napier and his deputies focused the attention of the Press on the ancient burgh. With the building of HMS *Black Prince* and PS *Persia* at Napier's and with the experimental work of David Kirkaldy into the tensile strength of iron and steel, any shipyard in the vicinity was assured of a knowledgeable and versatile workforce.

Every student of Clydeside is aware of the building of three paddle steamers by J. & G. Thomson each with the name *Iona*, and all for David Hutchison one of the forerunners of today's Caledonian-MacBrayne Ltd. The first in 1855 was sold in 1862 to the

The first Atlantic passenger liner with twin screws—the City of New York *built by J & G Thomson of Clydebank in 1888 for the Inman Line (John Smith Photographic Unit, UIE Clydebank).*

Confederate States for blockade running, and while running unlit from the Clyde to escape detection by Federal agents, was run down accidentally and sunk off Gourock. A replacement was built in 1863 and, after a season on the Clyde, had her saloons stripped off and was prepared for the trans-Atlantic voyage— no mean feat for a slim paddler only 244 ft (74 m) long and 25 ft (7.6 m) broad. After strengthening and storing she sailed for Ireland for final coaling

Built by John Brown of Clydebank, the Empress of Britain *was the embodiment of Canadian Pacific's plan to make the St Lawrence-UK route fashionable from 1931. This fast and remarkable ship sank in October 1940 after being bombed and then torpedoed (John Smith Photographic Unit, UIE Clydebank).*

and, after crew trouble which could not have been unexpected in a ship in such a situation, she sailed. Racking and working of the hull made her take water, and after her crew had been taken off by a sailing pilot cutter, she sank off Lundy Island. The third, built in 1864, became part of the Clyde steamer legend serving on the Clyde, around Oban and the inner Hebrides until 1935, and at the time of her breaking up was an almost perfect example of a classical Victorian passenger paddle steamer. She retained the saloons stripped of her predecessor, as these had been purchased to great advantage by Hutcheson's!

It must have been with reluctance that J. & G. Thomson heard that the Clyde Navigation Trust wished to take over their yard at Govan for the construction of No 1 Drydock. The acquisition was compulsory under the 11th Act of Parliament for the Improvement of the River Clyde, but with hindsight was to have the most beneficial effect on both the company and the river as a whole. In many parts of Britain similar acts, moved shipyards, as in Liverpool,

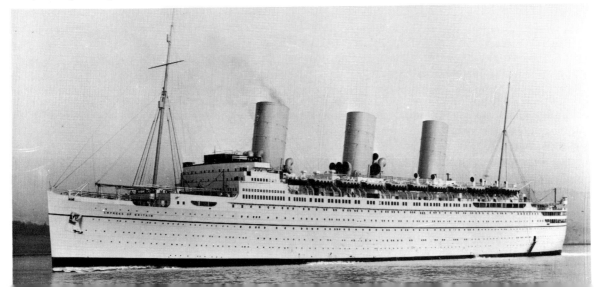

out from the centres of population while here the move was to a new yard on a green field site and to a stretch of water at the confluence of the Cart and the Clyde that allowed the very largest of ships to be built and launched safely.

George Thomson's sons James Rodger and George Paul were now in charge of the business, James senior having retired in 1864 and their father having died in 1866. Despite a family proclivity at that time for disagreement and quarrelling, they acted decisively, and co-operating with the Clyde Trustees, opened a new yard on the North Bank well away from Govan and continued their business during the time of upheaval and removal. The new Clydebank yard had room for expansion and it had water, the only initial problem was the redeployment of their manpower. This was overcome by the rapid building of tenements in the new area and by maintaining direct daily contact with Govan by their own iron paddle steamer *Vulcan* which had been built some years earlier by Robert Napier. By now logistics were a severe problem with more than 1,500 people employed.

Despite the ups and downs of the shipbuilding market, the company continued with a wide and varied order book. It is surprising that many vessels were not large, and not utilising the space now available. Rather they reflected the Thomson's desire to build ships with a high technical input, such as smaller passenger and cargo vessels, Clyde steamers like PS *Glen Sannox* and PS *Columba* and, in the 1870s, they went into the Admiralty market initially with gunboats and later torpedo boat destroyers and then slowly moving up the scale to cruisers and ultimately battleships.

One of the very direct advantages of the Clydebank site was the opportunity to lay out the yard properly and to set up good engine building facilities, which throughout the history of the company had a large measure of independence, and in fact continues today as John Brown Engineering Ltd, although with no direct marine engineering outlets.

In 1881 the Cunard Line were to take delivery of an unusual ship, the single-screw steamer *Servia*, with a length of 515 ft (157 m) and a breadth of 52 ft (15.8 m) giving the then fashionable 10:1 ratio for length to beam. Apart from the *Great Eastern*, the *Servia* was the largest ship in the world and was Cunard's first experience of using steel for construction. The machinery was a complex compound system, and alone it weighed 1,800 tons

or 10 per cent of the ship's displacement, but drove the ship at 17 knots with propeller revolutions at the low but efficient rate of 53 rpm. The *Servia* can also be remembered as one of the first ships to have automatic closing watertight doors in the bulkheads. Despite Cunard going to Fairfield for *Umbria* and *Etruria* they stayed loyal to Clydebank, as did White Star to Belfast and the Inman Line to Barrow-in-Furness. As a matter of interest, the fashion for long narrow ships quickly ended as the benefits in stability, cost and reduced power for broader vessels became apparent.

In 1890 the company became incorporated under the Limited Liability Act, and the shareholding became more diversified. This in turn led in 1897 to a change of title to the Clydebank Engineering & Shipbuilding Co Ltd. For just two years the shipyard operated with the name which was supposed to reflect an overall change in the balance of ownership, and in this period turned out well over 30 ships including the TSS *Moskva* for the Russian Volunteer Fleet and 20 barges for the same country.

In 1899 the company acquired the name John Brown & Co Ltd, the controlling organisation in Sheffield. John Brown's was one of Britain's main suppliers of armour plating, and to ensure an outlet for their product had looked at suitable shipyards to purchase, including Earle's of Hull and finally at the Clydebank yard. In 1899 they acquired the majority shareholding and a new and English name came to Clydeside. The situation and the size of the Clydebank yard was fortunate as their main rivals in the armour plating world, Messrs Vickers and Messrs Cammell had already obtained large yards in England in which their plating was used. Despite the change of name and of control, the Clydebank shipyard retained a remarkable degree of autonomy in arranging their affairs. It is interesting to note that John Brown & Co Ltd of Sheffield obtained a substantial part of the equity of the Belfast shipyard of Harland & Wolff Ltd around that time but never became involved in their day to day affairs.

Of John Brown himself, we know that he was a former Sheffield apprentice steel merchant who set up his own business at the Atlas Works in 1856. Through shrewd business arrangements with people like Henry Bessemer his career was assured and once on a firm base he then moved into armour plating to the extent that in 1867, a mere 11 years after setting up business, he had contracts for the armour of 75 per cent of all UK built ironclads. Ultimately the control passed from John Brown to others, but to this day in various engineering activities the name continues.

It is difficult to describe in simple form the output and strength of the great Clydebank yard from 1899 to its merger with UCS in 1968. A procession of close on 400 of the world's largest merchantmen and mightiest warships were to be launched across the Clyde and into the Cart, and after outfitting make their way down the Clyde. These included the battleships *Australia*, *Barham*, *Duke of York* and others, the battlecruiser *Hood* and the last battleship for the Royal Navy, HMS *Vanguard*, which made its way down river in 1946 once hostilities were over.

Among the superb merchantmen were the trans-Atlantic liners *Aquitania* and *Empress of Britain*, the Cape mail liner *Transvaal Castle*, the Swedish Amerika *Kungsholm*, the four Cunard sisters *Saxonia*, *Ivernia*, *Carinthia* and *Sylvania* of the 1950s, each with their unmistakable dome topped funnels from which the last Glasgow tramcars took the name 'Cunarders'.

Two interesting naval orders after the Second World War were the Royal Yacht *Britannia* and the assault ship *Intrepid* which, when nearly 20 years old, sailed with the Falklands Task Force. The *Intrepid* has a docking system at the rear for handling landing craft and similar vessels, and when built was far ahead of its time. The *Britannia* is by any standards a ship of grace and beauty, her superb lines enhanced by immaculate deep blue topsides set off by a chased gold line. Surely no country has such a fine ceremonial vessel, nor one which has journeyed so far?

Despite the tradition and expertise of building very large ships, John Brown's were faced with mammoth design problems when it came to the launching, outfitting and delivery to the Tail of the Bank of the QSS *Queen Mary*. In 1907 the *Lusitania* had been 760 ft (232 m) long bp, and in fully laden condition displaced 38,170 tons, in 1934 at the launch of the *Queen Mary* they had to contend with a ship nearly 30 per cent longer and displacing at launch 36,700 tons and with a further 1,200 tons of sliding ways and make up. With typical resourcefulness, a 200 in (5 m) model was constructed and launched into a part of the shipyard model tank in conditions closely simulating the Clyde. The naval architect of the shipyard, James McNeill (later Dr McNeill and later again Sir James), created an equation to represent the motion of the ship at launch and from this he predicted the ship would travel 1,194 ft after it was launched—in fact the vessel travelled 1,196 ft. The launch was later described by Professor Hillhouse in the following words; 'I can honestly and enthusiastically say that never in my life have I seen a more perfect or a more beautiful launch.' As Hillhouse, in addition to his academic duties at Glasgow University, was naval architect to the great rival shipyard Fairfield, there can be no greater praise!

For this launch the Clyde Trust dredged around the shipyard and widened the Clyde at the entrance to the Cart. Steel columns which had been used to strengthen the hull were taken out and placed round the stern of the *Queen Mary* in order that a protective barrage could be fitted to ensure no ship collided with her stern sticking out into the fairway. The river was widened by rockbreakers and dredgers at Dalmuir and the channel re-aligned for the great ship to make her progress to the sea.

Similar arrangements were made for the QSS *Queen Elizabeth* for HMS *Vanguard* and for TSS *Queen Elizabeth 2*. The *Vanguard* with a draft of 32 ft 5 ins (9.9 m) went down river on May 2 1946, steaming with several tugs at 4 mph to Dunglass and at 8 mph thereafter taking 146 carefully planned minutes to cover the river west of Clydebank passing shallows and narrow parts at the optimum moment on the high spring tide.

Mention must be made of the engine works at Clydebank. From the outset the Thomson family set up specially designed engine works, and had a clientele of many outside the normal marine field. In 1908 they obtained a license to manufacture the Curtis turbines from Mr Charles G. Curtis of New York; these were a great success and in 1920 were the prime movers in the massive 144,000 shaft hp installation on HMS *Hood*. When negotiations were in progress between Brown's and Curtis, one of the junior American engineers came over, joined the Clydebank staff and in 1938 became managing director. Stephen Pigott retired from the company in 1948 with a knighthood and a DSc from his old university—Columbia NY.

In the 1960s Brown's had a most interesting work output with ships as varied as the *Queen Elizabeth 2* and the bulk carrier *Vennachar*, the Swedish America liner *Kungsholm* and the self-propelled jack-up rig *Offshore Mercury*. During the unhappy period leading up to the integration into Upper Clyde Shipbuilders Ltd and the completion of the great

Above left The quadruple screw turbine liner Queen Mary *which served from 1936 until withdrawn in 1967. This ship represented the very best of the John Brown/Cunard tradition* (John Smith Photographic Unit, UIE Clydebank).

Left Photograph taken early during construction of *QSS* Queen Elizabeth *at Clydebank, 1936* (John Brown & Co Ltd).

Above John Brown's shipyard viewed from the South Bank of the Clyde around 1960 *(John Smith Photographic Unit, UIE Clydebank).*

Below After being named by Her Majesty the Queen, the new liner Queen Elizabeth 2 *enters the River Clyde on September 20 1967* (John Smith Photographic Unit, UIE Clydebank). *Inset* Admission Ticket to John Brown's shipyard for the launch of *TSS* Queen Elizabeth 2 *on September 20 1967* (John Brown Engineering Ltd).

THE CUNARD STEAM-SHIP COMPANY LIMITED
JOHN BROWN & CO. (CLYDEBANK) LIMITED

Launch of
Cunard Liner No. 736
from Clydebank Shipyard
on Wednesday, 20th September, 1967
at 2.30 p.m. *

This card admits **one person**
It is to be shown at Entrance Gate (Cart Street)
and given up on entering South East Enclosure
See back for directions

SOUTH EAST ENCLOSURE
(ENTER BY CART STREET)

* Gates open from 1 p.m. to 1.50 p.m.
Admission by ticket only.
Children under 7 years not admitted.

Cunarder, it seemed that the yard would be unlikely to return to passenger ship building and it would concentrate on either rig building or bulk carrier production. Both views in the event turned out to be true with several bulkers leaving Clydebank in the UCS period, but on the establishment of the Marathon Company at Clydebank in 1972, the policy of concentrating on jack up oil rigs became formalised, building these vessels to the proven design of the parent company in Houston, Texas.

The rigs are built on new berths at Clydebank, some at right angles to the former ones pointing to the Cart. Once the platform of the rig has been constructed, the spuds (or columns) are inserted and the platform winched up on its own spuds. The launch ways are laid under, and when complete the platform is lowered on to the ways and the spuds drawn up safely. After launching, outfitting and testing in the fitting out basin, the rig is towed down river for final trials at the Tail of the Bank. Here the spuds are lengthened, having been retained at a short length owing to the Erskine Bridge.

In 1980, the Marathon Company intimated its desire to withdraw from Clydebank and the French company UIE took over the facility. The workforce was streamlined and many of the former facilities available in the yard rented out to other commercial companies. As a low profile experiment in industrial management the work of UIE Shipbuilding (Scotland) Ltd will be interesting to watch in the years to come.

The exploration jack-up rig Uxmal *leaves the UIE Clydebank Shipyard in July 1981. After being taken to the Tail of the Bank her spuds were lengthened, trials carried out and she was then handed over to* PERMARGO *of Mexico (UIE Shipbuilding (Scotland) Ltd).*

Chapter 16

The ubiquitous diesel and some other engines

Exactly 100 years after the *Comet* had inaugurated steam navigation in Britain, a new ship was delivered by Barclay Curle & Co Ltd of Glasgow to the prestigious East Asiatic Co of Copenhagen. At the beginning of May 1912 a large gathering of shipbuilders, engineers, shipowners and well known people were invited by the builders on a cruise in the Firth of Clyde to view the vessel but, above all, to assess the revolutionary engine built to Danish design and in accordance with the principles established by the German engineer Dr Rudolph Diesel. The ship was the *Jutlandia*, a twin-screw motor vessel of 7,400 tons deadweight built for the Copenhagen-Bangkok mail and passenger route. While being the first large ocean-going motor ship built in Britain she missed by some weeks being the first in the world, that honour going to her sister TSMV *Selandia* launched at

In May 1912, just 100 years after the completion of the PS Comet, *the Clyde produced the first British-built ocean-going motorship. TSMV* Jutlandia *was built by Barclay, Curle & Co Ltd just some weeks after Burmeister & Wain of Copenhagen had built her sister ship* Selandia, *the world's first for the East Asiatic Company of Copenhagen. The* Jutlandia *set a pattern for motorships without funnels, a tradition maintained by the Danes until recent years.* (National Maritime Museum).

Burmeister & Wain's Copenhagen shipyard on November 4 1911.

Serious research into diesel engines commenced in the 1890s with many European companies looking into the possibilities of using oil engines with their theoretical higher thermal efficiency and in marine applications having the added advantage of easy storage of the fuel oil in special tanks or in the double bottom. Two companies led the research, MAN of Augsburg, Germany, and Burmeister & Wain of Copenhagen and, indeed, they have remained closely linked ever since, merging in the early 1980s. Both companies had experimental oil engines and slowly developed their techniques while simultaneously assisting the Russians and others with primitive diesel electric drives for canal and river craft. Around 1910 it was felt the time was ripe for the venture of faith and, with the help of the East Asiatic Co (known in Denmark as ØK), three ships were ordered, two in the home country and one from the Scottish shipyard. During the subsequent trials of *Jutlandia* she attained 12.6 knots on 2,810 ihp and was regarded as a complete success. The *Shipping World* magazine reported that, 'Ordinary Scottish oil was used, the particular quality being Oakbank slate oil of a specific gravity of 0.855'.

Mr James Gilchrist, chairman of Barclay Curle, in

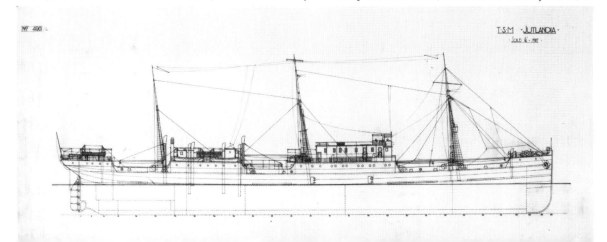

a speech at the time made the following interesting observations:

'When his firm began to build the *Jutlandia* they did so in fear and trembling, but also in full confidence that the Diesel engine, as it had been developed at that time, was one which would commend itself to the public. Since then they had given the engine their most careful attention, and had reached the conclusion that it had come to stay. If his firm had accepted all the offers which had been made to them since they started work on the *Jutlandia*, to build ships propelled by oil engines, they would have required half the Clyde to find room for the vessels. They had made up their minds, however, that they would not take any more orders until they had produced that ship. Now that they have done so, they could recommend to their clients the adoption of the Diesel engine. The *Jutlandia* could carry fuel to take her from the Clyde to South America and back without replenishing. She had no firemen, no coal bunkers, and no boilers, and it was estimated that on each round trip between Copenhagen and Bangkok £2,300 would be saved in the engine-room alone. This was quite apart from the profits to be obtained from the larger amount of additional cargo which she would carry.'

Mr Gilchrist's words were prophetic and were echoed in speeches by persons none other than Winston Churchill, then First Lord of the Admiralty, and Kaiser Wilhelm II of Germany. By 1980 practically no ship under construction had engines other than diesel excepting, of course, very specialist vessels like giant ice breakers with nuclear fuelled steam systems or diesel-electric drive, VLCCs with steam turbines and high speed naval craft with gas turbines.

The success of the *Selandia* and *Jutlandia* was seen in Copenhagen as the opportunity for capitalising first on the research work done and, second, on the

The steel motor coaster Innisshannon *built in 1913 by W. Chalmers & Co Ltd of Rutherglen for the Coasting Motor Shipping Co Ltd of Glasgow. This was one of the first diesel-engined coasters built, and was powered by a 4-cylinder Beardmore engine* (Wotherspoon Collection, Mitchell Library, Glasgow).

Clyde's pre-eminent position in world shipbuilding. As early as March 1912 a new company was incorporated with the head office in Glasgow and known as the Burmeister & Wain Oil Engine Co Ltd. The share capital was £0.55 million, a considerable sum at the time, and they became the British outlet for an organisation called the Atlas Mercantile Co Ltd which was designed to handle all B&Ws license rights worldwide.

This arrangement had barely two years to operate when the First World War commenced. Although several ships had diesel engines fitted and some interesting retrofits were organised, the tendency in Britain was to concentrate on known technology and to win the war. This unhappy situation was further complicated by B&Ws close associate on the Clyde—Barclay Curle & Co—being taken over in 1912 by Messrs Swan Hunter & Wigham Richardson of Wallsend-on-Tyne. The Atlas syndicate was liquidated and Burmeister & Wain decided from then on to issue the rights to manufacture their engines by licensing agreements made in Copenhagen, a situation that exists to this day. The B&W Oil Engine Company was taken over by Harland & Wolff Ltd and UK engines were built at their Glasgow and Belfast works and at such other places in the Commonwealth as they might agree to. For most of the time since then they have had John G. Kincaid & Co of Greenock and the Hongkong & Whampoa Co Ltd (now HUD Ltd) in this capacity.

The original engines were four-stroke single acting

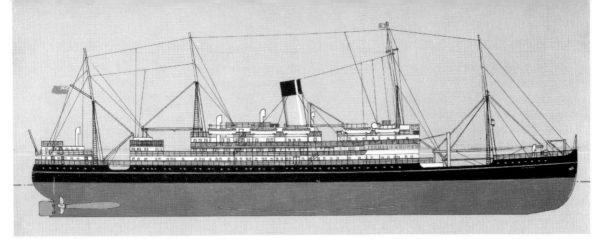

The Bibby Line of Liverpool had some of the most elegant liners sailing from British shores. Between the wars they continued the tradition of having four masts. The TSMV Derbyshire was built for them in 1935 by the Fairfield Company with twin Fairfield-Sulzer diesels, and the ship designed with the UK-India-Burma trade in mind. The press notices created mild amusement in that it was said her funnel was of streamlined design to reduce wind pressure. No mention was made of the additional high masts!

but with 70 years of continuous research and development the current B&W diesel is double acting, two stroke, turbocharged and uses lower quality heavy oil with solid injection. The fuel crises of 1973 and 1978 gave great impetus to integrated ship design and current large freighters have direct driven propellers turning at about 80 rpm, a speed both efficient from the propulsion point of view as well as that of the engine. The diesel engine is by far and away the most efficient and economical prime mover on the market and B&W Diesel claimed at the end of the 1970s that their 90 GB/GBE engine was the first to break the 50 per cent thermal efficiency barrier, far in excess of the theoretical 34 per cent thermal efficiency claimed by Dr Diesel in 1892.

Several large Clyde shipyards exploited the diesel engine and some of their licence arrangements are as shown:

Ailsa	Doxford			
Barclay Curle	Doxford	Sulzer		
Beardmore				Tosi
John Brown	Doxford	Sulzer		
Wm Denny		Sulzer		
Fairfield	Doxford	Sulzer	Stork	
Scott's	Doxford	Sulzer		Still
Stephen	Doxford	Sulzer		

In addition John G. Kincaid were Harland & Wolff/

B&W licensees, David Rowan were Sulzer builders and the now long-closed North British Locomotive Co were licensees of MAN and at one time had aspirations to move into the marine market.

Sadly, not one of these engines was a true Clyde bred machine. The Doxford, one of the most popular diesels of all time was a Sunderland design and only recently discontinued by decision of British Shipbuilders in their plan to rationalise slow speed diesel engine manufacture to Greenock and one plant in the North East. The Sulzer is from Winterthur in Switzerland and the Stork, a most promising development was stopped on the decision of the Dutch designers as they became Stork-Werkspoor. The Scott-Still was a 1920s development for which only two engines were built, both satisfactory, for installation on ships of the Blue Funnel Line.

In 1920 a small company called Fiat British Auxiliaries was founded at Govan, but with changes in policy and the passage of years it has come to be known as British Polar Engines, the manufacturer of diesels under license from Nohab Diesel of Sweden. With rationalisation it employs under 200 people and is one of the few such companies left on Clydeside. This gives an indication of the contraction in this industry.

Other well known but smaller engine works which have closed in recent years include Aitchison Blair of Clydebank, McKie & Baxter of Paisley, Murdoch, Aitken & Co of Glasgow and Rankin & Blackmore of Greenock. A much earlier company was Claude Girdwood of Hutchesontown. Shipyards which have closed since the war and had engine building capacity included Fleming & Ferguson, A. & J. Inglis, Lobnitz & Simons, although mostly based on steam engine manufacture.

At least two large Clydeside companies have been exclusive engine and boiler manufacturers. David Rowan & Co was founded by the original proprietor at Elliot Street in 1866 and under family guidance went to the forefront of engine manufacture. It became part of the Lithgow Group and brought great distinction on themselves and the City of Glasgow by building more engines (on an hp basis) on more than one annual return during the war than any other manufacturer! The Lithgow Group decided to merge Rowan's with the engineering division of Fairfield and much of the plant and equipment was moved from Elliot Street to Govan in the early '60s, and for a while the proximity of the Fairfield Dock was of great convenience saving the necessity of fitting engines on ships moored to public quays in Queen's Dock or at Finnieston. Fairfield-Rowan Ltd did not survive the Fairfield 1965 crash and the tools, including some of the best gear cutting machines in Europe, were sold off by the liquidators.

The other company is John G. Kincaid & Co Ltd of Greenock, founded in 1868 by a partnership of Kincaid, John Hastie and Robert Donald. In 1888 it became Kincaid & Co Ltd and was finally reconstituted with its present name in 1895. Their first B&W engine was built in 1924 and now they are a thriving company designated as slow speed diesel manufacturers by their holding corporation—British Shipbuilders.

The speed of acceptance of the diesel engine can be seen by the purchase of a diesel-engined vessel *Glenapp* of 7,374 gross tons by the Glen Line from Barclay Curle in 1918. Shortly thereafter she was sold to Elder Dempster as the *Aba* and the word was round that the diesel vessels were economical and dependable. The Union Steam Ship Company approached Fairfield for a 16,000-ton steamer to replace the *Aotearea* which had been lost on war service before entering the Canadian-Australasian service. Professor Hillhouse has been credited with persuading the owners that a diesel ship was essential and designing a vessel of great elegance and practical worth. Eschewing the contemporary fashion for neglecting funnels or fitting stumpy ones on motor ships, he fitted two smokestacks of considerable length taking the auxiliary exhausts up the forward one and the main engine exhausts up the after. The ship named *Aorangi*, the second of the name to come from Fairfield, was to serve for the best part of 30 years and ran throughout on six-cylinder two cycle Fairfield-Sulzer engines. There were four engines developing in all 12,000 bhp and driving quadruple screws, in itself an unusual combination.

In the same year the Vulcan Shipyard in Hamburg undertook a conversion to a 2,000 ton dw three hatch cargo vessel, appropriately named *Vulcan*. It had medium speed diesels which are efficient in their own right but have too high a rate of turn for an efficient propeller. On the *Vulcan* hydraulic torque converters were fitted—akin to gearing—and with this development it became feasible to use medium and ultimately high speed diesels on ships. An example of this was built by Denny of Dumbarton in 1939 with the Hebridean mail vessel *Lochiel* for David MacBrayne. Here twin propellers were driven by twin eight-cylinder Paxman-Ricardo diesel engines mounted on flexible mountings and then through reduction gearboxes with oil operated friction clutches. The *Lochiel* served the islands of Islay, Jura, Gigha and Colonsay for 30 years during which time she was once badly holed in West Loch Tarbert and sank a few hundred metres from the pier. Raised and refitted she continued sailing until withdrawn and sold. Today she continues in another role as a floating restaurant in the Bristol docks.

In 1965 the Ben Liner *Ben Ledi* was delivered by Charles Connell & Co. She set a new pattern in almost everything being 171 m long, carrying 13,450 tons deadweight and having a service speed of 21 knots. To speed cargo handling at Penang and other ports on her round voyage to the Far East she had comprehensive although conventional cargo gear but created a stir by having triple hatches through the upper, second and third decks. The choice of machinery was a nine-cylinder Barclay Curle/Sulzer and, for a ship of such high speed, this constituted formal recognition (if this was needed) that the diesel engine could tackle all foreseeable maritime requirements.

In the spring of 1911 the Sandpoint yard of MacLaren Brothers of Dumbarton produced a 50 ft motor yacht and, apart from her name *Electric Arc*, she would have excited little curiosity in the eyes of any bystander. As her name indicated she was powered by a multiple wound electric motor taking alternating power from a dynamo driven by a six-cylinder 45 bhp Wolseley engine. This pioneering effort was the result of Mavor & Coulson's great interest in extending electric power to sea and they were more than successful in drawing to the attention of marine engineers that electric installations were more flexible with regard to speed and power control than other engines and infinitely easier to reverse.

The *Electric Arc* worked on the River Forth for

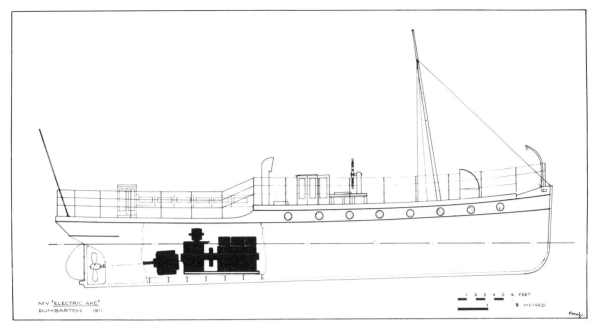

MV 'ELECTRIC ARC'
DUMBARTON 1911

1 2 3 4 5 6 FEET
1   2 METRES

Above *The Glasgow engineers Mavor and Coulson supplied revolutionary propulsion machinery to the 50 ft launch* Electric Arc *built in 1911 by MacLaren Brothers of Dumbarton. A 45 bhp Wolseley 6-cylinder petrol engine drove an alternating current dynamo which in turn supplied power to an ac propulsion motor. This vessel can justly claim to be the forerunner of the modern diesel-electric or turbo-electric driven ship.*

Right *The diesel electric paddle vessel* Talisman *undergoing repair on the slipway of Inglis Shipyard in 1952.*

the SMT Company, was requisitioned for war work and ultimately burned out. The effect was sufficient to generate interest and, in the 1930s, a series of electrically powered vessels were built on the Clyde. In 1931 David MacBrayne took delivery of the diesel-electric passenger ship *Lochfyne* from Denny of Dumbarton. The *Lochfyne* was one of the dreariest looking ships in the MacBrayne fleet but made up for lack of appearance by giving nearly 40 years of arduous service on the Clyde and in the Inner Hebrides. In the 1930s MacBrayne's had a large fleet of ships giving students the opportunity of seeing engines of almost every kind produced on the Clyde from a single-cylinder steeple on the *Glencoe* to a two-cylinder oscillating type on the magnificent *Columba*, and from diesel electric drive through to steam turbine. Dependent on the attitude of the marine superintendent the job of overseeing the

efficient running of such a fleet could be a joy or a Herculean task. In 1934 Denny's built two diesel electric paddle vessels for their own account to operate on the historic Queensferry Passage under the Forth Rail Bridge. Denny's had obtained the rights to this service and built the *Queen Margaret* (all riveted) and the sister ship *Robert the Bruce* identical in all respects except that she was the first all-welded ship built on the Clyde. The weight saving of 12 per cent in the welding raised the paddles above their optimum water line and the *Robert the Bruce* had to be ballasted. However, valuable experience was gained and the shipyard had the satisfaction of building two ships from one set of basic plans. Both ships operated satisfactorily until 1965 when withdrawn on the opening of the Forth Road Bridge. In 1935 the London and North Eastern Railway built the diesel electric paddle vessel *Talisman* at Inglis of Pointhouse, again a longevitous ship, but few other major contracts were completed before the war.

The most important and the first large electrically driven ship on the British register was the *Viceroy of India* which had her maiden voyage to Bombay in March 1929. Built by Stephen of Linthouse for P&O the *Viceroy* was outstanding both visually and technically. The propelling machinery consisted of twin propulsion motors taking three phase alternating current from British Thomson-Houston turbo alternators, in turn driven by high pressure steam. For ten years she gave superb service and was a symbol of all that was best in the old P&O fleet. Every cabin had an outside light and with a speed approaching 19 knots she remained a 'single operator' in the fleet. Sadly, on November 11 1942 she was torpedoed while off Oran.

On the resumption of peace time building after the Second World War little consideration was given to diesel electric or turbo electric propulsion and the best options at the time were turbine or diesel. With the dramatic increase in the cost of fuel oil this decision too has gone and the slow speed two-stroke diesel reigns supreme.

In this brief resume of marine engine developments attention must be paid to the gas turbine. This is an expensive and inefficient drive for a merchant ship but it has immense military value giving instant response and the ability to be at action speed on demand. Original gas turbine naval ships were steam propelled with gas turbines for suddenly required top speeds or for getting away from harbour when still raising steam. The latest naval ships have two types of gas turbine, first the emergency top speed machinery and then a more economical cruising turbine. Such arrangements while complex are suitable for the new maintenance philosophy of minimal interference while aboard and complete unit replacement either when necessary or when a certain level of running time has been reached. The abbreviations used to describe gas turbine engine rooms are given below: CODOG, Combined Diesel or Gas; CODAG, Combined Diesel and Gas; COGOG, Combined Gas turbine or Gas turbine (cruise or boost); COGAG, Combined Gas and Gas; COSAG, Combined Steam and Gas; CONAG, Combined Nuclear and Gas; COGAGE, Combined Gas turbine and Gas turbo electric.

In 1937 the Anchor Line took delivery of their first motorship, the twin-screw passenger/cargo liner Circassia *for the Glasgow-Liverpool-Bombay mail run. The following year the* Cilicia *joined the company and immediately after the war the identical* Caledonia. *All three ships, built by Fairfield, were immediately successful, and their machinery of Fairfield-Doxford type gave excellent service. In the mid-1960s the Anchor Line ceased the passenger side of the Indian trade and the three popular 'C-birds' were sold.*

Chapter 17

From Broomielaw to Bowling

North bank city yards

Shipbuilding in Glasgow is a complex web of relationships and is not something easily or succinctly defined. However, bearing in mind the need to describe these yards, it will be better if we consider first those on the north bank within the city boundary and, also, those easily reached by employees domiciled in Glasgow. For this reason this chapter will concentrate on the north bank companies on the 11-mile stretch from the Broomielaw in the heart of Glasgow to Bowling at the western end of the Forth & Clyde Canal.

It is amazing to reflect that Glasgow had had an identity for 12½ centuries before a proper shipyard, as we would now accept them, was opened on the upper river banks. It was around 540 AD that the young priest Mungo followed the cart bearing the body of Fergus to its place of burial in ground already long since consecrated as a graveyard on the banks of the Molendinar, a tiny tributary of the Clyde. This spot, now known as Blacader's, or Fergus Aisle in Glasgow Cathedral and a stone's throw from the original site of the college, can be regarded as the centre from which the ecclesiastical organisation later to become the Royal Burgh and later again the City of Glasgow developed. It was close to the Molendinar that Watt thought up his epoch-creating life's work and, also, if one carefully inspects the 19th century graveyards of the Necropolis and of St David's (Ramshorn) Kirk, that one appreciates much of the early engineering skills of Glasgow were first tested in this area.

By 1818 the industrial developments of the city made themselves felt on the river front and in that year one of the first properly organised shipyards was established in the city when John Barclay feued (a Scots word akin to renting) some ground at Stobcross. The yard was set up with a slip capable of lifting ships up to 200 tons, and this was later increased to 400

once his sons Thomas and Robert acquired the business, and with initiative and drive took advantage of Glasgow's burgeoning life as a seaport. In 1844 Robert became the sole partner but the following year invited Robert Curle and James Hamilton to join him. Twelve years later three further names were added, John Ferguson, Andrew McLean and finally Archibald Gilchrist who brought a family name to Clydeside that was to remain there for 120 years. In 1855 the yard at Clydeholm was acquired from J.G. Lawrie and in 1857 the manufacture of marine engines was commenced.

The business grew from strength to strength becoming known as Robert Barclay & Curle and in 1863 as Barclay, Curle & Company. In 1874 the work was concentrated at Clydeholm and the Stobcross site sold to the Clyde Trustees who required much of the land for the building of Queen's Dock which was opened in March 1880.

Steady development seemed the keynote of Barclay, Curle which became a limited liability organisation as early as 1884 and which developed an independent ship repair business around the same time. In 1902 they opened a ship repair office in Govan, strategically positioned close to the Govan Dry Docks, and this was extended in 1912 when the major opportunity of acquiring the new Elderslie shipyard and dry docks from John Shearer & Son was presented. It was at this period that Swan, Hunter and Wigham Richardson of Wallsend-on-Tyne acquired a major shareholding in Barclay, Curle, a shareholding which ultimately became in excess of 99 per cent. The shipyard continued to grow and in 1923 extended into the nearby Whiteinch and Jordanvale shipyards.

Until shipbuilding was discontinued in the mid-1960s about 750 ships were to enter the Clyde as products of Barclay, Curle, among them over 70 ships for British India including the troopers *Dunera* and *Nevasa* and the popular school ship *Uganda* which served as a hospital ship with the Falklands task force. Four Clyde paddle steamers were constructed for the North British Railway and the pioneer diesel powered twin-screw liner *Jutlandia* for the East Asiatic Company of Copenhagen. A ship with an unusual history was launched in 1883 being the iron steam yacht *Capercailzie* for John Burns, later to be Lord Inverclyde. The yacht was sold in 1891 to the Royal Navy and renamed HMS *Vivid* and was sold again around 1912 to the Royal Technical College, Glasgow, for £1,800. The college outfitted the yacht as a training ship, being their part in the 1912 *Comet* centenary celebrations— but it sank off Colonsay on its first cruise.

Barclay, Curle's ship repair business was one of the greatest in Britain. Almost no words are required when one quotes their First World War ship repairing statistics: 999 ships stemmed in drydock representing 2.9 million tons gross. 2,244 ships were repaired afloat of 6.7 million tons gross. The ship repair business ran down in the 1950s and by 1974 the business was closed and the drydocks handed over to Yarrow Shipbuilders.

The marine engine building business developed first at Stobcross before being transferred to Finnieston Quay. Later engines were built at Finnieston Street and boilers at Kelvinhaugh Street, but ultimately everything was transferred to the North British works which lay between the Barclay, Curle and Connell shipyards. In 1977 the last marine diesel engine was delivered, but British Shipbuilders have retained the name for the general engineering facility set up in 1978 for the production of the Sea Dart Missile system for the Royal Navy. In this very specialist role the company continues 16 decades after John Barclay set up his small business on the Glasgow waterfront.

Before leaving Elderslie the company of John Shearer is worthy of mention. Founded in 1890 by John Shearer, son of a Glasgow joiner, it operated for 17 years at Kelvinhaugh where the east end of Yorkhill Quay now stands and on premises previously occupied by Aitken & Mansell. In 1903 Shearer was knighted and two years later was laying out a new ship repair yard at Elderslie with associated dry dock. This far-sighted move had been accelerated by the Clyde Trust's wish to purchase Kelvinhaugh for further port development, a never-ending process of moving shipyards to make the city centre a unified dock system. Shearer's built about 46 ships, mostly coasters, as well as running a substantial repair business before it was sold to Barclay, Curle. A typical product of the yard was contract No 19 for the Glasgow shipowners William Robertson, being the raised quarterdeck coaster *Pearl*, 185 ft (54.6 m) long with triple expansion engines and costing £8,605.

At Lancefield Quay David Napier worked from 1821 to 1836, and from 1836 to 1841 Robert Napier occupied the site before expanding his business and moving to Govan Old Shipyard where the company was to work for a further 59 years. This was the shipbuilding site on the tidal river closest to the centre of Glasgow.

In 1840 another company operated at Lancefield of whom little is known. Their name was Hedderwick and Rankine and production was limited.

Kelvinhaugh had several shipbuilders and often more than one operated there at one time. They included Hunter and Dow of the 1830s, builders of small steam wooden built ships, and from 1840 to 1851 Robert Black worked having built the celebrated hydraulically powered slipway. He handed the yard over to Alexander Stephen & Sons who were commencing their Clydeside history after a hundred years of successful operation on the Scottish East Coast. In the 1850s John Barr had a business there, and from 1863 to 1876 Aitken & Mansell

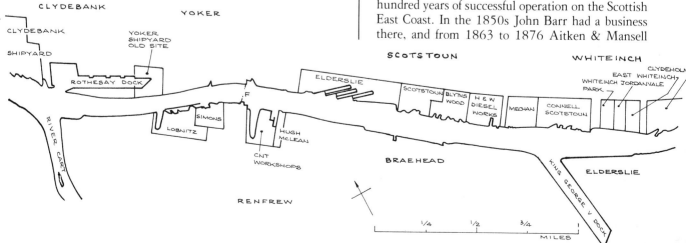

Below left *Map showing the relative positions of shipyards on the Clyde between Whiteinch and Clydebank.*
Below *Map showing the relative positions of the different shipbuilding establishments within the centre of Glasgow and including Govan.*
Right *The engine works and slipway of Barclay, Curle & Co at Stobcross, 1865 (National Maritime Museum).*

built about 30 ships there before transferring their business to Whiteinch. Finally the Union Shipbuilding Company built four small vessels at Kelvinhaugh around 1864.

The River Kelvin

The Kelvin rising in the Kilsyth Hills to the north-west of Glasgow is a river of unfailing interest, and in places of intense beauty. In the 19th century it passed areas of industrial activity like the busy Forth & Clyde Canal near Maryhill, the mills for paper, flour, flint and cotton at Kelvindale, Kirklee and Kelvingrove and ultimately the busy shipyards on either bank as it flowed into the Clyde.

On the west bank the Meadowside yard had a history of shipbuilding from 1847 till 1962, and the east bank a slightly shorter one, of just 100 years from 1862 till 1962. In all five companies have been involved on these two sites.

The Meadowside shipyard was first opened by David Tod and John MacGregor, who had commenced business on their own account as engineers just off the Broomielaw around 1834. They were former employees of Robert Napier having held junior management positions with him and probably acting from time to time as guarantee engineers. By 1836 they had set up a shipyard near Mavisbank Quay remaining there for 11 years before taking over the green field site at the mouth of the Kelvin, and selling their previous yard to the Clyde Trustees who were pursuing a policy of building quays on all available river frontage near the city centre. While at Mavisbank they carried out some notable jobs including the Clyde paddle steamer *Loch Goil*, reputedly engined by their former employer.

An early order of historic interest was the iron screw yacht *Vesta,* an elegant steamer 110 ft (35.5 m) on the waterline and rigged as a schooner. The machinery configuration was unusual being two oscillating engines applied to one shaft. Going on trial in 1848 the *Vesta* became one of the earliest ocean-going screw steamers built on the Clyde and set Tod and MacGregor's tradition of novel engine room layouts. The little ship obviously had caused trouble to the builders as David Tod remarked: 'I

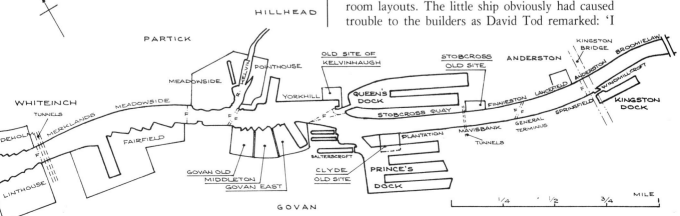

hope you will not bring us any more screw boats—we prefer paddle steamers'.

He must have changed his opinion later as by 1866 the company had constructed screw vessels aggregating 70,000 tons and in 1850 produced the SS *City of Glasgow*, a ship which was to be a milestone in north Atlantic travel, and proved that a thoughtfully constructed and well run ship could operate without government subsidy. Again the machinery was of novel design, being double beam engines on one side of the ship, balanced by a three to one reduction gearing on the other side driving the propeller shaft. The career of this fine ship ended in 1854 when she sailed from Liverpool with 480 persons aboard and was never heard of again.

The two partners obviously had strong financial backing as the *City of Glasgow* started as a speculative venture and, during the course of construction, became considered for the Inman Line fleet. The first four voyages were mainly to the account of Tod & MacGregor, but on obtaining good voyage profits the Inman Line took over and a long relationship between the two companies ensued.

The first proper dry dock in the City of Glasgow was opened at Meadowside on January 28 1858. The entrance in the River Kelvin can be seen to this day. The execution of this contract was daring for the time, and even the use of the Kelvin must have been a gamble for the shipbuilders. The dock was large, 144 m long on the floor, 19 m broad at the entrance and with 5.5 m depth of water at high spring tides. Surprisingly the dock remained in operation until 1962 and must have carried out thousands of dockings in every condition of weather over the years. In the first year of operation alone 30 ships were stemmed totalling 20,000 tons indicating the growth of Glasgow as a seaport.

Another innovation was two large sheds built over building berths. They were certainly the first in Scotland and, according to Frank C. Bowen, were known as the 'Meadowside Ship Palaces'. After storm damage they were pulled down and not replaced but, again, a style of shipbuilding had been tried, one which is now seen worldwide, with recent examples in Britain at Pallion in Sunderland, Hall, Russell in Aberdeen, Ailsa in Troon and Appledore in Devon.

David Tod died in 1859 and much of the drive seemed to leave the firm, but Tod and MacGregor continued for another 14 years. Important orders were received from the P&O Company and Cunard built their iron screw steamship *Cuba* at Meadowside in 1864. In 1873 the Inman Line placed an order in Birkenhead for a North Atlantic Liner and it signalled the end of this short lived but vital company. The shipyard was sold as a going concern for £200,000 in 1873.

The size of yard had enlarged slightly owing to the purchase of Thomas B. Seath's yard at Meadowside when they moved upriver to Rutherglen in 1856.

The new owners were David and William Henderson and the Anchor Line. For many years after the yard was known locally as 'the Anchor Line', and the Henderson brothers in shipping placed considerable business both for repair work and for new building in the shipyard. The Anchor Line orders varied from the iron screw tender *Express* (150 ft × 25 ft) built 1880, to the famous twin-screw North Atlantic liner *Columbia* of 1902 which continued the Anchor Line tradition of multiple tall black funnels. For most of her life *Columbia* sailed from Glasgow on Saturday afternoons on her routine run to New York via Moville in Ireland. In 1911 she collided with an iceberg crushing her bow for about 5 m and flooding No 1 Hold, but reached New York in safety. Shortly after the *Titanic* accident the same happened to the Allan liner *Corsican*, built by Barclay, Curle & Co, and she too survived with only minor bow damage, largely owing to travelling at only four knots when the impact occurred. Such accidents were more frequent than we realise now as ice routeing was only commencing and icebergs which roll over are practically impossible to detect in the dark. Wireless communications with ships was not common until the beginning of the First World War.

The most surprising feature of D. & W. Henderson was their wide range of construction from high class passenger liners to runs of batch-produced dumb barges. Such ranges in product make it difficult to keep balanced work loads for all trades in the yard, but many yards were perfectly happy to engage and discharge labour at short notice to meet their requirements. The variety of work may have been the result of employing an outstanding naval architect from 1882 to 1916, George Thompson, a man from Tayside who specialised in yachts. During his time Henderson's built several large sailing craft including the French five-masted barque *France* as well as racing yachts like *Thistle*, *Valkyrie II*, *Valkyrie III* and, of course, the famous King's *Britannia*. The yacht *Thistle* a contender for the

America's Cup, was not designed by Thompson but by G.L. Watson, and such secrecy surrounded her building that she was launched with canvas round the hull to hide the shape.

In 1890 the five-masted barque *France* was completed for Bordes et Cie of Dunkirk. This company had already come to the Clyde and had purchased from Russell & Co and from Barclay, Curle & Co but this ship, their largest, was able to carry 6,200 tons of guano in the nitrate trade. Sadly she was lost in the Atlantic in 1901 and her crew's fate never ascertained.

During the First World War standard merchant vessels were constructed and Henderson's were parent builders for the A and B designs of 8,000 tons deadweight and with triple expansion engines giving them a service speed of 11 knots. Of the ten parent builders only three were from the Clyde, the remainder being from Belfast or from the North-East—the home of the standard tramp ship.

At the end of the war trade fell away and the Meadowside yard obtained fewer orders at progressively less lucrative prices. Around 1933 Henderson's obtained an order for one and then two duplicate ships at prices well below the amount that even Lithgows or Burntisland were prepared to offer. Coupled with the collapse of the Anchor Line it became impossible for D. & W. Henderson to continue business and the company ceased to trade. The men were paid off, the unfinished contracts put to other builders and the apprentices transferred to Fairfield and other shipyards, and while in liquidation the shipbuilding assets sold to National Shipbuilders Security Ltd. NSS Ltd did not place the usual ban on construction for 40 years but held the yard in reserve, which was fortuitous, as various companies used the berths for landing craft construction during the war, mainly Sir William Arroll & Co and Redpath Brown & Co.

The name D. & W. Henderson did not die as the ship repairing assets and goodwill were purchased by Harland & Wolff Ltd of Belfast and the company continued until 1962. During the Second World War work was hectic, but with the reduction in up-river traffic and the restrictions imposed by both the Kelvin and the dock entrance, the company came on bad times and closure was announced in 1962. With hindsight it is difficult to see what else could have been done, but nevertheless, the slow death of the company through lack of investment was a sad sight for Glaswegians.

Among the industrial concerns that have been situated on the banks of the Kelvin was the Smithfields Iron Company at Pointhouse. In 1734 they were responsible for the organising of a ferry, crossing the river on a chain, taken over the fore end of the boat and manipulated by a spoked hand wheel. Previously rowing boats had been in use and even after the introduction of the ferry they continued for some years. Shortly after Inglis' shipyard was set up, the Clyde Trustees acquired the rights of the ferry and introduced a steam vessel working on chains between two sloping hards. Following a special Act of Parliament the roadways were raised and an elevated platform ferry was introduced with four propellers working at the corners. From all of this the legend of the Govan Ferry was born, and the shipyard of Pointhouse had means of attracting labour, not only from Partick, but from the Burgh of Govan on the south bank.

The brothers Anthony and John Inglis formed a business partnership in 1847 at the Whitehall Foundry in Anderston. Previously Anthony Inglis had been in business on his own account. The Whitehall Foundry was to remain with them for many years and, indeed, many years later the first set of Parsons turbines built under licence outside Wallsend-on-Tyne were constructed there. In 1862 ground at Pointhouse was acquired and the yard to which the company remained loyal throughout came into operation. There was no attempt to build a dry dock, but a patent slipway and a marine railway to accommodate ship movements throughout the yard were constructed. Normal berths for conventional launchings were also constructed and angled that new ships slipped into the mouth of the Kelvin.

Several fine sailing ships were constructed including the composite full rigged ship *Norman Court* in 1869, built initially for the China tea trade and lost in 1883 off Anglesey while returning to Greenock with a cargo of sugar from Java. Some years later the full rigger *Loch Etive* was built of iron at Pointhouse and in January 1878 sailed from the Clyde on her maiden voyage to Australia. She had an excellent record and remained on the British registry for 32 years before being sold. Her greatest reason for being remembered is that Joseph Conrad served on her for some time as third mate.

Shortly after the *Loch Etive* sailed the paddle steamer *Cosmos* was constructed for owners in Uruguay and she, too, had distinction, being the first vessel with electric lighting and prior to departure

was inspected by Lord Kelvin. The yard built up very good connections and, for anyone looking today at the small derelict site, it is difficult to imagine that around 40 steamers were built there for service in the British India Steam Navigation Fleet.

The Inglis family were very successful; on his death in 1884 Anthony Inglis was assessed on an estate of nearly £152,000 only 22 years after the shipyard had opened. His son John (1842-1919) joined the business after training at Glasgow University. In 1867 he married one of the Denny family and from then developed the lifestyle of a successful shipbuilder, living for the yard and for his family yachting holidays. He became an enthusiast on yacht design and is credited with the idea of designing and first using the integral keel shaped to the lines of a yacht.

John Inglis received an LL D from his old university and became a well-known figure in the West of Scotland. He was a director of the North British Railway, a company which incidentally owned part of the ground on which the yard stood. The North British Company and their successors, the LNER, ordered 13 passenger steamers from Inglis, the last one being the PS *Waverley* built in 1947 and engined by Rankin & Blackmore Ltd of Greenock. With the patent slip on the Kelvin many of these ships came back yearly to Pointhouse for their annual overhaul.

In 1935 the North British fleet were augmented by another paddle vessel from Inglis, the *Talisman.* Again new ground was covered as the vessel following close on the heels of Denny's *Robert the Bruce* and *Queen Margaret* was of diesel electric propulsion with optional bridge control. The new ship served for well over 30 years, and following part re-engining in 1939 and some reconstruction that improved her appearance in 1946, became a successful, but individual Clyde 'steamer'.

Just before his death in 1919 John Inglis sold the shipyard to Lord Pirrie's Harland & Wolff group. At the time he said that it was the best move as the future of the Clyde was uncertain, and that throughout his life he had campaigned against union militancy, and also against their restrictions regarding intakes of apprentices. Despite the change of ownership work continued at Pointhouse for another 43 years!

Nothing can dim their achievement in producing some beautiful ships and opening new commercial areas. In 1911 Inglis obtained their first Royal Navy contract, HM Destroyer *Fury* which was the first ship built for the Navy within the boundaries of the City of Glasgow. This had been preceded by the order for the Royal Yacht *Alexandra*, the first such vessel to be built by a commercial shipyard. The yacht was triple-screw and powered by Parsons steam turbines to give smooth performance in her specialised duties of private cruising and being a yacht in the Mediterranean. In 1925 she was sold to the Nordenfjeldske Company of Trondheim, Norway, renamed *Prins Olav* and put to cruising to the North Cape. In 1937 she became a *hurtigruteskip*, or fast route ship, working on the Norwegian coast, and then when well over 30 years old was lost at sea as a result of war action.

In all four Loch Lomond steamers have come from the yard. Two are worthy of mention, the PS *Prince Edward* and the PS *Maid of the Loch*. The *Prince Edward* was launched in May 1911, towed to Dumbarton and then with trace horses was drawn up the River Leven towards Loch Lomond. Unfortunately the empty hull stuck in the bottom near Renton and had to be covered and left until the spring floods of 1912, when with the help of traction engines she reached Balloch one year late for outfitting and the fitting of engines. Despite this she was a successful ship and was relieved only in 1953 when the *Maid of the Loch* was built at Pointhouse, knocked down and re-erected at Balloch for conventional launching.

The closure of the yard in 1962 ended a company which had built smaller specialist vessels ranging from clipper ships to East African anti-slaver patrol ships and from whale catchers to the Khedive of Egypt's yacht. Inglis had built on average five ships a year, and their name will long be remembered.

West of Clydeholm

Taking the various shipyards in sequence moving west from Clydeholm the first group of three are East Whiteinch, Whiteinch-Jordanvale and then Park. All three parcels of ground ultimately passed into the hands of Barclay, Curle but not before developing their own interesting histories. East Whiteinch belonged to Thomas Wingate from 1848 to 1878 and his brilliant career is already described in Chapter 3.

Whiteinch-Jordanvale was home for William Simons & Co from 1826 to 1860, and for Aitken & Mansell from 1876 to 1889 after their move from Kelvinhaugh. Robert Mansell (1828-1905) was a former student of Glasgow University and a pupil of

Robert Napier and joined James Aitken to found a company to build hulls only up to 4,000 tons. They built many blockade runners and were also remembered on the Clyde for pioneer work in the development of electric hand tools. John Reid & Company had the yard from 1891 to 1909 and their best work is described in the Greenock chapter. From 1916 to 1921 the yard was operated by a wholly-owned Belgian company known as Lloyd Royal Belge (Great Britain) Ltd associated with Brys & Gilsen Ltd. The yard was laid out by Donald Bremmer, a later director of Blythswood, and then about 20 ships were built before the yard passed into the hands of the Australasian Steam Navigation Co and finally sold to Barclay, Curle.

The Park shipyard was in the hands of a former Glasgow University student, J.G. Lawrie from 1854 to around 1875. Sixty-three ships were built including several full rigged vessels for the Loch Line of Glasgow. Lawrie is remembered as the first president of the fully united Institution of Engineers & Shipbuilders in Scotland for the sessions 1865-1867 and for being an early lecturer in naval architecture and marine engineering at Glasgow University around 1880 or 1881.

After Lawrie the Park shipyard was taken over by W.B. Thompson from the late 1870s to the mid-1880s and produced about 20 ships. William Bruce Thompson (1837-1923) is better remembered for opening the Caledon shipyard in Dundee in 1876. In the 1890s the yard had another lease of life when taken over by Ritchie, Graham & Milne who had commenced as engine and barge builders in Govan in 1891 and then moved to Whiteinch in 1895. They built nearly 400 vessels mostly barges, shallow draft steamers, stern and side wheelers as well as other interesting craft including the Royal Naval single screw tug HMS *Jaunty* of 1920. In 1922 while associated with the Rennie, Ritchie & Newport shipbuilding group, they suffered financially on the group's collapse and were forced to close.

Moving west the Scotstoun shipyard of Charles Connell had a long history being founded in 1861 and continuing until 1968 when absorbed into **Upper Clyde Shipbuilders**. The Scotstoun yard was reprieved on the setting up of Govan Shipbuilders, being a subsidiary with the unusual name of Scotstoun Marine Limited and operating under the general direction of Govan. In 1980 British Shipbuilders announced that it would go on a care and maintenance basis and, in effect, shipbuilding had come to an end after 120 years.

Again, westwards was the Blythswood Shipbuilding Company set up in 1919 with the objective of capturing part of the tanker building market. The founders were Hugh M. MacMillan, formerly of Fairfield and a member of the Dumbarton shipbuilding family, and Donald Bremner, formerly of John Brown's and of Dunlop, Bremner & Co. They were successful in obtaining contracts as the yard was being constructed and their first ship was the tanker *British Architect* and their first series run was for several ships of the 'Pacific Enterprise' Class for Furness Withy's cargo service to the west coast of South America. While the techniques in the yard were for the cheapest possible construction the directors realised that low cost building and the selling of ships by attractive lines and appearance was aided by meticulous drawing office work and, in particular, by careful use of half block model. In this they were successful and while tankers are not the most elegant of craft theirs were often in a high class of their own. Many ships were built for Eagle Oil including the *San Demetrio* of Second World War fame. The last ship to be built was the *Fingal*, contract No 140, for the Commissioners of the Northern Lighthouses, a ship based on Oban. Their demise was not a surprise as their low overheads and basic approach to shipbuilding, while admirable in every way, were not part of the market scene of the 1960s and '70s.

Yarrow shipbuilders to the west again purchased their yard in 1965 and extended over part of it, as described in Chapter 14.

At Yoker to the west of the Renfrew Ferry the shipyard of Napier, Shanks & Bell operated from 1877 to 1898 with as founder partners H.M. Napier (a grandson of Robert Napier), R.T. Napier, David Bell the noted shipbuilding historian, and a Mr Shanks. They built in all 84 ships and in 1898 on change of ownership were reconstituted as Napier & Miller. The new company built 70 further ships at Yoker but were forced to move to Old Kilpatrick once the Clyde Navigation Trust gave notice that they wished to build a new dock partly over their ground. The new dock was opened by the Princess of Wales on April 25 1907 and named Rothesay Dock in honour of her title Duchess of Rothesay. At Old Kilpatrick the company produced another 120 ships before being purchased and abruptly closed down in 1930 by National Shipbuilders Security Ltd.

Their production at Old Kilpatrick had included wartime aeroplanes and a wide range of ships including London County Council ferries and large vessels for the Norske Amerika Linje of Oslo. Their most historic ships were the barques *Sunlight* and *Rendova* built for Lever Brothers for the carriage of coconut oil from Rendova Isle in the Pacific to Port Sunlight. These two ships were the last square-rigged freighters built in the UK for British owners and both were lost in the First World War.

The shipyards at Clydebank and Dalmuir are dealt with elsewhere in this book.

At Bowling where the Forth & Clyde Canal goes into the Clyde there has been shipbuilding for a very long time. In 1851 a member of the Scott family of Greenock founded a yard combining two small firms operating on the West Littlemill site and the East Bay site. The yard with minor changes in name operated until 1979 when put on care and maintenance by British Shipbuilders and effectively closed. In close on 130 years it produced about 450 craft including tugs, barges, steam yachts, puffers and coasters. In 1965 they became a subsidiary of Scott's of Greenock and through this Scott Lithgow and ultimately British Shipbuilders.

In this brief survey the name of Sandeman and McLaurin has been left out so far. It is believed that this company operated from Whiteinch in the 1850s and built some ships for Handyside and Henderson and their later associate the Anchor Line.

Chapter 18

Govan and Linthouse

The father of Clyde shipbuilding

The years 1790 and 1791 saw the birth of two boys, cousins, endowed with the name Napier—David was the elder and Robert the younger. Their lives were to be closely associated for some years, and from their collective efforts were founded engineering and shipbuilding enterprises of such magnitude that ultimately Robert Napier became known as the 'Father of Clyde Shipbuilding'.

Firstly, David Napier spent his early years in Glasgow and around 1811, on the death of his father, took over the family foundry business in Howard Street. While not trained as an engineer according to the wont of the time, he had an all-round education and from this was fitted to take on both technical and administrative responsibility. His friendship with Henry Bell brought him the order for the boiler of the historic PS *Comet* which in turn brought about increased involvement in marine matters. In 1813 the business was moved to Camlachie, and there David Napier showed his originality and flair by designing a novel and successful hull form based on observations made aboard sailing packets on the Irish Sea, and by models carefully tested in the Camlachie Burn. Napier asked his kinsmen, the Dennys, to build the new ship, and the result was the *Rob Roy* of 1818 which instituted a regular steam service between the Clyde and Belfast. David Napier's renown as a marine engineeer spread far and wide and, as orders poured in, he decided to move to larger premises at Lancefield in Glasgow, leaving Camlachie to his cousin Robert.

During 15 years at Lancefield, David Napier produced many original ideas including steeple engines and feathering paddles. In either 1820 or 1822 the paddle steamer *Post Boy* was purchased by Napier and engined by him with surface condensers giving it freedom to ply in any waters, and, indeed, it was advertised to sail from Glasgow irrespective 'of wind, or weather, or tide'.

As has been mentioned elsewhere, David Napier set up various steamer routes, and his contribution to steam navigation is as important as his endeavours in marine engineering. However, it is said that in 1835 during a period when he had been depressed, he received the news that the ship *Earl Grey*, which had been engined by his company, had had a serious explosion killing and injuring many. This made him even more downhearted and he decided to wind up his affairs in Scotland. The Lancefield site was sold to his cousin Robert, and then with his sons, John and Francis, he set off for London, to set up business at Millwall. His departure from the Clyde was regretted, but his work with the *Marion* at Loch Lomond and the *Aglaia* at Loch Eck had laid the foundations of an industry.

*   *   *

Robert Napier wasted no time in reorganising the Camlachie Works after taking them over in 1821, in order that business might expand. To free himself from routine matters, he appointed a millwright, David Elder to be his manager, and from this came the long relationships between David Elder and his son John and the Napier business. In 1823 he was entrusted with his first marine engine contract for the PS *Leven*, and happily this engine can be seen to this day in Dumbarton. This enabled him to quote for further engines and from this the big breakthrough came in 1830 when he supplied engines for a steam yacht for the well connected T. Assheton Smith. The two men became friends and introductions followed which brought Napier work from the Hon East India Company, overseas governments and

Robert Napier (1791-1876), the Father of Clyde Shipbuilding (Wotherspoon Collection, Mitchell Library, Glasgow).

ultimately the Admiralty. In 1837, the Napier engines on the East India paddle ship *Berenice* brought glowing reports from all involved and Napier decided he must obtain Admiralty work, up till then a preserve of two or three English companies, and with surprising ease he obtained the orders for engines for HMS *Vesuvius* and HMS *Stromboli.*

In 1836, despite efforts by the Clyde authorities to repossess the Lancefield site, Robert Napier took it over from David and for the five years which followed some very exciting things took place with Napier's involvement in the setting up of the British and North American RMSP Company being the most important. Napier subscribed £6,000 towards the £270,000 required, and introduced many investors to Samuel Cunard.

Robert Napier had a large hand in the design of the first four Cunarders, and sub-contracting them to different shipbuilders made him decide to expand into shipbuilding, to work in iron and to discontinue passing work to other companies. The Govan Old Yard was built on land to the east of the parish church and in 1841 Robert Napier commenced shipbuilding in the heart of Govan—which was then a burgh in its own right and was to remain so until 1912 when it was swept into the Glasgow net.

David Elder remained engineering manager and Napier's relation William Denny joined for a short time as naval architect. Their first iron ship, PS *Vanguard*, was delivered in 1843, reputedly of the most beautiful form. Other original ships followed, more about which will be related later, and all the time Robert Napier strove to widen his influence by entertaining, by offering works training and at all times by giving good value for money in all the jobs he undertook. In 1850 the company moved to Govan East shipyard, and there the real life's work of Robert Napier came to fruition.

For 50 years Robert Napier & Sons operated from the Govan East Yard and for 26 of these until his death in 1876 Robert Napier had a profound influence. From the yard in 1855 came the beautiful PS *Persia* and then, in 1861, the ironclad *Black Prince* was launched just weeks behind the Thames-built HMS *Warrior* to which must be given the credit of being the first such British vessel. After Napier's death, Dr A.C. Kirk ran the company with other partners, and the developments continued with the SS *Aberdeen* and then a series of ships for the Royal Mail Steam Packet and in 1891 the magnificent TSS *Ophir* of the Orient Line which was later used by King George V, while still a prince, as the Royal Yacht for his Empire cruise in 1901.

Throughout this volume, reference is made to the work of Robert Napier. Without his drive and initiative the Clyde would have been a quieter place, and fewer of the shipbuilders who were to become great would have had the all-round training that made their businesses flourish. Truly, Napier was the father of the industry on the river.

The three Govan yards

From the 1830s three shipyards in the very centre of the Burgh of Govan were to have considerable influence on the prosperity of the area: from west to east they were known as the Old Yard, Middleton and Govan East. As its name would imply, the Old Yard to the east of Govan Old Parish Church was the first in existence and Messrs MacArthur and Alexander were the first tenants. Robert Napier took over in 1841 and remained until 1850 and in this short period did considerable building in iron and here perfected his techniques. Among the interesting ships built were the pioneer train ferries PS *Leviathan* and her smaller sister PS *Robert Napier*, so named after the designer and builder by the directors of the Edinburgh, Perth & Dundee Railway— later incorporated in the North British. The *Robert Napier* while only 140 ft (42.7 m) in length and having the remarkably low power of 112 hp, was designed to stern load around 16 railway waggons, and by careful scheduling was able to transport more than 50,000 trucks per year across the Firth of Forth. She was to operate for close on 40 years on the Scottish East Coast.

In 1850, Robert Napier moved his establishment to Govan East and the Old Yard was taken over by Messrs J. Napier and Hoey who remained for about eight years before handing the yard to Randolph, Elder and Co for their short stay from 1860 to 1864. For the two years from 1864, about 14 ships, some iron steamers and some composite sailing ships, were built while the yard was directed by the partnership of Dobie, Hedderwick and McGaw. In 1866, Mr

Dobie became the sole principal and for 18 years the yard was known as Dobie & Co, building well over 100 ships, including the barque *Forthbank* in 1877 for Andrew Weir and Co. Among their products were three ships for the widely advertised Twin Screw Line of Altantic Steamers owned by W.B. Hill and W.H. Nott and aptly named TSS *Notting Hill*, TSS *Ludgate Hill* and TSS *Tower Hill*. In 1884 with three ships on the stocks, the company went into liquidation, but with prompt action by the Allan Line which had contracted two of the ships, a new

An aerial view of the Clyde between Govan and Partick, probably around 1930. The Fairfield yard is just visible top left, and Govan Old Parish Church, one of Britain's oldest sites of worship, is clearly visible. Across the river three ships are on the stocks of D & W Henderson, and in the right foreground is the Govan yard of Harland & Wolff Ltd. Foliage on the few trees visible, and the clear atmosphere, would indicate that it is the time of the Glasgow Fair Holidays (Strathclyde Regional Archives).

company, the Govan Shipbuilding Company, was set up with the approval of the receiver, and the work in hand including SS *Carthaginian*, SS *Siberian* and the barque *Loch Trool* were completed. On good authority it is believed that further ships were built by the Govan S.B. Co which indicates either an adventurous spirit in the new partners or an order book of potentially profitable work at the time of bankruptcy. After lying idle for sometime the yard was taken over by Mackie & Thomson (of whom more is written in Chapter 20), and then in 1912 the ground was purchased by Harland & Wolff Ltd of Belfast.

Govan Middleton, was in the hands of Smith and Rodger from 1843 to 1864 and nearly 100 ships were delivered by these early iron shipbuilders. No doubt the iron techniques were introduced by Smith who was one of that numerous and distinguished group of engineers who had been pupils of Robert Napier. From 1864 until 1912 the yard was known as 'The Limited', being the London and Glasgow Engineering and Iron Shipbuilding Co Ltd, of which more is said in Chapter 19.

The East Yard was in the hands of Robert Napier and then William Beardmore until 1905, and in 1912, along with the other two yards, was combined to form the great Harland & Wolff complex. After Beardmore's vacated Govan East, the London and Glasgow Company obtained the land and had an outfitting basin cut at an angle of about 45 degrees to the line of the Clyde. The new basin was named the **Middleton Basin** after the Mid Yard, but to generations of Glaswegians was known simply as 'Harland's Basin'.

In 1912 Harland & Wolff were at a high point in their history, having delivered the world's largest and finest ship—the triple-screw liner *Olympic*—from their Belfast shipyard, and were completing her sister the *Titanic*. The disastrous loss of the *Titanic* should not conceal the fact that the 'Olympic' Class were ships of supreme elegance and highly refined engineering design—they were ships to be proud of. No ship in the world could have survived the damage which the *Titanic* suffered on April 15 1912, when 35 per cent of her bottom was ripped through in a matter of seconds, and the fact that she was representative of the finest British traditions of ship design and shipbuilding was forgotten in the fearful examinations which followed her sinking.

At this high point, Harland & Wolff were anxious to have a shop front on the world's premier ship-building river, and the opportunity to obtain the three Govan sites was too good to miss. This acquisition allowed them to rebuild the sites as an integrated steel fabrication and engineering ship factory with good tooling and superb hammerhead cranes, which became a showpiece on Clydeside. Despite being overshadowed by the Queen's Island shipyard across the North Channel, the Scottish end of the company produced a wide range of ships over 50 years including Royal Naval monitors in 1915 and the Norwegian heavy lift ship *Belisland* in 1962. Examples of their work included the Nelson Line passenger motorship *Highland Hope* which sailed to join her Belfast-built sisters, but was sunk shortly after, ferries for the Clyde Trust, the turbine steamer *Duchess of Hamilton* for the LMS Railway fleet, the tanker *British Trust* in 1937 and the British Phosphate Commissioners ship *Triaster* in 1955. On the whole the tanker and the cargo ship were the basic workload for the yard throughout the years.

Harland & Wolff's control on Clydeside grew and at its peak had several engineering establishments as well as the undernoted shipyards within the group: Caird & Co, 1916-36; Harland & Wolff Ltd, Irvine, 1914-15; D. & W. Henderson, 1935-62; A. McMillan & Sons Ltd, 1920-30; A. & J. Inglis Ltd, 1919-62.

The drastic effects of the 1930s recession began to be felt in Govan after the Second World War. The yard had suffered from lack of investment and had been worked hard throughout the war. Ship sizes started to increase rapidly in the 1950s, and it was apparent that to survive the building berths would need to be broadened and the cranes realigned and possibly replaced. As all major expenditure was authorised at Belfast, it became clear in the early 1960s that the yard was running down, and it was no surprise when closure was announced in 1962. Around the same time Inglis yard and Henderson's drydock were disposed of and Harland & Wolff began effecting their policy of concentrating their activities at Queen's Island.

Within months of the closure, the land was cleared and later considerable house building started on the historic Govan site. It is doubtful if many of the children in the area are aware that they are living on the spot where Robert Napier founded one of the world's great industries.

The outfitting basin was used for some years by Alexander Stephen for outfitting and for ship repair and was most conveniently sited for the Govan dry

Built in 1896 at Govan, the intermediate mail steamer Tintagel Castle served in the fleet of Donald Currie's Castle Mail Packet Company, later the Union Castle Line. In 1912 she was sold to the French, renamed Liger and broken up shortly after.

docks. In turn it passed into the hands of the go-ahead ClydeDock Engineering Limited and hopefully will remain a symbol of maritime enterprise in Govan for years to come.

As a postscript, it is interesting to note a proposal for a Clyde Barrage which emanated from Greenock Corporation in 1963. This idea involved the building of a sea wall with roadways on top, similar to the Dutch sea defences in the Delta Scheme, running from Greenock on the south shore to Ardmore Point. It was an interesting and imaginative scheme, and with shipping locks would have enabled ships to enter the River Clyde at any state of the tide. Many of the proposals were controversial, and the Clyde Shipbuilders were concerned about several aspects including the need for low tide in certain craneage jobs on the river to give maximum clearance from the ship to a crane in its highest position and, of course, for the need of low tide to fit the bottom launch ways on shipbuilding berths. This last requirement had, however, been met in Harland & Wolff's Govan yard as each berth had a dock gate, or caisson, which allowed the stern of ships to be worked in dry conditions irrespective of the tidal state of the river. The Govan yard is now gone and the Barrage Scheme has been consigned to the archives of the Greenock councillors.

The legacy of John Elder

When C. Randolph and R.S. Cunliff inaugurated a millwright business in Tradeston in 1834, little did they anticipate that it would be the forerunner of the world famous companies which from 1864 would occupy the site of the farm of Fairfield near the village of Govan. The company, originally known as Randolph & Co, became Randolph, Elliott & Co in 1837 and in 1852 when John Elder was assumed a partner it became Randolph, Elder and Co, and commenced marine engineering with conspicuous success as has been told already in this book. In 1860 the Govan Old Yard was occupied and shipbuilding commenced with some interesting ships including the SS *Macgregor Laird*, a passenger ship of 966 tons for the African Steam Ship Company (the forerunner of Elder Dempster of Liverpool) and named in memory of their founder.

In 1864 the Fairfield site was taken over and ship-building has gone on there continuously for 120 years. In 1868, both Randolph and Cunliff retired and John Elder became the sole partner, but this was to last for a short period and in 1869 his unexpected and early death not only robbed the Clyde of a great engineer and shipbuilder, but left a delicate situation at Fairfield. Mrs Isabella Elder, his widow, was a main beneficiary and effectively owned the shipyard,

John Elder & Co built the SS Etruria *in 1885. For 24 years this highly satisfactory vessel was to serve the Cunard Line well, and frequently had average speeds for crossing the Atlantic in excess of 19 knots.*

and she arranged that a partnership of Messrs J.F. Ure, J.L.K. Jamieson and William Pearce be set up to run the shipyard, and that in 1870 the name be changed to John Elder & Co.

The control of the company more and more came under Pearce, and the direction changed from that of a shipyard on the forefront of technical advance to a business that was prepared to exploit business opportunities—indeed in some cases, like the Atlantic Blue Ribband, to create them. This idea came from his appreciation that countless millions of people crossed the Atlantic, and that there was justification for creating an exclusive class of transport using expensive and speedy ships. The first Fairfield 'Atlantic Greyhound' was the SS *Arizona* delivered in 1879 to the Guion Line and which was to earn undying fame for three feats—first gaining the Blue Ribband by crossing from Queenstown to New York on her maiden voyage in 7 days 10 hours and 30 minutes, second by hitting an iceberg in 1879 at 16 knots and apart from telescoping 6 m of the bows surviving intact, and third by remaining in service until 1927, a period of close on half a century. She was followed by the Guion *Alaska* and then the Cunarders *Oregon*, *Umbria*, *Etruria*,

Campania and *Lucania*. By the time of his death, Pearce was knighted, had been MP for Govan and had left plans and proposals for a liner to cross the Atlantic in five days!

Just before the death of Sir William Pearce in 1888, the company was reconstituted and restyled the Fairfield Shipbuilding and Engineering Co Ltd, and continued under the chairmanship of some remarkable men including W.G. Pearce, Professor Francis Elgar and Alexander Gracie. The yard was kept at the highest standards with continuous investment in machinery and plant, and in 1911 the massive hammerhead crane was placed on the east side of the basin. Special efforts had been made to build ships quickly, and one typical result was the construction of the Caledonian Steam Packet paddle ship *Duchess of Fife* in 1903. The schedule was as follows: laid down, January 17; launched, May 9; trials, June 5.

While this was a small vessel, the times did represent an understanding that work throughput enabled large undertakings to remain buoyant, with good cash flow and high overhead recovery. The yard was ready for the First World War and produced in all 68 ships all for Royal Naval service, including the well known Train Ferry *TF3*, an output which was second only to John Brown & Co of Clydebank.

Following the death of Sir W.G. Pearce in 1907 his shares, which had been held by a college, were sold around 1918 and through this the Northumberland Shipbuilding Company gained control. Fairfield

Above left *Built at Fairfield in 1913, the* Empress of Asia *served in the Pacific until 1942 when sunk off Singapore by Japanese aircraft. This ship remained a coal burner all her days, as it is said she could not be spared from her route by Canadian Pacific to return to UK for conversion.*

Left *The Hudson's Bay Company motor coaster* Rupertsland *under construction at the Fairfield Shipyard in 1948. This ship was specially designed for the rigorous conditions of Canada, and was unusual for the time in having a hull entirely welded.*

Above *The fast motor cargo ship* Glenfalloch *about to be launched from the Govan shipyard of the Fairfield S & E Co Ltd in 1962. This ship was built for the Glen Line Limited of London, a subsidiary of Alfred Holt's Blue Funnel Line.*

having good liquid assets survived the Northumberland crash in 1926, but in 1935, believing themselves through the worst of the recession, discovered that on the bankruptcy of the Anchor Line, of whom they were creditors, they could not continue trading. At this point Sir James and Mr Henry Lithgow stepped in and purchased Fairfield as a going concern for the Lithgow group, a relationship which was to last 30 years. From 1935 work picked up and again in war Fairfield found itself a naval building yard, producing a host of cruisers and destroyers as well as HM Battleship *Howe* and HM Aircraft Carrier *Implacable.* The growth in world trade kept the yard busy and many fine ships were

produced including the liner *Empress of Britain* launched in 1955 and a series of ore carriers led by MV *Bomi Hills* in 1952 which were then the largest in the world.

Reconstruction of the yard followed, and while the steel fabrication facilities were completely updated, the building berths were left almost in their 1900 condition with the addition of road surfacing and good craneage. In 1962, the first of the four superb fast cargo liners was built for the Glen Line of London: they were the MV *Glenogle* and then her sister *Glenfalloch* from Fairfield and the *Glenlyon* from the Netherlands Dock and *Flintshire* from van der Giessen, Rotterdam. At the time these superb ships, built to the exacting specifications of the Blue Funnel Line, represented the highest standards in cargo ship design.

Two Fairfield-built ships must be mentioned before the next phase in the company history is told. They were the CPR liner *Empress of Ireland* and the *Athenia* of the Donaldson Atlantic Line, both of which were lost with considerable casualties. The *Empress of Ireland* was outward bound from Quebec to Liverpool when, near Rimouski on the St Lawrence on May 30 1914 with 1,477 persons aboard, in fog she was struck by the Norwegian freighter *Storstadt.* The accident occurred at 1.55 am when almost all passengers were in their cabins, and as the *Empress* had received a mortal blow amidships and sank in less than quarter of an hour, the loss of life was 1,014 persons, with a higher percentage of passengers dying than on the *Titanic* two years earlier. Percy Hillhouse, the naval architect of Fairfield, gave evidence at the public inquiry and cleared the shipyard of any suspicion of poor design or bad workmanship. The boiler rooms had flooded, (a distance greater than 30 per cent of the ship's length) and her only slim hope would have been if she had remained upright in the water as she settled, and if all sidelights had been closed securely. The onset of the First World War had a deadening effect on the publicity and Britain's third worst merchant ship disaster is therefore the least known.

The other ship *Athenia* had been built in 1923 along with her twin-screw sister *Letitia* for the Anchor-Donaldson Line, Glasgow to Montreal service. The two ships were efficient and popular and served continuously with only a change of owner's name in 1935 to Donaldson Atlantic Line on the collapse of the Anchor Line. Within hours of the outbreak of the Second World War a German U-boat positioned 200 miles west of Ireland torpedoed the *Athenia* outward bound from Glasgow and Liverpool with 1,418 persons aboard. The vessel sank in a few hours, becoming the first war casualty and 112 lives were lost including those of 28 Americans who were at that time neutral. The *Letitia* was brought into war service, survived the confict, and continued sailing into the 1950s as the New Zealand government emigrant ship *Captain Cook*.

Happily most Fairfield ships were longevitous and the builder's list reads like a roll call of some of the world's most interesting ships.

Suddenly on October 15 1965, after consultations with the Bank of Scotland, the Fairfield Company called in a receiver. On that evening almost all Scottish shipbuilders and engineers were attending the annual James Watt Dinner, an event regarded as an evening for entertaining one's clients or for being entertained and an opportunity for meeting old friends and renewing acquaintanceships. By no stretch of the imagination is it an evening for heavy business discussion, and apart from the principal speeches and the tradition of the silent toast 'To the Immortal Memory of James Watt', it is an undemanding evening with few dramatic overtones.

Few Clydesiders who attended the 1965 dinner will forget the evening or the courage and quiet dignity of the chairman James Lenaghan, the President of the Institution of Engineers and Ship-

builders in Scotland, and managing director of Fairfield. Many major shipyards throughout the world have collapsed since 1965 but on that evening it seemed unimaginable that Glasgow's largest shipbuilders, recent tenderers for the Cunard Q3 project, builders of the *British Commodore* (the largest ship built in the port of Glasgow) and with an order book of some magnitude, were unable to meet their financial obligations. The evening passed and the Immortal Memory was honoured, but a turning point in the politics of British shipbuilding had been passed, and things would never be the same again.

*   *   *

The old Fairfield yard, with its glorious traditions of building ships like *Livadia* and *Calais-Douvres* passed away, but with government help the labour force was kept together and in January 1966 a new company, Fairfields (Glasgow) Ltd, was set up largely financed by government and industry and, to a lesser extent, by the trade unions. The aim was to transform the shipbuilding scene by specialised industrial relations, good in-company communications and by introducing measured day work for all manual employees. Despite the violently opposing attitudes to the so-called Fairfield Experiment, most people will agree that the motivation in the yard in the early days indicated a desire at all levels to see change. Even traditional line managers agreed that there were better ways of handling industrial disputes than the stereotyped methods of many older shipyards, indeed many aspects of the current Employment Acts were thrashed out 'on the floor' of the Fairfield Yard, including what were then radical changes in the methods of employing and discharging labour.

One problem faced by Fairfields (Glasgow) Ltd was the heavy orientation of senior managers to production engineering and a real lack of senior men with professional shipbuilding expertise. Grave disquiet was felt by the shipbuilders at the introduction of measured day work and indeed this was dropped at the merger of the Upper Clyde yards.

In two years Fairfields (Glasgow) may have achieved little in measurable terms, but it did hasten in days when new ideas and styles of management were welcomed. No financial results were published but, possibly fortunately, all this was overtaken by the UCS merger.

*   *   *

Right *The last great liner to be built at Govan was the TSS* Empress of Britain, *shown here at Fairfield in June 1955 just before her launch by Her Majesty the Queen.*

Below *in 1928 Alexander Stephen & Sons delivered the twin screw steam tanker* Victolite *to the Imperial Oil Company of Canada.*

In the wake of the Geddes Report, the Upper Clyde shipyards formed a very insecure and unhappy alliance called Upper Clyde Shipbuilders Ltd. Initially it was to have been Yarrow, Connell and Stephen with John Brown's excluded because of their losses, Fairfields because of their partial nationalisation and Barclay, Curle because of impending closure by the parent company Swan, Hunter of Wallsend-on-Tyne.

With government help and inducements, the company was formed in February 1968 and the equity divided as follows: Yarrow, 20 per cent; Connell, 5 per cent; Fairfields, 35 per cent; Stephen, 10 per cent; John Brown, 30 per cent.

There were immense difficulties in concluding such an arrangement, as the only factor in common between the five participating companies was that they built ships. It is easy with hindsight to be unkind; perhaps it may be summed up best by saying that each company had a vested interest to watch and that all were suspicious of Fairfields—where 'brashness had replaced the old autocratic authority'. The situation was not helped by Yarrow's having an option to buy out of UCS, an option which they exercised and which, with the benefit of hindsight, may have been a good move on their part.

Problems piled on to UCS and barely 3½ years after being formed the receiver was called in. The subsequent 'work-in' has become a much talked of phenomenon, and indeed will become part of Clydeside's folklore, but it certainly assisted in keeping public attention on the Clyde yards and after prolonged negotiations the setting up of a new and successful shipbuilding company under government supervision.

* * *

Govan Shipbuilders Ltd, was formed in 1972, based on the Fairfield Yard and absorbing the works of Stephen and Connell. The Connell yard was managed under a separate company known as Scotstoun Marine Ltd, but under Govan's direct supervision and produced ships from 1973 to 1980 when closed by British Shipbuilders and placed on care and maintenance basis.

Govan Shipbuilders have been highly successful in increasing productivity and in producing fine modern ships with considerable technological content. Much of the sales drive has centred on the use of standard ships like the *Clyde*, the *Kuwait* and the *Cardiff* designs, but with flexible arrangements to meet owners' specialised requirements. Since incorporation, the company has delivered around 60 standard vessels as well as building specialist ships and carrying out successful retrofits on container ships.

There is little doubt that John Elder and Sir William Pearce would heartily approve of the style and drive of the company which is based in the Fairfield Yard.

Alexander Stephen

Based at Linthouse, from which arose the famous sobriquet 'Stephen of Linthouse' the company of Alexander Stephen & Sons Ltd, had a much further travelled base than most Scots realise. First founded in 1750, only five years after the Jacobite uprising, the company had moved from Burghead on the Moray Coast, to Aberdeen, to Arbroath and finally to Dundee. During their stay in Dundee they decided to set up another yard in Glasgow, which they hoped would have the great advantages of Clydeside ship-building skills coupled with the know-how of shipbuilders acccustomed to the whaling vessels and strongly built ships which left Scotland's East Coast. The site they chose in Glasgow was at the bottom of Kelvinhaugh where they both built and repaired ships from 1851 to 1870. In 1870 they transferred

Built by Alexander Stephen & Sons of Linthouse, the Clyde Shipping Company's coastal passenger and cargo liner Toward *goes on trials in 1923. The CSC, founded in 1815, is one of the oldest shipping concerns in the world. For coastal vessels, they have always used the names of lighthouses, and at the time this photograph was taken used two pennants for their houseflag, one with the lion rampant and the other with the Irish harp. This has been replaced by a blue pennant with a lighthouse and the initials CSC (National Maritime Museum).*

Built by Alexander Stephen & Sons Ltd the steam cable layer The Cable *proceeds on sea trials in 1924 before being handed over to the Australasia & China Telegraph Company.*

to new ground at Linthouse where they continued building until the late 1960s. (The Dundee yard was sold to the Dundee Shipbuilders Company Ltd, in 1894, and from this, the Panmure Shipyard, in 1901 came the famous *Discovery* of antarctic fame.)

The overall number of ships built is believed to be: at Aberdeen, 10 vessels from 1793 to 1829; at Arbroath, 33 vessels from 1830 to 1843; at Dundee, 97 vessels from 1844 to 1893; at Kelvinhaugh, 147 vessels from 1851 to 1870; at Linthouse, 547 vessels from 1870 to 1968. The Aberdeen totals are for known ships, but it is assumed many more were built as, indeed, they must also have been on the Moray Coast.

In many ways Stephen's could be likened to Denny of Dumbarton. They built custom requested vessels of unimpeachable quality, and while not in the forefront of technical development to the same extent as their friendly rival, they produced a remarkable number of firsts, including Sir Christopher Furness' steam yacht *Emerald* which was the first turbine vessel to cross the Atlantic and shortly thereafter the Allan Line's *Virginian* which made the first crossing by turbine passenger ship in 1905.

The ships by which the Linthouse Yard made its good name were the smaller passenger ships like the DFDS liners *Hellig Olav* and *United States* of 1903 or the *Pieter de Connick* built in 1881 for the White Cross Line of Antwerp. This latter ship was later sold to the ill-fated Danish Thingvalla Line, renamed *Norge* and ultimately became part of DFDS Skandinavien-Amerika-Linien, and while in their service was run on to rocks off the Island of Rockall on June 22 1904 with the loss of 620 lives.

The ultimate in elegance from the Stephen yard must be the beautiful ships built for Elders & Fyffes and the Imperial Direct West Indian Line for bananas and a limited number of passengers. These ships were of the highest standards, with their design carefully vetted for both technical and commercial considerations, as they had to run a liner trade to coincide with not only British and European market demand, but also the seasons in the West Indies. Typical of these was the TSS *Port Kingston* built for Elder Dempster & Co (an associate of Elders & Fyffes) in 1904 and the lovely *Golfito* built for Elders & Fyffes in 1949. It is interesting to note that the *Golfito*, along with her sisters, was powered by twin-screw turbine machinery and gave good service over the best part of 20 years on the Atlantic.

Three ships that typify the Linthouse 'marque' are the Aberdeen Line *Marathon* of 1903, a beautiful clipper bowed ship, which was so popular that in 1912 she was lengthened (and a second funnel added) to give more passenger accommodation. The second was the graceful two-funnelled *Gelria* of 1913 which was to the account of Koninlijke Hollandsche Lloyd, and which can be admired second-hand with the superb builder's model in

Glasgow Transport Museum. The third must be the *Aureol*, that fine ship for Elder Dempster's West African trade which must vie for the title of the most beautiful Clyde-built ship of the 1950s.

Among the companies which built at Linthouse was P&O, and they placed three very important orders with Stephen's in the late 1920s. One was for the pioneer turbo-electric *Viceroy of India* one of the company's most successful ships and for two smaller turbine ships, the *Corfu* and the *Carthage*.

The Royal Navy built many ships of all sizes at the yard including the very fast minelayers *Manxman* and *Ariadne* both capable of speeds in the upper thirties, and the aircraft carrier *Ocean* completed in August 1945 and which was the first to have a jet aircraft land and take off from its flight deck. Undoubtedly the most famous Stephen ship for the Admiralty was the sloop *Amethyst* which made the famous dash from the River Yangtse in 1949.

In 1968, when the *Port Caroline* left the ways at Linthouse bearing the yard No 701, it was the end of a great shipbuilding tradition. The goodwill of Simons-Lobnitz had been obtained and, while no

The fast minelayer HMS Ariadne *completed in 1943 by Alexander Stephen of Linthouse. This ship was a sister of the famous Linthouse-built HMS* Manxman *whose speed approached 40 knots in light displacement condition (Ralston photograph).*

more launches took place, at least two dredges were built for 'knocking down' and re-erection elsewhere.

Stephen's had for many years been the most liberal of employers and apprenticeships in the yard were sought after, especially as they had their own excellent training school. It is appropriate that British Shipbuilders (Training, Education and Safety) Ltd, have their school mid-way between the Fairfield and former Linthouse sites. There could be no greater memorial to the foresight of the earlier generations.

Far from their birthplace, the Elder Dempster liner Aureol *and a Ghana Ports tug pictured in 1966 at Tema. The* Aureol *was built by Alexander Stephen & Sons, the tug by Ferguson Brothers of Port Glasgow.*

Chapter 19

From boatyard to nationalisation

The development of commercial and business arrangements in shipbuilding is as instructive as technical developments are in naval architecture, and with two centuries of industrial development on the banks of the Clyde there is ample opportunity for this to be examined in detail. The earliest yards were one man or one family businesses with simple systems of management and control—a situation which is ideal for what might be referred to as low level technology. Manning levels were low, original design work was seldom carried out, research and development were non-existent, all part of an arrangement seen in every corner of the world and, indeed, suitable internationally for the building of local craft in timber.

For yards to develop, more structured arrangements were required as it was important that investors could see both potential profits and monitor the results of management. Therefore as shipyards enlarged and became more organised many came under the control of partnerships where each partner contributed finance and in return had a mutually agreed share in the management of the operation. With the coming of iron shipbuilding there was a need for expensive tooling and for the financing of large holdings of stock plates and sections. It was clear to both shipowners and shipbuilders that larger ships meant considerably larger cargoes and in the end more princely profits. New industries have a recognised syndrome; either financial returns of staggering magnitude on a given outlay, or of complete loss in a new field of venture—the 19th century shipyards had their share of both with the profitable shipyards making their gains either from the building of large ships or from exploitation of some new technological development. There were disadvantages to partnerships like difficulty in obtaining credit without acceptable security and the ever-present concern of each partner, that he was

liable at all times for the debts of the others, but despite these the bulk of the Clyde shipyards prior to 1900 worked in such circumstances and by and large were successful.

While partnerships, especially those of long standing and mutual trust, allowed for flexibility in financial investment there was a need for a simple way in which individuals could purchase or sell small shareholdings in a business venture. The Companies Act of 1855 met a great need and some shipyards quickly availed themselves of the opportunity to enlarge the number of people with a stake in the business and to limit their corporate liability. One of the first was the London and Glasgow Engineering and Iron Shipbuilding Co Ltd of Govan which took over Smith & Rodger's Middleton Yard in 1864. They chose a name which reflected the two areas where their principal shareholding interests lay.

Known in Glasgow as 'The Limited' the London and Glasgow Company built 270 ships from 1864 till 1912 when they sold their ground, engineering patents and interests to Harland & Wolff. Every ship built there was of iron or steel and their products ranged from ships for the Royal Navy like the cruisers *Monmouth*, *Cumberland* and *Roxburgh* around 1901, and the cruiser *Yarmouth* launched in 1911 to merchantmen as varied as the iron passenger coasting liner *Princess Royal* in 1876 for M. Langlands & Sons of Liverpool and Glasgow and the 1895 Cunarders *Sylvania* and *Carinthia*. 'The Limited' were fine engineers and had varied marine and general work including, in 1893, boilers for the yacht *Mahroussa*. For many years they were managed by David Kinghorn (1821-91) regarded at the time of his death as the doyen of shipbuilders and link between the old and the new technologies.

Traditionally most shipbuilding companies have remained private limited companies ensuring that shares were in the hands of a family and friends or possibly a holding company. Such arrangements made it possible for groups to be created with vertical integration, such as shipyards supplying their product to shipping and trading companies, all bound with similar interests. Examples on the Clyde include: D. & W. Henderson Ltd and the Anchor Line; Greenock Dockyard and Clan Line Steamers; William Hamilton & Co and T. & J. Brocklebank & Co Ltd; William Denny & Brothers and the Irrawaddy Flotilla Co; William Denny & Brothers and 'Paddy' Henderson; Ardrossan Dockyard and Coast Lines.

Less usual arrangements include small shipping companies like Ross & Marshall and Burrell & Son operating their own shipyards; Yarrow's shipyard controlling a consultancy group Y-ARD; major horizontal groupings like the massive 1920s Harland & Wolff combine including Caird & Co, D. & W. Henderson, A. MacMillan & Son and A. & J. Inglis.

Many companies which were making heavy weather of the depression in the 1920s and '30s sought to rectify matters by altering their Articles of Association, trying alternative areas of trading and often changing their name in the process, such as William Hamilton & Co (1928) Ltd as the proprietors of the Glen yard were known as from 1928 to 1933. The owning of ships by shipyards is more frequent than generally supposed and comes about for many reasons including speculative building when the market is depressed in the hope that the new ship can be sold later when demand is buoyant and the price higher. Some shipbuilders have been known to buy back second hand tonnage as part of a deal to capture new orders and others, particularly high technology companies like Denny's and Fairfield, have invested in the ownership of experimental and unusual vessels. One remarkable vessel was the paddle steamer *La Marguerite* completed in 1894 by Fairfield for management by a consortium of steamship owners with the title papers remaining with the Govan shipbuilder. She was 330 ft long (110.5 m) and with two-cylinder compound diagonal engines developing a remarkable 8,000 ihp, was able to steam at 22 knots. *La Marguerite* had a long and profitable life operating on the Thames/Kent/English Channel excursion trade before the consortium collapsed and Fairfield arranged her management under a new company created for the purpose—New Palace Steamers Limited.

The most important feature of a shipyard

endeavouring to move into the high class market is the establishment of design, estimation and sales procedures. In more recent years such requirements have developed into a need for marketing and, with a very few notable exceptions, this vital discipline was omitted by Clyde shipbuilders. Even Fairfields (Glasgow) Ltd which had almost every fashionable management aid from value engineering to organisation and methods within its walls, did not carry out forward evaluation and marketing studies largely on the grounds that such a service is very costly to a small or, in this case, medium size business. This ultimate department is to be found only in companies which have the most sophisticated financial arrangements and, indeed, the presence of marketing is a test as to whether a company is fully developed in management style or still has to rely totally on the intuition and experience of their chief executive.

Writing in 1968 Sir Wilfred Ayre of Burntisland recounted a situation in the early 1930s when 'a handful of builders were negotiating with a well known firm of Glasgow shipowners for a cargo steamer of 6,500 tons deadweight'. Ultimately the tenderers were reduced to the Burntisland Company, Lithgows Ltd and D. & W. Henderson of Partick. Neither Lithgow nor Ayre were prepared to further reduce price or offer further incentives and Henderson's were awarded, in fact, a two ship contract on accepting a £500 reduction in the price of the second ship. Henderson's asked for cash in advance for both vessels and obtained this, again on the strength of further price cuts. During construction of the ships Messrs D. & W. Henderson went into liquidation creating problems for many people, not least the Glasgow shipowner.

This brief, but sadly only too frequent kind of incident, clearly demonstrates the problems of the industry in time of recession and the very unfortunate effect that can be created by one or two shipyards in trouble, quoting unrealistic or indeed suicidal prices in a deadened market. In times like these the effect of Government work can be helpful and this has been offered to Scottish shipbuilders from time to time over 130 years, and with increasing frequency in the 1930s to overcome the slump and to prepare for the war that seemed looming on the horizon.

Several shipbuilders felt that something more positive should be done to avoid the law of the jungle and, with tacit support from the Bank of England, a means of rationing naval orders was attempted and, indeed, as early as 1928 the Shipbuilding Conference was founded as a means of trying to help the industry act in a concerted way. It was a small and unsure step aptly described by Professor Slaven in these words: 'The highly individualistic and independent ship-builders manoeuvred themselves uneasily into hesitant co-operation . . . under the pressures of the market in the 1920s.'

This movement amongst industrial leaders brought about consideration of means of eliminating unncessary competition from shipyards with redundant shipbuilding berths. With Government financial backing a new company was formed with a name that shortly was to become misrepresented, misunderstood and, indeed, rightly feared—National Shipbuilders Security Limited. To this day NSS Ltd conjures up partisan prejudice and is a symbol of disunity between owners and workforce.

It is certain now on looking back that while NSS Ltd created terrible problems and was brutal in closures it served a purpose. While it did not regenerate industry, as had been one of its aims, it probably helped to steer the industry clear of a worsening situation. The company was formed with capital borrowed on overdraft from the Bank of England, and this finance was used to purchase ship-yards with a view to their being closed permanently, dismantled or otherwise 'sterilised'. Further finance came from shipbuilders in levy form and from the small returns on resale of purchased interests and property. Shipbuilders in the scheme (and most were) undertook not to expand their activities from 1930 to 1940.

Several Clyde yards were affected, the largest being Beardmore which was then heavily in debt to the Bank of England. Effectively the closure of Beard-more's shipbuilding activities was a relief to the Government and the ending of an embarrassing commitment. The Clyde yards were hit hard at the beginning but by the end of the scheme it was applied fairly across the country. The Clyde yards affected were:

Wm. Beardmore, Dalmuir—1931 complete shipyard closure
Napier & Miller, Old Kilpatrick—1931 complete shipyard closure
Ardrossan Dry Dock, Ardrossan—1931 new yard closed
Barclay, Curle, Glasgow—1932 part yard closure
A. MacMillan, Dumbarton—1932 complete ship-yard closure

Bow McLachlan, Paisley—1933 complete shipyard closure
Dunlop Bremner, Port Glasgow—1933 complete shipyard closure
Ayrshire Dockyard, Irvine—1934 shipbuilding stopped
Fairfield, Glasgow—1934 part yard closure
D. & W. Henderson, Glasgow—1936 shipbuilding stopped
Harland & Wolff (Caird & Co), Greenock—1936 complete shipyard closure

As one of the directors of NSS Ltd was Sir James Lithgow, it was perhaps unfortunate that NSS Ltd purchased a restrictive covenant on the yard of Dunlop, Bremner & Co of Port Glasgow in 1933. This yard had come under the control of the Lithgows nearly 20 years before and this deal raised some public controversy and not a little private unrest at the time. However, it has to be said that the Port Glasgow yard had been idle for seven years and during that period had employed no men. The finance channelled to Lithgows turned out to be providential as, in 1935, James and Henry Lithgow stepped into the Fairfield collapse and by obtaining shares saved the great yard from oblivion. It is doubtful if these forthright and astute men received the real credit due for their subsequent actions.

The real sadness of NSS Ltd was that while owners of yards were compensated for allowing their business to be closed permanently and the sites to come under restrictive covenants for 40 years, there was no formal assistance given to the workforce. Conditions were desperate on parts of Clydeside and possibly worse on Tyneside with places like Jarrow full of unemployed people virtually devoid of hope. In the knowledge that Britain could easily absorb all the world's shipbuilding orders in one year and that foreign yards were in direct competition, a fatalistic belief developed that nothing could be done and there was no natural justice.

The worst was over in 1936 and by 1939 the position had changed. Inglis Shipyard which had been on the NSS waiting list had also been reprieved.

The period after World War Two did not run parallel to the experience of the 1920s. The shipyards were busy and some reconstruction and yard development was contemplated. In the 1950s Denny's laid out new steel fabrication facilities as did Barclay, Curle and Fairfield, but there was litle evidence of either shipbuilders or trades unions being

fully conscious of the increasing efficiency of European shipbuilding, Scandinavian in particular, and scanty attention was paid to the fast approaching industrial battle with the Japanese. It is a recurrent theme that lack of marketing was a major cause of the troubles not only of the Clyde but of the whole UK as well.

The Shipbuilding Inquiry of 1965-6, under R.M. Geddes, was a turning point. It recommended that shipbuilding be concentrated in four main groups in the UK and that techniques be adopted to select optimum markets and that once orders were obtained they be diverted to the most appropriate building yard. There were other far-reaching findings, some of which came to pass and others which were quietly buried. It was proposed that two major shipbuilding companies be set up on the Clyde, one in Port Glasgow and Greenock and the other at Clydebank and Glasgow.

The Lower Reaches company was formed in 1967 by the amalgamation of Scott's S.&E. Co and Lithgows Ltd and is known to this day as Scott Lithgow Limited. Initially it included Ferguson Brothers and Scott & Sons of Bowling, but the former is now independent within British Shipbuilders and Scott's of Bowling has been closed. This group has concentrated on the Kingston yard which has swallowed up the Glen yard, and on the Cartsburn/Cartsdyke complex. With some fine offshore vessels like the emergency support vessel *Iolair*, the dynamically positioned HMS *Challenger* and the dynamically positioned drillship *Ben Ocean Lancer* to its credit, the Scott Lithgow Group has the proven skill and experience for an offshore

TSS Empress of Canada *was a Canadian Pacific Liner with an interesting history. Launched by John Brown's in 1928 as the* Duchess of Richmond, *she served on the North Atlantic until 1940 when requisitioned as a troopship. In 1946 she was refitted at Fairfield and on completion of the work in 1947 emerged as* Empress of Canada *and in the postwar livery of the 'White Empresses'. In 1953 she caught fire at Liverpool and became a total loss. After righting she was towed to Italy in 1954 for breaking up.*

construction company and, indeed, has been so designated by British Shipbuilders.

The other group became known as Upper Clyde Shipbuilders Ltd formed in a much unhappier alliance between John Brown & Co, Charles Connell & Co, Fairfields (Glasgow), Alex Stephen & Co and with Yarrow as an associate. Ultimately Yarrow withdrew from UCS and following the collapse of UCS and the world famous work-in, a new company Govan Shipbuilders was formed. This is dealt with elsewhere.

On July 1 1977, Scott-Lithgow and Govan Shipbuilders were nationalised becoming members of the new Corporation. Yarrow Shipbuilders Ltd was taken over also leaving its former holding company Yarrow & Co which retained independence. The engine building facilities of Barclay Curle and John G. Kincaid were also nationalised as were Scott's of Bowling and Ferguson Brothers being part of the Scott Lithgow Group. Within a short period the Ailsa shipyard in Troon requested that it be taken over and from then has been a busy yard working in close liaison with Ferguson Brothers through their joint management structure.

Possibly the saddest aspect of nationalisation was the near two years of indecision which came about through the delaying tactics of the Opposition in the House of Commons. While it is the duty of the party in Opposition to act as watchdog it is tragic when a state of insecurity develops as it did in shipbuilding and as a result no massive investment was forthcoming from private enterprise or from public funds, and the centralised marketing which was to be a keystone of the new industry was delayed over two of the most vital years, mid-way between the two 'oil crises' of 1973 and 1978. The main delay in the passing of the Commons Bill was over the technicality of 'hybridity' or the nationalising of shipbuilding and ship repairing. Ultimately the Government gave way and dropped ship repairing from their requirements and Vesting Day for British shipbuilders was announced. Strange to relate the Opposition victory became pyhrric as many ship repairers automatically came within the groups to be nationalised, and at least one major independent ship repairing group sold out as quickly as they could to the new Corporation.

Now the vast bulk of the Clyde is within British Shipbuilders apart from a few companies of which ClydeDock Engineering Ltd founded at Govan on the old Harland & Wolff site in 1977 is the largest.

On May 19 1969, a National Demarcation Procedure Agreement was signed on behalf of the Shipbuilders and Repairers National Association and the Conferation of Shipbuilding Unions. It was a simple 19 clause agreement of only a few hundred words but it meant that, for the first time on a National basis, inter-union disputes would be made to follow a rigorously laid down procedure and for the first time in 100 years shipyards could plan on availability of manpower to carry out and complete contracts. The immediate results were not perfect—but over the following months and years there was a dramatic drop in the time lost at work through unofficial stoppages.

One might ask why it took so long to reach this situation, especially when eminent trade union leaders and shipbuilding executives had proposed similar arrangements for many years. There would appear to be three distinct reasons for this tardiness in coming to an acceptable peace formula. First, despite the warmth and loyalty that all shipbuilders traditionally feel for one another, there have always been men of an inflexible nature who have been bred in certain elements of what was misnamed 'Red

Clydeside', and also from a minority of the families which traditionally governed the 'family shipyards'. These few men from the extremes of industrial attitudes and thought have had a perverse effect on the evolution of industrial relations.

Secondly, the traditional tough trade union background in heavy industry, evolved loyalties which were first to their trade union group as distinct from those who worked in the same industry and were of another union. This situation came about through the third reason which had its roots in the financial structure of the shipyards. The Clyde shipyards, similar indeed to most others in Britain, were plagued with liquidity and cash-flow problems. As a result they were labour intensive units, where in times of economic prosperity there was full employment, high utilisation of yard facilities, good wages and the recovery of overheads for the shipyards. In bad times, with slack order books, shipyard owners could effect the quickest savings by reducing manpower and laying off or dismissing workmen. With around 20 trades in each yard—blacksmiths, riggers, joiners, riveters, platers and so on, fierce competition developed for each job, and over the years demarcation became an established method of preserving one's right to a livelihood. Indeed in the files of the Clyde Shipbuilders' Association, one finds large quantities of paper representing the early cases of the demarcation disputes.

Fortunately with the amalgamation of many unions, in particular the black squads into the Amalgamated Boilermakers' Society, and the development of closer ties and co-operation between unions, this form of dispute diminished and was further reduced by the 1969 Agreement. Certainly a new spirit came into many unions in the late 1960s, and a real desire to further their industry, as distinct from the union which served it and other industries besides. Gone are the days when shipbuilders developed a petulant attitude to one another in days of labour scarcity and, conversely, adopted a common front when groups of men had to be discharged at any place on the river.

By tradition, most managers were not involved in union activities, some recruited from the drawing offices had tenuous connections with the former Association of Engineering and Shipbuilding Draughtsmen which had been founded in Clydebank in the earlier years of this century, and others retained links with their former trades unions. The Nationalisation Bill in Westminster radically changed this, as managers realised that to have a coherent and accepted voice on the councils of the industry they would have to consider either forming a union or joining an existing trade union with management interests. Several major unions wooed the managers, and were discomfited when the managers formed their own Shipbuilding and Allied Industries Management Association. With a membership throughout UK of less than 2,000, it joined in with the larger and well established Engineers and Managers Association, and has been successful in forming a co-ordinated group of the managers, who have established their own ethos and collective voice.

In the late '60s, with the co-operation of both management and yard and local union organisation, agreements were made in which relaxations in demarcation and working practices were instituted in shipyards in return for cash payments, with the long term aim (now almost achieved) of parity of wages and complete interchangeability of work where necessary for production.

The shipbuilding employers have had various societies designed to co-ordinate their activities and to allow them to speak with one voice both on matters of industrial relations as well as on national matters affecting government policy. In 1889 a 'Federation of Shipbuilders and Engineers of England, Scotland and Ireland' was formed and no doubt closely studied the Shipbuilding and Engineering Companies Association first set up on the Clyde in 1866 by 24 subscribing firms. This latter body became the Clyde Shipbuilders' Association which was a powerful voice on the River until 1966, when the new Fairfields (Glasgow) Ltd,

declined to join and when the sharp run down in shipbuilding organisations was felt.

On a national scale the Shipbuilding Employers' Federation was founded in 1899, but the most important organisation was undoubtedly the Shipbuilding Conference set up in 1928 to attempt to rationalise the tendering for work, and to make a stronger political lobby for shipbuilding which in parliamentary terms always came secondary to the shipping interests of this country. In 1967 these two bodies, along with the Dry Dock Owners' and Repairers' Central Council, all amalgamated to form SRNA—the Shipbuilders' and Repairers' National Association, and for 10 years until nationalisation this body had the authority to speak for the shipyards, to negotiate with the unions at national level and was charged with the responsibility of furthering the interests of the industry at the highest levels.

SRNA was wound up in 1977, and British Shipbuilders assumed this role for their own companies and the new Shiprepairers and Shipbuilders Independent Association represented those smaller companies remaining in private ownership.

With trials successfully completed, the Anchor Liner Tuscania *has been handed over to her new owners by the shipbuilders. The Anchor Line flag has gone to the mainmast and the Fairfield flag to the courtesy position on the foremast. The* Tuscania *entered service in 1922 and throughout her service saw varied work on the Atlantic, to India and on trooping. In 1939 she was sold to the Greek Line and renamed* Nea Hellas. *Later renamed* New York, *this Govan-built liner was not broken up till 1961, 40 eventful years after launching.*

Chapter 20

Shipbuilders of the Firth

Shipbuilding on the Ayrshire Coast

It is appropriate that Ayr, the county town, is given the leading position in a review of shipbuilding on this lovely stretch of coastline, as according to ancient records building of ships has taken place here for at least 700 years. King Alexander II is believed to have had boats built at Ayr in the 13th century, King Robert the Bruce sailed from Ayr in the 14th after outfitting in the town and late in the 15th century ships were ordered to be built there by the Scots parliament. Fuller records are available for the 19th century and onwards and it is known that two small builders operated around the harbour area for a short time: D. & A. Fullarton who built several small sailing vessels in the 1860s including the barque *Calderbank* and the steamer *Carrick Mail*, and then in the 1870s the yard of M. Kellard known to have built smacks and similar craft. Another short lived venture of the time was the Ayr Shipbuilding Co.

Ayr took on a new significance as a building centre in 1883 when Messrs McKnight and McCredie set themselves up with a yard in the harbour. Within a year they built five ships—probably in steel—and then Samuel McKnight became sole proprietor of the business, which became well known for the next 18 years as S. McKnight & Co Ltd. They specialised in paddle steamers and coasters, and through their connections with P. & A. Campbell, they and their successors, Ailsa, built many fine white funnelled paddle steamers for the Bristol Channel. In all nearly 60 ships were built at Ayr before the yard was taken over by the Ailsa Shipbuilding Company of Troon. Ailsa operated the yard until the economic depression forced them to abandon the site in 1929 and to concentrate their sparse inter-war years orders at the Troon base.

From the national point of view it was fortunate that the Ayr yard was not dismantled, as 11 years later the patent slipway was brought back into use on the order of the Admiralty Merchant Repairs Department and for two and a half years was operated by the London Graving Dock Company. In 1943, control was transferred back to the Ailsa Company who continued to operate it until 1947 when once again the management changed to the Ayr Engineering & Constructional Company Ltd. This latter company had been formed in 1941, and to complicate the story was a subsidiary of the London Graving Dock! The Ayr slip continued for some years, but with the war over, and the run down of the Clyde steamer fleet, their traditional markets for ship repair had disappeared and once again closure was inevitable. The situation was exacerbated by the fact that the slipway, or marine railway for hauling ships out of the water, was just over 16.5 m broad (54½ ft) and therefore considerable amounts of business could not be attempted, especially as no inexpensive solution for broadening the slip could be devised.

The demise of Ayr and of the other long established shipbuilding town Dumbarton was particularly sad as, probably, they were Scotland's oldest shipbuilding ports, and arguably the oldest in Britain. This honour now goes to Sunderland where Wearside shipbuilding flourishes to the present day and where the history can be traced back as far as 1346.

Visitors to the National Trust for Scotland's great showpiece, Culzean Castle in Ayrshire, could be excused for not connecting it with shipbuilding. At the foot of the cliffs below the castle are various relics and a shed, which on closer examination inform the thoughtful person that this was once a site for ship construction. The Marquis of Ailsa (1847-1938) formed the yard shortly after succeeding to his title in 1870. He designed many of the small yachts and

other vessels which came from its slipway. One cannot fail to be impressed with the beautiful castle, the glorious scenery around, and on entering the castle the beauty of the lines of the half models displayed. The Marquis was not only a fine seaman and a good ship designer but seems to have had an ability to have the right men round him. For a while William Fife (3) was manager, and when the yard was moved ultimately to nearby Maidens, he was associated with Peter Wallace and also with Alexander McCredie the previous partner of Sam McKnight. In 1885 they took over the Troon shipyard and gave it the family name, the Ailsa Shipbuilding Company, as it continues to be known as to this day. Nearly a century has passed and over 500 ships have been launched from the yard which is a vital part of the economy of Troon.

The history of the yard is interesting, while not being in the vanguard of technical progress at the beginning of the century, they maintained their name by good solid workmanship and excellent customer relations. This is borne out by the large number of repeat orders throughout their history. The association with Ayr has been noted already, but it is worthy of remark that during the two ship-yard phases they had nine building berths, six in Ayr

The coastal steamer Maple *during her trials in 1914. Built at the Ayr shipyard of the Ailsa Shipbuilding Company, the new ship was handed over to the Laird Line Ltd of Glasgow. After the merger of the Burns & Laird Lines, this well known ship was renamed* Lairdsglen *in 1929 (Wotherspoon Collection, Mitchell Library, Glasgow).*

and only three in Troon. In 1903 the last sailing ship was built at Troon, a steel barque, and in 1907, to signify their total allegiance to powered vessels, an engine works was completed. On the death of the Marquis of Ailsa in 1938 the company passed into the hands of the Hutchison family and at one time Sir James Hutchison, the MP for Kelvinside, Glasgow, was chairman. In the late 1970s along with many other shipyards worldwide the Ailsa Company had difficulties in securing orders and for a short time there were many anxious families in Troon. The Nationalisation Act did not include Ailsa as their turnover put them just below the mark for takeover on vesting day. This was an invidious situation and, early in 1978, some months after the nationalisation of the bulk of the industry, Ailsa requested that they, too, join the State Corporation.

British Shipbuilders responded positively, took over Ailsa, and shortly after arranged that they form a joint management structure with Ferguson Brothers of Port Glasgow. This arrangement left the two shipyards with their own local management, but with an administrative holding company Ferguson-Ailsa Limited for design and marketing affairs. The first major contract for the new company was the gas tanker *Traquair* for the Anchor Line, Glasgow which was built in two parts, one half at Port Glasgow and the other half at Troon. This ship was joined at the Greenock dry dock and went into operation in 1982.

The shipyard in Troon has been in operation since 1811 and had been through various phases of ownership prior to Ailsa taking over. They included the Portland Shipbuilding Company, named after the fourth Duke of Portland who developed Troon in the early 1800s and the Troon Shipbuilding Company which occupied the yard for 20 years before the Ailsa company commenced operations.

Among well known Troon ships was the paddle steamer *Glen Usk* built for P. & A. Campbell in 1914. This attractive vessel not only served as a minesweeper from 1915 to 1919, but her design became a pattern for Admiralty minesweepers during the First World War. The Campbell fleet was set up by brothers Captain Peter and Captain Alec Campbell who, after running steamers on the Clyde moved to Bristol, but remained loyal to the yards north of the border, and even more so to those on the Clyde for the bulk of their new construction. Their last Clyde built ship was the paddle steamer *Cardiff Queen* built by Fairfield at Govan in 1947.

In 1957 Ailsa built the twin-screw motor car ferry *Glen Sannox* for the Caldeonian Steam Packet. In the mid-1970s this ship was upgraded and re-engined in Aberdeen by Hall Russell & Co Ltd and as some wags put it, just a retaliation for the complete rebuilding of the Hall Russell ferry *Clansman* which was carried out by the Troon company, when the *Clansman* was split, lengthened and heightened in a major piece of ship surgery at the beginning of the 1970s.

*　　　*　　　*

The Steele family, forefathers of Robert Steele of Greenock, commenced shipbuilding in Saltcoats, but the shipbuilding activities of the resort were limited to wooden smacks and small traders mostly in the 18th century. Shipbuilding was carried out to a considerable extent in neighbouring Ardrossan from about 1825. In the last century, work was carried on by Barr and Shearer, Peter Barclay, Barclay Robertson and Archibald Boyd.

The biggest shipbuilder at the time was the Ardrossan Shipbuilding Company founded in the 1870s. They were a continuation of Barr and Shearer and are to be remembered specially for building the first iron ship constructed at the port in 1888. In 1899 control of the company passed to several men from Tyneside and the name was changed again to Ardrossan Dry Dock and Shipbuilding Company. In 1913 the controlling interest again became Scottish and efforts were made to redevelop the site known as the North Yard from which ships were launched into the fitting out basin, a non tidal area of impounded water. The new directors also set about planning a new South Yard with ships launching into the sea. The work commenced in 1916 after Government approval had been received with provision for five building berths. To allow larger vessels in the old yard the tidal basin entrance was widened to 17.5 m (57 ft).

Sadly the amount of investment never justified itself as, by the early 1920s, work was running dry. In 1925 the title was changed yet again to that of Ardrossan Dockyard Ltd and it remained as such until closure in 1964. In 1931 National Shipbuilders Security Ltd purchased the (new) South Yard, which had not been able to pay for itself. This yard was closed with a 40-year restriction on building on the site. The North Yard was allowed to continue shipbuilding, but with a restrictive covenant forbidding the building of ships longer than 275 ft. The ownership of the Dockyard ultimately passed jointly to Coast Lines Ltd and to the Greenock engine builders John G. Kincaid & Co Ltd. Investment in the yard was kept at a low level and despite the building of some notable coasting ships after the Second World War, closure came as no surprise in 1964.

At the end of the 40-year covenant, a small shipbuilding enterprise McCrindle Shipbuilding commenced work in the South Yard. The first ship launched was the *Maid of Glencoul* for Highland Region ferry services.

Small yards were found round the coast: Ninian's and Richardson's at Largs, and the very much more famous yard of William Fife & Son at Fairlie. This company was founded around 1812 when William Fife launched his first vessel the 51-ton cutter yacht *Lamlash*. As a young man Fife had worked at his

father's business of wheelwright and had built rowing boats in his leisure hours, effectively teaching himself the trade, for which generations of Clydesiders and, indeed, those from other parts of the world, were to acclaim him a master. His son and grandson followed and, while the trading name is extinct, the company entity continues in the Fairlie Yacht Slip.

In 1814 Fife built the PS *Industry* for a Glasgow leather merchant and in 1815 it was sold to the newly formed Clyde Shipping Company. The *Industry* survived as a hulk to the 1920s. Her second engines are retained to this day by Glasgow Museums. Among the famous ships designed were the Americas Cup challengers *Shamrock I* and *Shamrock III*.

At Girvan the wooden fishing boat building yard of Alexander Noble & Sons Ltd was founded in 1946. This was developed on a green field site, with proper shipways built in 1948, in 1956 and again in 1973. A most readable description of the yard and its work is to be found in the National Maritime Museum's monograph *Scottish Inshore Fishing Vessel Design and Construction.*

Irvine is another Ayrshire town which is not associated in the public mind with shipbuilding, yet records show many small yards operated there during the 19th century. Outfits like Gilkison, Thomson of the 1820 period, Calderwood, the Scottish Iron Works, the Co-operative Iron Works and McGill & Gilmour who built SS *Fairy Queen* in 1893 for James Aitken, the Forth and Clyde Canal excusion operator of Kirkintilloch. From 1870 until 1872 a yard called the Irvine Shipbuilding Company existed, but despite their pretentious name only turned out a few small schooners. They were followed from 1898 to 1912 by the Irvine Shipbuilding & Engineering Company, which had an output of 31 ships of the coaster and fishing vessel type. In 1912 the yard was taken over by Mackie & Thomson of Govan and a new era began.

Mackie & Thomson vacated their site on the upper reaches in 1912 in order that Harland & Wolff might make the old Govan shipyard into a single unit. They had been set up in 1888 by William Mackie, formerly chief draughtsman to Stephen's and Robert Thomson, and from 1888 to 1912—a

Opposite page and right *The liquid gas carrier* Traquair *for the Anchor Line Limited, Glasgow, was constructed in two parts. The after section was built by Ailsa Shipbuilders Ltd, Troon, and launched in August 1981—their first night time launch. The forward section was subcontracted to Ferguson Brothers (Port Glasgow) Ltd and launched the same month. The two sections were positioned together at the Inchgreen Drydock on 23 August 1981. By September 15 the link up was complete, the main engine installed and the* Traquair *towed away for the installation of her liquid gas cargo tanks (The Anchor Line).*

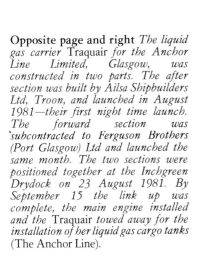

period of less than a quarter of a century—they produced nearly 450 ships at Govan, moving into the then fast growing market of steam trawlers and drifters which were replacing the British sailing fleets at the turn of the century. Their productivity was remarkable, an example being 25 vessels launched in 1896, 38 in 1897 and 34 in 1898. Their first steam trawler was the *Silver King* of 1889, only a few years after this type had been introduced in East Anglia. Their most famous ship must be the four-masted barque *Olivebank* built in 1892 for the Bank Line of Andrew Weir & Co Ltd and their most unusual, the steel schooner rigged barge *King Coal* which was built in an unsuccessful attempt to cheapen coal transit across the North Sea.

On the purchase of their Govan yard by Harland & Wolff Ltd they moved to the Irvine yard, operating there until 1928 producing just over 70 new ships. In 1928 as business prospects became progressively gloomier, the yard was purchased by the brothers James and Henry Lithgow. (By this time William Mackie was long dead and his partner Thomson nearing 70 years.) In an effort to brighten the image at Irvine, the name was changed to the Ayrshire Dockyard Co Ltd. Lithgow type procedures were introduced, ships were built 'on spec' and several vessels ultimately sold to the Clan Line, to Hogarths the Ardrossan-registered tramp operators and similar fleets. However, with the deepening recession, ship-building ceased. In 1934 the yard was sold to National Shipbuilders Security Ltd and closed down apart from the ship repairing function. During the Second World War the yard was used for major ship conversions. Harland & Wolff Ltd also operated in Irvine for about a year during the First World War, and it is recorded that four ships were constructed.

Around the coasts of the Firth of Clyde many other small ship, boat and yacht building enterprises abound. In Rothesay alone at least four firms have built or repaired ships in the area on which the pier now stands. Alexander Black leased the town slip and later this was held in the names of George and James Burns the brothers better known for their Irish Sea steamers and their involvement with Samuel Cunard. Robert MacLea and J. & J. Fyfe built small ships in the harbour area up until the 1870s while further round at Port Bannatyne the Bute Slip Dock was set up by the famous Glasgow naval architects and yacht designers Alfred and Charles Mylne.

Small yards have been situated near Dunoon in Lochfyne, at Sandbank and Rhu. At Rosneath on the western side of the Gareloch, Peter R. McLean built some fine small ships and in 1910 the yard was taken over by the now defunct company of James A. Silver. Silver's with the original hand of James Bain at the drawing board produced some of the most elegant motor cruisers ever built in Britain, each with individuality and yet all revealing the marque of their shipyard.

McGruer & Co Ltd of Rosneath and formerly of Clynder are an alive organisation with a history going back into the 19th century. McGruer's, it is believed, started off as itinerant boat builders on the shores of Western Scotland but eventually developed their own yard at Rutherglen next to that of Thomas Seath. In 1911 they transferred to Rhu near Helensburgh from Tighnabruich where they had been associated with the boatbuilder Smith. The Clynder yard made a name for superbly designed and built ships and Ewing McGruer Senior and his son of the same name became renowned for their success designing and building yachts of the 'Gareloch' Class, the International Six Metre Class and the first International Dragons ever built outside Scandinavia.

During the First World War they operated a factory in London making hollow struts for aircraft using their specialist skills developed in the making of hollow wooden masts and spars. The first aeroplane to fly the Atlantic had McGruer struts as did the airship *R34*. During both wars the company produced fast motor launches, naval pinnaces and torpedo boats and in 1942 they built an experimental semi-hydrofoil. In peace time work has been on yachts mostly but with several hydrographic survey launches and pilot boats. In 1952 the prestige order for the barges for the Royal Yacht *Britannia* was received. The company now under third generation George McGruer (Denny and Glasgow University trained) is still in the yacht business but also in the high class commercial market.

In the lochs around the Clyde, shipbuilding activities were found for short periods when steamers were erected on their shores and launched to serve the tourist trade and the Royal Mail. An example of such a transient yard was that of Duncan Young at Port Sonacham in Loch Awe. It is recorded he built the wooden screw steamer *Queen of the Lake* for David Hutcheson's service on the Loch. With no industrial structure in the area and a very limited market in steamers for the Loch such ventures fade into obscurity.

The mail ship from Aberdeen sets off for the Shetlands. From 1960 until 1977 the work was handled by the St Clair built by the Ailsa Shipyard, Troon.

Campbeltown

In a book entitled *Glasgow and its Environs* published in 1891 a paragraph reads: 'As an example of the enterprise of the firm, it may be mentioned that there is a telephone wire from the yard to the Post Office at Campbeltown, whence messages are transmitted by telephone, whereby great saving of time and effort is effected'.

The Campbeltown Shipbuilding Company had the unique telephone number of 'No 1 Campbeltown'. Whether the telephone helped or not, it is pleasing to record that in over 45 years they produced 110 ships of up to 4,500 tons each. When the depression of 1922 forced the yard to close, one of the bravest endeavours in Clyde shipbuilding came to an end. The company had been founded by Archibald MacEachern in 1877 after returning to his native town from a tour of duty in Africa. MacEachern came from that mould of West Highlanders who have the initiative to go overseas, earn money in amounts undreamed of in their native shores and return not just to spend it at home, but to use it to create employment and wealth in their communities. Others like John McCaig of Oban come to mind as similar benefactors of their areas. Campbeltown had some illustrious people around that time, not the least of whom was William MacKinnon the founder of the British India Steam Navigation Company, an organisation that ordered several hundred ships from Scottish yards over the best part of a century.

Campbeltown has had shipbuilding activities since 1700, and it is possible that the industry was continuous in the town until the closure of the yard in 1922. The site at Trench Point was ideal, with good water for easy launching into Campbeltown Loch, ample local coal supplies from the nearby Macrihanish Colliery and abundant good labour. One drawback was the need to bring iron and later steel supplies, engines and small parts to town by sea. The ending of the venture put 300 men out of work, and created serious distress in the Mull of Kintyre.

All other ventures in Campbeltown have been of boat building type, like those of Wardrop and of Wylie, but in 1968, an enterprise with far reaching results was commenced. The new company named Campbeltown Shipyard Ltd was founded on the old Trench Point site, and was set up to build steel vessels, in particular standard fishing craft. After 18 months of operation the financial condition of the company was such that the Highlands and Islands Development Board felt it necessary to bring in outside help. The shipyard became part of Lithgows (Holdings) Limited, and in fact it remains a part of the Lithgow Group to this day, remaining outside nationalisation despite Lithgow's large shipyard at Port Glasgow coming under state control. One of the exciting features of this yard is the entirely covered slipway capable of building two vessels up to 40 m long simultaneously. Modern shipbuilding techniques are used throughout—the success of the venture can be judged in that there has been a steady work output with about 60 ships delivered to-date and a workforce increasing over the years to around 200.

Chapter 21

The canals and specialist sites

Puffers

There are small trading craft which are unique and indigenous to every coastal region of Europe. The Clyde is no different, as for over 100 years small steam coasters served the lighterage needs of the river, and the freight delivery services of the West Highlands. These craft, known as puffers, displaced the early sailing gabbarts of the Ayrshire coast and the Western Isles and took over the role of the scows and dumb barges of the canals. It is estimated that only 400 were built, but despite this low number left an indelible mark on the folklore and literature of West Scotland—indeed they almost rival the place in prose and art attained by the China Clippers, a group of ships even smaller in number and flourishing for a vastly foreshortened period.

The first puffer is ascribed to the foresight of James Milne, the engineer to the Forth & Clyde Canal in 1856, when he converted an iron barge, the *Thomas*, to a screw steamer using a two-cylinder steam engine and a 3 ft diameter boiler. Like most barges of the time her cargo capacity was around 80 tons, and it was found that her reliability while trading between Glasgow and Falkirk was such that it was financially better to operate powered craft than to rely on trace horses. Within a few years there were over 20 puffers, mostly long, low flush-decked iron barges, probably double ended. Their tall funnels and tiller steering set a tradition that was to remain in evidence in some craft right up to the 1950s.

Mundanely described as steam lighters, puffers were often built with the restraints of the Forth & Clyde and Crinan Canals in mind. While the former was in use, the length was limited to 66 ft 6 ins. This canal, 35 miles in length, and with a four mile branch in Glasgow had 39 locks and could take vessels no longer than 68 ft 6 ins, 19 ft 6 ins broad and with a draft on the canal not exceeding 8 ft. As

this waterway crossed the central belt of Scotland, owners of small fleets of coasters had to make the decision either to build to puffer size, or to build considerably larger and neglect the trading opportunities offered by the area. A second type of puffer was later developed with a length of 86 ft 6 ins and with the Crinan Canal in mind.

The puffers were built in many places, but mostly in the Clyde area. Around 40 came from Scott & Sons of Bowling and smaller numbers from Ferguson Brothers of Port Glasgow, McMillan of Dumbarton, Wishart of Port Glasgow, the Scottish Iron Works at Irvine, George Brown of Greenock, and surprisingly two each from Scotts of Greenock and Denny of Dumbarton.

The shipowners Ross & Marshall Ltd had a small shipyard at Cartsdyke West in Greenock from 1899 to 1925. They built and repaired small coasters on their slip, much of the work being to their own account, and the last new construction reported in the Shipbuilding Conference returns of 1920 was their own SS *Warlight* bearing their traditional affix *'light'*.

The most colourful story of puffer building must be that of the Hamilton family, who built their first puffer on the high water mark at the head of Brodick Bay in 1895. Typical of the 19th century and earlier, a sawpit and steambox were set up on the beach and the keel laid. Frames were erected and then cladded with steamed timbers. This ship, the *Glencloy*, started their pattern of naming, and it is interesting to note that the last steam operated puffer trading on the Clyde until the 1960s was named *Invercloy*.

Puffers were built to be mini bulk carriers, and Hebridean workhorses. A flat bottom was essential for discharging coal on an open beach, or for dredging gravel from a river bank. Ample and

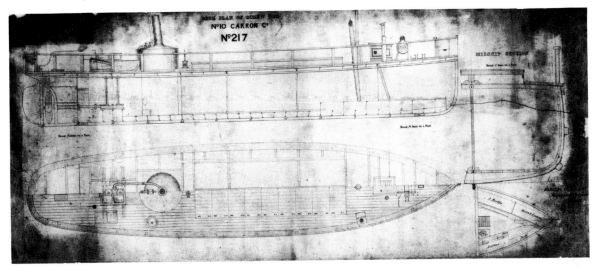

Steam Lighter No 10 *built in 1871 for the Carron Company of Falkirk by Barclay, Curle & Co of Glasgow. The Clyde puffers evolved from vessels of this type* (National Maritime Museum).

efficient craneage was in the form of a high derrick and a simple steam winch. It was usual to carry a crew of four, with the skipper sleeping in a tiny cabin under the steering tiller and the remainder in the triangular shaped fo'c's'le. Little space was required for a small engine, a vertical boiler and side coal bunkers in the bluff hull shape leaving a large rectangular shaped hold which ultimately carried 140 tons deadweight in the last of the Forth & Clyde puffers.

For 20 years shipbuilding flourished in the little town of Kirkintilloch on the banks of the Canal. In 1877, the MacGregor family set up their yard to build small wooden vessels, mainly for the canal trade. In 1901 they launched their first steamship and continued building powered ships in steel until their closure in 1921. P. MacGregor & Sons built many puffers and in 1912 the motor coaster *Innisagra*, one of the very first small diesel engined ships to be constructed, with five sisterships to follow. Their products were not confined to British waters, with many ships finding their way to far flung places, and South America in particular. As is usual in small ship delivery, various means were employed, such as bolted up construction, and then all parts numbered, knocked down and packed for delivery, or piggy back delivery when a small vessel

in whole or possibly in two parts is carried to its ultimate destination on the deck of a steamer from Glasgow. Despite these possibilities, a surprising number of vessels made their own way over the Atlantic, and owing to their size carried sails to assist in conserving fuel for the long trip.

Further along the canal was the busy shipyard of J. & J. Hay, which had a longer life span than its near rival. John Hay was a local farmer, and to assist in his business obtained a horse drawn barge which gave him both assistance and enjoyment. Being forward looking he developed the water transport side of the enterprise, ultimately purchasing some puffers, and in 1868 the interests of a small yard at Kirkintilloch. Hay's shipyard was for 90 years the operational centre of an ever growing fleet, and it is believed that over 100 puffers were built there of which 60 were for his own company. Launching was carried out sideways into the canal with very steep declivity (slope) on the launch ways and the last ship being *Chindit* in 1945 almost certainly the last traditional puffer built. Hay's fleet were named after national groups like *Dane*, *Boer* and *Saxon*.

The evolution of puffer from early canal barge with coal-fired boiler, single- or twin-cylinder simple steam engine, without condenser, using canal water and exhausting to the atmosphere (hence the name puffer) came a long way in 100 years. They were never at the forefront of technical advance, but the accolade of distinction must surely have come when at the beginning of the Second World War the Admiralty Merchant Shipbuilding Department selected the puffer as the most straightforward and

economical design for the large fleet of lighters which were required for the duration of hostilities. Using Scott of Bowling's design for the *Anzac* and *Lascar* of 1939, the plans were prepared for the successful VIC lighters of which 90 were built, mostly in England.

Apart from the Coastal Motor Shipping Company's ten motor puffers of 1912 and 1913, no serious attempt was made to use the internal combustion engine. This was reasonable in that the steam puffers were very simple and until some years ago, coal was plentiful, and indeed was one of the main cargoes to the Hebrides. In 1953, Hamilton & McPhail ordered the *Glenshira* from the Bowling Shipyard; with an overall length of 83 ft 6 ins, a five-cylinder British Polar diesel, 190 tons of cargo and by previous standards very excellent crew accommodation. The new vessel was ideal for the Clyde to

Hebrides trade using the Crinian Canal. With the running down and ultimate closure of the Forth & Clyde Canal, the *Glenshira* somehow underlined the fast approaching end of the puffers. In 1967 trading by steam vessels ceased and by the late 1970s few vessels remained in the trade. In 1982 the *Spartan*, a diesel-engined conversion, was handed over to the West of Scotland Boat Museum Association and the puffer era was over.

Other canal shipyards

From early days in the history of the Forth & Clyde Canal, there was shipbuilding at Kelvindock, Maryhill just east of the magnificent aqueduct over the Kelvin Valley. To this day the canal at Maryhill is of great interest, with a ladder of locks, large circular basins for both turning ships and impounding water and the few remains of the shipyard. At the

Above left *Broadside launches were unusual in the Clyde district, but were essential from time to time on the Forth & Clyde Canal. Here the puffer* Briton *takes to the water in Hay's Shipyard, Kirkintilloch, on November 30 1893* (Courtesy of J. M. Hay).

Above *The beautiful motor puffer* Pibroch *in Prince's Dock, Glasgow, 1970. This vessel, owned by Scottish Malt Distillers, carried raw materials to Islay and returned to Glasgow with whisky. She was built by Scott's of Bowling in 1957. The floating crane in the background is TSS* Newshot, *built in 1943 at Paisley by Fleming & Ferguson Ltd.*

Right *The Clyde puffer* Lascar *loading coal at Queen's Dock, Glasgow, in 1960. This was one of several conversions to diesel power.*

end of the 19th century it was an area of activity with constantly passing ships, and even in the Second World War several hundred men were employed there on the repair of small vessels and, of course, the ubiquitous landing craft.

The earliest shipbuilder at Maryhill was a Mr Morrison, of whom little is known. Various members of the Swan family were involved from 1857 until just short of 1890. It is probable that the dry dock was built in Morrison's time, but in 20 odd years their output and influence was considerable, and with building being carried out at other sites, the Swan's had many interests. It is known that they built at least one small vessel at Firhill in Glasgow, and in the Glasgow Museum's list of Clyde Built ships 11 vessels were stated as originating from Kelvindale, that is on the canal banks west of the aqueduct. They ceased building in wood in 1865 and from 1870 to 1874 ran a shipyard at the Woodyard in Dumbarton, where over 30 ships were built many of them using fabrications and parts prepared at Maryhill, an ingenious way of overcoming the restrictions of the canal!

The Maryhill yard was then in the hands of Marshall & Co for 20 years, of Richard Munro for just over one decade, and with the McNicoll Brothers from 1922 to the 1950s. The last launches of two puffers, *Kype* and *Logan* took place in 1921 although it is understood that the McNicoll's built some very small steel hulls during their tenure of the dock.

On the Monkland Canal, the arm running past Firhill and on to Port Dundas, several small ship-builders have flourished while others scraped a mere existence. Among these William Burrell & Son operated from 1875 to 1903, building over 50 ships, and from 1881 to 1884, they too operated the Lower Woodyard in Dumbarton, it coming into their possession being creditors of the previous owners R. Chambers & Co. At Blackhill both Cumming & Swan and their associated D.M. Cumming operated at Firhill, builders by the name of Ferguson built a few ships in the 1864 period and at Port Dundas itself W. Jackson operated, building the puffer *Basuto* in 1902, a vessel which operated on the Manchester Ship Canal until the 1970s.

Rutherglen

Of the generations of young people who have read and enjoyed Arthur Ransome's book *Swallows and Amazons*, few will associate one of the lake ships in the story with Clyde shipyards. The ship in question

The launching of PS Isle of Arran *from the Broomloan Shipyard of T. B. Seath in May 1892. This Clyde paddle steamer was one of the larger vessels built in the reaches above Glasgow Green, and this contributed, no doubt, to the size of crowd gathered. The* Isle of Arran *gave satisfactory service for 44 years, the last three of which were on the River Thames. Seath sent his ships down river and through the Glasgow bridges before fitting funnels, bridges and masts. Machinery was installed usually at Greenock or Glasgow* (Rutherglen Museum).

is the houseboat belonging to Captain Flint believed to be the *Esperance*, one of several ships on Lake Windermere built by T.B. Seath & Co of Rutherglen. The *Esperance* was Seath's 99th ship and constructed in 1869.

The story of Thomas Seath and his shipyard has an almost fairytale-like quality, perhaps not rags to riches, but certainly the story of a workman for whom toil was no stranger, and who enjoyed considerable success and in his later years prosperity of a high order. His unique shipyard can claim many products in good working order, even after the ravages of a century. In the last few years his hull No 209 has been recovered from Loch Rannoch, having had a working history of less than one year, and spent 99 years in the depths of the loch. The vessel is the iron steam yacht *Gitana*.

Seath was born at Prestonpans in 1820, and around 1828 came to Glasgow with his parents. His father was employed on coasting steamers, to be joined later by his son who rose through the ranks and ultimately obtained his coastal master's certificate. Throughout his life Seath seemed torn between his desires to build ships and to operate and serve on them. In 1853 he took over a building site on the west bank of the mouth of the Kelvin where Tod & McGregor and D. & W. Henderson were later to become established. In three years he built three ships one of which PS *Artizan* was for the Glasgow to Rutherglen service on what was then known as the Upper Clyde Navigation. This paddle steamer drawing only 27 ins ($\frac{2}{3}$ m) had Seath as captain, owner and chief engineer, controlling the engines by levers passing from the bridge to the engine room. The vessel sailed from the Old Weir at Glasgow Green to Rutherglen Quay.

In 1856 he moved the business to a yard off Broomloan in Rutherglen, three miles upstream from the Green, and nowadays the haunt of oarsmen and the mooring place for converted yachts. During the next 46 years he was to prove that the restrictions and inadequacies of the place and the shallowness of the river at that point were not a hindrance to progress, but a challenge to be met and overcome. These difficulties were to give him invaluable experience in the design and construction of river and shallow draft vessels, and his 300 Rutherglen-built ships gave him a worldwide renown as a specialist builder. His *Artizan* was later replaced on the Rutherglen service by the paddle steamers *Royal Burgh* and *Royal Reefer*, and from then on

Above SS Conway, *an ice-breaking maintenance barge built in 1894 by Napier Shanks & Bell of Yoker for the Crinan and Caledonian Canal Commissioners* (Wotherspoon Collection, Mitchell Library, Glasgow).

Left *Thomas B. Seath (1820-1903) one of the most colourful Clyde shipbuilders and a world-acknowledged expert on shallow draft and river steamers. Throughout his life he was torn between the desires to build fine ships, and to operate them* (Wotherspoon Collection, Mitchell Library, Glasgow).

Above right *A rare photograph of the twin-screw steamer* Clutha No 1 *proceeding down the Clyde. The shipyard in the background is the Kelvinhaugh Slip occupied by John Shearer & Son from 1890 till 1907. The* Clutha's *were owned and operated by the Clyde Navigation Trust from 1884 till 1903 and were built in Rutherglen, Dumbarton and Port Glasgow* (Wotherspoon Collection, Mitchell Library, Glasgow).

Right *A view of the weir dividing the River Clyde at Glasgow Green. This, the second weir, was constructed at the foot of Saltmarket in 1895, the previous one having been built at Hutchesontown Bridge in 1851 and demolished in 1880.*

there was a constant succession of barges, coasters, passenger steamers and steam yachts. Among the yachts were two special orders for the King of Siam and the King of Burma.

In April 1884 the Clyde Trust introduced a river passenger service on small steamers named *Clutha*'s from the Roman name for the Clyde. Altogether 11 were built and their names were *Clutha I* through to *Clutha 12* with No 11 missing. Seath made the initial design and built the first six with iron hulls. All were twin-screw ships giving them good manoeuvreability, and the remaining five, constructed of steel were built by Murray Brothers of Dumbarton and Russell & Co of Port Glasgow. The operating schedule was from Victoria Bridge in the city with calls at: Glasgow Bridge, Springfield Lane, Stobcross, Highland Lane, Pointhouse, Water Row, Meadowside, Sawmill Road, Linthouse, Whiteinch.

The great chronicler of the Clyde, Sir James Marwick, noted that in 1900 they carried 2.85 million passengers. However, the extension and efficacy of the Glasgow Tramway system had its effect, and the *Clutha* service came to an end in November 1903.

In 1885 Seath submitted plans to the Admiralty for a warship 150 ft by 30 ft and with a hull divided into many watertight compartments, as is now the practice in naval ships. A rockered keel was introduced to give quick turning and a 2 ft armour belt round the topsides designed either to break up missiles on impact, or to deflect them off harmlessly. This ship was never built and, indeed, the Broomloan yard would have been hard pressed to build it on the Upper Clyde.

Something like 16 steamers for the Clyde or the Scottish Lochs were built at Rutherglen. In 1888, as a sub-contract, Seath constructed the hull of a paddle

The beautiful sailing yacht Clunies Ross *photographed prior to her launch at Rutherglen in 1893. Two features are noteworthy—the steep declivity of the launch ways at the yard of Thomas B. Seath and the interesting cradle arrangement under the hull of the new ship* (Rutherglen Museum).

steamer for the North British Railway. On completion the new ship entered service causing little stir or sensation but 60 years later, when retired from the fleet, the *Lucy Ashton* had earned affection from Clydesiders for her regular and dependable functioning in all conditions and weather. Her story did not end there as is related elsewhere in this book.

As can be seen from his portrait, Seath was a man of energy, initiative and enthusiasm. Despite physical disabilities, he was never defeated and brought credit to the river and his profession. He died in 1903, a year after the yard had had its first idle period. The business name continued for a while as his sons set up a consultancy service, but the shipyard was sold.

In 1903 the yard became known as William Chalmers & Company, but the type of product remained unchanged. In 1913 and 1914, they produced motor coasting ships, and then plunged into the war effort of the Great War. It was said that they had 20 building berths and at different times used all of them for very varied wartime contracts.

In 1919 the yard was bought over again by the Rennie, Ritchie and Newport Shipbuilding Company, which controlled Ritchie, Graham & Milne of Whiteinch, and also a shipyard at Wivenhoe in Essex. The yard was reconstructed, four building berths set out and post-war shipbuilding commenced. Unhappily the onslaught of the depression was felt particularly strongly in the small ship market and, in 1922, the company went into voluntary liquidation. So ended 66 years of fascinating history, industrial effort and technological development and so ended a singular shipyard.

Wartime fabrication sites

The exigencies of war create positive and far reaching effects. In shipbuilding, naval architects realised that steel fabrication was an art in its own right, and this furthered a trend whereby steel construction firms were expected to contribute their very specialised expertise to the war effort. One such company, then called the Motherwell Bridge & Engineering Co Ltd, laid out a new shipyard at Alloa on the River Forth, and from that site delivered over 100 of the largest and most complex Landing Craft to be built in the United Kingdom. Parts were fabricated on the east coast also at their main works situated half a mile from the lovely stretches of the Clyde in what is now Strathclyde Park. Parts of frigates were prepared,

mostly for John Brown of Clydebank, and using a Lobnitz-generated design they built sections of the great floating Mulberry Harbours, so effectively used in the retaking of Normandy in 1944.

Similar work was carried out by another old established Motherwell engineering firm, Alex Findlay & Co Ltd. Their produce and output was similar to the Bridge Company, except that their final fabrication and erection was carried out at Old Kilpatrick, in the former Napier & Miller Shipyard specially adapted for the purpose and reopened despite the National Shipbuilders Security bond, by special Government decree. The steel output of Findlay's was massive by any standards, and in April 1944 alone topped 1,000 tons! Their labour force which had been 400 in 1939, rose to 1,700 in 1945 with a further 1,800 employed indirectly.

Redpath, Brown & Co Ltd built barges and landing craft on the waste ground at the former Henderson yard in Meadowside. P. & W. McLellan Ltd used an old yard on the Cart at Paisley and Sir Wm. Arroll & Co with fewer ships in their output used various launching sites on both sides of the country.

From all this a clear lesson emerged, that repetitive and relatively large output steelwork should be left to the professional fabricators. They can offer the specialised, critical and analytic view of the work to be performed, leaving the complex 'shipbuilding' jobs to the shipyards with their long history of problem solving.

The non-river side buildings

Throughout the late 19th century and through the early years of the 20th, there was a steady and, indeed, in some cases spectacular production of lake and shallow draft river craft for the Mission fields of Africa. The clients included the London Missionary Society, the Baptist Missionary Society and other similar groups—the Universities Mission to Central Africa, however, have left to posterity not only a glowing description of their aims and objectives, but also a delightful booklet on 'knock down shipbuilding' in their volume entitled *The Building of Chauncy Maples*, published in London in 1903.

A replacement was required for the mission station ship to serve on the then Lake Nyasa, and following negotiations and preliminary design work, the contract was awarded to Alley & MacLellan of Glasgow around 1897. The lake is very deep in places, is 350 miles long and up to 40 miles broad, and therefore the requirement was for an excellent sea boat and one that could approach the shore with safety and ease. The chief engineer on the mission station produced preliminary plans, and after consultation with a naval architect in the United Kingdom, the final brief became:

Length bp	120 ft 0 in	36.58 m
Length oa	127 ft 0 in	38.71 m
Beam	20 ft 0 in	6.10 m
Draft	5 ft 11 in	1.80 m
Speed	10 mph	

The ship and engines were assembled at the Polmadie iron works and the engines were run in 1899, with the power absorbed by a dynamometer. A contemporary photograph shows the contract in almost completed state in Glasgow with masts and funnel erected, and even the staysails bent on.

All the parts, plates, bolts and components were marked, taken to pieces and then sent for galvanising in hot zinc dip. On completion of this everything was put in 3,500 packages, the vast bulk of which was under ½ cwt and the largest the boiler at 9½ tons. SS *Hollingside* shipped the packages to the Zambesi from where they were transported to the lake and there re-erected using 35,000 rivets. After prolonged trials, the ship was accepted and early in 1902 dedicated, being named after a bishop who had lost his life in the lake in 1895.

Of as much interest as the foregoing is the costing. Alley & MacLellan made the following estimates:

Hull, engines and galvanising	£9,000
Transport: Glasgow/Lake Nyasa	£5,500
Re-assembly	£2,000

At £16,500, the *Chauncy Maples* was an expensive commodity in the 1900s, when a Clyde puffer could be built for a sum between £1,200 and £2,100. However, she was custom-designed and built, zinc coated and delivered almost by hand to a water thousands of miles from her birthplace. No doubt she gave good service, and almost inevitably it must be added that the builder either made a loss or in working for a religious organisation restricted themselves to a nominal profit.

Alley & MacLellan were the largest of the non-river side builders. In 1918 they became part of the Beardmore group, regaining their independence in 1937, having by then shed their Shrewsbury activities to the Sentinel Wagon Company Ltd.

Other similar companies included Hall Brown, Butterly & Co, Davidson & Wood, J. Howden, J. Norman and Wood & Mills.

Shipbuilding in concrete

An interesting but short-lived enterprise was witnessed on the Clyde at the end of the First World War. A small company called the Scottish Concrete Shipbuilding Company was set up and built a few ships near the west of Greenock.

This was one of several similar operations which began at the same time at Aberdeen, Barrow, Liverpool, London and elsewhere, partly as the result of the wartime Ministry of Shipping's initiative in setting up a programme for the construction of concrete ships. Their aim was to produce a fleet of barges, lighters and coasters capable of carrying 150,000 tons of cargo for the war effort without using the normal quantities of steel which was in short supply. The Armistice of November 1918 led to the abandonment of the scheme, but several of the new companies, including the Clyde one, continued in production for a while, but in the course of a few years all were closed.

The earliest successful concrete ships were built in Norway and with the builders bravely allowing the technical Press to monitor both the building and the subsequent operation. The first ship to obtain a Norwegian certificate for deep sea trading is believed to be the motor coaster *Namsenfjord* of 182 tons deadweight, completed in August 1917, and over the following four or five years, Scandinavian yards were to build such ships up to 2,000 tons. It was claimed that first cost was 25 per cent reduced, that repairs were simpler and quite correctly that fireproofing, insulation and corrosion resistant properties were better. Two styles of construction were used, one where prefabricated, pre-stressed sections were assembled on site, and the other, used by yachtbuilders to this day where a steel mesh is set up between two temporary skins into which is poured a Portland cement mix.

British shipbuilders, including Mr Maurice Denny of Dumbarton and Mr Walter Pollock of Faversham, Kent, showed much interest in the system. However, for a variety of reasons including the unwillingness of shipowners to experiment during the start of the depression in the 1920s and possibly through inflated claims for the efficacy of the system, this promising venture came to nothing.

Chapter 22

A new breed from the Clyde

It takes a brave man to foretell the future but, equally, a responsibility is shirked if one does not look ahead and consider the future of a professional field. The shipbuilding industry on the Clyde has had its misfortunes and periods of serious industrial depression but a close study of the business over 150 years can instil confidence in the student as the achievements in a comparatively short span of time are remarkable. In recent years a criticism has been heard that British—and indeed Clyde—shipbuilding has lacked the orientation given by marketing studies. Observations of past practice would tend to bear this out, especially when one realises that over the last 80 years Britain has consistently built around one million compensated gross tons of shipping per year, but our contribution to world shipbuilding has fallen from 60 per cent of the total at the turn of the century to as low as 3 per cent in recent years. As we pass through the worst shipbuilding recession of all time it is encouraging to note that our percentage share of the market has shown a small but nevertheless upward movement and in the early 1980s our position had improved to around 4 per cent.

In the past 150 years by determination, effort, genius and some good luck, the River Clyde was made navigable and as physical impediments to its use were overcome by engineering skill then it has become usable by the largest ships afloat. Glasgow became Scotland's premier seaport and for many years held an enviable place in the rankings of world shipping centres. With changes in the patterns of trade this is no longer the case and the role of Glasgow has altered, as has that of many similar towns and cities in Europe. In every case this has required a rethinking of their corporate affairs.

The River Clyde remains navigable and while the numbers of shipyards on its banks and shores has fallen from the peak of nearly 70 one hundred years

ago it still has a fine industry of a diversified nature based on the traditions of the founding forefathers. The Clyde has seen hundreds of shipbuilding establishments come and go, some famous, others unknown, big and small, some advanced technologically, others noted for their plain, unadorned but satisfactory workmanship—and mercifully very few where standards were known to be consistently poor. All these yards and the tens of thousands of men employed in them have given cause for the description 'Clyde-built' to be one indicating the highest praise.

This tradition is carried on in more establishments than people realise and a quick survey is in order. Starting in Glasgow the first shipyard is that of Govan Shipbuilders capable of building the most complex ships up to 70,000 tonnes deadweight. The yard has become noted for good steelwork standards and productivity and for introducing into the merchant sector modular outfitting, or the outfitting of steel units while still in the fabrication areas. Series production of cargo ships has been attempted in a major way with over 20 'Cardiff' Class bulk carriers and a similar number of 'Kuwait' Class general cargo ships were built in the past decade. The role of Govan is that of builder of ships with high quality steelwork coupled with advanced technological design. The very best of the traditions laid down by Elder and Pearce are found in Govan and the early shipbuilders would not be disappointed with the imaginative design work coming from this British Shipbuilders yard.

On the north bank about two miles west there is Yarrow Shipbuilders Ltd, another British Shipbuilders company and one that is dedicated to the building of defence vessels. Over the past years this yard has been so designed that it is capable of series production of some of the most advanced naval vessels and, currently, is building the Type 22

frigates of the 'Broadsword' Class. Yarrow has expanded both west and east in recent years and the three former Elderslie dry docks are now available as a frigate outfitting complex, a GRP manufacturing facility and one conventional dry dock. The importance of Yarrow to the Royal Navy was borne out by the fact that at the last Royal Naval Review in 1977 there were more Yarrow built ships there than from any other shipbuilder.

At Clydebank the shipyard is operated by UIE Shipbuilding (Scotland) Ltd part of a French industrial group. They have specialised in jack up rigs and are licensees for the manufacture of Marathon Le Tourneau rigs. UIE is working in a new technological field but based in the yard where some of our finest merchant liners and largest warships have been built.

At Greenock and Port Glasgow British Shipbuilders have their large Scott Lithgow group of yards. Here

The 35,000-tonne deadweight bulk carrier Selkirk Settler *is launched from Govan Shipbuilders in 1983. This motor vessel, the first of three sister ships, is designed to operate in the North American Great Lakes, but during the winter three-month freeze up will be brought through the St Lawrence Seaway to operate on deep sea charters. This ship is typical of the high value specialised tonnage for which Govan Shipbuilders have built up a great reputation (Govan Shipbuilders).*

the oldest shipbuilding company in the world is now constructing offshore vehicles and other specialised tonnage. The yard and its products would be unrecognisable to the workforce of 100 years ago, as indeed would be the technology of self positioning ships regularly featured in their products. Their facilities are enhanced by a very large dry dock.

Ferguson Brothers (Port Glasgow) Ltd and their

British Shipbuilders partner, Ailsa Shipbuilders of Troon, deal with the smaller vessels required from the Clyde such as roll-on-roll-off ferries, fishery protection vessels, gas tankers and trawlers. The two companies work in close co-operation and are building in a sector of the market which is likely to expand in the long term.

Several repair companies and one or two smaller shipyards and boat building establishments conclude this brief survey. A very considerable number of people are still employed despite the cutbacks since the war and Clyde output is varied and of high quality.

It is imperative that the industry be looked at positively and thoughtfully. Professor Slaven in a recent paper said: 'The history of British shipbuilding clearly demonstrates that industries which plan for stability and neglect growth eventually invite extinction. Survival is an admirable business objective—but it demands active planning for growth and flexible responses to changed conditions.'

The ability of the Clyde shipyards to change their markets, their operating techniques, their industrial relations methods and their production systems cannot be questioned. In the past 20 years the yards have done all this and at the same time become highly safety consicous and, indeed, successful in reducing accident rates.

It is now up to the shipyards themselves to ensure that their marketing strategy is correct and to be training and updating staff to keep them in the technological forefront as it is in this area and this area only that European yards will be able to compete with the up and coming shipbuilders of the future— the Chinese and Koreans.

The need to rethink markets is brought out by developments in North Sea Oil technology: changes and simplification to oil rig design affect production areas critical to Clydeside and the ever-increasing efficiency and economy of pipelaying is for the first time calling into question the long-term future of the oil tanker, but in its place will be required the pipe laying barge and the hardware of the oil field and this market is open to the imaginative and innovative engineering company.

Government planning which recognises the vital role of shipping and shipbuilding is essential. The Falklands campaign brought to our notice the very fine dividing line between ships of the Royal and Merchant Navies, and the need for adequate and positive defence of our merchant ships in any future war has to be legislated for. It is many years since merchant ships built for United Kingdom account had any defensive arrangements such as gun stiffening or de-Gaussing equipment fitted in the shipyard before delivery, and possibly the time has come again for a positive consideration of the requirements of large expensive and complex multi-purpose vessels which will have to operate in a missile conflict. Even more worrying is the run down in merchant ship tonnage, and direct action over several years will be needed to rectify the shortfall. For this a concerted will must be shown by shipowners, shipbuilders, the Government, but above all by the population of this country, spearheaded by those who live in seaports or major shipbuilding areas.

For successful shipbuilding operations, a marketing policy is essential but, as has been seen in the past few years, this has had to be discarded by many nations, including those in the Far East, as the downturn in world trade has created a situation which shipyards are prepared to accept almost any work to keep their labour force together and to remain in business. Despite these bad times shipbuilders are still looking to the future and it may be interesting to close this book with a brief consideration of some of the products which may come in the future from the Clyde shipyards.

One can be confident in asserting that for many years to come the main means of powering ships will remain the diesel engine, with its high thermal efficiency (over 50 per cent), slow speed and cheapness relative to other forms of propulsion. With its slow speed, enabling propellers to be directly driven at their most efficient revolutions, the diesel engine has still several stages of development to go through before it is overtaken by other technologies or before world sources of oil have dried up.

In the longer term as oil reserves decline there will be a concerted move to return to coal fired ships with steam turbines as their main machinery. The turbine technology is well understood and mastered, but modern automatic coal firing using mechanical conveyors and fluidised bed furnace grates is a new field of study offering the opportunity for continuous development and a steady market outlet. Already this is under development in various parts of the world with, in particular, the Australians exploiting it for the massive bulk carriers used to export their coal stocks, and the Canadians and Americans for their Great Lakes freighters.

The gas turbine will remain an expensive form of

propulsion, but for certain applications it will be favoured, especially where high speed take-offs from a cold start are required, as in the case of defence vessels. Despite the fact that their efficiency may increase, they will come under increasing competition from medium speed diesel engines. The gas turbine engine room does, however, point to the concept of the engine room, where maintenance is aimed mostly at the complete replacement of major components at predetermined times, with full refurbishment carried out ashore.

Sail power will be seen in increasing amounts, but possibly less than anticipated by its ardent supporters. The use of the wind to drive very large vessels will be very difficult technically, and the most likely form of development may be the use of auxiliary sails to assist the main engine during periods of steady running in suitable conditions. The justification for sail power at sea is solely the reduction in fuel costs—an important factor when one considers that oil prices are unlikely ever to reduce in real terms—but the arguments that it saves a scarce commodity, while true, are not important in practical terms as marine transport uses only a few per cent of current world oil consumption.

The future of commercial nuclear vessels is much more problematic, and despite the safe use of this kind of power in hundreds of ships operated by the navies of Russia, the USA, France and the United Kingdom there is likely to be fierce public opposition to the use of British commercial waters by these ships. The two or three attempts to have viable operations using nuclear ships for trade have so far ended without positive results. Perhaps, here more than anywhere else, a new technological breakthrough will be needed before the Red Ensign will fly from the stern of a nuclear powered ship. The final decision on this will be as much political as economic.

The technology of shipbuilding and of ships has undergone a revolution in the last quarter century, with the contents and outward appearance of ships changing dramatically. Such changes will increase, and there will be the continuous introduction of labour and maintenance saving materials and ideas.

The Type 22 Class frigate HMS Broadsword on Contractors' Sea Trials in the Kilbrannan Sound, 1979. The village of Carradale on Kintyre is in the background. This Yarrow-built ship has twin controllable pitch propellers powered by Rolls Royce Olympus and Tyne gas turbines. (Yarrow Shipbuilders Ltd).

The emergency support vessel Iolair *on trials on the Clyde in 1982. This ship was built by Scott Lithgow Ltd of Greenock and Port Glasgow for BP operations in the North Sea* (Scott Lithgow Ltd).

Already the mandatory annual dry docking of ships to clean and apply fresh anti-fouling to the bottom is almost a thing of the past with the new self polishing paint coats which continuously offer a fresh smooth surface to the sea. The navigating bridge has changed beyond the wildest dreams or hopes of a watch keeping officer of the 1950s, and steadily there has been a vast reduction in the numbers of men serving aboard.

The types of ship at sea change along with the pattern of world trade. The most obvious difference in recent years has been the reduction in demand for oil tankers, a trend which may well continue with the expertise developed in the past decade for oil and gas pipe laying in deep and hostile waters. There has been a trend for ships to be designed for specific trades only, and more and more ships will be delivered which have been designed for operation on two- or sometimes three-leg round trips with cargoes arranged even before the keel was laid in the shipyard.

By and large ships will become more expensive, less labour intensive and requiring high investment. One exciting possibility is the appearance on the high seas of the sophisticated cruise and study liner, designed with submarine 'moon pools' and every possible aid for educational and recreational adventure cruising.

While new materials are being used increasingly, steel is likely to remain unchallenged for a long time as the principal component of construction. In the past few years there has been witnessed an evolution in ship design but, apart from the introduction of welding and prefabrication, the techniques of shipbuilding have stood unchanged in many ways from the time Thomas Wilson built the iron barge *Vulcan* near Glasgow in 1819. It is possible that new styles of shipbuilding may emerge from Western Europe as a by-product of the difficult times through which they are passing, and it is to be hoped that the Clyde may take the lead here: the river which gave modern shipbuilding its sure foundation has people well trained and amply endowed to lead in such a technological revival.

On a note of optimism, this book ends with the certainty that the story of Clyde shipbuilding has many, many more chapters to be written.

Appendices

1 Bibliography

Abbreviations used

Trans IES   Transactions of the Institution of Engineers in Scotland.
Trans IESS   Transactions of the Institution of Engineers and Shipbuilders in Scotland.
Trans INA   Transactions of the Institution of Naval Architects.
Trans RINA   Transactions of the Royal Institution of Naval Architects.
Trans NECIES   Transactions of the North East Coast Institution of Engineers and Shipbuilders.

Chapter 1: The River Clyde

British Ships and Shipbuilders, George Blake, Collins, London, 1946.

British Shipbuilding, Joseph L. Carozzi, Syren & Shipping Ltd, London, 1919.

The Clyde, a Hundred Years Ago, John Tweed (1872), Reprinted by The Molendinar Press, Glasgow, 1973.

Clyde Barrage Project—a Preliminary Investigation, Corporation of Greenock, 1963.

Clyde Built, John Shields, William MacLellan, Glasgow, 1949.

Clyde Navigation: a History of the Development and Deepening of the River Clyde, John F. Riddell, John Donald, Edinburgh, 1979.

Clyde Shipbuilding from Old Photographs, J. Hume & M. Moss, Batsford, London, 1975.

The Development of the West of Scotland 1750-1960, Anthony Slaven, Routledge & Kegan Paul, London & Boston, 1975.

Down to the Sea, George Blake, Collins, London, 1937.

Design and Equipment of the Clyde Trustee's New Granary at Meadowside, G.H. Baxter, Trans IESS, 1914-15.

Engineering Work of the Clyde Lighthouse Trust, D. Alan Stevenson, Trans IESS, 1945-6.

European Shipbuilding: One Hundred Years of Change, Conference Editors: F.M. Walker and A. Slaven, Marine Publications International Ltd, London, 1983.

The Firth of Clyde, George Blake, Collins, London, 1952.

Gap of Danger: The Story of the Ocean Weather Ships, John D. Drummond, W.H. Allen, London, 1963.

Glasgow, J.M. Reid, B.T. Batsford Ltd, London, 1956.

Glasgow's Herald 1783-1983, Alastair Phillips, Richard Drew Publishing, Glasgow, 1982.

A Hillhead Album, Glasgow W.2., H.B. Morton, Trustees of Dr. C.A. Hepburn, Glasgow, 1973.

A History of the River Clyde and the Development of the Port of Glasgow, W.F. Robertson, Trans IESS, 1948-49.

Improvement Works on the Clyde Estuary, D. & C. Stevenson, Proceedings International Engineers Congress Sect 2, Glasgow, 1901.

Kingston Dock: Its Improvement and Reconstruction, P.D. Donald, Trans IESS, 1916-17.

Machinery of Clyde Trustees No 3 Graving Dock, G.H. Baxter, Trans IESS, 1898-9.

The Old Quay Walls of Glasgow Harbour, W.M. Alston, Trans IESS, 1902-3.

Presidential Address (Clyde Weir etc), J.M. Gale, Trans IES, 1868-9.

Provision of Ore Handling Facilities at General Terminus Quay Glasgow, G. Gray, A. Young, Trans IESS, 1957-8.

The Purification and Improvement of the River Clyde, J. Struthers, Trans IESS, 1890-1.

The River Clyde and Harbour of Glasgow, W.M. Alston, Proceedings International Engineering Congress Sect 2, Glasgow, 1901.

The River Clyde and the Clyde Burghs, Sir James D. Marwick, James Maclehose, Glasgow, 1909.

Scenic Aspects of the River Clyde, Summer Exhibition Catalogue Glasgow Art Gallery and Museum 1972, 1972.

Scottish and Scandinavian Shipbuilding Seminar, Kuuse and Slaven, University of Glasgow, 1980.

The Second City, C.A. Oakley, Blackie, Glasgow, 1967.

Ships of the Clyde, H.M. Le Fleming, Adlard Coles, Southampton, 1960.

Steamers of the Clyde, G. Stromier and J. Nicholson, George Outram, Glasgow, 1967.

The Third Statistical Account of Scotland: Glasgow, J. Cunnison, J.B.S. Gilfillan, Collins, Glasgow, 1958.

Tides and Tidal Phenomena, A.C. Gardner, Trans IESS, 1933-4.

The Upas Tree: Glasgow 1875-1975, S.G. Checkland, University of Glasgow Press, 1976.

Chapter 2: Early shipbuilding

The Clyde Passenger Steamer from 1812 to 1901, James Williamson, James MacLehose & Sons, Glasgow, 1904.

Early Clyde Built Steamers, W.J. Millar, Trans IESS, 1880-1.

A History of Naval Architecture, John Fincham, Whittaker & Co, London, 1851.

The Merchant Schooners Vols 1 & 2, Basil Greenhill, National Maritime Museum, Modern Maritime Classics Reprint, London, 1978.

Sailing Craft of the British Isles, Roger Finch, William Collins, Sons & Co Ltd, London and Glasgow, 1976.

The Scottish Inshore Fishing Vessel: Design, Construction and Repair, Alexander Noble, National Maritime Museum, London, Monograph No 31, 1978.

Ship Models 3; Clyde and Other Steamers Art Gallery and Museum, Glasgow, 1971.

The Shipwright's Vade-Mecum: A Clear and Familiar Introduction, to the Principles and Practice of Shipbuilding Etc, 2nd Edition, London, 1822.

Working Boats of Britain: Their Shape and Purpose, Eric McKee, Conway Maritime Press, London, 1983.

Chapter 3: The steam engine

The Birth of the Steamboat, H. Philip Spratt, Charles Griffin & Co Ltd, London, 1957.

British Paddle Steamers, Geoffrey Body, David & Charles, Newton Abbot, 1971.

By Royal Charter: The Steam Conquistadores, A History of the Pacific S.N. Co, John E. Lingwood, 'Sea Breezes', March and April 1977.

Early Clyde Built Steamers, W.J. Millar, Trans IESS, 1880-1.

Early Days of Engineering in Glasgow, Robert Harvey, The Old Glasgow Club, 1919.

Fairfield 1909, 'Engineering', London, 1909.

History and Development of Machinery for Paddle Steamers, G.E. Barr, Trans IESS, 1951-2.

A History of Mechanical Engineering, Aubrey F. Burstall, Faber & Faber Ltd, London, 1963.

A History of Technology Vol 5 1850-1900, Oxford, 1958.

John and Charles Wood, Frank C. Bowen, 'Shipbuilding & Shipping Record', March 1 1945.

The Late Mr John Wood and Mr Charles Wood, Naval Architects Port Glasgow, J. Scott Russell, Trans INA, 1861.

A Marine Engineering Review T.W.F. Brown, Trans RINA, 1960.

Marine Engineering, Descriptive Catalogue, Science Museum, London.

The Mechanical Engineering Industry of Clydeside: Its Origin and Development, C.A. Oakley, Trans IESS, 1945-6.

A Memoir of John Elder, W.J. MacQuorn Rankine, Robert Maclehose, Glasgow, 1883.

Powered Ships: The Beginnings, Richard Armstrong, Ernest Benn Ltd, London & Tonbridge, 1974.

Reports Relative to Smith's Patent Screw Propeller as Used on Board the Archimedes Steam Vessel etc, Captain Edward Chappell RN, James Ridway, London, 1840.

Sailing Directions and Anchorages: West Coast of Scotland, Clyde Cruising Club and Gilmour & Lawrence Ltd, Glasgow, 1974.

The Screw Propeller and Other Competing Instruments for Marine Propulsion, A.E. Seaton, Charles Griffin & Co Ltd, London, 1909.

The Sea Carriers 1825-1925, The Aberdeen Line, L. Cope Cornford, The Aberdeen Line, 1925.

Steam at Sea, K.T. Rowland, David & Charles, Newton Abbot, 1970.

The Steam Engine, R.J. Law, Science Museum, London, 1965.

West Highland Steamers, C.L.D. Duckworth and G.E. Langmuir, T. Stephenson & Sons, Prescot, 1967.

William Symington: Inventor and Engine Builder, W.S. Harvey and G. Downs-Rose, Northgate, London, 1980.

Chapter 4: Shipbuilding in iron

The Iron Ship, Ewan Corlett, Moonraker Press, Bradford on Avon, 1975.

The Modern Practice of Shipbuilding in Iron and Steel Vols 1 & 2, Samuel J.P. Thearle, William Collins, Sons & Co Ltd, Glasgow, 1886.

Practical Ship Building Vols 1 & 2, A. Campbell Holms, Longmans Green & Co, London, 1904.

Chapter 5: Sailing ships

Masts, Mast Making and Rigging of Ships, Robert Kipping, John Weale, London, 1853.

Sailing Ships: Their History and Development, G.S. Laird Clowes, HMSO, London, 1932 and 1959.

Sails and Sailmaking, Robert Kipping, Crosby Lockwood & Co, London, 1880.

The Tea Clippers—Their History and Development 1833-1875, David R. MacGregor, Conway Maritime Press, London, 1983.

Robert Steele & Company, F.C. Bowen, 'Shipbuilding & Shipping Record', January 22, 1948.

Chapter 6: Building on a sure foundation

Ancient History of Ship Regulations, Sir Westcott S. Abell, Trans IESS, 1920-1.

The British Corporation Register of Shipping and Aircraft 1890-1946, A Brief History, Glasgow, 1946.

The Doxford Turret Ships, L. Gray and J. Lingwood, The World Ship Society, Kendal, 1975.

The Five Hundred Year Book of the University of Glasgow 1451-1951, J.R. Hamilton, The University, Glasgow, 1951.

The Glasgow University Department of Naval Architecture 1883-1983, J.F.C. Conn, Conference Paper National Maritime Museum, 1983: *European Shipbuilding—*

One Hundred Years of Change.

A History of a Faculty: Engineering at Glasgow University, C.A. Oakley, Glasgow University, 1973.

The Institution's First President William John MacQuorn Rankine, James Small, Trans IESS, 1956-7.

The K Boats, Don Everitt, George Harrap & Co Ltd, London, 1963.

Lloyd's Register of Shipping 1760-1960, George Blake, London, 1960.

The New Science of Strong Materials—Or Why Don't You Fall Through the Floor, J.E. Gordon, Penguin Books, Harmondsworth, 1968.

Ship Stability and Trim, Percy A. Hillhouse, John Hogg, London, 1918.

Steel Ship Building, Fred M. Walker, Shire Publications Ltd, Aylesbury, 1981.

Steel Ships: Their Construction and Maintenance, Thomas Walton, Charles Griffin & Co Ltd, London, 1901.

Structures—Or Why Things Don't Fall Down, J.E. Gordon, Penguin Books, Harmondsworth, 1978.

Shipbuilding, Theoretical and Practical, W.J.M. Rankine and Others, William Mackenzie, London, 1866.

Useful Rules and Tables, W.J.M. Rankine, Charles Griffin & Co, London, 1876.

The Worshipful Company of Shipwrights 1782-1982, W.D. Ewart and A.G. Hopkins, London, 1982.

Chapter 7: The cradle of steam navigation

The Arcform Ship: Trials and First Voyage Performances, Sir Joseph W. Isherwood, Trans NECIES, 1933-4.

Blackwood & Gordon of Paisley & Port Glasgow, F.C. Bowen, Shipbuilding and Shipping Record, August 12 1948.

Blue Funnel, F.E. Hyde, Liverpool University Press, 1957.

Brocklebanks 1770-1950 Vols 1 & 2, J.F. Gibson, Henry Young & Sons Ltd, Liverpool, 1953.

Bruusgaard Kiösterud & Co, Drammen, Norway, 1959.

Caird of Greenock, F.C. Bowen, Shipbuilding & Shipping Record, September 22 1949.

The Clyde Drydock Project, J.W. Dalgliesh, Trans IESS, 1962-3.

Construction of Very Large Tankers in Two Parts, A. Ross Belch, Trans RINA, 1976.

Duncan of Port Glasgow, F.C. Bowen, Shipbuilding & Shipping Record, October 18 1945.

Dunlop Bremner & Co, F.C. Bowen, Shipbuilding & Shipping Record, March 9 1950.

George Brown & Co (Marine) Ltd, Privately published handbook, Greenock, c 1938.

James Lithgow—Master of Work, J.M. Reid, Hutchinson of London, 1964.

John & Charles Wood, F.C. Bowen, Shipbuilding & Shipping Record, March 1 1945.

John & James Reid, F.C. Bowen, Shipbuilding & Shipping Record, June 27 1946.

John Scott Russell, George S. Emmerson, John Murray, London, 1977.

The Modern System of Naval Architecture, J. Scott Russell, 3 Vols, Day & Son, London, 1865.

Murdoch & Murray of Port Glasgow, F.C. Bowen, Shipbuilding & Shipping Record, September 27 1951.

Saga of Scindia, N.G. Jog, Scindia S.N. Co Ltd, Bombay, 1969.

Seventy Adventurous Years: The Bank Line 1885-1955, Journal of Commerce, Liverpool, 1956.

The Trade Makers: Elder Dempster in West Africa 1852-1972, P.N. Davies, George Allen & Unwin Ltd, London, 1973.

Two Hundred and Fifty Years of Shipbuilding by the Scotts at Greenock, 4th Ed (First under this title), Scotts, Greenock, 1961.

Chapter 8: Ship design

Architectura Navalis Mercatoria, Fredrik Henrik af Chapman, Stockholm, 1768, Reprint 1971 published by Adlard Coles Ltd.

Basic Naval Architecture, K.C. Barnaby, Hutchinson, London, 1949.

Basic Ship Theory, K.J. Rawson & E.C. Tupper, Longmans, Green & Co Ltd, London, 1968.

The Design and Construction of Ships, J.H. Biles, Charles Griffin & Co Ltd, London, 1908.

A History of Engineering Drawing, P.J. Booker, Northgate Publishing Co Ltd, London, 1979.

Manual of Naval Architecture, W.H. White, John Murray, London, (5th Ed), 1900.

Naval Architecture, Brian Baxter, Teach Yourself Books, London & Norwich, 1959.

Naval Architecture, Cecil H. Peabody, John Wiley & Sons, New York, 1904.

Theory of Naval Architecture, A.M. Robb, Charles Griffin & Co Ltd, London, 1952.

Chapter 9: Paisley and Renfrew, birthplace of dredgers

A Century of Shipbuilding 1810-1910, Wm Simons & Co Ltd, Renfrew.

Dredgers and Dredging, C. Prelini, Crosby Lockwood & Son, London, 1912.

Dredging of Harbours and Rivers, E.C. Shankland, Brown, Son & Ferguson Ltd, Glasgow, 1949.

Practical Dredging, H.R. Cooper, Brown, Son & Ferguson Ltd, Glasgow, 1958.

Chapter 10: The shipbuilding process

BSRA Resistance Experiments on the Lucy Ashton, Sir Maurice E. Denny, Trans INA, 1951.

On Compass Adjustment on the Clyde, Sir Wm Thomson, Trans IESS, 1876-7.

The Life of William Thomson: Baron Kelvin of Largs (Vols 1-2), Silvanus P. Thompson, Macmillan & Co Ltd, London, 1910.

Speed Trials and Service Performance of the Cunard Turbine Steamer Lusitania, T. Bell, Trans INA, 1908.

The Stability of Ships, Sir Edward J. Reed, Charles Griffin & Co, London, 1885.

The Thankless Years, W.G. Riddell, Art & Educational Publisher, London, 1948.

Theory and Design of British Shipbuilding, A.L. Ayre, Thomas Reed & Co, Sunderland, c 1921.

Trials of Steamships at the Measured Mile, E.J. Reed, Trans INA, 1867.

Trials Performances of a Torpedo Boat Destroyer, Sir Harold E. Yarrow, Trans IESS, 1934-5.

Chapter 11: The steam turbine

The Golden Years of the Clyde Steamers (1889-1914), A.J.S. Paterson, David & Charles, Newton Abbot, 1969.

The Marine Turbine Part I 1897-1927, Ingvar Jung, National Maritime Museum Monograph, London, 1982.

Ravenscrag, the Allan Royal Mail Line, Thomas E. Appleton, McClelland & Stewart Ltd, Toronto, 1974.

Chapter 12: Dumbarton

The 'Cutty Sark', Her Designer and Builder, Hercules Linton 1836-1900, Robert E. Brettle, W. Heffer & Sons Ltd, Cambridge, 1969.

Denny: Dumbarton 1844-1932, Published privately by Wm Denny & Bros Ltd, Dumbarton, 1932.

The Denny List (Vols 1-4), Compiled by D.J. Lyon, National Maritime Museum, Greenwich, 1975.

Fundamentals of Welding Design as Applied to Ship Structures, E.W. Cotton, Lectures Organised by Admiralty & Clyde Shipbuilders' Association, Glasgow, 1944.

The Irrawaddy Flotilla Company, H.J. Chubb & C.L.D. Duckworth, National Maritime Museum Monograph No 7, London, 1973.

Irrawaddy Flotilla, A. McCrae & A. Prentice, James Paxton Ltd, Paisley, 1978.

The Life of William Denny, Shipbuilder, Dumbarton, Alexander B. Murray, Hodder & Stoughton, London 2nd Ed, 1889.

McMillan of Dumbarton, F.C. Bowen, Shipbuilding & Shipping Record, July 12 1951.

Paddy Henderson, Dorothy Laird, George Outram & Co Ltd, Glasgow, 1961.

Presidential Address, W.P. Walker, Trans IESS, 1967-8.

Vane Wheel Propulsion, Maurice E. Denny, Trans IESS, 1922-3.

Chapter 13: Small craft

Blow Five—A History of the Alexandra Towing Company Limited, W.B. Hallam, JOC Publications, Liverpool, 1976.

The Campbells of Kilmun, Iain Hope, Aggregate Publications, Johnstone, 1981.

The Campbeltown and Glasgow Steam Packet Joint Stock Company Ltd, Centenary History, Published by the company, Campbeltown, 1927.

The Clyde Passenger Steamers, Kenneth Davies, Kyle Publications, Ayr, 1980.

Clyde River and Other Steamers, C.L.D. Duckworth & G.E. Langmuir, Brown, Son & Ferguson, Glasgow, 1946.

Clyde River Steamers of the Last Fifty Years, Andrew McQueen, Gowans & Gray, Glasgow, 1923.

Clyde Shipping Co Ltd—A History, Alan D. Cuthbert, Privately Published, Robert Maclehose, Glasgow, 1956.

The Clyde Steamers, Desmond Banks, Albyn Press, Edinburgh, 1947.

Clyde Steamers at a Glance, John Marshall, Albyn Press, Edinburgh, 1948.

Cycloidal Voith-Schneider Propulsion, E.C. Goldsworthy & A. Betts Brown, Trans IESS, 1957-8.

Dinosaur Down Below, Ian W. Muir, Peveril Publications, Neilston, 1980.

Mersey Built Blockade Runners of the American Civil War, Arthur C. Wardle, *The Mariner's Mirror*, Vol 28 No 3, July 1942.

Notes on the Development of Tug Boat Machinery During the Past 46 Years, G. Baird, Trans NECIES, 1935-6.

Screw Tug Design, A. Caldwell, Hutchinson's Scientific Technical Publications, London, 1946.

Small Seagoing Craft and Vessels for Inland Navigation, A. Koorda & E.M. Neuerberg, H. Stam & Co, Haarlem, The Netherlands, 1957.

Tugs of the Admiralty Wartime Merchant Ship Programme, A. Caldwell, Trans IESS, 1946-7.

Tunnel Type Vessels, A.R. Mitchell, Trans IESS, 1952-3.

The Victorian Summer of the Clyde Steamers (1864-1888), A.J.S. Paterson, David & Charles, Newton Abbot, 1972.

William Symington: Inventor & Engine Builder, W.S. Harvey & G. Downs Rose, Northgate, London, 1980.

Chapter 14: The Clyde, wars & the Royal Navy

Alfred Yarrow—His Life and Work, Lady Yarrow, E. Arnold & Co, London, 1923.

Beardmore—The History of a Scottish Industrial Giant, Hume and Moss, Heineman, London, 1979.

The Black Battlefleet, G.A. Ballard, Nautical Publishing Co Ltd, Lymington, 1980.

The British Submarine, F.W. Lipscomb, Conway Maritime Press, London, 1975.

British Warships Illustrated, A.C. Hardy, A. & C. Black Ltd, London, 1935.

Cockatoo Island, R.G. Parker, Nelson, 1977.

Construction and Operation of the Military Ports in Gareloch and Loch Ryan, Sir Bruce G. White, Trans IESS, 1948-9.

The Development of HM Submarines, MOD Ship Dept, BR 3043, A.N. Harrison, 1979.

Fifty Years of Warship Building on the Clyde, J.H. Biles, Trans IESS, 1908-9.

Forty Years of Dreadnoughts—Built on the River Clyde,

Ian Johnston, Privately Published, Foulis Archive Press, c 1980.

The K Boats, Don Everitt, George Harrap & Co, London, 1963.

Lectures on Naval Architecture and Engineering with Exhibition Catalogue, William Collins, Sons & Co, Glasgow, 1881.

Modern History of Warships, William Hovgaard, Reprinted 1978, Conway Maritime Press, London.

A River Runs to War, John D. Drummond, W.H. Allen, London, 1960.

The Second City, C.A. Oakley, Blackie & Son Ltd, Glasgow, 1967.

Special Wartime Fabrication Methods Employed in the Construction of Small Vessels, R.L. Aitken, Trans IESS, 1946-7.

Steam, Steel and Torpedoes, Vol 8 of 'The Ship' Series, David Lyon, HMSO, London for NMM, 1980.

Technical Change and British Naval Policy 1860-1939, Bryan Ranft and others, Hodder & Stoughton, London, 1977.

Tunnel Type Vessels, A.R. Mitchell, Trans IESS, 1952-3.

Yarrow & Co Ltd; 1865-1977, Glasgow, 1977.

Chapter 15: The Clydebank story

British Passenger Liners of the Fine Oceans, C.R. Vernon Gibbs, Putnam, London, 1963.

Family Engineers, Eric Mensforth, Ward Lock Ltd, London, 1981.

Lusitania, Colin Simpson, Penguin Books, Harmondsworth, 1974.

Metamorphosis, Presidential Address Re: John Brown's, J.A. Turner, Trans IESS, 1981-2.

North Atlantic Seaway Vols 1-5, N.R.P. Bonsor, Brookside Publications, Jersey, 1980.

River Work for the Queen Mary, A.C. Gardner, Trans IESS, 1936-7.

Steel and Ships: The History of John Brown's Sir Allan Grant, Michael Joseph, London, 1950.

Chapter 16: The ubiquitous diesel and some other engines

A Century of Burmeister & Wain, Johannes Lehmann, A/S Burmeister & Wain, Copenhagen, 1948.

Diesel Electric Paddle Boat 'Talisman', G.A. Inglis, Trans IESS, 1935-6.

Electric Propulsion of Ships: Description of the Electric Arc, Mavor & Coulson Ltd, Glasgow, 1911.

Power for the Fleet: The History of British Marine Gas Turbines, C.E. Preston, Eton Publishing, Eton, 1982.

The Role of the Diesel Engine in Shipbuilding, J. Hetmar, Conference Paper National Maritime Museum, 1983, 'European Shipbuilding—One Hundred Years of change'.

Chapter 17: From Broomielaw to Bowling

Anchor Line 1856-1956, R.S. McLellan, Anchor Line Ltd, Glasgow, 1956.

The Ben Line 1825-1955, George Blake, Wm Thomson & Co, Edinburgh, 1956.

Bruusgaard Kiøsterud & Co, Drammen, Norway, 1959.

Craigendoran Steamers, Alan Brown, Aggregate Publications, Johnstone, 1979.

Development of Shipbuilding on the Upper Reaches of the Clyde etc, Barclay Curle & Co Ltd, Glasgow, 1911.

Inglis, Glasgow, John G. Inglis, Privately published, 1977.

Shipping Enterprise and Management 1830-1939: Harrisons of Liverpool, F.E. Hyde, Liverpool University Press, 1967.

Talisman—The Solitary Crusader, Alan Brown, Aggregate Publications, Johnstone, 1980.

Tod & Macgregor and D. & W. Henderson, F.C. Bowen, Shipbuilding & Shipping Record, May 22 1947.

Wilhelm Wilhelmsen 1861-1961, E. Ytreberg, Wilh Wilhelmsen, Oslo, 1961.

Chapter 18: Govan and Linthouse

Atten Sømil Fra Rockall, Michel Nielsen, Samlerens Forlag, Copenhagen, 1978.

Canadian Pacific 1891-1961, George Musk, World Ship Society, London, 1961.

David Napier, Engineer 1790-1869, Autobiographical Sketch With Notes, James Maclehose & Sons, Glasgow, 1912.

The Donaldson Line 1854-1954, A.M. Dunnett, Jackson Son & Co, Glasgow, 1960.

Fairfield 1860-1960, Souvenir, Govan, Glasgow, 1960.

The Fairfield S. & E. Co Ltd, Govan, Souvenir, Govan, Glasgow, 1919.

The Govan Yard, F.C. Bowen, Shipbuilding & Shipping Record, February 15 1951.

The History of the Bibby Line, E.W. Paget-Tomlinson, Bibby Line Ltd, Liverpool, 1969.

The Life of Robert Napier, James Napier, Blackwood, Edinburgh, 1904.

The Log Book of an Engineer and Shipbuilder (During Six Reigns), Alex. S. Maclellan LL D, Published privately in Glasgow, 1958.

Robert Napier, F.C. Bowen, Shipbuilding & Shipping Record, January 26 1950.

Robert Napier—The Father of Clyde Shipbuilding, J.M. Halliday, Trans IESS, 1980-1.

Shipbuilding Between the Wars—An Accountant's View of the Experience of the Fairfield Company, Hugh B. Peebles, Conference Paper National Maritime Museum, 1983, 'European Shipbuilding: One Hundred Years of Change'.

Stephen of Linthouse 1750-1950, John L. Carvel, Alex. Stephen & Sons Ltd, Linthouse, Glasgow, 1950.

Train Ferries of Western Europe, P. Ransome-Wallis, Ian Allan, London, 1968.

Chapter 19: From boatyard to nationalisation

The British Shipbuilding Industry 1870-1914, S. Pollard

and P. Robertson, Harvard University Press, Cambridge Mass, 1979.

British Shipping, R.H. Thornton, Cambridge University Press, 1959.

British Shipping & World Competition, S.G. Sturmey, Athlone Press, University of London, 1962.

Brocklebanks 1770-1950, J.F. Gibson, 2 Vols, Henry Young & Sons Ltd, Liverpool, 1953.

Crisis on the Clyde—The Story of the Upper Clyde Shipbuilders Jack McGill, Davis-Poynter Ltd, London, 1973.

Productivity in Shipbuilding, Report of the Patton Committee, 1962.

The Right to Work—The Story of the Upper Clyde Confrontation, Alasdair Buchan, Calder & Boyars, London, 1972.

Self-Liquidation: The National Shipbuilders Security Ltd, and British Shipbuilding in the 1930s, A. Slaven (University of Glasgow), Paper given at Queen Mary College, London, 1981.

Shipbuilding Inquiry Committee 1965-66 Report, Chairman: R.M. Geddes, HMSO, London, 1966.

A Shipbuilder's Yesterdays, Sir Wilfrid Ayre, Privately published, Aberdour, 1968.

Trade Unions & Industrial Relations in the British Shipbuilding Industry, James McGoldrick, Conference Paper National Maritime Museum, 1983, 'European Shipbuilding—One Hundred Years of Change'.

Welding—the Quiet Revolution, D. McKeown, Conference Paper National Maritime Museum, 1983, 'European Shipbuilding—One Hundred Years of Change'.

Chapter 20: Shipbuilders of the Firth

B.I. Centenary 1856-1956, George Blake, Collins, London, 1956.

Contributions to Scottish Maritime History, John Crichton Jr, Ayr E. & C. Co Ltd, Ayr, 1950.

Eighty Six Years—Plus: The History of the London Graving Dock Company Ltd, Edgar Hurd, London Graving Dock, 1976.

Glasgow & Its Environs, Stratten & Stratten, London, 1981.

Kintyre, Alasdair Carmichael, 1974.

Lectures on Naval Architecture & Engineering, Glasgow Exhibition 1880-1, William Collins, Sons & Co Ltd, Glasgow, 1881.

Motor Yachts & Motor Yachting on the Clyde, F.L. Maclaren, Trans IESS, 1926-7.

The Old Scots Navy 1689-1710, James Grant, The Navy Records Society, 1914.

Rothesay Harbour 1752-1975, Ian Maclagan, Vol 19, Trans Buteshire Nat History Society, 1976.

Salt Water Palaces, Maldwin Drummond, Debrett, London, 1979.

Where Ships are Born: Sunderland 1346-1946, J.W. Smith & T.S. Holden, Thomas Reed & Co Ltd, Sunderland, 1953.

Chapter 21: The canals and specialist sites

BSRA Resistance Experiments on the Lucy Ashton, Sir Maurice Denny, Trans Institution of Naval Architects, London, 1951.

The Building of Chauncy Maples, A.E.M. Anderson-Morshead, Universities' Mission to Central Africa, London, 1903.

Burrell: A Portrait of a Collector: Sir William Burrell 1861-1958, Richard Marks, Richard Drew, Glasgow, 1983.

The Canals of Scotland, Jean Lindsay, David & Charles, Newton Abbot, 1968.

The Clyde Puffer, Dan McDonald, David & Charles, Newton Abbot, 1977.

Coasters & Small Craft in the Wartime Merchant Shipbuilding Programme, T.W. Davis & J. Lenaghan, Trans IESS, 1946-7.

Kirkintilloch Shipbuilding, A.I. Bowan, Stathkelvin District Libraries & Museums, Bishopbriggs, Glasgow, 1983.

The Monkland Tradition, T.R. Miller, Thos. Nelson, London, 1958.

The River Clyde and the Clyde Burghs, Sir James D. Marwick, James Maclehose & Sons, Glasgow, 1909.

The Rutherglen Yard, F.C. Bowen, Shipbuilding & Shipping Record, July 14 1949.

Seagoing & Other Concrete Ships, N.K. Fougner, Oxford Technical Publications, London, 1922.

Chapter 22: A new breed from the Clyde

The Development of the Offshore Engineering Industry in UK & Europe, Neil S. Miller & Douglas Faulkner, Conference Paper National Maritime Museum, 1983, 'European Shipbuilding: One Hundred Years of Change'.

Training for Shipbuilding, Brian N. Baxter, Conference Paper National Maritime Museum, 1983, 'European Shipbuilding: One Hundred Years of Change'.

2 Statistics

Notes

1 Numbers of ships built and total gross tonnages are based on launching returns for the world and for the United Kingdom.

2 The graphs are designed for comparison purposes only and have been compiled with information drawn from the following sources: Lloyd's Register of Shipping Statistical Tables; The Glasgow Herald Trade Review; University of Glasgow, Department of Economic History; The National Maritime Museum, Greenwich.

3 Minor discrepancies arise through certain countries not submitting returns, eg, USSR and the People's Republic of China.

4 All naval and military work is excluded.

5 Tonnage is based on gross tons, which closely represents all enclosed spaces in the ship based on 2.832 m^3 or 100 cu ft to the ton.

6 Inconsistencies are to be found in 19th century British shipbuilding returns reported in various journals, but are usually the result of different bases for accounting.

7 In recent years there has been a change in most published tables from launching to completion of contract. In this case, however, launching is used.

8 In an effort to make annual shipbuilding returns more meaningful, and for tonnage to more closely correspond to the work input in the ship, the Association of West European Shipbuilders agreed coefficients for gross tonnages in 1968. Should these coefficients be applied to the British totals, and should naval work be added, then the United Kingdom's relative position will be improved considerably. The coefficients are:

Cargo

under 5,000 tons dwt	1.60
5,000 tons dwt and over	1.00
passenger-cargo	1.60
high speed cargo	1.60
container ships	1.90

Tankers

30,000 tons dwt and under	0.65
30-50,000 tons dwt	0.50
50-80,000 tons dwt	0.45
80-160,000 tons dwt	0.40
160-250,000 dwt	0.35
over 250,000 tons dwt	0.30

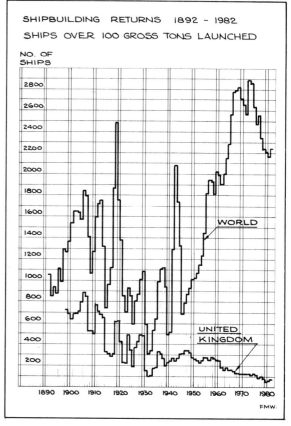

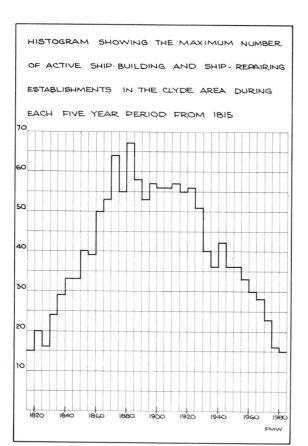

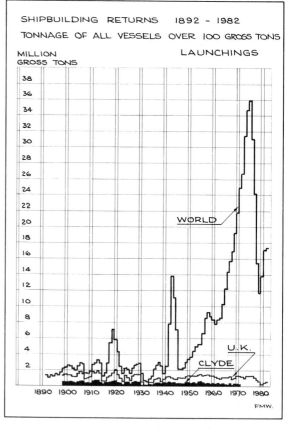

Multi-purpose ships	0.80	*Refrigerated cargo*	2.00	
Bulk carriers including ore/oil		*Fish factory ships*	2.00	
under 30,000 tons dwt	0.60	*Gas carriers and chemical tankers*	2.20	
30-50,000 tons dwt	0.50	*Passenger ships*	3.00	
50-100,000 tons dwt	0.45	*Ferry Boats*	2.00	
over 100,000 tons dwt	0.40	*Fishing vessels and miscellaneous vessels*	1.50	

3 Shipyards and ship repairing establishments of the River Clyde and the surrounding area

No	Shipyard	Dates	Location	Approx no of ships built*	Remarks
1	The Abercorn Shipbuilding Co		Abercorn, Paisley		See Hanna, Donald & Wilson.
2	James Adam & Son (Shiprepairers) Ltd	1871-	Gourock		Founded as yacht builders.
3	Ailsa Shipbuilding Co (Ltd in 1901)	1885-	Troon	530	Now part of British Shipbuilders.
4	Ailsa Shipbuilding Co Ltd	1902-29	Ayr		Ayr yard formerly S. McKnight & Co.
5	Aitken & Mansell	1863-76	Kelvinhaugh, Glasgow		Kelvinhaugh Slip 1870-6.
6	Aitken & Mansell	1876-89	Whiteinch, Glasgow	230	
7	Alley & MacLellan Ltd	c 1890-1960	Polmadie, Glasgow	500	Builders of knock down ships.
8	American Marine & Machinery Co Inc	1964-9	Phoenix, Paisley	12	Took over Fleming & Ferguson.
9	Anderson & Gilmour	1840s	Glasgow	4	
10	Anderson & Lyall	1880s	Govan, Glasgow		Small vessels, eg, for Loch Tay.
11	ANDOC (Anglo Dutch Offshore Concrete Cons.)	1975-8	Hunterston		Proprietors of oil rig yard.
12	Arclay	1860s	Cartsdyke mid, Greenock		Yacht builder.
13	Ardrossan Dockyard Ltd	1925-64	Ardrossan	90	Owned by Coast Lines and Kincaids.
14	Ardrossan Drydock & S.B. Co Ltd	1899-1925	Ardrossan	150	South yard purchased NSS Ltd 1931.
15	Ardrossan Shipbuilding Co	1870s-1899	Ardrossan	175	Formerly Barr & Shearer.
16	Argyll Ship & Boatbuilding Co Ltd	1970s	Renfrew	5	Formerly Hugh McLean & Sons
17	Sir William Arroll & Co Ltd	1941-5	Meadowside, Glasgow		Wartime builders: also at Alloa.
18	Atlantic Engine Co (1920) Ltd	1920s	Old Kilpatrick		Small vessels.
19	Ayr Engineering & Constructional Co Ltd	c 1947	Ayr		Took over slipway for London GD.
20	Ayr Shipbuilding Co	1870s	Ayr	3	Small sailing vessels.
21	Ayrshire Dockyard Co Ltd	1928-34	Irvine		Formerly Mackie & Thomson. Acquired by NSS Ltd 1934.
22	Ayrshire Marine Constructors	1979-	Hunterston		Builders of *Maureen* oil field base.
23	John Barclay	1818-44	Stobcross, Glasgow		Ultimately became Barclay, Curle.
24	Peter Barclay & Son	1860s	Ardrossan		Builders of schooners and smacks.
25	Robert Barclay & Co	1844-45	Stobcross, Glasgow		Ultimately became Barclay, Curle.
26	Robert Barclay & Curle	1845-63	Stobcross, Glasgow		Ultimately became Barclay, Curle.
27	Barclay, Curle & Co	1863-74	Stobcross, Glasgow		

*Where information is not available this column is left blank.

No	Shipyard	Dates	Location	Approx no of ships built	Remarks
28	Barclay, Curle & Co (Ltd in 1884)	1855-	Whiteinch, Glasgow	750	1912 amalgamated with Swan, Hunter & WR. Owners Elderslie Dry Docks 1912-74. Ceased shipbuilding 1967.
29	Barclay Robertson & Co	1870s	Ardrossan		Builders of schooners and smacks.
30	J. Barnhill	1844-7	Cartsdyke, West Greenock	5	
31	J. Barr	1840s	West, Renfrew		Became Barr & MacNab.
32	John Barr	1850s	Kelvinhaugh, Glasgow	4	
33	Barr & MacNab	1838-1840s	Abercorn, Paisley		Builders iron Clyde paddle steamers.
34	Barr & MacNab	1840s-1847	West, Renfrew		Last vessel *Blue Bonnet*.
35	Barr & Shearer	1840s-1870s	North, Ardrossan	20	Became Ardrossan SB Co.
36	William Beardmore & Co Ltd	1900-05	Govan, Glasgow	170	Formerley R. Napier & Sons.
37	William Beardmore & Co Ltd	1905-30	Dalmuir		1938 Dalmuir site for shipbreaking.
38	Bergius Launch & Engine Co	1908-39	Glasgow	1,185	Custom-built launches.
39	Birrell, Stenhouse & Co	1874-89	Upper Woodyard, Dumbarton	46	Sailing vessels mostly.
40	Alexander Black	1840s	Rothesay		Lessee of repair slip.
41	Robert Black	1840-51	Kelvinhaugh, Glasgow		Yard taken over from A. Stephen. New slip dock 1850.
42	Blackwood	1860s	Glasgow		
43	Blackwood & Gordon	1846-52	Paisley		
44	Blackwood & Gordon	1852-60	Cartvale, Paisley	34	
45	Blackwood & Gordon	1860-1900	Castle, Port Glasgow	209	Closed from 1887-9. Became Clyde SB & E Co Ltd.
46	Blythswood Shipbuilding Co Ltd	1919-64	Scotstoun, Glasgow	140	Tanker specialists. Yard acquired by Yarrow & Co.
47	John Bourne & Co	1853-5	Ladyburn, Greenock	3	Early users of Lloyd's Rules for iron ships.
48	Bow, McLachlan & Co Ltd	1900-33	Thistle, Paisley	180	Commenced as engineers 1872. Purchased by NSS Ltd 1933.
49	Archibald Boyd	1870s-1890s	Ardrossan		Builders of schooners and smacks.
50	Boyd & Turner	c 1865	Castlegreen, Dumbarton	1	
51	George Brown & Co (Marine) Ltd	1900-83	Garvel, Greenock	285	Associate company: Cargospeed Ltd.
52	John Brown & Co Ltd	1899-1968	Clydebank	350	Builders of some of the world's greatest ships. Formerly Clydebank E&S Co Ltd. Became part of UCS.
53	Brys & Gilsen Ltd		Whiteinch, Glasgow		See Lloyd Royal Belge (GB) Ltd.
54	George & James Burns	1848-53	Rothesay		Lessees of repair slip.
55	Wm Burrell & Son	1875-1903	Hamiltonhill, Glasgow	50	Puffers, etc, on F&C Canal.
56	Burrell & Son	1881-4	Low Woodyard, Dumbarton	20	Associate of Hamiltonhill Company.
57	Bute Slip Dock Co Ltd	1913-68	Port Bannatyne, Bute		Founded by Alfred & Charles Mylne.
58	Caird & Co	1840-67	Cartsdyke Mid, Greenock		Commenced as engineers early 19th century.
59	Caird & Co (Ltd in 1888)	1863-1922	Westburn E, Greenock	360	1916 acquired by Harland & Wolff.

No	Shipyard	Dates	Location	Approx no of ships built	Remarks
60	Caird & Co Ltd	1871-1922	Westburn W, Greenock		Known as H&W after 1922.
61	Calderwood	*fl* 1868	Irvine		
62	A.G. Cameron	*fl* 1861	Cartside, Greenock	2	
63	Campbell & Co	1880-1	Thistle, Paisley	5	Became J. McArthur & Co.
64	Campbeltown Shipbuilding Co Ltd	1877-1922	Trench Point, Campbeltown	110	
65	Campbeltown Shipyard Ltd	1968-	Trench Point, Campbeltown	60	Part of Lithgow Group. Builders of standard fishing vessels.
66	Carmichael MacLean & Co	1895-8	Cartsdyke W, Greenock	30	Last contracts completed by Russell & Co.
67	R & A Carswell	1816-32	Greenock	30	Proprietor formerly of Steele & Carswell.
68	Cartsdyke Dockyard Co Ltd	1966	Cartsdyke, Greenock	2	Holding arrangement during transfer of Greenock Dockyard to Scott's.
69	William Chalmers & Co Ltd	1903-20	Broomloan, Rutherglen	90	Formerly C & McK Govan. Seath's yard.
70	Chalmers & McKivett	1899-1903	Govan, Glasgow		Formerly Chalmers, Scott & McKivett.
71	Chalmers, Scott & McKivett	1896-9	Govan, Glasgow		Builders of tugs, small vessels, etc.
72	R. Chambers & Co	1877-81	Low Woodyard, Dumbarton	17	Bankrupt & succeeded by Burrell.
73	Chambers Brothers	*c* 1889	Dumbarton		Lifeboat builders.
74	Chambers Brothers	1896-1900	Cartsdyke W, Greenock	2	Small vessels.
75	Clan Line Steamers Repairing Works Ltd	1890-1948	Finnieston, Glasgow		Shiprepairers & Chandlers. Became Scottish Lion R&E Co Ltd.
76	Clyde Navigation Trust	-1905	Dalmuir		Workshop & Slips became Beardmore's.
77	Clyde Navigation Trust	1907-	Pudzeoch, Renfrew		Now Clydeport Authority.
78	Clyde Shipbuilding Co	1864-6	Ladyburn, Greenock	5	
79	Clyde Shipbuilding & Engineering Co Ltd	1900-29	Castle, Port Glasgow	115	Sold to James Lamont & Co
80	Clydebank Engineering & Shipbuilding Co Ltd	1897-9	Clydebank	36	Previously J. & G. Thomson Ltd. Became John Brown & Co Ltd.
81	ClydeDock Engineering Ltd	1977-	Govan, Glasgow		Ship repairers.
82	Charles Connell & Co Ltd	1861-1968	Scotstoun, Glasgow	510	Became Scotstoun Division of UCS.
83	Co-operative Iron Shipbuilding Co	*fl* 1874	Irvine	2	
84	Cornwallis	1820-1	Greenock	2	
85	Wm Craig & Co	1840s	Glasgow		
86	Crawford	1860s	Greenock		
87	J. Crawford	1884	Sandpoint, Dumbarton	3	Completed H. Murray's last contracts.
88	Culzean Steam Launch & Yacht Works	1870s	Culzean		Founded by Marquis of Ailsa at Culzean Castle.
89	Culzean Steam Launch & Yacht Works	1880s-1887	Maidens, Girvan		
90	D.M. Cumming Ltd	1880s-1920s	Blackhill, Glasgow	18	On Monkland Canal.
91	W.S. Cumming	*c* 1882	Blackhill, Glasgow		Became D.M. Cumming.
92	Cumming & Swan	1870s	Blackhill, Glasgow		Became W.S. Cumming.

No	Shipyard	Dates	Location	Approx no of ships built	Remarks
93	Cunliffe & Dunlop	1869-81	Inch, Port Glasgow	84	Became D.J. Dunlop & Co.
94	Dalmuir Dry Dock Co Ltd	1907	Dalmuir		Battleship drydock project of Beardmore. Never completed.
95	Darroch & Espie		Glasgow		
96	Davidson & Wood	1860s	Glasgow		Works sited away from river.
97	Davie & McKendrick	*c* 1889			
98	Alexander Denny & Brother	1849-59	Albert, Dumbarton	48	Iron shipbuilder, mostly steamers.
99	Archibald Denny	1853-66	Churchyard, Dumbarton	40	Worked with brother Alexander until 1853.
100	William Denny & Son	1818-19	Woodyard, Dumbarton		William Denny was builder in 1814 of PS *Margery*, the first steamer on
102	William Denny & Son	1819-26	Albert yard, Dumbarton		the Thames.
103	William Denny & Son	1826-33	Woodyard, Dumbarton		
104	William Denny & Brothers	1844-67	Woodyard, Dumbarton		Known as Denny Brothers until 1849. One of the best recorded
105	William Denny & Brothers	1844-9	Churchyard, Dumbarton	1,460	shipyards and with a worldwide reputation for all round excellence.
106	William Denny & Brothers (Ltd in 1918)	1867-1963	Leven, Dumbarton		
107	William Denny & Brothers (Ltd in 1918)	1865-1963	Victoria, Dumbarton		
108	Denny & McLean	1853-66	Churchyard, Dumbarton	53	
109	Denny & Rankin	1838-44	Woodyard, Dumbarton		Builders in wood until 1852.
110	Denny & Rankin	1844-65	Victoria, Dumbarton	200	
111	A.M. Dickie & Sons	1890s-1950s	Tarbert, Lochfyne		Yachts & fishing craft.
112	Dobie & Co	1866-84	Govan, Glasgow	118	Liquidated during construction of Allan Liners.
113	Dobie, Hedderwick & McGaw	1864-6	Govan, Glasgow	14	Became Dobie & Co.
114	Donald & McFarlane	1867-1868	Cartvale, Paisley	4	
115	H. Dubord	*c* 1850	Glasgow		
116	Duncan	1830s	Greenock	6	
117	Robert Duncan & Co	1830-41	Greenock		Builders of the first Cunarder PS *Britannia*.
118	Robert Duncan & Co	1862-1934	East, Port Glasgow	400	Taken over by Lithgows 1914.
119	Duncanson	1830	Glasgow		
120	David J. Dunlop & Co	1881-1911	Inch, Port Glasgow	110	Became Dunlop, Bremner & Co.
121	Dunlop, Bremner & Co Ltd	1911-26	Inch, Port Glasgow	80	Sold to Lithgows during First World War. 1926 voluntary liquidation. 1933 restricted covenant on yard by NSS Ltd.
122	John Elder & Co	1870-86	Fairfield, Govan, Glasgow	180	Became Fairfield S & E Co Ltd, formerly Randolph, Elder & Co.
123	Fairfield Shipbuilding & Engineering Co Ltd	1886-1965	Govan, Glasgow	580	Became Fairfields (Glasgow) Ltd.
124	Fairfields (Glasgow) Ltd	1966-8	Govan, Glasgow	10	Became Govan Division of UCS Ltd.
125	Fairlie Yacht Slip Ltd		Fairlie		Yacht builders. Successors to Wm. Fife & Son.

No	Shipyard	Dates	Location	Approx no of ships built	Remarks
126	Ferguson	1860s	Firhill, Glasgow	3	Canal side builders.
127	Ferguson Brothers (Port Glasgow) Ltd	1903-	Newark, Port Glasgow	310	Taken over by Lithgows 1961.
128	Ferguson-Ailsa Ltd	1981-	Troon & Port Glasgow		British Shipbuilders holding company for Ailsa and Ferguson Brothers.
129	William Fife & Son	1812-1930s	Fairlie		Eminent yacht builders.
130	Alex. Findlay & Co Ltd	1941-5	Old Kilpatrick & Motherwell		Wartime fabrication at Motherwell and erection at Old Kilpatrick.
131	Firth of Clyde Dry Dock Co Ltd	1960s	Greenock		Later became part of Scott-Lithgow.
132	Fleming & Ferguson (Ltd in 1898)	1885-1969	Phoenix, Paisley	690	Dredgers & specialist ships.
133	R. Foster	1881	Cartside, Greenock		
134	D. & A. Fullarton	1860s	Ayr	5	
135	John Fullerton & Co	1866-1928	Merksworth, Paisley	270	
136	J. & J. Fyfe	1870s	Rothesay		Schooners, etc.
137	Gilkison, Thomson & Co	*fl* 1819	Irvine		Builder of brigantine *Jean*, the first ship for Allan Line.
138	Govan Shipbuilders Ltd	1972-	Govan, Glasgow		Part of British Shipbuilders. See also Scotstoun Marine Ltd.
139	Govan Shipbuilding Co	1884	Govan, Glasgow	7	Took over Dobie & Co after liquidation completed last 3 ships. Yard became Mackie & Thomson.
140	Grangemouth & Greenock Dockyard Co Ltd	1900-08	Cartsdyke Mid, Greenock	44	Became Greenock & Grangemouth.
141	Greenock Dockyard Co Ltd	1920-34	Cartsdyke Mid, Greenock		Closely associated with Clan Line Steamers Ltd.
142	Greenock Dockyard Co Ltd	1934-66	Cartsdyke East, Greenock	110	1966 integrated with Scott's S & E Co.
143	Greenock & Grangemouth Dockyard Co Ltd	1908-20	Cartsdyke Mid, Greenock	47	Became Greenock Dockyard.
144	Gush	1871	Cartside, Greenock		
145	Hall-Brown, Butterly & Co	1892-1912	Govan, Glasgow		Engineers: Constructed some barges, etc.
146	S. Halliday	1740-60	Westburn, Greenock		
147	G. & G. Hamilton	1895	Brodick, Arran	1	Wooden puffer built on beach.
148	William Hamilton & Co (Ltd in 1928)	1871-1963	Glen, Port Glasgow	520	Associated with Lithgows and Brocklebank Line. Integrated with Lithgows 1963.
149	Hanna and Donald	1851-70	Abercorn, Paisley		Became Hanna, Donald & Wilson.
150	Hanna, Donald & Wilson	1870-95	Abercorn, Paisley	32	Company in liquidation *c* 1895. Work continued till 1901 possibly under name of Abercorn SB Co.
151	Harland & Wolff Ltd	1912-62	Govan, Glasgow	300	Govan Yard formed from 3 shipyards.
152	Harland & Wolff Ltd (Caird Greenock Yard)	1922-36	Westburn, Greenock	12	Formerly Caird & Co. Purchased 1936 by NSS Ltd.
153	Harland & Wolff Ltd	1914-15	Irvine	4	
154	J. & J. Hay	1868-1958	Kirkintilloch	100	Shipbuilding and puffer maintenance. Known around 1866 as Crawford & Co.
155	A.C. Head	1940s	Greenock		Fabricators of landing craft.
156	Hedderwick & Rankine	*fl* 1840	Lancefield, Glasgow		

No	Shipyard	Dates	Location	Approx no of ships built	Remarks
157	D. & W. Henderson & Co Ltd	1873-1962	Meadowside, Glasgow	470	Closely associated with Anchor Line. 1935 shipbuilding ceased and yard purchased by NSS Ltd. Ship repairing interests purchased by Harland & Wolff. Discontinued 1962.
158	J. Henderson & Son	1847-61	West, Renfrew		Became Henderson, Coulborn & Co.
159	Henderson, Coulborn & Co	1861-74	West, Renfrew		Became Lobnitz, Coulborn & Co.
160	Henderson, Spence & Co	1866-70	Churchyard, Dumbarton		Formerly Archibald Denny.
161	Laurence Hill & Co	1853-69	Inch, Port Glasgow	76	Very progressive small yard.
162	J.W. Hoby & Co	1850-60	East, Renfrew	8	
163	Hood, Rowan & Co	1840s	Glasgow		Known as Rowan & Co and William Hood, Rowan & Co.
164	J. Howden & Co (Ltd in 1907)	1862-	Glasgow	2	Sited away from River. Builders of wooden craft and flying boats at Whiteinch and Old Kilpatrick 1914-18.
165	John Hunter	c 1815	Port Glasgow		
166	Hunter & Dow	1830s	Kelvinhaugh, Glasgow		
167	Hutsons Ltd	1875-1950s	Kelvinhaugh, Glasgow		Sub-contractors of hulls.
168	A. & J. Inglis Ltd	1847-62	Anderston, Glasgow		Engineers.
169	A. & J. Inglis Ltd	1862-1962	Pointhouse, Glasgow	500	1919 became part of Harland & Wolff.
170	Irvine Shipbuilding Co	1870-2	Irvine	4	Sailing vessels for coastal trade.
171	Irvine Shipbuilding & Engineering Co	1898-1912	Irvine	31	Trawlers, coasters etc.
172	W. Jackson & Co	1850s-1900s	Port Dundas, Glasgow		Barges, lighters etc.
173	William Johnston	1836-41	Greenock	4	
174	M. Kellard & Co	1870s	Ayr		Smacks & sailing coasters.
175	Kirkpartrick, McIntyre & Co	1863-7	Cartside, Greenock	16	Iron steamers.
176	Lambie	1896	Greenock		Yacht Builder.
177	James Lamont & Co Ltd	1870-	East India, Greenock	74	Shiprepairers.
178	James Lamont & Co Ltd	1929-79	Castle, Port Glasgow		Shipbuilding activities 1938-79.
179	James Lang	c 1815-1822	Dockyard, Dumbarton		Became Lang & Denny. Builders of PS *Comet* (2).
180	Lang & Denny	1822-39	Dockyard, Dumbarton		
181	J.G. Lawrie	1854-75	Whiteinch, Glasgow	63	Lawrie active in Glasgow academic life.
182	Lithgows Limited	1918-35	Bay, Port Glasgow		Lithgows have absorbed the ship-building interests in Port Glasgow of Duncan, Hamilton, Reid, Rodger and Russell.
183	Lithgows Limited	1936-72	East, Port Glasgow		
184	Lithgows Limited	1963-9	Glen, Port Glasgow		
185	Lithgows Limited	1918-69	Kingston, Port Glasgow		
186	Lithgows Limited	1926-69	Inch, Port Glasgow		
187	Lloyd Royal Belge (Great Britain) Ltd	1916-21	Whiteinch, Glasgow	25	Also known as Brys & Gilsen Ltd. Yard sold to Barclay Curle.

No	Shipyard	Dates	Location	Approx no of ships built	Remarks
188	Lobnitz & Co Ltd	1895-1957	West, Renfrew	1,178	No of vessels includes previous companies on site. 1957 amalgamated with Simons.
189	Lobnitz Coulborn & Co	1874-95	West, Renfrew		Became Lobnitz & Co.
190	London & Glasgow Eng & Iron SB Co Ltd	1864-1912	Govan, Glasgow	270	One of earliest limited liability companies. Yard sold to Harland & Wolff.
191	London Graving Dock Co Ltd	1941-5	Ayr		Former Ailsa site operated by LGD for wartime repair work.
192	Love	18th c	Greenock		
193	Lyon & Foster	1869-71	Cartside, Greenock	2	
194	J. Macadam	1880s	Govan, Glasgow		Small steam launches, etc.
195	John MacAlister	1820s-1838	Albert, Dumbarton		Wood shipbuilder.
196	Robert McAlister & Son	c 1885-	Sandpoint, Dumbarton		Continues as a yacht slip.
197	Sir Robert McAlpine & Sons Ltd	1974-	Ardyne, Argyll	3	Concrete North Sea Platform site.
198	J. McArthur & Co	1882-1900	Thistle, Paisley	136	Took over yard of Campbell & Co. Succeeded by Bow, McLachlan. Possibly commenced 1880 at Inchinan.
199	MacArthur and Alexander	1839-41	Govan, Glasgow		
200	John McAuslan	1839-51	Bridgend West, Dumbarton		On River Leven above bridge at Dumbarton.
201	Charles McBride	1871-7	Cartside, Greenock	4	
202	McCrindle (Shipbuilders) Ltd	1970s	South, Ardrossan		First use of yard on expiry of NSS restrictive covenant.
203	McCulloch & Paterson	1869-71	Glen, Port Glasgow	10	
204	MacDonald	1820s	Greenock		
205	McFadyen	1872-4	Bay, Port Glasgow	13	
206	A. McFarlane	1831-44	Woodyard, Dumbarton		
207	T. McGill	1825-51	Bay, Bowling		Small craft. Also known as D. McGill.
208	McGill & Gilmour	1887-95	Irvine	20	Also known as J.H. Gilmour.
209	P. MacGregor & Sons	1887-1921	Canal Basin Kirkintilloch	120	Built first British motor coaster *Innisagra*.
210	McGruer & Co Ltd	1911-1983	Clynder, Helensburgh		Yacht builders. Commenced earlier in Rutherglen next to Seath's.
211	McGruer & Co Ltd	1970s-	Rosneath		Now centralised at Rosneath.
212	McIntyre	1877	Cartside, Greenock	1	
213	H. McIntyre & Co	1877-85	Phoenix, Paisley	123	Yard taken over by Fleming & Ferguson.
214	McKellar & McMillan	1872-6	Low Woodyard, Dumbarton	15	Founded by Archibald McMillan.
215	J. McKenzie	c 1837	Paisley		
216	McKirdy	1820-40	Cartsdyke, West Greenock		
217	S. McKnight & Co Ltd	1884-1902	Ayr	59	Yard sold to Ailsa SB Co. Became S. McKnight & Co.
218	McKnight, McCredie & Co	1883-4	Ayr	5	Builders PS *Marion* 1816.
219	Archibald MacLachlan	c 1812-18	Woodyard, Dumbarton		
220	MacLaren Brothers	1908-26	Sandpoint, Dumbarton		Builders MV *Electric Arc* 1911.

No	Shipyard	Dates	Location	Approx no of ships built	Remarks
221	Robert MacLea	1853-72	Rothesay	30	Smacks & schooners.
222	Hugh McLean & Sons Ltd	1880-1943	Govan, Glasgow	5,010	Small craft running into thousands.
223	Hugh McLean & Sons Ltd	1933-71	Renfrew		Also believed at Gourock.
224	Peter R. McLean	1900s	Rosneath		Yacht builder.
225	P. & W. McLellan (Ltd in 1890)	1811-	Pollokshields, Glasgow		Builders of Landing Craft at Paisley during Second World War (Thistle Yard).
226	D. McLeod	1855	Greenock		
227	Archibald McMillan & Son (Ltd in 1890)	1834-1930	4 sites, Dumbarton	500	Part of Harland & Wolff 1920-1930. Purchased NSS Ltd 1930.
228	McMillan	1851	Cartsdyke, West Greenock		
229	James McMillan	1850s-1860s	Greenock	18	
230	McMillan & McDonald	1865-7	Greenock		
231	McNab & Co	1863-72	Westburn, Greenock	18	Yard sold to Caird & Co to enlarge the Greenock yard.
232	McNicoll Brothers	1922-1950s	Maryhill, Glasgow	2	Large scale repair work during Second World War.
233	MacPherson and MacLachlan	1740-60	Greenock		
234	McTaggart	1820s	Greenock		
235	Mackie & Thomson (Ltd in 1907)	1888-1912	Govan, Old Glasgow	44	Prolific output of trawlers etc. Govan yard sold to Harland & Wolff. Irvine yard became Ayrshire Dockyard.
236	Mackie & Thomson Ltd	1912-28	Irvine	74	
237	Malcolm	1900s			Yacht builder.
238	A. Malcolm	1940s	Port Bannatyne		Wartime landing craft builders.
239	Marathon Shipbuilding Co (UK) Ltd	1972-80	Clydebank	11	Jack up rigs and drill ship conversions.
240	Marine Craft Constructors Ltd	1950s	Dumbarton		Small vessels.
241	Marine Investment Co	1865-7	Ladyburn, Greenock	2	
242	Marshall and Co	1890-1910	Maryhill, Glasgow		
243	Martin	1814	Port Glasgow	2	
244	Mechans Ltd	1862	Scotstoun, Glasgow		Builders of mass produced lifeboats, etc, operated munitions factory during First World War.
245	Menzies	1840	Glasgow		
246	Meurice	1840s	Dockyard, Dumbarton		
247	Millen Brothers	1919-1950s	Paisley		Barges and knock down craft.
248	Miller	1880s	Dumbarton		
249	G. Mills	1830s	Bowling		Later known as Mills & Wood.
250	Milne & McGilvary		Paisley		Barge builders. Possibly known as Milne, Milne, Milne & McGilvary.
251	Morris & Lorimer Ltd		Sandbank, Dunoon		Yacht builders.
252	Morrison	early 19th c	Maryhill, Glasgow		
253	Morton Wylde & Co	1870	Woodyard, Dumbarton		Never completed a ship.
254	Motherwell Bridge & Engineering Co Ltd		Motherwell	110	Erected vessels on River Forth at Alloa 1940-5.
255	Muir	1860s	Dumbarton		Boat builders.
256	James Munn	1760-1820	Greenock	6	

No	Shipyard	Dates	Location	Approx no of ships built	Remarks
257	John Munn	1840s	Glasgow		
258	D. Munro & Son		Blairmore, Dunoon		Loch Fyne skiffs, etc.
259	Richard Munro & Co	1910-22	Maryhill, Glasgow		Taken over by McNicoll Brothers.
260	P. Murchie	1837-52	Bay, Port Glasgow		
261	Murdoch & Murray (Ltd in 1909)	1875-1912	Port Glasgow	260	Became Port Glasgow SB Co Ltd.
262	Henry Murray & Co	1867-82	Kingston, Port Glasgow	100	Small steamers.
263	Henry Murray & Co	1881-4	Sandpoint, Dumbarton	10	2 ships completed by Crawford.
264	Murray Brothers	1883-91	Westbridge or Phoenix Park, Dumbarton	16	Henry Murray a partner. Builders of 4 *Clutha*s.
265	Murries and Clark	1831-44	Westburn, Greenock	18	Also known as Murries.
266	Napier & Crichton	1840s	Glasgow		
267	Napier & Miller Ltd	1898-1906	Yoker, nr Glasgow	70	Site taken over for Rothesay Dock.
268	Napier & Miller Ltd	1906-30	Old Kilpatrick, nr Glasgow	120	Purchased by NSS Ltd. Alex. Findlay of Motherwell used site in 1940s.
269	Napier Shanks & Bell	1877-98	Yoker, nr Glasgow	84	Became Napier & Miller.
270	David Napier	1821-1836	Lancefield, Glasgow		Built *Post Boy* 1822 with surface condensers. Moved to London and R. Napier took site.
271	James Napier & Hoey	1850-8	Govan Old, Glasgow		Yard sold to Randolph & Elder.
272	Robert Napier & Sons	1836-41	Lancefield, Glasgow		Prolific builder of superb ships.
273	Robert Napier & Sons	1841-50	Govan Old, Glasgow	470	
274	Robert Napier & Sons	1850-1900	Govan East, Glasgow		Became Wm. Beardmore 1900.
275	Neilson & Co	1850s	Whiteinch, Glasgow		
276	John Neilson	1830s	Hamiltonhill, Glasgow		Builders 1831 Iron PS *Fairy Queen*.
277	T. Nicol	1820s	Greenock		
278	Ninian	1890s	Largs		Yacht builders.
279	Alexander Noble & Sons Ltd	1946-	Girvan	80	Traditional wooden fishing vessels.
280	J. Norman	1860s	Broomhill, Glasgow		Small vessels. Non-river site.
281	Thomas Orr, Junior	1883-99	Greenock	20	Small vessels, steam launches.
282	Matthew Paul & Co	1880s	Dumbarton	2	Engineers. Built at least 2 screw yachts.
283	Port Glasgow Shipbuilding Co Ltd	1912-27	Port Glasgow	45	Previously Murdoch & Murray. Yard closed and dismantled.
284	Porter & Morgan	1740-60	Greenock		
285	Portland Shipbuilding Co	1860s	Troon	2	
286	Randolph, Elder & Co	1860-4	Govan Old, Glasgow		Commenced marine engineering 1852.
287	Randolph Elder & Co	1864-70	Fairfield, Glasgow		Became John Elder & Co.
288	Redpath Brown & Co Ltd	1940s	Meadowside, Glasgow		Used former yard as Landing Craft assembly site.
289	John Reid & Co	1847-63	East, Port Glasgow		Builders of successful clipper ships

No	Shipyard	Dates	Location	Approx no of ships built	Remarks
290	John Reid & Co	1863-85	Glen, Port Glasgow	300	and yachts.
291	John Reid & Co	1876-90	Newark, Port Glasgow		Yard sold to William Hamilton.
292	John Reid & Co Ltd	1891-1909	Whiteinch, Glasgow		Reconstitution of Port Glasgow business.
293	Reid & Hanna	1816-51	Paisley		Engineers & iron boat builders.
294	Reid & Hanna	1833-6	Greenock		
295	Rennie, Ritchie & Newport SB Co	1920-2	Broomloan, Rutherglen	5	Part of large shipbuilding group which collapsed 1922.
296	D. Richardson	1890s	Largs		Small vessels, yachts.
297	J.H. Ritchie	1820s	Port Glasgow		Associated with the Woods.
298	William Ritchie	18th c	Saltcoats		Went to Belfast 1791.
299	Ritchie, Graham & Milne	1891-5	Govan, Glasgow	370	Barges and shallow draft ships.
300	Ritchie, Graham & Milne	1895-1922	Whiteinch, Glasgow		Many knock down jobs.
301	Alexander Robertson & Sons (Yachtbuilders) Ltd	1876-	Sandbank, Dunoon		Built first Scottish constructed RNLI lifeboat 1935.
302	Robertson & Co	1865-9	Cartsdyke, Greenock	28	
303	A. Rodger & Co	1891-1912	Bay, Port Glasgow	120	Business reverted to Russell & Co.
304	Ross & Marshall Ltd	1899-1925	Cartsdyke, Greenock	14	Part of coastal shipping company.
305	Russell	1867-8	Ladyburn, Greenock		
306	Russell & Co	1874-91	Bay, Port Glasgow		Early builders of hulls to standard form.
307	Russell & Co	1879-1900	Cartsdyke, Greenock		
308	Russell & Co	1882-1918	Kingston, Greenock		Successful large cargo sailing ships.
309	Russell & Co	1912-18	Bay, Port Glasgow		Became Lithgows Ltd.
310	D.M. Russell Marine (Rosneath) Ltd	1979-	Rosneath		Formerly James A. Silver.
311	Sandeman & McLaurin	1850s	Whiteinch, Glasgow		
312	Sanderson & Co	1840s	Glasgow		
313	Scotstoun Marine Limited	1973-80	Scotstoun, Glasgow		Subsidiary of Govan Shipbuilders.
314	Scott	1850s	Rutherglen		
315	Scott & Sons (Bowling) Ltd	1851-1979	Bowling	490	Production ceased 1979.
316	Charles Scott	1860s	Greenock		
317	J.E. Scott	1874-79	Cartsdyke, Greenock	20	
318	Scott & Linton	1867-70	Woodyard, Dumbarton	9	Hull builders of *Cutty Sark*.
319	Scott Lithgow Ltd	1969-	Greenock & Port Glasgow		Sold by BS 1984 to Trafalgar House.
320	Scott, MacGill & Duncan	1850	Bowling		See Scott & Sons.
321	Scott & MacGill	1850s	Bowling		See Scott & Sons.
322	Scott's Shipbuilding & Engineering Co Ltd	1711-	Various yards, Greenock	900	Oldest shipbuilding organisation in the world. (Ltd in 1899.)
323	John Scott				
324	James & William Scott				

No	Shipyard	Dates	Location	Approx no of ships built	Remarks
325	Scott, Sinclair & Co				Various names under which Scott's
326	John & William Scott				has operated.
327	John Scott & Sons				
328	Scott & Co				
329	Scottish Concrete Shipbuilding Co	1917-20	West End, Greenock	10	Concrete coasters and dumb barges.
330	Scottish Iron Works Co	1870s	Irvine		Coasters.
331	Scottish Lion Ship Repairing & Eng Co Ltd	1948-71	Glasgow		Clan Line Repairers.
332	T.B. Seath & Co	1853-6	Partick, Glasgow	3	Including Seath's own PS *Artizan*.
333	T.B. Seath & Co	1856-1902	Broomloan, Rutherglen	300	Small vessels.
334	John Shearer & Son	1890-1907	Kelvinhaugh, Glasgow	46	Small coasters.
335	John Shearer & Son	1905-12	Elderslie, Glasgow		Laid out first Elderslie Dry Dock. Taken over by Barclay Curle.
336	James A. Silver Ltd	1910-70	Rosneath		Yacht builders: distinctive motor vessels.
337	Simmonds & Co	1850s	Glasgow		
338	William Simons & Co	1810-12	Cartside, Greenock		
339	William Simons & Co	1812-18	Isle aux Noix, Montreal		
340	William Simons & Co	1818-26	Cartside, Greenock		
341	William Simons & Co	1826-60	Whiteinch, Glasgow		Builders of elevating deck ferries, dredges and hopper barges.
342	William Simons & Co (Ltd in 1888)	1860-1957	East, Renfrew	812	Amalgamated with Lobnitz 1957.
343	Simons Lobnitz Ltd	1957-63	Renfrew		On closure, goodwill taken over by Alex. Stephen and by Seadrec. Yachts.
344	W. Smith	1860s	Greenock		
345	Smith & Rodger	1843-1864	Govan, Glasgow	90	Became London & Glasgow Co.
346	James Steele	18th c	Saltcoats		Father of Robert Steele.
347	Robert Steele	1765-96	Saltcoats		Became Steele & Carswell at Greenock.
348	Robert Steele & Co	1816-55	Rue End, Greenock		
349	Robert Steele & Co	1851-83	Cartsdyke, Greenock	270	Builders of famous clipper ships.
350	Steele & Carswell	1796-1816	Greenock	34	Became Robt. Steele & Co.
351	Stenhouse & Co		Dumbarton		See Birrell, Stenhouse & Co.
352	Alexander Stephen & Sons	1851-70	Kelvinhaugh, Glasgow	140	Formerly of Burghead, Aberdeen, Arbroath and Dundee. Founded 1750.
353	Alexander Stephen & Sons Ltd	1870-1968	Linthouse, Glasgow	540	Became part of UCS in 1968.
354	Stuart & Rennie	1820s	Greenock		
355	David Swan	1840s	Glasgow		
356	J. & R. Swan	1870-4	Woodyard Upper, Dumbarton	33	Same family as Swan's of Maryhill.
357	Swan		Maryhill, Glasgow	54	Variously known as:
358	Swan	1857-88	Port Dundas, Glasgow	1	David Swan Jr; J.H. Swan; J.R. Swan; W. Swan.
359	Swan		Kelvindale, Glasgow	11	

No	Shipyard	Dates	Location	Approx no of ships built	Remarks
360	Tarbert Boatyard Ltd	1980s	Tarbert, Lochfyne		
361	R. Taylerson	1858-9	Port Glasgow	1	
362	Taylor & Mitchell	1898-1900	Garvel, Greenock	4	
363	W.B. Thompson & Co	1880-6	Whiteinch, Glasgow	20	Associated with Thompson of Dundee—later the Caledon Yard.
364	James & George Thomson	1851-72	Govan, Glasgow	124	Land taken over for Govan Dry Docks.
365	James & George Thomson Ltd (Ltd in 1890)	1872-97	Clydebank	140	Became Clydebank E & S Co Ltd.
366	Thomson & Spiers	1840-2	Cartsdyke, Greenock	8	
367	Timbercraft	1940s	Rhu		Minor landing craft.
368	Tod & MacGregor	1834-47	Mavisbank, Glasgow	160	Opened drydock 1858.
369	Tod & MacGregor	1847-73	Meadowside, Glasgow		Became D. & W. Henderson.
370	Troon Shipbuilding Co	1860s-1885	Troon	25	Wooden sailing vessels.
371	UIE Shipbuilding (Scotland) Ltd	1980-	Clydebank		Part of French industrial group. Jack up rig specialists.
372	Union Shipbuilding Co	1860s	Kelvinhaugh, Glasgow	4	
373	Upper Clyde Shipbuilders Ltd	1968-71	Clydebank		Formerly John Brown & Co Ltd.
374	Upper Clyde Shipbuilders Ltd	1968-71	Govan, Glasgow		Formerly Fairfields (Glasgow) Ltd.
375	Upper Clyde Shipbuilders Ltd	1968-71	Linthouse, Glasgow		Formerly A. Stephen & Sons Ltd.
376	Upper Clyde Shipbuilders Ltd	1968-71	Scotstoun, Glasgow		Formerly C. Connell & Co Ltd. Known as UCS. Yarrow as an associate company.
377	Wardrop	1880s	Campbeltown		Small vessels.
378	W. Watson	*fl* 1882	Ladyburn, Greenock	1	Fish carrier SS *Talisman*.
379	Wavebreaker Marine (Scotland)	1980s	Glengarnock		
380	Thomas Wilson	*fl* 1819	Blackhill, Glasgow		Canal boat builder at Faskine. Builder of iron boat *Vulcan* 1819.
381	Thomas Wingate & Co	1837-48	Springfield, Glasgow	200	Commenced as engineers 1823. Reputedly built first triple expansion in engine in 1872.
382	Thomas Wingate & Co	1848-78	Whiteinch, Glasgow		
383	Wishart	1860s	Port Glasgow	2	Puffer.
384	Charles Wood	1835-40	Dockyard, Dumbarton		Also built at Port Glasgow and at Prince Edward Island, Canada.
385	Charles Wood	1840-43	Castlegreen, Dumbarton		
386	John Wood & Co	1780-1810	Rue End, Greenock		Builders of PS *Comet* 1812 and PS *Tug* 1817. Built 81 steamers.
387	John Wood & Co	1810-53	East, Port Glasgow		
388	Wood & Mills	1830s	Glasgow		Non-river site.
389	R. Wylie	*c* 1905	Campbeltown		Small vessels.
390	Yarrow & Co Ltd	1906-77	Scotstoun, Glasgow	1,000	Formerly of Isle of Dogs and of Poplar, London. International ship-building group. 1968-71 associate of UCS.
391	Yarrow Shipbuilders Ltd	1977-	Scotstoun, Glasgow		Part of warship division of British Shipbuilders.
392	Duncan Young	1860s	Port Sonachan, Argyll		Erecting small vessels for Loch Awe.

Appendix 4

Houseflags of some companies with shipbuilding interests on the River Clyde

1 Ailsa Shipbuilding
   Co Ltd

2 Allan Line

3 Anchor Line

4 Barclay, Curle
   & Co Ltd

5 British Shipbuilders

6 George Brown & Co
   (Marine) Ltd

7 John Brown
   & Co Ltd

8 Burrell & Son

9 Clan Line
   Steamers Ltd

10 Charles Connell
   & Co Ltd

11 William Denny
   & Brothers Ltd

12 Fairfield S & E
   Co Ltd

13 Govan Shipbuilders

14 Harland & Wolff Ltd

15 J. Hay

16 James Lamont
   & Co Ltd

17 Lithgows Ltd

18 Ross & Marshall
   Ltd

19 Scotts S & E Co Ltd

20 Scott Lithgow Ltd

21 T. B. Seath & Co

22 Alexander Stephen
   & Sons Ltd

23 Upper Clyde
   Shipbuilders Ltd

24 UIE Shipbuilding
   (Scotland) Ltd

25 Yarrow & Co Ltd

Index

An O Class submarine built by Scotts of Greenock for the Royal Australian Navy, on sea trials on the Clyde in 1970 (Scott Lithgow Ltd).